ENCYCLOPEDIA
OF THE USSR

ENCYCLOPEDIA OF THE USSR

1905 TO THE PRESENT
LENIN TO GORBACHEV

Warren Shaw
and
David Pryce

CASSELL

126456

Cassell Publishers Ltd
Villiers House, 41/47 Strand, London WC2N 5JE

Copyright © 1990 Warren Shaw and David Pryce

First published 1990

Distributed in the United States by
Sterling Publishing Co. Inc.
387 Park Avenue South, New York, NY 10016–8810

Distributed in Australia by
Capricorn Link (Australia) Pty Ltd
PO Box 665, Lane Cove, NSW 2066

British Library Cataloguing in Publication Data

Shaw, Warren
  Encyclopedia of the USSR 1905–1990.
  1. Soviet Union, 1894–
  I. Title   II. Pryce, David
  947.083

ISBN 0–304–31813–8

Typeset by Butler & Tanner Ltd, Frome and London
Printed in Great Britain by Butler & Tanner Ltd

CONTENTS

≡ MAPS ≡

≡ INTRODUCTION ≡

On 18 January 1918 the Bolsheviks under the leadership of Lenin dissolved the Constituent Assembly and instituted one-party rule in Russia. On 7 February 1990 the Central Committee of the Communist Party under Chairman Mikhail Gorbachev repealed Article 6 of the Constitution and abandoned the Party's claims to the monopoly of power, thus opening the way for multi-party democracy.

Between these two dates, the bibilical span of a man's life, is the most extraordinary story of the twentieth century and one which has profoundly affected the lives of everyone now living. The story begins with the abortive 1905 revolution, shortly followed by the successful revolutions of 1917, the fall of the Tsar and the establishment of communist rule under Lenin. After Lenin's death, under the brutal dictatorship of Stalin, the backward peasant economy was transformed into a major industrial super-power, and the world was divided into two power blocs, each possessing a terrifying nuclear arsenal.

In 1956 Khrushchev revealed the enormity of Stalin's crimes and the extent of his tyranny. A vast number of political prisoners were then freed, but under Brezhnev the initial impulse towards greater freedom was once again suppresssed. It was not until Mikhail Gorbachev was declared General Secretary in 1985 that the startling changes now taking place in Russia and the whole Eastern bloc began.

Gorbachev introduced the twin concepts of perestroika and glasnost. Perestroika has both political and economic significance. Politically it has led to the formation of the Congress of People's Deputies, and the emergence of dozens of new political parties, many of whose candidates, twenty years ago, would have been confined in labour camps. In economic terms Gorbachev aims to introduce elements of the market economy through the formation of co-operatives and joint ventures with the West and even to create a Moscow stock exchange.

In the wider world Gorbachev created an immensely favourable impression. His unilateral announcement of cuts in conventional arms and his wide-ranging agreements with the USA on nuclear forces lowered international tensions. At the same time he presided over the collapse of the communist regimes in Eastern Europe, starting with Hungary and Poland and followed by the Romanian revolt against Ceaucescu in December 1989, and his death by execution. For that wider world, the culmination of the dramas in Eastern Europe was the dismantling of the Berlin Wall and the imminent reunification of East and West Germany.

In some ways it is possible to compare Gorbachev's situation with that of Stolypin, the reforming prime minister of Tsarist Russia at the beginning of the century. Both inherited a rigid bureaucratic system with an oppressed peasantry and an inefficient industrial structure. Both attempted to introduce elements of a market economy and democracy. Stolypin was assassinated, probably with police collusion. Gorbachev's popularity and prestige within the Soviet Union are threatened by having liberated the twin forces of nationalism and democracy in the country.

Gorbachev has problems which Stolypin did not face. For the first time in its history the republics that make up the Soviet empire are using their rights under the constitution to declare their independence, while in the Caucasus and in Central Asia bitter ethnic struggles have broken out. A command economy responds only sluggishly to attempts at reform and the queues for food and consumer goods grow longer, while Gorbachev's opponents – both radical and conservative – become more vocal. Boris

Yeltsin, now president of the RSFSR, the largest of the republics, has accused him of being both too radical and not radical enough. Lithuania has opted for sovereignty, as have the RSFSF, the Ukraine and Georgia. Further declarations of independence by the republics are inevitable.

The situation is threatening and unpredictable. Whether the Soviet Union can change its nature both constitutionally and economically without disintegrating is hard to say: there are no real historical parallels. The possibility of extreme reaction – even of a return to a hard line regime backed by the army – must exist, though the Red Army has no tradition of intervening in politics. It may be that some form of federation will emerge.

Whatever happens, the changes that have taken place in the USSR and Eastern Europe in such a short period of time are astounding and have brought the possibility of a better life to so many millions after years of dark and terrible repression.

≡ AUTHORS' NOTE ≡

Our intention in writing this book is to give the interested reader or student detailed background information on the Soviet Union from the 1905 revolution to the present time in compact and accessible form. We are primarily concerned to plot the political and economic developments in the USSR and deal with its external relationships and our selection of topics and choice of biographies are directed towards this end. We neither pretend nor aspire to a total account of all aspects of Soviet life: such a vast enterprise is quite beyond the scope of a single volume.

The book is divided into three main sections: a chronology starting in 1905 and extending to the close of the 28th Communist Party Congress in July 1990, an encyclopedia of topics, and a selection of biographies, the latter two being in alphabetical order. There is some cross-referencing in the encyclopedia when the need is apparent. The index will assist the reader in finding particular items of information and act as an additional aid to cross-reference.

The transliteration of Russian names used has been that which we judged to be most familiar to the reader. Thus we have not used the academically acceptable American Library of Congress system which would give, for example, Trotskii rather than Trotsky. Since the Russian alphabet has more letters than English, a direct transliteration is not possible and each European language has its preferred spellings: thus for Khrushchev the French might have Krouchtchev and the Germans Chruschtjow. For Muslim names we have used the form that reaches us through Russian texts.

CHRONOLOGY

1905

Dates are given in 'old style' (13 days' difference) up to 14 February 1918. Imperial Russia adopted the Julian Calendar in 1700 – just as the rest of Europe was abandoning it in favour of the Gregorian Calendar. The Bolsheviks joined the rest of the world's calendar in 1918.

Where no specific date is shown the events in any month are given in the order of their occurrence.

The Russian Empire is at war with Japan. In 1896 the Russians had arranged a treaty with the Chinese Empire to run the Trans-Siberian railway through Manchuria to Vladivostok, in return for guaranteeing China's territorial integrity and paying off her debt to Japan. Russia now came into conflict with Japan over Korea and Port Arthur. The Imperial Russian army and navy are incompetent in the face of the new Japanese forces.

1 January	The surrender of Port Arthur by the Russians to the Japanese is announced and popular discontent with the war breaks out.
22 January	Bloody Sunday: The Orthodox Church priest Father Gapon, organiser of a workers' union but also having an association with the police, leads a march to the Tsar's Winter Palace in St Petersburg with a petition to the Tsar. Troops, called in anticipation of trouble, open fire on the marchers, killing about 150. The reaction to the massacre is a general strike.
17 February	Grand Duke Sergei, Governor of Moscow and uncle to the Tsar, is killed in the Kremlin by a bomb planted by the 'Combat Section' of the Socialist Revolutionaries (SRs).
1–9 March	The Japanese army routs the Russians at the Battle of Mukden.
29–30 March	The police discover the Combat Section's dynamite store in St Petersburg and arrest most of the members.
April–May	The 3rd Congress of the Social Democrats (RSDLP) is held in London. This is a congress of only Bolsheviks, the Mensheviks hold their congress in Vienna.
2 May	Striking workers at a large textile mill in St Petersburg elect a group of workers to carry their demands to the owners. It is the first of the workers' soviets, the pattern of which will spread.
27 May	The Battle of Tsushima: the Imperial Russian fleet, having sailed from the Baltic, around South Africa and across the Indian Ocean, meets the Japanese fleet and is mostly destroyed in three quarters of an hour's action in the Sea of Japan.
14 June	The crew of the battleship *Potemkin* of the Black Sea fleet mutiny, kill many of the officers and sail from port, shelling Odessa before taking refuge in Romania.
June	There are general strikes in Odessa and other major cities.
	Soviets are organised in cities and, after the harvest, peasant 'republics' are declared in the countryside with the help of the SRs, the landlord moved off his estate and his house perhaps burnt down.
29 August	By the Treaty of Portsmouth, New Hampshire, after the mediation of the American President, Theodore Roosevelt, and negotiation by the Tsar's prime minister, Count Witte, the war against Japan is ended with Russia giving up Port Arthur, all claims on Korea, half the island of

Sakhalin and the southern half of Manchuria. These losses are a scar on Russia's memory for 50 years.

7 October A railway strike throughout the Empire is called by the large and effective union of its workers. To end the chaos caused by the strike, trains are sent from east and west of the Trans-Siberian railway with officers and soldiers who are ordered to disarm and execute any mutinous troops who join the strikers.

October A soviet is set up in St Petersburg to co-ordinate the workers' strikes. The SRs and Social Democrats dominate these and the Menshevik Trotsky is a leading figure. It lasts 50 days before being suppressed.

17 October The Tsar issues a manifesto, declaring an amnesty and agreeing to a popularly elected Duma. Freedom of the Press, free speech and religious toleration are also promised. Under the amnesty many political prisoners are released, including those arrested in March. The Tsar issues the manifesto drafted by Witte.

The Duma will not be able to control the army or navy or to get foreign loans and (under the new Article 87 of the Fundamental Laws) the Tsar's government can make any laws it likes if it deems the situation is an emergency.

The State Soviet, a Council of Ministers made up of nominated members – officials and others from zemstvos, universities, the church, etc. – is made into an upper house to balance the elected Duma and to join in passing or rejecting its proposals.

October The Constitutional Democratic (Kadet) Party is formed from zemstvo unions and illegal liberal organisations. It had first been founded in Stuttgart in 1902 and named the Liberation Party. It is a middle-class liberal party which reckons that the revolution has now been achieved. It sees a democratic parliamentary future ahead, with liberal capitalist economic policies, and will oppose the 1917 October Revolutionaries. In 1905, led by Milyukov, it demands free elections for a national assembly.

1 November The religious mystic Rasputin goes to stay in the Tsar's household, holding the Tsarina, fearful for her haemophiliac son, under his influence.

November The St Petersburg Soviet calls for a general strike, but without total success.

The moderate Octobrist Party is formed by Guchkov to ensure the success of the Duma and the continuance of the Tsarist regime. It represents large commercial interests and supports the Tsar's October Manifesto, becoming a majority party in the 3rd and 4th Dumas.

8 November Lenin arrives in St Petersburg, but the Bolsheviks have had little role in the revolt.

3 December The government feels strong enough to break up the St Petersburg Soviet and arrest the leaders. Trotsky is sentenced to exile but he escapes.

9–19 December A Moscow soviet, where Trotsky is a leader, brings out workers on strike, which leads to rioting and the army suppresses it brutally.

December The 1st Conference of the Social Democrats is held at Tammerfors.

1906

January
The army makes punitive expenditions against risings, particularly in the Baltic provinces, where the Letts and Estonians have attacked their German landlords. Hundreds or probably thousands of executions are carried out.

April
The 1st Duma is elected. The SRs have large numbers elected under the name of a Peasant Union (since many of the SRs themselves are hunted by the police), the Bolshevik Social Democrats boycott the elections while the Mensheviks have success among the factory workers, but the Kadets are the dominant party.

The Duma presents its proposals, including land reform, to the Tsar, but there is doubt if it had any such constitutional right. One of the Tsar's ministers lectures them on their inadmissible demands and the Duma passes a vote of censure. There being no constitutional precedent, the ministers do not resign.

April
The 4th RSDLP Congress (known as the 'Unity' Congress) is held in Stockholm. There is a Menshevik majority.

20 July
When the Duma, frustrated by the government's refusal to consider its land reforms, decides to appeal to the people, it is dissolved and Stolypin is appointed prime minister.

Stolypin uses Article 87 to rule, setting up courts martial which deal out death sentences. He also uses his powers to give all (male) peasants voting rights.

25 August
A bomb attempt by the SRs combat section on Stolypin's house fails, but severely injures his daughters. From then on he lives as a guest of the Tsar in the Winter Palace.

9 November
Stolypin, aiming to build peasant support, gives them the right to claim as their own parts of the common village land. Later the Bolsheviks will claim that the number of kulaks is thus being deliberately increased and encouraged.

November
The 2nd Conference of the RSDLP (the 1st 'All-Russian') is held at Tammerfors.

1907

January
Lenin moves to Finland.

5 March
The 2nd Duma is elected and meets with many of the same members. The Kadets continue to dominate but there are nine party groupings. The SRs enter under their own party name and the Social Democrats have both Menshevik and Bolshevik deputies.

A new small group is the Union of the Russian People, established in 1905, avowedly nationalistic, monarchist and anti-Semitic, the open front for the Black Hundreds, led by Purishkevich.

April–May
The 5th RSDLP Congress is held in London, over 300 attending, 105 of whom are Bolshevik, 97 Menshevik and the remainder from other organisations, including the Jewish Bund.

3 June	The Duma is dissolved after an Imperial manifesto accuses it of having plotted against the Tsar. There had been two attempts by the Okhrana to implicate SRs and Social Democrats with acts of treason. The 65 Social Democrat deputies are arrested and exiled to Siberia.
16 June	A new electoral law restricts the suffrage to landowners and the professional classes. The 3rd Duma, predominantly right of centre with Guchkov of the Octobrists leading the largest party, 153 deputies, and a stronger right-wing representation of 50 from the Union of the Russian People and 89 Nationalists. Of 442 deputies only 54 were Kadets, 20 Social Democrats and 13 SRs, with 18 Polish deputies and others of minority interests.
July–August	The 3rd Conference of the RSDLP is held at Korka in Finland.
November	The 4th Conference of the RSDLP is held in Helsingfors (Helsinki).

1908

The Social Democrats are now all driven from Russia, some to Western Europe and some to Siberia.

December	The 5th Conference of the RSDLP is held in Paris. The Bolsheviks, led by Lenin, accuse the Mensheviks of failing to follow the policies of the party and of collaborating with the Duma.

1911

31 August	Stolypin, chairman of the Council of Ministers, is shot at a Kiev theatre by Bogrov, a revolutionary who also acts as a police agent, and dies a few days later.

1912

January	The 6th RSDLP Congress is held in Prague. The Bolsheviks constitute themselves a separate party, finally splitting with the Mensheviks and electing a Central Committee. Lenin, Ordzhonikdze, Sverdlov, Zinoviev and (in his absence) Stalin were the leading members. They are now the Russian Social Democratic Labour Party (Bolshevik).

The 4th Duma is elected by a narrow franchise, consisting exclusively of substantial property-owning men who, in general, favoured a Western parliamentary democracy. The extreme right despises it and the left are represented only by the moderates who have avoided exile. Apart from parties representing minorities (Lithuanians, Ukrainians, etc. and 30 Muslims who were aligned with the Kadets), the balance of parties is:

Social Democrats (12 Mensheviks and 6 Bolsheviks)	3%
Trudoviks (Socialist Populists)	2%
The moderate left (Kadets and Progressives)	25%
Octobrists and other centrists	31%
The moderate right and Nationalists	21%
The extreme right	15%

April — At the Lena gold fields a strike of 2,000 workers is met by troops who fire on them and kill at least 200. This massacre sparks off strikes throughout the Empire. Kerensky is sent to the gold fields by the Duma to investigate.

The newspaper *Pravda* is founded as the organ of the Bolsheviks.

1914

1 May — On May Day an estimated half-million workers march in cities of the Empire, where a million and a quarter are on strike.

15 June — The heir to the throne of the Austrian Empire, Archduke Franz Ferdinand, and his wife are shot at Sarajevo in Austrian Bosnia. Many are convinced that this is an assassination inspired by Serbia, and Austria demands war against Serbia. There is a chain rection throughout Europe as nations look to their defences and allies.

Summer — Baku oil workers strike.

13 July — Austria and Serbia declare war.

In the St Petersburg general strike workers put up barricades against the police.

17 July — The Tsar decides, after hesitation, on mobilisation in view of the Austro-Serbian crisis and fear of pre-emptive strikes. This continues the chain of military reactions in Europe, compelling Germany towards war.

19 July — Russia and Germany declare war after Russia declines to halt its mobilisation.

25 July — Austria declares war on Russia and invades Russian Poland.

2 August — Russian troops invade East Prussia and Galicia. Their aim is not simply defensive, but to annex 'Russian' lands in the Austrian Empire. They are also honouring their agreement with France to attack Germany 'in the rear'.

16 August — Germans defeat and rout the Russian army at Tannenberg, and inflict further heavy defeats at the Masurian Lakes. But the Austrian reverses in Galicia, where the Russians capture Lvow, mean that German forces have to be moved to their support.

18 August — The capital of Russia is renamed Petrograd, since 'St Petersburg' sounds German.

16 October — The Black Sea ports of Odessa and Sevastopol are bombarded by the Turkish navy and war with Turkey starts. This closes the Black Sea to Russia, which can now only receive munitions through Murmansk and Archangel or Vladivostok.

6 November   Five Bolshevik members of the Duma are arrested and exiled to Turkestan for urging Russians to fight their government rather than the Germans. The arrests spark off the protests they had been intended to suppress.

10 November   Although the Russians force the Austrians back in Galicia, the Germans take Lodz. Already the Russian army is running short of guns and munitions.

December   A Turkish army under Enver Pasha invades the Caucasus, intending to raise revolt there. It is heavily defeated by the Russians at Sarikamish.

═══ 1915 ═══

January   Enver Pasha, left with one-seventh of his army, falls back to re-form.

200 Finns, with an independent Finland in mind, go for military training in Germany. In May 1916 they become the '27 Königliche Preussische Jäger' battalion, which grows to about 2,000 men and is sent to the German eastern front near Riga.

February   The Russian 10th Army is encircled by the Germans at Masuria, while the Austrian attacks in the Carpathians collapse.

March   In counter-attacks against the Austrians, the Russians take Przemysl in Galicia with 120,000 Austrian prisoners.

24 April   Thousands of Armenians near the Russian borders are killed in preventive measures by the Turks. Officials and teachers are particular targets.

May   Austro-German offensive defeats Russians in Galicia, forcing a retreat.

July   A further offensive towards Russian Poland leads to over a million Russian casualties.

20 July   The All-Russian Union of Zemstva for the Relief of Sick and Wounded Soldiers is formed, which co-ordinates the supply of necessary resources and helps with hospitals and supplies. Its chairman is Prince Lvov. This network of voluntary organisations and local committees becomes a focus of criticism of the government's conduct of the war.

22 July   Germans take Warsaw.

1 August   The Duma, with strong feelings on the conduct of the war, meets and proposes the creation of a Defence Council.

22 August   The leaders of the Duma's central and liberal groups meet and form a 'Progressive Bloc'. They call for a 'government of confidence'.

23 August   The Tsar assumes command of the armies, moving to the Stavka (leaving Palace politics in the hands of the Tsarina and the notorious, unpopular Rasputin). His move is against the advice of the Progressive Bloc and the Council of Ministers.

The Tsar appoints the commander of the north-west front, General Alekseev, his Chief of Staff.

The Russian army retreats 125 miles (200 km) east of Warsaw.

8 September   Progressive Bloc puts forward a reform programme calling for an end to

religious and racial discrimination, the lifting of restrictions on trade unions and an amnesty for political offenders.

15 September   In the face of Russian defeats, the Union of Zemstvos and industrialists call for a reorganisation of the war effort. The Progressive Bloc in the Duma presents its case but the Tsar responds by dismissing the ministers who show sympathy with the bloc.

16 September   Tsar prorogues the Duma.

The socialist congress in Zimmerwald, Switzerland, calls for the end of the imperialist war. Lenin and the Bolsheviks form an international committee (the nucleus of the Third International) and, in contrast to the Mensheviks of Martov, want the war to be turned into a civil war in which the workers would seize power.

1916

February   An attack on the German front fails with a costly retreat, but it succeeds in taking pressure off the French on the western front.

April   Russian troops push through Turkish Armenia to Trebizond.

A socialist conference is held at Kienthal, Switzerland.

4 June–
October   The Brusilov offensive (the only offensive of World War I to be named after its commander!) gains some territory south of the Pripet, crossing the Dniester, and taking half a million Austrian prisoners, but it results in a further million Russian casualties. Pressure on the French at Verdun is relieved, and Romania comes into the war on the side of the Allies.

25 June   Decrees for a military call-up of non-Russian peoples, previously exempt, cause resentment, anger and revolt in Russian Asia. In Turkestan and Kazakhstan many thousands of Russians are killed in riots.

September–
October   The food shortages and heavy war casualties lead to strikes in Russian cities and mutinies by soldiers at the front. Proposals to conscript soldiers in Russian Central Asia cause a revolt among the Kazakhs and Kirgiz which is suppressed, but some of the rebels take to the hills and, in rebellion against Russian rule, form a basis for the future anti-Bolshevik Basmachis. It is these people that the revolutionaries of 1917 mistakenly expect to join their cause.

November   Admiral Kolchak's mining of the Bosphorus Sea blocks Turkish trade and regains control of the Black Sea for Russia.

31 December   Rasputin murdered by aristocrats in the palace. His influence over the Tsarina was suspected of being morally evil and pro-German.

By this time in the war, 14,600,000 Russians have been put in uniform: 6,900,000 of them in the field, 2,000,000 in the rear and the remaining 5,700,000 wounded, prisoner or dead. There are also 60,000 Russian troops assisting French armies in France and Salonika who will only hear of the 1917 Revolution through French newspapers.

9 January	300,000 workers stage a strike in Petrograd commemorating 'Bloody Sunday' of 1905.
14 February	The Duma meets and the Progressive Bloc calls, unsuccessfully, for a government which would have national confidence.
22 February	With severe food shortages and an atmosphere of revolt, there are riots in Petrograd. Police fire on the crowds.
23 February	On International Women's Day women from textile factories come on to the streets calling for bread, bringing others out to join them, some 50,000 in all. The Cossacks show a reluctance to charge the crowds. The next day nearly 200,000 come on the streets. Although they are dispersed, the hesitancy of the Cossacks is noticed.
25 February	Soldiers start to join with the strikers and demonstrators; the Tsar orders the suppression of the trouble.
26 February	More soldiers mutiny and join the people, providing weapons for the demonstrators.
	Tsar prorogues the Duma.
27 February	Prince Golitsyn, Chairman of the Council of Ministers, and the cabinet resign. The Progressive Bloc forms a Provisional Committee of the Duma and proclaims that as a Committee of State they have replaced the Tsarist government and taken responsibility for national and public order.
	The Petrograd Soviet of Workers' and Soldiers' Deputies is formed with Chkheidze, the leader of the Mensheviks in the Duma, as chairman. It is an informal body of between 2,000 and 3,000 members, modelled on the 1905 Soviet and occupying part of the same building, the Tauride Palace, as the Duma. The most dominant person is Tsereteli, a Menshevik.
28 February	*Isvestia* calls on people to take power.
	Tsar Nicholas leaves the Stavka to join his wife and family at Tsarskoe Selo.
1 March	Petrograd Soviet declares the army is under its control and in Order No. 1 calls for soldiers' soviets and so removes the authority of officers over men. The order is circulated through the whole army although it was intended for Petrograd only.
2 March	A Provisional Government is agreed between the Provisional Committee and the Petrograd Soviet. It has Prince Lvov at its head as prime minister and commissars replacing the ministers, who are mostly arrested. The Ministry of Foreign Affairs is under Milyukov, War under Guchkov and Justice under Kerensky. Tsar Nicholas II abdicates in favour of his brother Grand Duke Michael and confirms the new government. He and his family are in Tsarskoe Selo, effectively as prisoners.
3 March	Grand Duke Michael refuses to become Tsar.
4 March	A Ukrainian Rada (council) is established in Kiev, mainly by socialists.
11 March	Grand Duke Michael is removed from his post as Commander-in-Chief and replaced by General Alekseev.

12 March	The Provisional Government abolishes the death penalty in the army.
3 April	Lenin returns to Petrograd from exile by the 'Sealed Train'. He is met at the Finland Station by Chkheidze, the Menshevik president of the Petrograd Soviet, as a matter of courtesy.
7 April	Kuropatkin, the governor-general of Turkestan, is arrested and a Turkestan Committee of the Provisional Government is organised.
	An All-Russian Conference of Soviets is in session and votes to continue the war. The Bolsheviks, led by Stalin and Kamenev of the Petrograd Soviet, are pressing for the Provisional Government to open peace negotiations, but Lenin opposes this. He argues for no support for the government in any way; there can be no peace without the overthrow of capitalism. This, the 'April Theses', becomes the Bolsheviks' policy.
	1st Kazakh Conference, nationalist and anti-Russian, is held at Orenburg.
16–23 April	A Congress of Muslims of Turkestan makes nationalist resolutions, but no action is proposed.
24 April	The 7th Conference of the (Bolshevik) Social Democrats meets openly in Petrograd for the first time. Lenin elaborates on his 'April Theses'.
May	Meeting of the 1st All-Russian Congress of Peasant Deputies of 1,350 elected deputies.
3–5 May	Petrograd troops mutiny against the pro-war ministers Guchkov and Milyukov, who resign from government.
	Kornilov resigns his command in Petrograd.
5 May	A revised government under Lvov includes socialists and Kerensky becomes Minister of War.
22 May	General Brusilov appointed Commander-in-Chief, replacing Alekseev, who reverts to his post as Chief of Staff, in order to launch an offensive against the Germans.
June	1st All-Russian Congress of Soviets in Tiflis, where there are SR and Menshevik factions, formally united but rivalling each other. Bolsheviks are elected to the soviet.
10 June	The Bolshevik Central Committee calls for street demonstrations, but these are forestalled by Chkheidze's warnings and abandoned. Tsereteli calls for the disarming of the Red Guards but he is overruled.
18–26 June	An offensive on the southern front with 44 divisions is opened by Brusilov, with initial success. However, it results in losses of 60,000 men and further mutinies. Kornilov insists on an end to the offensive and is made Commander-in-Chief, replacing Brusilov.
18 June	Menshevik and SR leaders of the 1st All-Russian Congress of Soviets call for demonstrations in support of the offensive, but the demonstrators, with Bolshevik organisation, show hostility to the war.
19 June	A general congress (the 'Krug') of the Don Cossacks, held in Petrograd, elects General Kaledin as the Ataman.
June	The Ukrainian Rada sets up a General Secretariat which assumes some of the functions of government.
July	The Tsar and family are moved to Tobolsk.

2 July	Kadet ministers resign when the Provisional Government proposes a treaty with the Ukrainian Rada. They see it as a movement to separate the Ukraine from Russia.
3 July	The July Days: soldiers, sailors from Kronstadt and workers, in all over 30,000, demonstrate in Petrograd against the war, because of low wages and in hatred of the government. They are called out by Bolsheviks, who in the event do not appear, and are led on the march by the Left SR Maria Spiridonova, but dispersed after speeches by Trotsky. Troops and workers who follow find no rising and the day ends in disorder.
4 July	After further disorder the Provisional Government issues warrants for the arrest of leading Bolsheviks, partly on the grounds of their supposed support from Germany. Lenin flees to Finland.
9 July	Prince Lvov resigns and Kerensky becomes prime minister. He forms a new government.
12 July	Provisional Government reintroduces capital punishment and courts martial for the army at the demand of Kornilov.
18 July	Kornilov appointed Commander-in-Chief to replace Brusilov.
21–26 July	The 1st Kazakh Conference is held, but its anti-Russian nationalism attracts only narrow support.
26 July–3 August	The 6th Bolshevik Party Congress, with Lenin still in Finland, decides that any possibility of transfer of power to the soviets is now impossible and that a 'revolutionary proletariat' must seize power when possible.
3 August	Kerensky resigns, but forms a new government.
5 August	In Belorussia a Rada is formed with a largely Socialist Revolutionary policy, hoping to become something like an autonomous republic under the Petrograd Provisional Government.
12–15 August	Kerensky holds a State Conference in Moscow to settle differences between the moderate left, the centre and the right, Chkheidze and Tsereteli supporting him. Kornilov comes and is greeted as a hero and demands greater powers to control anarchy.
21 August	The Russian army on the Baltic is broken and Riga falls to the Germans. Petrograd military district is put under Kornilov.
27–29 August	The Kornilov affair: troops moving towards Petrograd are suspected by Kerensky of being a *coup d'état*. The reason for the moves remain obscure, but Kerensky orders the arrest of Kornilov and other generals. Kornilov claims he is acting in the defence of the Russian people with no political ambition. As Kornilov's cavalry approach Petrograd, the Red Guards are seen as the people's defence against a military counter-revolution. Kerensky assumes the position of Commander-in-Chief of the Russian army.
31 August	Petrograd Soviet has a Bolshevik majority.
1 September	Kornilov submits to arrest. With other generals he is moved to detention in Bykhov.
5 September	Moscow Soviet has a Bolshevik majority and elsewhere Bolshevik groups are getting control of towns such as Tsaritsyn.

9 September	General Alekseev resigns as Chief of Staff in protest against the treatment of Kornilov.
12 September	In Tashkent Bolsheviks and SRs attempt a take-over from the Provisional Government.
20 September	A 'South-Eastern Union' of Cossacks is declared, pledging the independence of the various Cossack groups and hostility to the Bolsheviks.
21 September	The Bolshevik Central Committee decides to take part in Kerensky's 'Pre-Parliament'.
25 September	Trotsky becomes chairman of the Petrograd Soviet Praesidium, which now has a Bolshevik majority among the soldiers' delegates.
6 October	The Duma and State Council are formally dissolved.
	A Kuban Rada declares its independent existence.
7 October	Kerensky organises a 'Pre-Parliament', anticipating the elected Constituent Assembly due in November. The 'Pre-Parliament' meets but its lack of purpose produces no effective action. In Petrograd the Bolsheviks collaborate with it, but Lenin in Finland urges them not to do so but to aim to seize power.
10 October	Lenin, clandestinely in Petrograd at a meeting of the party Central Committee, wins over a majority to his policy of taking power since now, unlike in July, the Bolsheviks have a majority. Kamenev and Zinoviev still hope for a parliamentary victory, but the Central Committee approves of an insurrection in principle.
20 October	Although he is aware of the Bolsheviks' preparations, Kerensky does not order defensive preparations. He probably believes his troops are adequate. The Bolsheviks set up a Military Revolutionary Committee, organised by Trotsky, with commissars appointed to military units who will issue orders and control stores of ammunition. There are 20,000 Red Guards, 60,000 Baltic sailors and 150,000 soldiers of the Petrograd garrison under the control of the Military Revolutionary Committee.
23–25 October	An armed rising is called by the Bolshevik Central Committee's Military Revolutionary Committee. Red Guard detachments occupy, without bloodshed, key points in Petrograd: the telephone exchange, the post office, the railway stations. Summoned by the committee, some 5,000 sailors and soldiers from Kronstadt land in the city and a further 3,000 land in the next four days.
	The Winter Palace, where the government is in session, is threatened by the guns of the cruiser *Aurora* and of the Peter and Paul Fortress, used as military headquarters by the Revolutionary Committee. Red Guards, soldiers and sailors surround the Palace which after a little resistance surrenders. The ministers are taken into custody but Kerensky has already left, looking in vain for military support.
	Petrograd remains outwardly calm, with restaurants and theatres open: Chaliapin sings *Boris Godunov* at the opera house.
25 October	The 2nd All-Russian Congress of Soviets opens with a socialist (but not Bolshevik) majority.
	A Don Cossack State proclaimed by Ataman Alexei Kaledin. It boycotts the Congress of Soviets on the grounds that the Provisional Government is the only valid authority.

26 October	The All-Russian Committee for the Salvation of the Country and the Revolution set up by the Praesidium of the Pre-Parliament. On it are Mensheviks and SRs and others, including trades unions.

The Congress of Soviets elects a Council of People's Commissars, Sovnarkom, with Lenin as its head and including Stalin as Commissar for Nationalities. All the members are Bolsheviks, although they are later joined by Left SRs. It becomes the effective, decision-making body ruling the nation.

27 October   The 3rd All-Russian Congress of Soviets issues two decrees.
    The Decree on Peace: calling for an immediate just peace without indemnities; neither the Western Allies nor the Central Powers took any notice of this.
    The Decree on Land: all land declared the property of the people and to be redistributed by village soviets; this was Socialist Revolutionary rather than Bolshevik policy and although it had popular appeal, it tended to increase the proprietorial instincts of the peasants. Promulgated on the 57th anniversary of Tsar Alexander's decree emancipating the serfs, one of its clauses defines the object of a socialist agricultural programme as being to develop the collective system of agriculture, as it was more economic in respect both of labour and products, at the expense of individual holdings.

29 October   Officer cadets, under orders from the Committee of Salvation, attempt a counter-rising but it fails with heavy casualties.

Kerensky is in Pskov and tries to raise an anti-Bolshevik force.

30 October   Cossack troops are defeated in an attempt to move into Petrograd by a force of sailors, workers and Red Guards.

1 November   In the city of Tashkent Bolsheviks and SRs regain control; there are no Muslims among them.

2 November   Ataman Kaledin assembles an anti-Bolshevik army of Don Cossacks under the command of General Alekseev. This forms the first 'White' army on the Don.

Decree on the rights of nationalities issued by the Petrograd Soviets.

Transcaucasian Commissariat is set up by the Musavet Party in Azerbaijan.

3 November   Bolsheviks with 30,000 Red Guards take power in Moscow after several days' fighting and after reinforcements arrive from Petrograd. The majority of the troops stay neutral.

6 November   The Ukrainian Rada declares an independent republic and groups soldiers of Ukrainian origin into an army. The Rada takes repressive measures against Bolsheviks.

10 November   The 2nd All-Russian Congress of Peasant Deputies meets in Petrograd. The delegates are equally SR (led by Chernov) and Bolshevik combined with the Left SR (led by Spiridonova). Spiridonova is elected to the chair, rather than the popular Chernov, by the soldier deputies because they hate the war and Chernov's 'Defensist' position. The congress breaks up and many of the SRs leave Petrograd; Chernov goes to Samara and later Ufa.

12 November   Elections to the Constituent Assembly are carried out. The Bolsheviks had promised them. 41,000,000 votes were recorded:

	Seats
Social Revolutionaries	370
Bolsheviks	175
Left Social Revolutionaries	40
Mensheviks	16
Kadets	17
Other minority national groups	89
Total	707

(These figures are from Soviet sources; SR historians differ slightly.)

13 November   A Tatar Constituent Assembly assumes authority in the Crimea, led by the Tatar National Party and Kadets.

15 November   Estonia proclaims sovereignty.

In Belorussia an armoured train and troops from Petrograd arrive and a Bolshevik *coup d'état* succeeds. The Rada acquiesces and Bolshevik rule is established.

20 November   Krylenko, a young Bolshevik soldier and lawyer nominated to take command of the army, arrives at Mogilev, storms the Stavka and arrests the general staff of the army and shoots General Dukhonin, the acting Commander-in-Chief, when he refuses to start armistice negotiations with Germany.

21 November   Dzerzhinsky sets up the Commission for Combating Counter-Revolution and Sabotage, Cheka, in the offices of a former insurance company in Lubyanka Street, Moscow. It is directly under the authority of Sovnarkom.

22 November   The 'All-Turkestan Muslim Congress' at Kokand declares southern Central Asian autonomy.

23 November   Led by nationalists resisting 'russification', Finland proclaims independence.

26 November   Eight SRs join Sovnarkom with the Bolsheviks.

28 November   The old Provisional Government, in hiding, issues a call for the Constituent Assembly to meet.

2 December   An armistice is agreed with Germany.

2–3 and 5–13 December   The 2nd and 3rd Kazakh Conferences are held at Orenburg, under the protection of the Cossack General Dutov. He uses the Conferences to take Orenburg for the anti-Bolshevik cause. The conferences fail to attract support for Kazakh rights.

3 December   Bolsheviks occupy the Stavka at Mogilev.

An 'Appeal to Muslim workers of Russia and the East' is issued by Lenin, but without noticeable effect.

6 December   Kornilov and the generals escape from detention in Bykhov and, singly, reach the Don headquarters of the Volunteer Army commanded by General Alekseev.

9 December	Russo-German negotiations for a peace treaty start at Brest-Litovsk.
18 December	The Volunteer Army agrees to be under the military command of Kornilov, but political relations with both civil authorities and foreign powers to be under Alekseev.

1918

5–6 January	The Constituent Assembly opens. But the Bolsheviks and the Left SRs withdraw when their resolution that the assembly should have only limited power is defeated. Red Guards stop delegates entering the assembly and it disperses.
9 January	Ukrainian Rada declares independence.
15 January	The Workers' and Peasants' Red Army established by decree.
	Independence is declared by the 'Baltic Knighthoods' under German influence.
	The Bolshevik Revolutionary Committee for the Don demands that power be handed over to them, and Kaledin finds that the Volunteer Army is not prepared to support him.
26 January	The Siberian Regional Duma in Tomsk is dissolved by the local soviet and they create an anti-Bolshevik provisional government, claiming to rule Siberia.
February	The Russian Muslim assembly in Kazan proposes an autonomous Volga-Ural Muslim state, but non-Muslim Russian socialists block it.
	A new 'Red Fleet' is decreed. One effect is to remove many of the sailors from Kronstadt as the Black Sea fleet is reorganised.
	Ottoman Turkish troops move into the Caucasus to protect Muslims against Armenian revenge.
1–14 February	Gregorian Calendar introduced.

All dates are now given in the 'new style', in common with the rest of the Western world.

6 February	Red troops from Tashkent, with Armenian Dashnak troops in support, attack the Turkestan Muslim autonomous government in Kokand. There is a massacre in the city and the resultant dispersal of Central Asians is part of the cause of the formation of Basmachi groups. The Red troops' attack on Bokhara is beaten back.
8 February	Soviet troops occupy Kiev.
9 February	Ukraine concludes a peace treaty with the Central Powers, Germany and Austria, who recognise its independence.
10 February	The Russians break off their negotiations with the Central Powers, the Bolshevik Central Committee having voted for Trotsky's proposal of 'neither peace nor war', that is to declare the war at an end but not accept the Austro-German annexations.
11 February	Kaledin commits suicide.
16 February	Lithuania declares independence.

18 February	Germans resume fighting in the Ukraine. They control the Donets coal area.
	Attempts to install a Soviet government on the Don are frustrated by the anti-Bolshevik Cossack Krug (assembly), who prefer a Don-Caucasian Union with German help.
23 February	After the All-Russian Congress of Soviets had voted in January to create their own military organisation, the Workers' and Peasants' Red Army, mass meetings are held and in Petrograd alone 60,000 volunteer. This day is now celebrated as 'Red Army Day'. Facing the threat to their revolution of the German advance, Lenin issues the proclamation 'The Socialist Fatherland is in Danger'.
24 February	The Central Committee and the All-Russian Congress of Soviets accept the German terms for peace. Trotsky resigns as Commissar for Foreign Affairs and becomes Commissar for War.
	Estonia declares independence, while Latvia waits for changes in its circumstances.
	The Volunteer Army, with a strength of about 4,000 men, is led out by Kornilov on the 'Ice March' across the steppes south towards the Kuban.
25 February	The Red Army occupies the Don capital and most of the Cossack forces submit.
	The main body of the Finnish Jäger battalion (formed in 1915), about 2,000 well-equipped and German-trained men, arrives in Finland, providing the nationalist General Mannerheim with an anti-Bolshevik and anti-Russian force.
1 March	Treaty of Friendship with the 'Finnish Socialist Republic' signed. But this is a short-lived revolutionary government and the Finnish nationalists continue to fight.
2 March	Germans re-occupy Kiev and restore Rada rule.
3 March	Treaty of Brest-Litovsk between Russia and the Central Powers (the German and Austrian Empires) is signed by Sokolnikov, because major Bolshevik figures will not risk putting their name to it. Russia cedes Poland, territory on the Baltic and allows independence for Finland and the Ukraine. There are supplements to the treaty signed with Bulgaria, Romania and Turkey. Russia surrenders to Turkey: Kars, Ardahan and Batum. The Left SR vote against the treaty and resign from Sovnarkom. The treaty is later invalidated after the 1918 Allied victory.
	In Baku there are race riots, continuing through the month, between Armenians and Azeri Muslims: 3,000 are killed.
6–8 March	The 7th Party Congress is held in Petrograd. The Party is now the 'RCP(B)' – Russian Communist Party (Bolshevik).
10 March	An offensive against the Whites in Finland starts. Germany supports the Finns with troops.
12 March	Soviet government moves from Petrograd to Moscow. The Kremlin becomes the seat of national government.
15 March	The Brest-Litovsk Treaty is ratified by the 7th Party Congress.
25 March	The nationalists in the Belorussian Rada see the opportunity for independence and meet to declare a national republic.

27 March	The first group of the Czech Legion, the military unit formed in 1916 of Czech prisoners of war and émigrés, which it has been agreed will be returned to their home by the only possible route, begins to leave by rail across Siberia to Vladivostok.
April	Bolshevik and left-Menshevik soviet established in Baku.
5 April	Allied troops land at Murmansk (their declared purpose being to protect the dumps of Allied arms and ammunition there). A Japanese contingent lands at Vladivostok shortly afterwards.
13 April	Kornilov, leading the anti-Bolshevik Volunteer Army, is killed by a shell and Denikin takes his place as military commander.
	Germany takes Odessa.
14 April	The Finns, led by Mannerheim with German support, take Helsinki.
22 April	The 'Democratic Federal Republic of Transcaucasia' declares independence, with Turkish and German troops present, as an outcome of the Treaty of Brest-Litovsk.
	Turkish troops move into the territory around Kars ceded to Turkey under the treaty. They continue deep into the Caucasus, to Tiflis and Erevan.
23 April	Germany makes a trade agreement with the Ukraine.
29 April	The Germans throw out the Rada and set up their own Ukrainian government under Hetman Skoropadsky, a wealthy landowner and a relation of the German army commander.
30 April	German troops take the Black Sea naval base of Sevastopol and demand the return of the Russian fleet, which the Bolsheviks order back to port, but the sailors scuttle the ships. In the Crimea the Germans install a puppet government.
	The Turkestan Autonomous Soviet Socialist Republic is declared by Lenin and Stalin (as Commissar for Nationalities).
4 May	The Bolsheviks make an armistice with the German-controlled Ukraine.
8 May	Germans in Rostov.
11 May	A 'North Caucasian Federal Republic' is founded by Georgian Mensheviks in Tiflis.
14 May	A fight between some Hungarians and Czechs at Chelyabinsk causes the Czech Legion to take up arms in its defence, which brings the Czechs into conflict with the local soviet.
15 May	The Finnish nationalists take the last Bolshevik-held fort on the Karelian isthmus.
25 May	Trotsky orders that any armed Czech found on the Penza–Omsk line is to be shot imediately. This gives the Czechs even greater determination to defend themselves since they see Trotsky and the Bolshevik government as allies of their enemies, the Germans.
26 May	Transcaucasian independence: the Georgian Soviet Democratic Republic is proclaimed by Irakly Tsereteli and recognised by the Moscow Soviet in August. This starts the break-up of the single Caucasian Republic into three – Georgia, Armenia and Azerbaijan.
28 May	Azerbaijan establishes its own government. It starts negotiations with the new Turkish leader Kemal Atatürk.

29 May	Although the Red Army strength is now 300,000 through volunteers, conscription is introduced. Denikin's Russian Volunteer Army is controlling much of the south, having pulled back into the steppes from the Kuban, but taking Novorossiisk after the fleet has sailed. He plans to move to control Azerbaijan, but the British presence blocks him.
30 May	Armenia announces its independence.
1 June	At Omsk an SR-dominated West Siberian Commissariat, with its own white and green flag (snow and forest), profiting from the activity of the Czech Legion, proclaims the autonomy of Siberia, continuing from the establishment of the Siberian Regional Duma set up in January and in support of the Constituent Assembly. By the end of the month this is taken over by the right-wing government of western Siberia.
8 June	The Czechs move to Samara, their presence allowing the SRs to form a government accepting the authority of the Constituent Assembly. The SRs hope to establish an all-Russian, pro-Allies and anti-Bolshevik government.
12 June	An armistice is signed with the Ukrainian regime of Skoropadsky.
13 June	A Revolutionary Military Council is established east of the Ural Mountains to deal with the Czech Legion.
14–20 June	The Menshevik and Right SRs are expelled from the Kronstadt Soviet, as they have been throughout Russia.
18 June	Committees of Poor Peasants are set up. Their purpose is to extract grain from the kulaks and the rich.
26 June	Kerensky appears unexpectedly at a British Labour Party conference in London. He says that the Russian people are fighting and will continue to fight against tyranny (meaning Germany).
June	Turkey makes an agreement with the Azerbaijani Musavet Party and moves towards their objective, Baku.
July	A Transcaspian government set up at Orenburg, mainly by anti-Bolshevik railwaymen. When the British leave Baku in September, this government is without protection.
4 July	4th Congress of Soviets: Spiridonova leads an attack on the Brest-Litovsk Treaty.
10 July	Constitution of the Russian Soviet Federal Socialist Republic (RSFSR), adopted by the 5th All-Russian Congress of Soviets (convened immediately after the 4th Congress), is published.
16 July	The German Ambassador von Mirbach is shot and killed in Moscow by two Left SR members under the orders of Spiridonova. They are also Cheka officials.
16–17 July	At Ekaterinburg, fearing an anti-Bolshevik attack (in fact the approach of the Czech Legion), Tsar Nicholas, Tsarina Alexandra, four daughters and a son are shot by their Cheka guards.
	Abortive anti-Bolshevik risings in Yaroslav (also in other centres, Rybinsk, Murom, Kazan, Kaluga and Vladimir) organised by the former SR Savinkov.
25 July	The Czech Legion enters Ekaterinburg.
2 August	Government set up in Archangel under Chaikovsky, with about 13,000 Allied troops landing.

6–7 August	The Czech Legion (now seen by the Bolsheviks as White forces) moving from Samara capture Kazan, where they find the Tsarist government's gold reserves. It would have advanced south to Saratov, but it was halted by the brilliant partisan leader Chapayev.
	Denikin advances towards the Volga River and besieges Tsaritsyn, where Stalin is sent as the Party's representative. With him are Budyenny, Ordzhonikidze and Voroshilov. They successfully withstand the siege.
14 August	British forces land at Baku, ostensibly to defend the area against the Turks, but also to protect the oil fields.
	Japanese, with British and Americans, land at Vladivostok; some 20,000 troops involved.
16 August	The capital of the Kuban is taken by Denikin's troops.
26 August	Lenin shot and injured by Fanya Kaplan, a Right SR.
	Denikin occupies the Black Sea port of Novorossiisk, where the Imperial fleet has already been scuttled.
2 September	The Revolutionary Military Council of the Republic is set up under Trotsky to control all military operations, but, given the communications, local councils continue to act on their own.
5 September	Sovnarkom issue a decree giving sweeping powers to the Cheka. This is the beginning of the 'Red Terror'.
8 September	Conference at Ufa of non-Bolshevik governments.
10 September	Trotsky's Red Army recaptures Kazan.
14 September	The British leave Baku, with a local anti-Bolshevik administration in charge.
15 September	The Musavet Party in Baku makes an alliance with the Turks (who are seen as enemies by the Armenians and Georgians).
20 September	26 Bolshevik 'Commissars', the leaders of the earlier attempt at control of the area, are taken from Baku and shot. British complicity assumed in this. The only survivor of the Bolshevik leadership there is Mikoyan.
23 September	White forces at Ufa set up the Directorate, an All-Russian Provisional Government of five members.
25 September	The leaders of the Volunteer Army and the Georgian Republic meet and debate their responsibilities, the Georgians arguing that the army was there solely to fight the Bolsheviks, not to determine states' rights or borders.
8 October	The Red Army takes Samara and the Whites are forced back to the east of the Urals.
9 October	The Directorate, forced from Ufa, sites its capital at Omsk.
11 October	The SR Central Committee at Ekaterinburg calls on the party to resist the rightist tendencies of the Directorate at Omsk.
October	Alekseev, who has been ailing a long time, dies and Denikin assumes both military and political command of the Volunteer Army.
11 November	Armistice between the Allies and Germany.
November	Soviet government, following the armistice between Germany and the Allies, denounces the Brest-Litovsk Treaty.

17 November	Another British contingent arrives at Baku, being met by an Azerbaijan Musavet government, which it cannot recognise unless it admits to being a part of Russia. Latvia, with a strong working-class movement and strong sympathies with the Bolsheviks on the one hand and Baltic German nationalists supported by Freikorps (German ex-soldiers organised into efficient fighting units) on the other, only now declares independence.
18 November	Omsk Directorate overthrown by officers, with the tacit approval of the Allied officers there, and Kolchak assumes full powers as 'supreme ruler' of all Russia.
25 November	An Allied naval squadron receives the surrender of the German fleet at Sevastopol (which was seized Tsarist ships).
14 December	The Skoropadsky puppet regime collapses in the Ukraine. The Ukrainian Social Democrat Petlyura re-emerges as Commander-in-Chief. With his forces growing rapidly to 100,000, allied with the anarchist Makhno's peasant guerrillas, he takes the capital Kiev.
17 December	France lands troops in Odessa as part of a plan to maintain order and ensure the evacuation of the Germans.
	The Ukrainian Directorate proclaims the restoration of independence. Petlyura's forces advance rapidly towards Odessa, where he stops outside the city, not wishing to be in conflict with the French. But elements of the Volunteer Army try to persuade the French troops into action against the Ukrainians, declaring them to be enemies of Russia.
23 December	The Central Committee decides to establish a Belorussian Soviet Socialist Republic.
29 December	A coalition government for Azerbaijan in Baku is accepted by the British who also have outposts at Batum and Tiflis. The Georgians are assured by the British that they too will receive a form of recognition.

1919

1 January	Belorussian Soviet Republic is formally declared.
3 January	The Red Army takes Riga in Latvia, where Baltic Germans have been in power, and Kharkov in the Ukraine.
5 January	An agreement is alleged to have been signed between the Bolsheviks and the German communist Karl Liebknecht to assist with 'Russian Gold' the establishment of a 'German Soviet Republic'. Karl Radek is in Berlin with the hope of raising the German revolutionaries and is arrested. During this month German soldiers murder Liebknecht and Rosa Luxemburg after an attempted rising in Berlin.
6 January	The Osipov coup d'état in Tashkent: a young ex-Tsarist officer working for the Bolsheviks but hostile to the Muslims and disillusioned with the regime declares Bolshevik rule in Central Asia at an end, but in two days the Red Guards in the town – mostly railway workers – have reversed the position. Osipov gets away with the money from the Central Bank and is never heard of again.

16 January	The Ukrainian Rada declares war against the soviets.
January	The 'Russian Political Conference' is held in Paris, consisting of senior Imperial Russians abroad at the time, including ambassadors. Prince Lvov is designated chairman. It is hoped that this body will co-ordinate the governments in Russia: South (Denikin), Siberian (Kolchak) and Northern (Chaikovsky). Unity is never achieved nor is recognition of the conference by the Western Allies achieved, since it is seen as one of a stream of representatives from minority nationalities with good claims to be heard. Thus Russia does not have a seat at the Versailles peace conference.
	Red Army takes Orenburg, its way to Central Asia being opened by Kolchak's defeat there. However, Kolchak's offensive in March rules out any chance of the Red Army linking forces with Tashkent.
6 February	Red Army takes Kiev. Petlyura's force has lost Makhno's partisans, who now are siding with the communists.
	Antonov-Ovseenko, the Red Army commander, moves rapidly through the southern Ukraine.
15 February	Denikin assumes supreme command of White forces in south-eastern Russia.
March	Polish armies under Pilsudski advance into Lithuania, the Ukraine and Belorussia. Belorussia is proclaimed part of Poland. At the same time the Belorussian Soviet Republic declares that Lithuania is merged into it.
2–7 March	Communist International holds 1st Congress in Moscow. The Comintern is formed in the expectation of the Revolution spreading throughout the world.
13 March	Kolchak starts an offensive from the Urals, hoping to advance to the north-west, linking with the White forces around Archangel.
18–23 March	8th Russian Communist Party (Bolshevik) Congress in Moscow. A Secretariat and Politburo are set up; both are already functioning in effect although the Politburo, with the Orgburo, is not formally in the Party's statutes until December 1919. Stalin is a member of both bodies.
21 March	The withdrawal of Allied troops from Russia is decided. The plans for a Franco-Ukrainian offensive are abandoned in the face of Antonov-Ovseenko's advance and the French troops landed at Odessa withdraw.
27 March	Foch's plan for an anti-Bolshevik crusade is rejected by the Allied Supreme Council.
5 April	British troops decide to leave Transcaucasia, having helped Armenia occupy territory, such as the province of Kars. They have found themselves a buffer between the nationalist Georgians and the insistence by Denikin on Russian imperial rights.
8 April	French troops leave Odessa, having been under pressure since mid-March from pro-Bolshevik partisans. The French are also anxious to leave since they do not accept Denikin's right to rule there. The city is crowded with refugees, but the French manage to evacuate 30,000 as well as 10,000 of the Volunteer Army.
	The Ukrainian Soviet Republic is formed.
10 April	Red Army enters the Crimea.

15 April	The People's Commissariat for Internal Affairs (NKVD) officially institutes labour camps run by the Cheka.
April	General Miller in Archangel acknowledges Kolchak's authority.
24 April	Beginning of the Russo–Polish war. The Poles destroy Bolshevik rule in Lithuania.
30 April	Sevastopol evacuated by the French, taking with them the Crimean government, after having agreed a truce with the Red Army.
4 May	Kolchak is defeated on both his centre and southern fronts.
19 May	The Denikin offensive starts. The Volunteer Army is now named the Armed Forces of South Russia. The army at this date has 64,000 men in the line but will soon grow to its largest with 150,000 men.
22 May	Riga, Latvia, is cleared of Bolshevik forces.
26 May	The Armenians declare their territory, combined with former Turkish lands, the Armenian Republic.
	A Georgian Soviet Democratic Republic is proclaimed and recognised by the Moscow Soviet in August.
30 May	Denikin retakes Kharkov in the Ukraine.
June	The advance of General Yudenich's north-western White army forces the evacuation of over 16,000 women and children from Kronstadt. Its mainland fortress of Krasnaia Gorka mutinies and defects to the Whites.
4 June	The Social Democrat Petlyura's Ukrainian nationalist forces take the key Galician town of Kamenetz Podolsk. The Galicians, however, seeing Polish troops moving eastward into the Ukraine, prefer to ally themselves with Denikin.
9 June	Red Army under Frunze takes Ufa.
14 June	Mensheviks and SRs are expelled from the Central Executive Committee of the Soviets. The Mensheviks (who are the Russian Social Democratic Labour Party) have maintained their ideals and gained popular strength but have no political power, newspapers nor armed force. They continue to gain seats on soviets throughout the country and to hold, individually, senior posts, especially in trade unions until 1921.
16 June	Krasnaia Gorka is recaptured and a purge begins on Kronstadt: hundreds are shot after a brief court martial.
1 July	Wrangel captures Tsaritsyn, having accepted command of the army of the Caucasus, largely Cossack, on Denikin's right flank.
10 July	A Kirghiz Revolutionary Committee is appointed.
12 July	USA orders the recall of all its military missions in southern Russia since they are becoming involved in what is seen to be the local problems of recognising statehood.
15 July	Red Army takes Chelyabinsk, putting Kolchak's Siberian army on the retreat.
23 August	Denikin takes Odessa.
August	British troops leave Azerbaijan via Iran and their troops in Georgia move to Batum for evacuation.

31 August	Denikin takes Kiev.
19 September	Allied troops evacuate Archangel.
20 September	Denikin's Whites, the AFSR centre group, take Kursk after the failure of a Red Army offensive.
28 September	The White General Yudenich's offensive reaches the suburbs of Petrograd.
14–20 October	Denikin takes Orel, and his army moves towards Tula, the last major city before Moscow. But he is forced back, starting a general White retreat as Budyenny's Red Army cavalry break through between the Volunteer and Don forces.
14 November	Yudenich is defeated by the energetic defence of Petrograd. He receives no help from the Finns nor from the Estonians.
15 November	Petlyura is given full authority as head of the Rada.
	Omsk taken by Red Army. Kolchak abdicates in favour of Denikin.
17 November	The White army loses Kursk and the centre commander at Kursk is replaced by Wrangel, who also takes command of the Volunteer Army.
December	8th (7th All-Russian) Conference of the Party is held in Moscow.
6 December	Petlyura goes to Warsaw for talks with the Polish government.
12 December	Kharkov taken by Red Army.
16 December	Kiev taken by Red Army and a reorganised Bolshevik regime takes power in the Ukraine.
24 December	A Menshevik and SR group take over Irkutsk in Siberia.
31 December	An armistice is signed in Estonia with the Soviet government.

1920

January–February	The soviets now gain control of most of eastern Siberia.
January	Sovnarkom issues a plan for the general mobilisation of labour, including work books which will state if the owner is carrying out socially useful work. The mobilisation of labour is extended to returning troops and Trotsky and Bukharin suggest the militarisation of labour to solve the problems of industry.
4 January	Kolchak resigns as 'supreme ruler' of all Russia, abdicating in favour of Denikin, and appoints Semenov commander of the White forces in the Far East.
8 January	Rostov is taken by Red Army. This is Denikin's last stand and his troops retreat into the Crimea.
15 January	Czech Legion hands over Kolchak to a 'Revolutionary People's Army' in Irkutsk, which, although Menshevik and SR, is in sympathy with the Bolsheviks.

31 January	General Rozanov overthrown, bloodlessly, in Vladivostok.
1 February	An armistice is signed in Latvia with the Soviet government.
2 February	A peace treaty with Estonia is signed at Tartu (known in German as Dorpat). This follows negotiations after the defeat of Yudenich in November 1919. It is seen by Chicherin as a first experiment in peaceful co-existence with bourgeois, capitalist states.
7 February	Kolchak executed in Irkutsk.
19 February	The northern White government of General Miller in Archangel falls.
February	Frunze takes command in Central Asia and captures Khiva; the Khanate of Khiva is declared a people's republic.
March	9th Party Congress. The Orgburo of the Central Committee, which includes Stalin and the three secretaries, now controls the placing of Party officials.
9 March	The Kirghiz Revolutionary Committee liquidates all nationalist opponents.
4 April	Wrangel takes over from Denikin, and starts reorganising the civil administration in the Crimea.
6 April	The 'Far Eastern Republic' is founded, made up of the territories east of Lake Baikal, north of Mongolia and Manchuria to the sea, including Vladivostok. Its capital is Chita. Although nominally independent, it is Bolshevik controlled and acts as a buffer against possible Japanese or Chinese ambitions. Although recognised as a separate state by the soviets, it returns to the RSFSR in 1921.
21 April	Polish–Ukrainian treaty of friendship signed.
24 April	Polish–Soviet war; Poles under Pilsudski invade the Ukraine.
27 April	Ordzhonikidze enters Baku and the independent government of Azerbaijan is ended. A Provisional Revolutionary Committee is formed.
29 April	A declaration of 'friendly relations' is signed with Japan.
6 May	Poles take Kiev.
7 May	Peace is agreed with the Georgian Republic.
11 May	A treaty is made with Turkey and the Republic of Armenia under its Dashnak government.
6 June	Wrangel launches an offensive northward out of the Crimea. He tries to make the Ukrainian partisans allies, but Makhno simply hangs his envoy.
12 June	Kiev retaken by Red Army.
July	Batum (ceded to Turkey under the Treaty of Brest-Litovsk) is occupied by Georgia after British troops leave.
	The peasants of Tambov, 260 miles (420 km) south-east of Moscow, take to arms in protest against Bolshevik rule: within the year there are up to 10,000 of them. Their leader is A S Antonov and their opposition is not halted until Lenin receives a delegation in February 1921.
11 July	The Red Army retakes Minsk from the Poles.
12 July	The Treaty of Moscow with Lithuania, recognising its independence. Vilnius (in Polish Wilno), occupied by the Red Army, is ceded to Lithuania.

19 July	After the treaty with Lithuania, parts of Belorussia are handed over to Lithuania.
	2nd Congress of the Comintern. Lenin advocates communist support for the overthrow of the colonialist 'feudal–landlord' order. This supposes that the national movements may not be communist, but should be supported to take power and then be taken over themselves at a second stage. The Indian communist M. N. Roy argues that the bourgeoisie and nationalist movements in colonies are essentially reactionary and that a workers' and peasants' revolutionary movement is needed. Lenin's argument prevails and the nationalist movements are deemed revolutionary. The revised Marxist slogan is adopted: 'Workers of the world, and of oppressed nations, unite!'
26 August	The Kirghiz Autonomous Soviet Socialist Republic is set up in Orenburg. The name Kirghiz is later dropped and Kazakh used for this territory (the Kirghiz people are to the south).
10 August	Western Allies sign the Treaty of Sèvres with the Turkish Ottoman Empire, ending its rule of land outside Asia Minor; the Armenian Republic is given parts of Turkey. The new ruler of Turkey, Kemal Atatürk, refuses to accept the treaty.
	The Soviet Union makes a military agreement with the Armenian Republic.
11 August	The treaty of Riga signed with Latvia, confirming Soviet relations with the third of the Baltic republics.
17 August	Red Army units approach Warsaw but are beaten back by a Polish counter-offensive. This ends the last real hope of the communist revolution spreading to the rest of industrialised Europe.
September	The 9th Party Conference.
13 September	The 'Khorezmian People's Socialist Republic', the former Khanate of Khiva, is recognised by the Soviet Union.
21 September	Russo–Polish peace talks start.
September	Frunze's Red Army troops enter Bokhara after four days' fighting and the Emir flees to Afghanistan; a Soviet Republic of Bokhara is declared (later included in Uzbekistan with Khiva).
28 September	Turkey attacks the Armenian Republic after its intervention in Turkish Anatolia over persecuted Armenian minotities. In a two-month campaign 200,000 Armenians are killed.
	A Comintern Congress of Peoples of the East is held at Baku. It includes delegates from Turkey, China and Russian Central Asia. The argument that the eastern, Muslim world has a different class structure and that the nationalist *petit bourgeoisie* were the key to revolution was rejected and ignored in Moscow.
	The congress also promised that independent Asian countries would have its co-operation, while colonial countries would be urged to revolt.
9 October	Polish troops occupy the Lithuanian capital Vilnius and hold it until 1939 as part of Poland, by League of Nations agreement.
12 October	Russo–Polish peace treaty.

14 October	Finland and Russia sign a peace treaty at Tartu. While the Arctic port of Petsamo is given to Finland, along with the Karelian isthmus as a boundary, part of Karelia is included as an autonomous republic in the RSFSR. Finnish fortifications are also to be demolished.
28 October	Frunze, sent to deal with Wrangel, attacks on the north Tauride front.
2 November	Wrangel is defeated and forced back into the Crimea.
11–14 November	Wrangel's forces ae evacuated from the Crimea: 150,000 refugees are taken to Turkey; 60,000 of them are soldiers but as an army they are soon dispersed. The remnants of the Imperial Russian navy are sailed to French Tunisia and maintained there for several years still recruiting and training.
23 November	Lenin introduces a policy of concessions to the hostile capitalist world surrounding the Soviet Union. Trade relations are to be established and a breathing space gained.
29 November	The Soviet Union mediates between Turkey and Armenia and in the process sets up a new Soviet Armenian government and accepts an earlier agreement on the partition of Armenia and Azerbaijan which produces the anomalous status of Nagorny Karabakh.
December	7th Congress of Soviets of Workers', Soldiers' and Peasants' Deputies. SRs and Mensheviks attend.
	Sovnarkom decrees that payment for rations is to be abolished, thus confirming the statement made earlier by the All-Russian Central Executive Committee of the Soviets (VTsIK) welcoming moneyless transactions 'with a view to total abolition of the monetary system'.
2 December	Turkey signs treaties recognising their national status and frontiers with both the Dashnak Armenian Republic and the Soviet Armenian Republic.
20 December	The Ukrainian Soviet Socialist Republic signs a Treaty of Alliance with the Soviet Union.
30 December	Last of the Czech Legion leave Vladivostok and the operation is officially ended.

1921

16 January	The Belorussian Republic is recognised and an alliance with Soviet Russia signed.
February	Baron Ungern-Sternberg captures the Mongolian capital Urga, hoping to use it as an anti-Bolshevik base against Siberia.
13 February	The last appearance of the anarchists in Russia as their survivors are released from prison for the day of Kropotkin's funeral.
14 February	A peace treaty with Lithuania is signed.
	Lenin meets a delegation from Tambov, where the peasants have been in revolt since the summer of 1920.
16 February	The Soviet Union moves troops into Georgia, with Stalin supervising the occupation.

20 February	A treaty of friendship is signed with Persia (Iran).
21 February	The Red Army moves into Dushambe, the capital of the future Taji-kistan.
22 February	Gosplan, the State Planning Commission, is established.
	Demonstrations in Petrograd, where food and fuel have become scarce.
24 February	Petrograd factory workers strike.
25 February	The Menshevik Georgian Soviet Democratic Republic is overthrown in Tiflis, with help from the Red Army, ending its independence. It becomes the Georgian Soviet Socialist Republic. With Armenia and Azerbaijan it is joined into the Transcaucasian Federation in 1922.
	Zinoviev is put in charge of a Defence Committee to deal with the Petrograd demonstrations.
27 February	Martial law is proclaimed in Petrograd.
	A delegation of Kronstadt sailors visits Petrograd and returns to report the failure of Bolshevik rule and to demand a non-party conference.
28 February	A treaty of friendship with Afghanistan is signed.
	The sailors of the battleship *Petropavlovsk* at Kronstadt call for free elections of new soviets, freedom of speech, the liberation of all socialist political prisoners, equal rations for all and full rights for land-holding peasants and small industrialists who are not employers.
1 March	Kalinin, the nominal head of state, goes to Kronstadt to appeal to the sailors, and to warn them. The outcome is a mass meeting which elects a non-Bolshevik revolutionary committee. There are 16,000 sailors, soldiers and workers in revolt under the slogan 'Soviets without Communists'. They send delegates to Petrograd.
8 March	An attempt by Soviet troops to take Kronstadt fails.
	In Petrograd the Defence Committee takes emergency powers and troops are gathered to storm the naval base.
8–16 March	10th Party Congress: there are now nearly three-quarters of a million Party members, but there is a 'cleansing' operation, removing a quarter of a million members in the first Party purge. Lenin announces the New Economic Policy (NEP). There is a resolution passed against 'party factions'.
11 March	Turkish troops occupy Batum.
16 March	A trade agreement is signed with Great Britain, having been negotiated since May 1920. This marks a major change in the Soviet State's status, for it is *de facto* recognition by a major international power. Other states follow to share any advantage of the new trade area.
	A treaty is signed with Turkey, giving Batum to the Soviet Union and Kars and Ardahan to Turkey.
	Stalin is elected to the Politburo and Orgburo of the Party's Central Committee.
17–18 March	Under Trotsky's Defence Committee, Tukhachevsky and Kamenev mobilise a force of 50,000 which, under heavy machine gun and artillery covering fire, goes over the ice to enter Kronstadt. 8,000 sailors escape

	to Finland, thousands of others are drafted to other naval units or labour camps and hundreds are rounded up and shot.

18 March   The Treaty of Riga between Russia, the Ukraine and Poland ends the war between them and defines their frontier. Poland gains a frontier further to the east than the earlier proposed 'Curzon Line'.

25 March   United States Secretary of State Hughes, in response to an approach by Litvinov, states that no trade relations are possible as long as Russia does not recognise 'the sanctity of private property, the sanctity of contract, and the rights of free labor'.

April   Famine in Volga region.

10 April   The Soviet Union fails to gain the co-operation of China over the Ungern-Sternberg regime in Mongolia and sets up a nominal communist Chinese government.

6 May   A Soviet–German agreement is signed, giving openings for trade. A secret agreement is also made to start the manufacture of German Junkers aircraft in Russia, financed by the German government. Three factories are built.

May   10th Party Conference.

21 May   An alliance with the Georgian Soviet Socialist Republic is signed.

27 May   Ungern-Sternberg in the Mongolian capital Urga declares himself 'Emperor of all Russia' and moves his Cossack and Chinese troops into the Soviet Union, where a Mongolian People's Republic government in exile is waiting. After brutal fighting, in which all prisoners are killed, Ungern–Sternberg is captured.

Independent Mongolian republics are set up as the autonomous protectorates of Inner Mongolia and Outer Mongolia (with Urga renamed Ulan-Bator as its capital).

26 June   *Pravda* reports that 25 million people in Russia are starving.

12 July   3rd Comintern Congress. The emphasis is on the search for new tactics, seeing the lack of progress towards a world revolution. Lenin says the main task is winning over the majority of the working class but he also expresses his hopes for nationalist revolutionary movements in Asia.

A rebellion by the people of Soviet East Karelia is supported by the Finns who, with Estonia, appeal to the League of Nations for a settlement.

13 July   Maxim Gorky issues an appeal to the world for aid for the Russian famine.

23 July   Herbert Hoover, chairman of the American Relief Administration (ARA), offers assistance to the starving, which the Soviet government accepts.

August   Tannu Tuva, a minor Tsarist Russian protectorate on the border of Mongolia, is established as an independent people's republic. The territory had been abandoned by Russian officials in 1918, taken over by Chinese rulers and used by White Russian troops. It will become an autonomous region within the RSFSR from 1944.

20 August   Famine relief agreements are signed with the American Relief Administration and the Red Cross. In the next two years the ARA feeds 11 million people and clothes millions more. Fridtjof Nansen, for the Red

Cross, raises huge sums of money and ships over 90,000 tonnes of food, but his plea to the League of Nations to take a lead in the relief of Russia fails.

August–
September
The Turks under Mustapha Kemal Atatürk decisively defeat the Greek occupation forces in Anatolia. This transforms the weakened Turkish Ottoman Empire into the strong modern republic of Turkey on the border of the Soviet Transcaucasian Federation.

15 September Ungern-Sternberg put on trial in Novosibirsk and shot.

13 October The Soviet–Turkish Treaty of Kars agrees on the borders with Turkey of Armenia, Azerbaijan and Georgia.

5 November A Soviet-Mongolian People's Republic treaty is signed, the Soviet Union no longer recognising Chinese authority there.

8 November Enver Pasha, who had escaped from Turkey to live in Russia, arrives at Bokhara, sent by Lenin to persuade the Muslim population away from support for the rebel Basmachis, but instead he joins them, planning to lead a holy war.

7 December An agreement with Austria, on the lines of the German agreement of May, is signed.

December 11th Party Conference.

1922

2 January Turkey signs a treaty of friendship with the Ukraine.

January–
March
Soviet troops crush the revolt which started in July 1921 in East Karelia.

February The Cheka is reorganised as the GPU.

14 February Enver Pasha captures Dushambe, then raids Bokhara and gains control of most of the former kingdom.

March–April 11th Party Congress. It defines the limits of the NEP, the state retaining control of large-scale industry, national transport and foreign trade, about which Lenin later showed great optimism.

3 April Stalin is elected Party General Secretary.

Lenin in convalescence after an operation to remove two bullets from the shooting in August 1918.

Arrest of Patriarch Tikhon and the dissolution of the Orthodox Church Holy Synod.

10 April The Genoa Conference of 34 nations (but not the USA) on economic reconstruction opens. Chicherin counters claims against Russia with accounts of the damages caused by intervention during the Civil War. The right of the RSFSR to represent the other Soviet republics is accepted, being a step towards the Union of Soviet Socialist Republics.

18 April The Treaty of Rapallo is signed by the Soviet Union and Germany, mutually renouncing reparations for war damage and establishing diplomatic and economic relations. One outcome is the establishment of the clandestine, German-staffed flying school at Lipetsk in central Russia.

29 April	The Soviet Union gives Turkey arms, ammunition and a credit of 100 million gold roubles to re-establish its army, thus enabling Turkey to end its war with Greece victoriously.
May	Enver Pasha, leading 7,000 Basmachi, demands the withdrawal of Soviet troops from Turkestan. He is in touch with King Amanullah of Afghanistan.
26 May	Lenin suffers a stroke, losing his power of speech. Stalin becomes the principal link between Lenin and the Politburo.
1 June	A new agreement with Finland is made to try and settle their frontier disputes.
14 June	Enver Pasha is defeated by the Red Army and his forces dispersed.
17 July	The Afghan Ambassador leaves Bokhara, accused of actively assisting the Basmachis. The Emir of Bokhara and his entourage remain in Afghanistan, but Amanullah abandons any hope of detaching Bokhara from the Soviet Union.
4 August	Enver Pasha is killed fighting, ending his insurrection.
August	12th Party Conference.
	Trials of Socialist Revolutionaries held in Moscow.
26 September	Stalin disputes the status of national minorities in the future Soviet Union with Lenin, convalescing at Gorky. Stalin, organising the federation of the Russian, Ukrainian, Belorussian and Transcaucasian Republics, proposes that they all come into a 'Russian Federation' and that minorities would be adequately represented, but with 'Great Russian' dominance.
2 October	Lenin returns to Moscow.
5 October– 5 December	4th Comintern Congress. The slogan of the 3rd Congress is repeated 'to the masses', with tactics for implementing 'united fronts', that is persuading workers' movements to voice support for revolution. Delegates are given the task of winning over the majority of the working classes of Europe and America.
20 November	'Far Eastern Republic' (former eastern parts of the Tsarist Empire) is dissolved and joins the RSFSR.
13–23 December	Lenin has further strokes, but he continues working and dictates his 'Letter to the Congress', also known as his 'Testament', with the often-quoted adverse comment on Stalin, his praise of Trotsky and the ambiguous remarks on Zinoviev and Kamenev.
30 December	The Union of Soviet Socialist Republics (USSR) is formed by the federation of the republics of Russia, Ukraine, Belorussia, Transcaucasia, Khorezm, Bokhara and the Far Eastern Republic.
31 December	Azerbaijan enters the USSR (as the Azerbaijan Socialist Soviet Republic) along with Georgia and Armenia, part of the Transcaucasian Federation.

1923

4 January	Lenin dictates a codicil to his 'Letter', warning of Stalin's ambition and proposing his removal from the General Secretary post.
9 March	Lenin's third stroke. It renders him permanently without speech.
11 March	Frunze becomes Chief of Staff to the Red Army.
April	12th Party Congress. The economic crisis of the 'scissors', as described by Trotsky, in which the cost of manufactured goods rose and the peasants' incomes collapsed.

Stalin, ignoring Lenin's arguments, reports on Party organisation and national minorities. The 'living Church', accepted by the Party, declares the Patriarch of the Orthodox Church unfrocked and abolished. This 'official' Church dies away in two years. Patriarch Tikhon, after imprisonment, calls on his followers to observe civic loyalty. |
June	ARA, the American Relief Administration, ends its operation in Russia.
6 July	The Soviet constitution published.
24 July	Treaty of Lausanne, signed between Turkey and the Western Allies, determining its frontiers, including that with Armenia.
October	Borodin arrives in China as a special representative of the Soviet Union. His aim is to reform the ruling party of Sun Yat-Sen, with Blyukher accompanying him to found a military academy and to strengthen the Soviet Union's position in China.
21 October	A communist rising in Germany, in which Radek is involved, fails to materialise and the army takes control in many centres. Radek escapes from Hamburg. The failed risings are an impetus to Hitler's first attempt at an anti-communist *coup d'état* in Munich in November.
5 December	Trotsky publishes a letter warning that the revolutionaries might degenerate into bureaucrats, since officials are now appointed from above rather than elected. This makes public the conflict between himself and Stalin (who is responsible for the appointments).

1924

January	13th Party Conference: Stalin openly attacks Trotsky for being against the Party organisation and inciting Party members against it.
21 January	Death of Lenin. The three who had been leading the Party during his illness (Stalin, Zinoviev and Kamenev) block Trotsky's gaining a majority in the Politburo.

The Mongolian People's Republic is established as a Soviet protectorate. |
| 1 February | USSR recognised by Great Britain as 'the *de jure* rulers of those territories of the old Russian Empire'. |
| 3 February | Rykov is elected prime minister of the RSFSR.

USSR recognised by Italy and Sweden. |
| February | New bank notes are issued as part of a struggle against inflation, ending the successful gold-backed unit of currency, the chervonets, introduced in 1921 to deal with the collapse of the Imperial rouble. |

April	Stalin's *Foundations of Leninism* published.
23–31 May	13th Party Congress: Zinoviev demands Trotsky's recantation of his 'permanent revolution'. Many of the delegates are new to the Party and strongly influenced by the economic distress and so support the status quo rather than revolutionary proposals. The Trotskyite 'Left Opposition' is isolated.
	The Central Committee decides to support Stalin and to suppress Lenin's 'Testament' recommendation to remove him from the post of General Secretary.
	Petrograd is renamed Leningrad.
May	A treaty is signed between the Soviets and China, giving the Soviets rights – as had Tsarist Russia – over the railway through Manchuria.
	The Turkestan Republic is replaced by Turkmen and Uzbek Soviet Republics.
17 June– 8 July	The 5th Comintern Congress decides that all communist parties should be 'Bolshevised', that is remodelled on Russian lines. The failure of the German rising of 1923 is examined and blame is put on Radek for working with Social Democrats.
24 October	The 'Zinoviev letter' published in Britain. It purported to be a secret directive from the Comintern to the British Communist Party and was confirmed as such by British intelligence. There are anxious reactions arising from a fear and misunderstanding of international Bolshevism. The letter leads to the crushing of Britain's socialist Labour Party at the next election and years of mistrust of the USSR.
28 October	France recognises the USSR.
November	Publication of Stalin's *Trotskyism or Leninism?*.
December	Abortive communist coup in Estonia.

1925

21 January	Japan recognises the Soviet regime and its forces finally leave eastern Russian territory.
26 January	Trotsky is dismissed as Commissar for War and replaced by Frunze, who had been high in Lenin's favour. Frunze and Tukhachevsky start a programme to reorganise the Red Army.
15 March	The Tajikistan Autonomous Soviet Republic is formed as part of the Uzbek SSR.
April	14th Party Conference. Stalin presents his thesis 'Socialism in one country'. Bukharin says 'We must tell the peasants, enrich yourselves.'
August	The Central Committee issues a resolution on the control of literature. Some writers see this as the Party's protection against extremists and zealots.
October	Frunze dies after an operation and is succeeded as Commissar for War by Voroshilov, Stalin's wartime comrade.

12 October	A further trade agreement is made with Germany.
December	14th Party Congress: the Party is now called the All-Union Communist Party (Bolshevik) – AUCP(B). It becomes known as the CPSU(B), the Communist Party of the Soviet Union (Bolshevik), keeping that name until 1952. Kamenev and Zinoviev are defeated when they oppose Stalin's industrialisation plan and fail in their vote of no confidence in Stalin.

1926

January	Kirov is made Party Secretary in Leningrad, ousting Zinoviev after the Central Committee orders new elections.
	Stalin publishes his *Questions of Leninism*, an anthology of his writings which becomes a standard Party textbook.
24 April	Treaty of Berlin with Germany, agreeing on non-aggression.
12 June	The British government protests to the Soviet Union over gifts of money to help strikers in Britain.
14 July	Zinoviev is expelled from the Politburo.
20 July	Dzerzhinsky, the head of the GPU, dies and is replaced by Menzhinsky.
31 August	A treaty with Afghanistan, agreeing that neither would join in any pact or trade agreement directed against the other, ends the hostility between the regimes.
28 September	Treaty of neutrality and non-aggression signed by the Soviet Union with Lithuania.
19 October	At the 15th Party Conference Stalin attacks the 'United Opposition'; Zinoviev is removed as chairman of the Comintern and Kamenev is replaced as Commissar for Foreign Trade by Mikoyan.

1927

17 January	Trotsky and Kamenev are expelled from the Politburo, admitting their disloyalty to the Party, following the 15th Party Conference. The Politburo now consists of Stalin, Bukharin, Rykov and Tomsky (the so-called 'moderates'), with the newly added members Kalinin, Molotov and Voroshilov.
April	4th Congress of the Soviets of the USSR.
May	Great Britain breaks off diplomatic relations (until 1929) after the raid on the Soviet trade office in Arcos House during which documents are found confirming Soviet support for British strikers.
29 July– 9 August	The Central Committee discuss the 'United Opposition' letter criticising Stalin.
October	Trotsky and Zinoviev expelled from the Central Committee and then from the Party. Stalin arranges this with the Central Committee, and the Rabkrin, the supervising body established by Lenin in 1920.

| December | 15th Party Congress: Trotsky and his supporters are refused a hearing; complete recantation is demanded. Stalin delivers the main report of the work of the Central Committee. Collectivisation is agreed. Diplomatic relations with China are broken off, as Chiang Kai-Shek's nationalists defeat the communists and the Comintern agent Borodin is forced to flee. |

1928

January	Stalin visits Siberia and issues orders to obtain grain by force from the peasants.
16 January	Trotsky is banished from Moscow, being put on a train at night by the GPU and sent to Alma Ata in Central Asia.
27 January	Kamenev and Zinoviev publish, as a capitulation to Stalin, a denunciation of the Trotskyites in *Pravda*.
	Collectivisation starts.
May	The public trial of mining engineers accused of sabotage at the Shakhty mines in the Donbas. Among them are Germans and it is suggested that they are included to show that the Soviet Union was not dependent on German aid.
	Gorky returns to the USSR.
July–August	6th Comintern Congress. Social Democrats are labelled 'Social Fascists' and declared the main enemy of Soviet communism.

1929

January	Bukharin's article in *Pravda* advocates non-violent co-operation between peasant and industrial worker.
	Trotsky is expelled from the USSR and is exiled to Turkey.
9 February	Litvinov, on behalf of the USSR, joins the Kellogg–Briand Pact, 'outlawing' war.
April	Stalin attacks the 'new bourgeoisie' and the 'moderates' (Bukharin and others) at the Central Committee, accusing them of counter-revolution and consorting with the Left Opposition.
	16th Party Conference. The 1st Five Year Plan (1928–33) is presented, with optimistic output targets for the industrialisation of the USSR.
October	The 'Wall Street Crash'. This confirms to the Soviet Union the imminent collapse of the democratic capitalist world.
November	Bukharin is removed from Politburo by the Central Committee.
	Stalin announces a programme of mass collectivisation and the 'liquidation of the kulaks as a class'.
December	Blyukher's Far Eastern army defeats the Chinese, who withdraw from Manchuria, allowing the railway to operate.

The Right Deviationists (Bukharin and his colleagues) make a public confession of their errors.

5 December   Tajikistan ASSR becomes a union republic of the USSR, being separated from Uzbekistan.

11–16   The Kazakh Party Central Committee decides on collectivisation and
December   the resettlement of nomads: 544,000 of 566,000 households are to be 'settled' by 1933.

1930

February   Decree on collectivisation, describing the categories of kulak to be dealt with in the process of deportation or confiscation of goods. By this time half of all the peasants are officially said to have joined collectives. In fact many left after a few weeks, but the process continues until by 1936 90 per cent of peasant households are collectivised.

March   Stalin's article 'Dizzy with Success' calls for moderation in the programme of collectivisation.

10 March   Kazakhstan declares that it has achieved 56.6 per cent collectivisation, but only 20 per cent resettlement of nomads. There is armed resistance to the programmes, fighters are either called 'Basmachi' or blame is put on the 'Alash Orda' of ten years earlier.

June–July   16th Party Congress adopts the slogan. 'The Five Year Plan in Four Years'. Molotov becomes chairman of the Council of People's Commissars and Litvinov, succeeding Chicherin, Commissar for Foreign Affairs.

               Opening of the Turkestan–Siberia railway.

October   Unemployment is stated not to exist any more in the USSR.

November   The trial of the 'Industrial Party', engineers accused of working for France, trying to wreck the Soviet economy and overthrow the government.

1931

June   Stalin's 'Six Points' speech to industrial managers, declaring that the period of 'wrecking' was past, calling for a new attitude to the intelligentsia, and to managers and technicians.

               Ex-Mensheviks and ex-SRs working in Gosplan on the Five Year Plan are accused of working with émigré Mensheviks in a plot to retard industrial development. They are tried and sentenced to imprisonment.

18 September   Japan invades Manchuria. Japan assures the Soviet Union that its action would be limited and would not touch the eastern Chinese railway.

8 December   Japan demands the Chinese soldiers who had fled into the Soviet Union and been interned should not be repatriated. These soldiers are later rearmed by the Soviet Union and sent against Chiang Kai-shek in northern China.

1932

21 January	Non-aggression pact with Finland.
January–February	17th Party Conference.
5 February	Japanese troops occupy the former Russian city of Harbin.
18 February	Japanese invasion of Manchuria ends with a new state, Manchukno, being proclaimed as a Japanese puppet. Non-aggression pact with Latvia.
April	Famine in Kazakhstan and Kirghizia, partly as a result of farmers having slaughtered their herds. As the Kazakh, Kirghiz, Bashkir or Chuvash people die, they are replaced by immigrating Russians.
23 April	A Central Committee Decree on Literary–Artistic Organisations abolishes all existing groups.
May	Writers' Union Organising Committee starts, with the new creed of 'socialist realism'.
4 May	Non-aggression pact with Estonia.
29 June	Non-aggression pact with China.
	Zinoviev and Kamenev expelled and exiled to Siberia.
	Dnieprostroi Dam is completed.
	Famine. In the Ukraine it is particularly severe, but Stalin refuses to admit its existence.
25 July	Non-aggression pact with Poland.
8–9 November	Suicide of Nadezhda Alliluyeva, wife of Stalin.
29 November	Non-aggression pact with France.
December	A system of internal passports is set up, collectivised farmers are forbidden them, preventing their movement from the farms.

1933

	Zinoviev and Kamenev are allowed to return, while Tomsky, Rykov and Bukharin recant their errors, Bukharin, admitting his responsibility for the 'rightist' opposition of 1928–29.
January	The Communist Party orders a purge of its members, mainly to weed out undesirables who have joined since 1929. A new central Purge Commission is formed. By the end of 1933 one-third of the Party (1,149,000), have been examined, of whom one in six are expelled. This purge is similar in its methods to earlier Party purges.
	Recruitment to the Party is suspended.
April	Japan stops all rail traffic between Manchuria and Siberia. The region is infested with armed bands of ex-soldiers and the Soviet Union offers to sell its share of the railway to Japan.
April	Metro-Vickers trials: the accused are Russian technical experts and five British engineers who are charged with being agents of foreign capitalism.

25 May	An order, from Stalin and Molotov, is issued to release half of those in labour camps as a result of collectivisation. This is seen as a sign of liberalisation.
2 August	The White Sea Canal, largely dug with labour from camps, is opened.
5 September	Baranov, the commander of the Red Air Force, is killed in a plane crash.
	There are famine conditions. The Ukraine suffers particularly.
	2nd Five Year Plan, 1933–37. It includes much development in the east, a second track on the Trans–Siberian railway, the Baikal–Amur railway, metallurgical works and electric power stations on the River Amur.
November	USA and USSR establish diplomatic relations.

1934

January	Japanese troops attacking northern China move through the Mongolian People's Republic, causing a serious military incident. The Japanese claim they are on Manchurian territory, the Soviet Union says it is the invasion of their ally.
January–February	17th Party Congress, the 'Congress of Victors'; Soviet economic success is hailed. Zhdanov, an expert in ideology, elected Secretary of the Central Committee. Yezhov, a director of the 1933 Party purge, becomes chairman of the Party Control Commission.
	The 2nd Chinese Congress of Soviets (being held at the same time) is praised as the best section of the Communist International, although the Chinese party is losing ground to the nationalist Kuomintang.
22 February	Bukharin becomes editor of *Isvestia*.
	A Soviet polar expedition explores north of the Chelyushkin Cape.
8 June	The 'Law on the Betrayal of the Motherland' is issued, making the death penalty obligatory for those found guilty and making members of a family collectively responsible for violations of the law.
July	GPU reorganised as the NKVD. The NKVD are forbidden to pass death sentences without the authority of the Soviet Union Procurator.
17 August	1st Congress of Soviet Writers. Leading speakers are Gorky, Radek, Bukharin and Zhdanov.
18 September	USSR is admitted to the League of Nations.
October	The Chinese communist army is forced to abandon its territories and starts on the 'Long March' of 5,000 miles (8,000 km) to the east and north of China.
November	The Central Committee abolishes food rationing and approves private plots and personal livestock on collective farms.
1 December	Kirov is murdered in Leningrad by Nikolayev. Zhdanov is sent to replace him as Party Secretary. Stalin visits Leningrad. Arrests are made of suspects and supposed accomplices accused of being Zinoviev supporters. This begins a new Terror.

1935

22 January	Zinoviev, Kamenev and 17 others are arrested, for complicity in the murder of Kirov.
March	The British Foreign Minister, Eden, visits Moscow.
23 March	The Chinese eastern railway, between Manchuria and Siberia is, after long negotiations, sold by the Soviet Union to Japan.
9 April	Trade agreement with Germany signed, which contradicts Soviet official hostility to fascism.
13 April	Campaign to verify all Communist Party members' documents is announced. It is due to be completed in October.
May	The Moscow Metro, the underground railway, is opened. Khrushchev, First Secretary of the Moscow Obkrom, is awarded the Order of Lenin for his part in its construction.
2 May	Laval, the French Minister of Foreign Affairs, visits Moscow and signs a mutual assistance pact.
4 May	Stalin in a speech declares 'cadres decide everything', stressing the importancce of training and developing Party workers, the need to stimulate the rank and file and to break through Party bureaucracy.
16 May	Assistance pact made with Czechoslovakia.
June	Czechoslovak President Beneš visits Moscow.
July–August	7th Comintern Congress, in Moscow. Under the pressure of the rise of Hitler's Nazi Germany, General Secretary Dimitrov calls for a change of tactics, promoting 'popular fronts' and co-operation with democracies against fascism. The Chinese leader Mao Zedong is elected to the Executive Committee.
July	A Constitutional Commission formed, to revise the 1924 constitution, under Stalin's chairmanship, with Zhdanov, Molotov and others regarded as loyal to Stalin, but also including Bukharin and Radek.
31 August	The coal miner Alexei Stakhanov is reputed to have hewed 102 tonnes of coal in a day, overfulfilling his quota by 1,400 per cent. The Stakhanovite programme is announced, urging workers to achieve such over-production and be rewarded with honour and money.
22 September	Conventional ranks are re-introduced for officers in the Red Army.
October	The Chinese communist 'Long March' ends at Yenan, south of Soviet Mongolia.
November	The verification of Communist Party membership is completed: of 1,800,000 checked 9 per cent (160,000) are expelled.
December	A series of incidents on the Mongolian border are described as invasions of Manchukuo by the Japanese.

1936

12 March	Mutual assistance pact signed with Mongolian People's Republic, giving warning to Japan to keep out of Mongolia.
June	The new constitution is published. It provides for wider suffrage in elections to Soviet bodies, including the new Supreme Soviet.
18 June	Maxim Gorky dies. Stalin believes that this is murder.
August	The Soviet Union accepts the Anglo-French proposal for a non-intervention agreement in the Spanish Civil War. At the same time Stalin decides on involvement in the Spanish Civil War.
19–24 August	A public show trial convicts Zinoviev, Kamenev and 14 others of the Kirov assassination plot. All are shot.
26 September	Yagoda is replaced by Yezhov in the NKVD. The Great Purge, the Yezhovschina, starts.
November	8th All-Union Congress of Soviets gives formal approval to the new Stalin constitution.
	The Soviet Union is now declared to have reached the stage of 'socialism' on the road to 'communism'.
	Zhdanov makes a threatening speech against the Baltic states' plan to ally themselves for defence.
	Enrolment to the Communist Party (frozen since 1933) is restarted.
25 November	Germany and Japan sign the Anti-Comintern Pact. This binds each not to enter into any political treaty with the Soviet Union and, if either is threatened by the Soviet Union, to support the other.
	Suicide of Tomsky.
5 December	The new Soviet constitution is adopted.
	The Kazakh ASSR becomes a union republic.

1937

January	Radek and 16 others are publicly tried for treason. Thirteen, including Radek, are executed.
1 February	Ordzhonikidze commits suicide at the intimation of his arrest.
	The Central Committee receives reports from Stalin, Molotov and Yezhov on the need for a purge of class enemies from the Party and the state.
11 May	Marshal Tukhachevsky dismissed. The purge of the Red Army starts.
May	Political commissars reintroduced into the Red Army.
June	The Soviet Union occupies two islands in the Amur River in Manchuria and Japan, occupying the opposite bank of the river, demands their evacuation. There are clashes between patrols and gunboats in the area. When the Soviets withdraw, the Japanese, in spite of protest, occupy the islands.

11 June	Marshal Tukhachevsky and eight other senior army officers are executed after a trial for 'breach of military duty and oath of allegiance, treason to their country, treason against the peoples of the USSR, treason against the workers' and peasants' Red Army'.
7 July	Japan begins its invasion of China. This is a relief to the Soviet Union, removing the threat of a direct war with Japan.
21 August	A Soviet–Chinese non-aggression pact is signed with the Kuomintang government. It is not one of assistance, only pledging not to attack or become an ally of an attacker. After the treaty the Soviet Union sends over 400 aircraft and flying instructors to China. A supply road into central China is built. The Chinese government and the Chinese communists now have a form of truce and alliance.

1938

January	The Central Committee tries to curb 'errors' in the purge of Party and state.
	Khrushchev is appointed acting Party Secretary in the Ukraine, to clear out nationalists and suspected dissenters. He is made a 'candidate member' of the Politburo.
March	Bukharin, Yagoda, Rykov and others are put on a public trial for treason. They are found guilty and shot.
13 March	The Russian language becomes a required subject in all schools throughout the USSR.
	All heads of oblasts (provincial governments) have been removed and replaced at this stage of the purge.
18 July– 10 August	'Lake Khasan incident', there is fighting on the Manchuria–Korea–Siberia border, at Chankufeng, south of Vladivostok, against the Japanese. The Soviet Union had started to build a submarine base when the Japanese occupied the hill dominating it. The battle comes near to full war and it is ended by a truce, both sides claiming victory. Japan is disappointed that Germany does not offer to come to its aid.
2 September	The Soviets ask the French to have a joint-staff military conference on assistance to Czechoslovakia.
27 September	Stalin assures the Czech president, through the leader of the Czech communists, Klement Gottwald, that the Soviet Union will assist him against Germany even if the French do not co-operate. Soviet troops are massed in the Ukraine and the Romanians permit Soviet planes to overfly. Poland refuses to collaborate with the Soviet Union and, when Germany gains concessions, occupies part of Czechoslovakia, Teschen.
30 September	The 'Munich agreement' between Germany, Italy, France and Britain gives Czech territory to Germany. Stalin is angered at the Soviet Union's being left out and assumes that France and Britain will take Germany's side against the Soviet Union.
	The *Short History of the CPSU* published, emphasising or exaggerating Stalin's role.

November	Marshal Blyukher, the successful commander in the east, is arrested and shot.
December	Yezhov is disgraced and Beria takes over the NKVD.

1939

3 January	A new military oath is administered to all the Red Army.
10–15 March	The annexation and division of Czechoslovakia by Germany, with Hungary taking Ruthenia.
10–21 March	18th Party Congress. Stalin speaks of the Great Purge as a thing of the past. He declares that the Soviet Union will fight to help nations defending their independence and blames France and Britain for appeasing Hitler and the Japanese with concessions and for turning down offers of collective security.
	Mao Zedong sends the Party greetings from a China at war with Japan.
18 March	Stalin proposes a conference with Britain, France, Poland and Balkan countries to discuss ways to stop Hitler. The British turn down the idea and propose that Britain, France, Poland and the Soviet Union declare their support for any threatened European nation. Litvinov agrees if the other nations do too, but Poland refuses for fear of provoking Hitler.
23 March	Lithuania returns the Baltic port of Klaipeda (Memel) to Germany.
17 April	Stalin proposes a Soviet–Anglo–French agreement, but Britain, fearing this might provoke Hitler, turns it down.
2 May	Litvinov, the advocate of an alliance with the West, is replaced by Molotov as Commissar for Foreign Affairs. Stalin is abandoning hope of an alliance with the West and it is also possible that he thinks that Litvinov, as a Jew, might not be able to negotiate with the anti-Semitic Nazi Germany.
20 May–16 September	In a major encounter at Khalkin-Gol, the Red Army blocks the Japanese advance in Manchuria.
20 May	Molotov tells the German ambassador that the Soviet Union wishes for better relations with Germany.
2 June	Molotov gives the British and French ambassadors a draft treaty guaranteeing the independence of small European states. When Britain hesitates on the details, this is taken as rejection.
18 July	The Soviet Union offers to discuss a trade agreement with Germany.
11 August	A Franco-British military mission arrives in Moscow to discuss co-operation.
19 August	A Soviet-German trade agreement is signed. Hitler would like at least a week to pass before the next treaty is signed, but his programme for war on Poland is already rolling.
20 August	The Red Army under General Zhukov go on the offensive against the Japanese on the Manchurian–Mongolian border, completing the victory at Khalkin-Gol.
23 August	Stalin agrees to a treaty with Germany and in Moscow Molotov signs a

non-aggression pact with Ribbentrop, who flies from Germany. Spheres of influence are secretly included, acknowledging the Soviet Union's interest in the Baltic and south-east Europe, with Poland divided on the Vistula, giving back to the Soviet Union those parts of the Ukraine and Belorussia lost in 1920.

25 August   The Anglo-French military team leave Moscow for home, their negotiations now being useless.

Communist parties throughout the world are in shock and now have to change their line and explain the Soviet's abandonment of the Popular Front tactic and the treaty with the hated fascists.

31 August   All Japanese are driven out of Mongolia, defeated by an army with superior mechanisation, tanks and artillery.

1 September   Germany attacks Poland, aiming immediately for Danzig, while bombers attack cities, including Warsaw, and airfields. By the end of the day the Polish air force is almost destroyed.

3 September   France and Britain issue ultimatums which expire and bring these nations to war with Germany.

15 September   A cease-fire and a neutrality agreement are signed with Japan.

17 September   The Red Army moves west into Poland, after only four hours' notice to the Germans, taking the agreed parts of the Ukraine and Belorussia, 78,000 square miles (200,000 sq km) of land and over 12,000,000 people. Soviet casualties are small. Between 180,000 and 250,000 Polish soldiers surrender to the Red Army. Most are sent east for detention. Of 15,000 army officers arrested, 4,000 were shot in 1940.

28 September   Boundary and friendship treaty with Germany, including secret protocols on the resettlement of Ukrainians and Belorussians, signed by Stalin and Ribbentrop.

On the same day an 'assistance pact' with Estonia is signed by Molotov, providing for 25,000 Soviet troops to be placed there.

5 and 10 October   Assistance pacts are made with Latvia and Lithuania. The Baltic republics are forced to accept Soviet bases with troops stationed in them.

12 October   Discussions with Finland start in Moscow, with Stalin and Molotov demanding that Finnish territory in the Leningrad area be ceded for the Soviet Union's defence.

3 November   Communist activists in the newly acquired territories in the Ukraine and Belorussia form committees and arrange for a popular vote for them to be taken into the Soviet Union. NKVD men remove to Kazahkstan or Siberia local administrators, officials, businessmen and others they think may be opposed to the Soviet Union. Soldiers found in civilian dress are arrested and sentenced to eight years' hard labour; from these are later recruited a new Polish army. Estimates of the number removed vary from a half-million to one and a half million.

9 November   The Soviet–Finnish talks break down, since the Finnish parliament does not trust Soviet dealings.

12 November   Talks between Ribbentrop and Molotov start in Berlin to discuss their world-wide interests.

30 November   After declaring that Finland was threatening it, the Soviet Union bombs Helsinki and invades Finland.

The Soviet 7th Army proves to be ill-trained and ill-equipped for the sturdiness of the Finnish defence lines and the severe winter.

14 December   The USSR is expelled from the League of Nations without any nation voting in its support.

31 December   The Japanese ambassador returns to Moscow and agreement is reached with Japan on the final payment by Manchukuo for the Chinese eastern railway, on fisheries and on the start of a new trade agreement.

1940

January   General Meretskov is removed from overall command of the Finnish war and Timoshenko made Commander-in-Chief.

15 January   The Red Army launches an attack on the Finnish 'Mannerheim Line', preceded by a heavy artillery barrage.

31 January   Relations with Japan, though improved, are still imperfect and the Japanese demand that the Soviet Union ceases to support its enemies in China. The Soviet Press is again attacking Japan, particularly on border matters.

11 February   An agreement with Germany guarantees it food and raw materials from the Soviet Union, with reduced freight charges on the Trans-Siberian railway for imports from Manchukuo. In return Germany is asked for examples of her most modern aircraft, warships, guns, machinery and equipment.

17 February   Soviet tank forces sweep around the 'Mannerheim Line' and drive back the Finnish troops.

27 February   Norway and Sweden refuse passage to Finland of an Anglo–French force.

12 March   Finland stops fighting against the Soviet Union and signs the original treaty to which extra demands are now added. The Finnish army has lost 25,000 men, but the Red Army casualties are much greater, possibly 200,000, reflecting appalling military blunders. German military opinion rates the Red Army very low.

March–May   Over 4,000 Polish officers are shot by the NKVD in Katyn Forest, near Smolensk. The discovery is made in 1943 and blamed on the Germans. Later examination proves the contrary.

9 April   Germany invades Denmark and Norway. Anglo–French forces try unsuccessfully to hold back the invasion.

7 May   Timoshenko is promoted to marshal of the Soviet Union and Voroshilov, Commissar for Defence, is demoted to deputy chairman of the Defence Committee.

10 May   Germany invades the Netherlands and Belgium, overrunning them and sweeping on into France.

16 May   Timoshenko issues 'Directive No. 160' to the Red Army, with a new strict disciplinary code, restoring officers' ranks and insignia, saluting and the wearing of medals. The role of the political commissar in the

army is limited. Some 4,000 purged officers are released and reinstated in the service.

3 June	The British army completes its evacuation from France at Dunkirk.
8 June	The last British troops leave Norway.
9 June	The Soviet Union and Japan agree to cease fighting on the Manchurian–Mongolian border.
15 June	Soviet forces move into Lithuania, following a series of border 'incidents'. With NKVD teams, Vyshinsky goes to Latvia, Zhdanov to Estonia and Dekanazov to Lithuania, where they arrange for new governments to be formed and elections to be held. Leading officials, businessmen, soldiers and policemen are deported to Siberia.
22 June	France signs an armistice with Germany.
28 June	Germany indicates to Romania that its provinces of Bessarabia and Bukhovina are likely to be claimed by the Soviet Union, and the Red Army moves into them.
21 July	Newly elected governments in Estonia, Latvia and Lithuania, supposedly with over 99 per cent support, are formed and all ask to be incorporated into the USSR.
20 August	Trotsky is assassinated in Mexico.
27 September	Without informing the Soviet Union, Germany, Italy and Japan sign a Tripartite Pact which they say does not affect their previous agreements with the Soviet Union.
2 October	By a Decree nearly 1,000,000 youths between the ages of 14 and 17 are directed to industrial training schools. The Decree ends free education in secondary schools, heavy fees being introduced for those who wish to remain.
26 October	Soviet troops occupy islands at the mouth of the River Danube, putting pressure on both Romania and Bulgaria.
October	German troops enter Romania ostensibly to train its army, but do not go into the provinces of Bessarabia and Bukhovina, which are annexed by the Soviet Union.
12–14 November	Molotov visits Berlin and is offered an agreement dividing Europe and Asia, with parts of China and India in the Soviet sphere, and he suggests also Bulgaria, Turkey, Afghanistan, Iran and Iraq. He also demands that German soldiers leave Finland, which would be in the Soviet sphere. Germany offers to add the Soviet Union to the Tripartite Pact with Italy and Japan which had been signed in September. At the end of the meetings, in an air-raid shelter, when Ribbentrop declared that Britain was finished, Molotov asked, 'Then why are we in this shelter, and whose are those bombs that are dropping?'
26 November	Stalin replies to Hitler's treaty offer by listing his sphere of influence demands in Europe and Asia.
18 December	Hitler issues the orders for 'Barbarossa', the invasion of Russia.
23–29 December	The Red Army commanders hold a conference in Moscow, which is followed by a war game simulating a German attack. The result leads to an increase in tanks for the army.

1941

15–20 February	Bulgaria allies itself to Germany, joining the Tripartite Pact. German troops immediately enter the country.
20 March	The head of the GRU tells his department to regard all claims that war is imminent as either British or German deceptions.
25 March	The Tripartite Pact is signed secretly with Yugoslavia, but the next day the news causes a *coup d'état* in Belgrade and the government is turned out.
March–April	Matsuoka, the Japanese Foreign Minister, visits Moscow then Germany and Italy, returning to Moscow. He reassures Stalin that Hitler does not plan to attack him and signs an agreement on peaceful relations and acceptance of present frontiers.
6 April	The new Yugoslav government signs a pact with the Soviet Union. The same day German troops cross the frontier into Yugoslavia and dash through to Greece.
13 April	Neutrality pact with Japan signed by Stalin and Matsuoka.
2 May	Sorge, the Soviet GRU spy in Japan, signals Germany's intention to invade. His later information suggests 22 June as the invasion date. The Soviet spy network in Western Europe, known as the Rote Kapelle, also warns of German invasion plans, at first giving 15 May as the date, then telling of its postponement to 22 June. Through another Soviet spy group, the 'Lucy Ring' in Switzerland, the British try to send information they have on the June invasion plan. These warnings are ignored by Stalin.
6 May	Stalin becomes chairman of Sovnarkom, the Council of People's Commissars.
4 June	The commander of the Red Army Special Military District in Belorussia reports German troop concentrations on the border.
11–17 June	Trade agreements are signed with Japan, to ensure the flow of goods for Germany over the Trans-Siberian railway.
13 June	The Soviet news agency, Tass, issues a statement decrying rumours of war between Germany the the Soviet Union.
	Timoshenko asks Stalin's permission to alert and redeploy forces on the border. Stalin refuses permission.
21 June	Bearing news from German deserters, Timoshenko and Zhukov go to Stalin demanding action against the German troops on the border. Stalin only allows a limited and unspecific warning to go out, but it is transmitted too late.
22 June	'Barbarossa', the German invasion plan, is put into operation. At 3 am the Black Sea fleet reports attacks on Sevastopol harbour, and the Baltic fleet attacks in the Gulf of Riga. Admiral Kuznetzov, Commissar for the Navy, in the Kremlin, cannot get news to Stalin.
	At 3.30 am Minsk military district tells Zhukov that Ukrainian towns are being bombed and the Baltic military district reports raids on Lithuania. Zhukov reached Stalin's office and is ordered to assemble the Politburo. The Germans have sent specially trained units ahead to destroy communications and secure bridges.

At 4.30 am Stalin orders the German embassy to be telephoned for information. The German ambassador meets Molotov and transmits a message which is in effect a declaration of war.

At 7.15 am Timoshenko issues Defence Commissar's Directive No. 2, ordering forces to fight back, but restricting air activity and forbidding pursuit over the border.

Before noon the German air force claims to have destroyed more than 800 Soviet aircraft on the ground. In all, probably 1,800 are destroyed during the day.

At 12.15 pm Moscow Radio broadcasts a brief message by Molotov stating that German troops have attacked and calling on citizens to rally to the Party and to Comrade Stalin.

23 June German troops, having marched 40 miles (65 km) through Lithuania, now enter Latvia.

In the Ukraine the advancing German armoured forces meet resistance instead of the expected collapse of the Red Army. The Soviets fall back on the Pripet Marshes, an easily defended area.

24 June The Red Army attempts a counter-attack near Grodno in Belorussia, but without air or artillery cover the Soviet losses are very heavy.

25 June Finland declares war on the Soviet Union. It advances to the old 1939 frontier on the Karelian isthmus and to the River Svir between Lakes Ladoga and Onega, where the line stays until 1944, for in spite of a strong German presence the Finns only make such military operations as are in their interest and play no part in Hitler's grand strategy. Marshal Mannerheim declines an offer to take command of the German troops there, since that will demote him, in effect, to being one of Hitler's generals.

The Red Army makes a stand on the River Dvina, but the Germans cross the next day.

26 June The US Secretary of State, Sumner Welles, announces that the Neutrality Act will not be invoked against the USSR, meaning that the USA may supply munitions.

27 June Hungary declares war on the Soviet Union. Its troops are to form a link with the German armies in Poland and Romania.

28 June Riga falls, although the Red Army escapes, leaving large quantities of equipment and tanks.

Minsk is taken by the Germans.

29 June Ribbentrop suggests to Matsuoka that Japan takes the opportunity of seizing Vladivostok, but Japan maintains its neutrality. American ships are sent to the port of Vladivostok, carrying supplies. When Japan and America are at war, the ships will fly Soviet flags and continue to sail; Japan thus tries to demonstrate its neutrality to the USSR.

Bialystok, attacked and cut off on the first day, falls to the Germans. Two Soviet armies are encircled in the same area.

30 June A State Committee of Defence is appointed with Stalin as its chairman and Molotov, Malenkov, Voroshilov and Beria as members. It will control the wider aspects of the war, political and economic as well as military.

3 July	Stalin gives his first wartime broadcast to the people. While defending the Soviet-German Pact as securing a year of peace, he calls on the people to defend the country and not allow anything, whether a machine, an animal or a sack of grain, to fall into German hands. He calls on the Soviet Union to fight a 'patriotic war'.
7 July	The British Prime Minister Churchill sends a personal message to Stalin, offering assistance.
8 July	The Soviet defence line on the pre-1939 frontier with Poland is pierced and the Germans are within 90 miles (145 km) of Kiev.
9 July	Vitebsk is surrounded and taken.
10 July	Stalin becomes chairman of the Stavka which has been under Timoshenko since 23 June. Three army areas are organised: north-west, Voroshilov with Zhdanov as the political adviser; west, Timoshenko and Bulganin; south-west, Budyenny and Khrushchev.
	The German Army Group North starts an offensive drive from Estonia towards Leningrad, where the Soviet north-west armies have lost much material but have survived as a large fighting force.
	The Germans marching towards Kiev are attacked in the flank by Red Army units from the Pripet Marshes and their supply lines cut.
11 July	German and Romanian armies advance towards the Dniester River, where the Red Army is waiting and heavy rain and thick mud only allow slow progress.
12 July	A military pact is signed in Moscow between Britain and the Soviet Union.
16 July	Smolensk is captured and another encirclement of Soviet armies is delayed because the Germans are too widely spread out.
18 July	Agreement with the Czechoslovak government in exile in London to work together in the conduct of the war and to agree to the formation of national troop contingents in the Soviet Union.
19 July	Stalin takes over from Timoshenko as Commissar of Defence, while he takes command in Leningrad. Hitler orders his Army Group Centre to advance on Moscow, but without their armour, one part being sent towards Leningrad and the other south to the Ukraine.
29 July	Zhukov advises withdrawing and surrendering Kiev. Stalin relegates him to the reserve armies.
	President Roosevelt sends his personal representative, Harry Hopkins, to Moscow to discuss military supplies with Stalin. Hopkins is impressed by Stalin's determination and realistic appraisal of the Soviet Union's chances and convinces Roosevelt that US help would be used effectively.
30 July	Agreement with Polish government in exile in London, similar to the agreement with the Czechs earlier in the month.
2 August	20 Soviet divisions are cut off near Uman in the southern Ukraine.
5 August	300,000 men and 3,000 tanks are surrounded and captured near Smolensk. In Belorussia the Germans have advanced over 500 miles (800 kms) and taken about 600,000 prisoners.
8 August	Stalin is officially named Supreme Commander.
	100,000 Soviet soldiers are captured at Uman.

23 August	Voroshilov's north-west area is broken up into a Leningrad front, under Popov and Zhdanov, and Karelian front and a north-west front.
25 August	The Soviet Union and Britain enter Iran, to deny it to Germany.
	In a move to cut Leningrad off and link with the Finns, the Germans take Novgorod and cross the Volkhov.
26 August	Taking stock, the German army records 440,000 casualties (including 94,000 dead), but only 217,000 reinforcements. Units are beginning to beg for refitting and restaffing.
31 August	300,000 Germans of the Autonomous Volga Republic ordered to move east.
4 September	All Estonia and nearly all the southern coast of the Gulf of Finland are cleared of Soviet troops by the German army.
5 September	Hitler decides that Leningrad is a secondary theatre and orders an attack on Moscow before the onset of winter. Armoured forces are therefore brought back from the Ukraine. 'Directive 35' on the attack is issued the next day.
11 September	Zhukov takes command of the Leningrad front. The western front is given to Konev and the Bryansk front to Eremenko.
13 September	Budyenny is removed from his command when he asks to be allowed to retreat beyond Kiev.
16–26 September	Around Kiev, about 80 miles (130 km) in width and depth, the Red Army is encircled. Kiev falls and 450,000 soldiers are made prisoner.
24 September	The Germans fail to get into the Crimea at the Perekop isthmus.
26 September	German total casualties are now 534,000. Frontline generals report anxiety that the Red Air Force is beginning to be active again and that anti-tank guns are proving ineffective against Soviet tanks, particularly the T34.
28 September	A high-level Anglo-American supply mission to Moscow, including the British newspaper magnate and cabinet minister Lord Beaverbrook and Averell Harriman, Roosevelt's envoy, agrees to send munitions, accepting that the requests will not be justified or explained.
30 September	The German offensive on Moscow begins, moving around Bryansk to reach Orel in four days.
6 October	On the Black Sea coast another 106,000 Soviet troops are captured. The route to the Caucasus is now only thinly guarded.
	The first snow falls on the German Army Group Centre.
7 October	Zhukov returns to Moscow on Stalin's orders, taking command of first the 'reserve' front and then the west front. Budyenny is briefly missing in the chaos.
8 October	There is a Japanese campaign to end Germany's war with the Soviet Union, so that Germany can direct her energies against Britain and the British Empire. Japan's new cabinet feel that Russia's difficulties may induce her to reduce support for China, but that war against her would not be in Japan's interest: neutrality is observed until 1945. The Soviet Union is able to withdraw troops from Asia to the west.
9 October	The German army reports supply shortages of 30,000 tonnes a month

and its inability to deal with captured weapons or munitions. Some of these will fall into the hands of partisans. Heavy snow and rain are now falling and transport of Army Group Centre is becoming bogged down.

11 October	The German Army Group South is also stopped north of Taganrog by bad weather.
16 October	Non-essential civilians (many in panic) evacuated from Moscow, Stalin, the Stavka and his government remaining.
	Odessa is evacuated. Its 80,000 troops and many of the 350,000 civilians move to the Crimea.
17 October	Taganrog is taken and the Germans reach the Donets basin – the main coal-mining area of the Soviet Union – at Kharkov, and approach Rostov.
18 October	German tanks are at Moscow's second defence line, 60 miles (95 km) from the city, but snow is now slowing down progress.
18–28 October	The Germans, short of tanks on this front, attack the Perekop isthmus, which is heavily fortified and where the Red Air Force have local control. Although they break through, taking over 100,000 more prisoners, they meet more resistance in the Crimea, where the Soviets have both air and sea command.
19 October	A state of siege declared in Moscow.
31 October	The German Army Group Centre, exhausted, cold and unable to advance further, is given a fortnight's pause for reinforcement.
October–November	75,000 Karachai people are deported from their Caucasian home to the east.
5 November	A German army attacks towards Rostov.
	In the Crimea a Sevastopol Defence Command is set up, with a garrison of about 50,000 and strong defences round the city.
7 November	Stalin speaks publicly in Moscow on October Revolution Day.
8 November	Tikhvin, near Leningrad, is taken, but counter-attacks regain part of the town and the German advance is held.
15 November	With clear frosty weather, and harder ground, the Germans resume the move towards Moscow.
18 November	Leningrad is besieged, but Lake Ladoga now freezes over and lorry convoys bring supplies over it.
20 November	Rostov is captured, but Timoshenko's reorganised south-west area counter-attacks successfully.
28 November	The Germans cross the Moskva–Volga Canal and are 25 miles (40 km) north-west of Moscow.
30 November	Hitler issues an order to his troops around Rostov to stand firm and sacks his general, but the Germans retreat from Rostov back to Taganrog.
December	380,000 Kalmyks are deported from their autonomous republic in the RSFSR, north-west of the Caspian Sea, to Soviet Central Asia.
	The Russian Orthodox Church pledges its support for the war.
	Stalin and the Polish General Sikorski sign a Polish–Soviet Declaration of Friendship and Mutual Aid.
5 December	Zhukov counter-attacks outside Moscow, with the support of half the

strength of the Far Eastern Command, which has been transferred west to the Urals: nearly a million experienced, trained and well-equipped soldiers.

6 December   Britain declares itself at war with Finland after long diplomatic attempts to persuade Finland not to support Germany. Finland in fact does little more in the war than regain its 1939 frontier.

The Russian counter-attacks north of Moscow succeed (to Zhukov's surprise, since he does not appreciate the exhaustion and lack of equipment of the Germans) and drive 20 miles (30 km) to the German rear. To the west of Moscow the Germans also retreat 15 miles (24 km).

7 December   The Japanese attack the USA at Pearl Harbor, bringing the United States into the war.

11 December   Hitler declares war against the USA. This act of solidarity with Japan ensures that America becomes an enemy and the war ally of the Soviet Union. However, the Soviet Union declines to give the USA air bases in Siberia, since it would invite war with Japan.

13 December   Soviet armies attack on the right of Timoshenko's south-west area and capture, for the first time in the war, quantities of German soldiers and weapons.

15 December   Parts of the government evacuated from Moscow are now ordered to return.

16–19 December   The British Foreign Secretary, Anthony Eden, visits Stalin but avoids discussion on post-war European frontiers and fails to get any promise on war against Japan.

20 December   A 'stand and fight' order is issued by Hitler, though withdrawals continue.

25 December   At Sevastopol the German attack, in bad weather, meets low morale among the the Soviet troops.

26 December   Finding a gap between the German armies, the Red Army in the Tula area advances quickly to Smolensk, but after five days, frost and lack of supplies stop them. However, the Stavka orders another move from the north-west front to envelop the Germans.

Red Army detachments from the Transcaucasus are landed on the eastern end of the Crimea, holding the Kerch peninsula. The effect is to break off the siege of Sevastopol, where the defences are crumbling.

1942

1 January   A revised German army handbook on the Red Army is issued, recognising that the Soviets had greater abilities to recover and re-equip from stocks that had been planned for.

7 January   To the east of Leningrad an offensive is launched from the Volkhov River to relieve the city. The Soviets advance slowly for a month to within 40 miles (65 km) to the east of Leningrad.

9 January   Launching a winter offensive on Stalin's orders, on the north-west front, the Red Army begins its advance of 200 miles (320 km) towards Velikye

Luki and Vitebsk and German armies have to retreat to avoid encirclement. The arms of the Soviet pincer are 100 miles (160 km) apart.

13 January   Under General Vlasov, a specially strengthened army moves through the centre of the German pocket.

21 January   To reinforce the flanks of the Soviet attack, units are moved from the centre, relieving the pressure of Vlasov's offensive. The Germans are able to stand and fight back.

28 January   Stalin designates the Crimea as a front, giving the siege of Sevastopol priority.

1 February   Zhukov is given command of the western area. The advance and completion of encircling movements cannot now be done by the overstretched Red Army.

8 February   The Red Army succeeds in cutting off about 90,000 Germans at Demyansk, south of Lake Ilmen. The Germans mount a large air supply operation which ensures their troops' survival: 230 aircraft are used at first and eventually 600 are deployed, flying in over 270 tonnes a day and taking 22,000 wounded out and bringing 15,000 reinforcements in.

27 February   The Soviet attempts to drive the Germans from Sevastopol and the Kerch peninsula die out. German attacks are equally unsuccessful.

20 March   A further Soviet attack beyond Moscow is ordered but within ten days it is stopped. The Red Army is exhausted and stuck in the spring mud.

18 April   Five US airmen of the Doolittle bomber raid on Tokyo make a forced landing in the Russian Far East and are interned. They are joined by other US airmen who land in the Soviet Union and are interned in a special camp near Tashkent as part of the Soviet Union's neutrality in the American war against Japan. In 1943 their 'escape' through Iran is arranged, probably by the NKVD border guards.

21 April   A specially created corps forces a narrow corridor through to the encircled Germans at Demyansk, who are then reinforced and act as a springboard for the later offensive.

May   A central partisan staff is established in the Stavka. In 1941 there had been stragglers or units cut off from the main force who made uncoordinated attacks on convoys or camps. Now partisan actions are to be part of the Red Army's plans, although their effect is not fully felt until 1943.

12 May   Timoshenko starts a spring offensive with an attack aiming at Kharkov. His left wing, to the south, does not drive home armoured attacks as he planned.

15 May   In the Crimean spring offensive, the Germans take the Kerch peninsula. Romanian soldiers are now conducting the Sevastopol siege. Hitler's objectives are no longer Moscow and Leningrad but to destroy the Red Army to the west of the Don and take the oil fields of the Caucasus.

26 May   A 20-year Treaty of Alliance is made between the Soviet Union and Britain.

29 May   Timoshenko's failed offensive ends with the loss of Kharkov, two Soviet armies being surrounded and cut to pieces and 214,000 being made prisoner.

June	General Vlasov and his army, cut off in the forests north of Lake Ilmen, are driven out and he is captured along with 33,000 men.
7 June	The Germans return to the siege of Sevastopol. There is desperate fighting.
10–26 June	In two operations, the Germans force the Soviet armies of the south-west back towards the Don River.
28 June	The Germans, with heavy air support, attack in the direction of Voronezh.
July	Hitler moves to his advanced HQ at Vinnitsa to watch his troops advance into the Crimea, the Caucasus and over the Volga at Stalingrad.
4 July	Sevastopol finally falls. Hitler is so pleased that he proposes to move the victorious troops to the siege of Leningrad.
	The loss of the Crimea leads to a new Soviet command being made: the north Caucasus front, commanded by Budyenny. Timoshenko's south-west command is reduced in size with parts being directly controlled by the Stavka.
6 July	Voronezh is taken and the Germans cross the Don. Soviet troops avoid being trapped and regroup on their side of the river.
8 July	German armour crosses the Donets River, but again the Red Army avoids being trapped and retreats intact, although Hitler is convinced that it must have been destroyed.
12 July	The Stavka creates the Stalingrad front under Timoshenko, with Khrushchev as the political adviser. Timoshenko is replaced shortly afterwards.
23 July	Rostov is taken, but again the Red Army falls back in good order, though weakened.
25 July	The Germans attack from three bridgeheads over the Don River. One army swings north towards Stalingrad. To the south, on a 100-mile (160 km) front, it breaks through Soviet defences and a rapid advance starts.
	Budyenny's Caucasus command is now mixed with the south front with him in nominal command.
28 July	Stalin issues an order of the day, 'Not a step backwards', that the Red Army should yield no more ground west of the Don. Although it leads to a large number of casualties, it results in a small bridgehead over the Don being held.
August	Voroshilov is made Commander-in-Chief of the partisan movement.
12–16 August	Churchill meets Stalin in Moscow and discusses the war, particularly the possibility of an Anglo-American second front being opened in Europe.
12 August	The Stalingrad front is put under General Eremenko of the south-east front.
18 August	The Germans reach the mountain passes entering the Caucasus.
23 August	A force heavily supported by the German air force crosses the Don and reaches the Volga River north of Stalingrad. The evacuation of the civilian population and the fortification of the city now begin.

1 September The advance in the Caucasus halts at the Terek River to wait for reinforcements.

12 September General Chuikov is selected by Khrushchev to command the 62nd Army on the Stalingrad front. This army will hold the city.

14 September The Germans under von Paulus nearly succeed in taking Stalingrad. With street-fighting, the Red Army begins to make small gains, supported by covering fire from the far side of the Volga River.

28 September The Stavka gives Rokossovsky the Don front north of Stalingrad and Eremenko, with Khrushchev, the Stalingrad front.

2 November The Caucasus offensive gets within 5 miles (8 km) of Ordzhonikidze – the furthest east reached by the invading army.

8 November Hitler receives the news of the Anglo-American landings in North Africa. This and the news of the defeat of his army in Libya at El Alamein by the British distracts him from Russia and when the Soviet offensive comes, his generals will have to wait indecisively for his instructions.

17 November Zhukov sent to co-ordinate the offensive against the German Army Group Centre.

19 November General Vasilevsky, who has been assigned the leadership of the Stalingrad counter-offensive, attacks and in four days encircles the 6th German Army there. The Germans expect the attack but are surprised by the strength of it. Von Paulus is ordered to defend his position in Stalingrad; he has six days of supplies and he is promised an airlift based on the experience of Demyansk in February. There are about 250,000 Germans and Romanians encircled there.

25 November The German air force attempts to airlift 700 tonnes a day to their 6th Army, but ice and fog, and losses of 488 aircraft bring the full total lifted by mid-December to only 3,300 tonnes.

12 December A German army under Manstein tries to reach Stalingrad but is halted 40 miles (65 km) away. Without artillery or infantry support, his armour is outgunned and runs out of fuel.

16 December On the south-west front, north of Stalingrad, an Italian army on the Don is broken and abandons its positions; the Red Army under General Vatutin makes an advance of 150 miles (240 km).

18 December In Stalingrad the Germans decide against attempting a break-out, hoping to hold out longer.

19 December Although now threatened in the rear, a German force gets within 30 miles (50 km) of Stalingrad.

24 December The breakthrough north of Stalingrad reaches the main airfield supplying the beleaguered Germans.

27 December The German Army Group Don is itself nearly encircled by Eremenko's advances through the Romanians in the south and by Vatutin in the north. These advances also threaten Rostov and all the German forces north of the Caucasus.

The Germans create a 'Russian National Army' under the captured General Vlasov.

7 January	Forward units of Eremenko's army reaches the HQ of the German troops in the Caucasus, 30 miles (45 km) from Rostov and the Germans start to leave the area. The Soviets are now powerful enough to stop them.
12 January	The siege of Leningrad is lifted by a narrow passage south of Lake Ladoga but the front outside remains unchanged.
	Roosevelt and Churchill hold a conference at Casablanca in North Africa, to which Stalin is invited but does not go, given the pressure of the war and his belief that all his allies should do is to attack in the west. The outline plans produced at Casablanca mean that the USSR will continue to bear the brunt of the fighting until the next year, 1944.
13 January	On the Voronezh front the Hungarian army is attacked, smashed and its line broken. Zhukov and Vasilevsky are briefly attached to this front for the offensive and Zhukov draws up plans to move on to Kharkov.
17 January	The Stalingrad siege is now fought at minus 30°C, German rations are reduced to 7 oz (200 g) of horse-meat and 3 oz (75 g) of bread, the pocket is half its original size and only one supply airfield remains. Aircraft have 300 miles (480 km) to fly and only bring 60 tonnes a day.
23 January	German munitions on the Russian front are reported dangerously low. From 3,300 tanks used at the invasion of June 1941, there are now only 495 battle-ready tanks on the eastern front and the Soviet KV and T34 tanks are proving superior. The Red Air Force is increasing in number and improving in fighting quality. However, the Germans have the new 'Tiger' and 'Panther' tanks and new fighter planes on the way.
31 January	The German von Paulus is promoted to field marshal, but despite this encouragement, he surrenders at Stalingrad with 91,000 soldiers and 24 generals (16,700 had already surrendered and 70,000 had died).
16 February	Kharkov, evacuated by the Germans, is taken. However, counter-attacks throw back the Red Army on the Voronezh front.
6 March	Stalin styles himself marshal of the Soviet Union.
12 March	Kharkov is retaken and the Soviets recoil, losing the initiative they have held since November.
April	The NKGB is made independent, relieving Beria's NKVD of state security and concentrating it on public order, and the smooth functioning of the war economy. The special NKVD sections are removed from the army and converted to an independent organisation (this develops into SMERSH).
26 April	Stalin breaks off diplomatic relations with the Polish government in exile in London in protest at its accusations after the discovery of the Katyn Forest massacres.
15 May	The Comintern is dissolved, encouraging the Americans to believe in the end of Russia's international ambitions.
1 July	Hitler assembles his commanders and prepares them for a new offensive in Russia. The Stavka recognises that there will be a German offensive and decides to wait for this and then counter firmly, using a reserve force placed opposite the Kursk salient. The front commanders are

Rokossovsky of the central front, Vatutin the Voronezh front and Konev with the steppe front in reserve.

5 July–23 August	The biggest tank battle in the history of warfare takes place in and around Kursk where, on 10 July, the German offensive is halted by Rokossovsky's artillery and effective anti-tank weapons, with the demoralising use of anti-tank rockets from aircraft.
10 July	Anglo-American forces land on Sicily. This is the first landing on Europe by the Western Allies.
12 July	The western and Bryansk fronts attack towards Orel and Kharkov.
25 July	Mussolini, the Italian leader, is arrested and a new Italian government is formed. Italy no longer wants to fight, forcing the Germans into a war on two European fronts. Needing troops for Italy, Hitler orders his Army Group Centre to evacuate its salient at Orel.
3 August	On the Voronezh and Donets fronts the Red Army surprises the Germans and moves towards Kharkov, which it reaches on 13 August.
	Stalin makes his only wartime visit to a fighting front, south-west of Moscow.
5 August	Orel is retaken.
6 August	Soviet papers start a campaign to show that the only effective anti-Japanese force in China is the communist army and not the Chiang Kai-shek nationalists.
23 August	Kharkov falls, but the Red Army's advance comes to a halt.
26 August	Rokossovsky attacks from beyond Kursk as part of a general, broad front Soviet attack and the Germans fall back to the Ukraine and in the south.
8 September	Orthodox ecclesiastical administration and church seminaries are allowed to be re-established. Metropolitan Sergius is elected Patriarch and is officially received by Stalin.
21 September	Moving rapidly, at 15 miles (24 km) a day, the Red Army reaches the Dnieper River and soon holds 400 miles (640 km) of its eastern bank, and makes a number of crossings.
9 October	The German forces in the Crimea are isolated; Hitler has decided to hold it as a protection for Romanian oil and lest its loss should change the attitude of neutral Turkey.
15–30 October	Conference of Allied Foreign Ministers (Britain, China, USA and USSR) in Moscow. The USA demands that China shall be one of the four major countries to sign the 'Declaration of the Four Nations on General Security'. This is the first agreement to demand unconditional surrender from Germany, but it also gives the possibility of negotiating with other enemies, and provides for the administration of both liberated lands and former enemy countries.
November	Tito, the communist leader of Yugoslavia, achieves Allied recognition.
	The Karachai Autonomous Region is dissolved because of the belief that it had collaborated with the Germans and the surviving people deported eastwards.
6 November	After breaking through from a Dnieper bridgehead, Kiev is retaken.
26 November	Exhaustion and mud stop further movement and a German counter-attack halts the Soviets.

28 November– 1 December	Allied conference at Teheran, without China on Stalin's insistence. Stalin demands a second front by the Anglo–Americans in 1944 and tells Roosevelt and Churchill that Russia will join the war against Japan, but only after the defeat of Germany. Post-war Europe is discussed. The Soviet Union demands and gets the promise that its borders will be at least those of June 1941 and that part of East Prussia will be included. Poland will not have any part of the Ukraine or Belorussia. The Soviet Union claimed those parts of Poland east of the 'Curzon Line' and it is allowed to move its borders westwards to the Oder River. It is agreed that Finland will maintain its national identity. On the Far East, Stalin requires an ice-free port and Dairen is suggested with Soviet use of the Manchurian railway.
	Roosevelt proposes to Stalin a post-war international organisation of about 40 nations with a small group of nations with themselves, Britain, China and a few others, as an executive committee. This is the seed of the United Nations.
24 December	The winter campaign starts from the Ukraine.
27 December	The Kalmyk Autonomous Republic is dissolved after claims that it had collaborated with the German occupiers and its people deported to the east.

1944

5 January	Under Konev, the Red Army's Ukraine offensive starts against fierce German opposition, but surrounds large numbers of them south of Kiev.
12 January	Following a broadcast of the Polish government in London affirming its rights to former territory, Molotov asserts that the people of all Belorussia and the Ukraine have chosen to join the USSR and that the Poles should enter into an agreement with the Soviet Union about future frontiers. He also points out the anti-Soviet tone of statements by Polish generals and leaders of the underground.
14 January	The Soviet offensive starts from the bridgehead west of Leningrad and in followed by attacks to the south which cut off the Germans in Novgorod.
27 January	The relief of Leningrad after 870 days of siege.
29 January	Vatutin's troops on the Ukraine front cross the 1939 Polish frontier.
February	400,000 Chechen and 75,000 Ingush Sunni Muslims are deported from their Caucasus home to Kazakhstan and western Siberia as a result of their anti-Soviet uprising following the German occupation of their area in 1942. They are rehabilitated in 1957.
4 February	The Germans encircled in the Ukraine are supported by air-drops. A relief force gets near them and there is a break-out. Half escape but return to the German army with an infectiously low morale.
15 February	Hitler agrees to a retreat on the Baltic coast out of Russia into Estonia. Both sides now get into defensive positions, with their main forces in Belorussia and the Ukraine.

23 February	Finland secretly discusses terms with the Soviet Union through its ambassador in Sweden, Kollontay.
24 February	Soviet forces regroup to complete the clearing of the Ukraine. Here the partisans are no longer all pro-Soviet, some being nationalist Ukrainians and some anti-German and anti-Russian Poles. Khrushchev (with Brezhnev as his deputy) sets the NKVD to weeding out the Ukrainian nationalist UPA (Ukraine Insurgent Army).
29 February	Vatutin is shot and killed by Ukrainian partisans. Zhukov replaces him.
6 March	An encircling movement in the south Ukraine aims at Odessa. Although Zhukov moves his army 200 miles (320 km) in six weeks, the Germans escape.
8 March	The Kabardino–Balkar Autonomous Republic temporarily loses the 'Balkar' part of its name, as the 40,000 Turkic speaking Balkars from the Caucasus Mountains are deported to the east of the Soviet Union for collaboration with the Germans. They are permitted to return to their lands after 1957.
9 March	The Romanian border is reached.
30 March	Japan closes down her concessions in the north of Sakhalin Island and a five-year fishery agreement is signed. With the war in both west and east turning against the Axis, Japan is anxious not to quarrel with the Soviet Union.
8 April	The Soviet attack on the Crimea starts. Hitler has ordered the Crimea to be defended.
10 April	Odessa is retaken.
5 May	In the Crimea all but Sevastopol is cleared of German and Romanian troops.
10 May	Sevastopol's defences collapse after heavy artillery and air bombardment and the city is taken.
June	The Crimean Tatar Autonomous Republic is dissolved and 200,000 Crimean Tatars are deported, accused of having helped the Germans in the occupation of their country.
6 June	Anglo-American 'D-Day' landings on the Normandy beaches of France. At this time the Germany army is deployed with 54 divisions in the west, 27 in Italy, 25 in the Balkans, 15 in Scandinavia and 164 on the Russian fronts.
9 June	An attack on Finland drives the Finns back to their 1940 lines on the Karelian isthmus.
10 June	The US ambassador to the Soviet Union, Averell Harriman, asks for air bases in the Far East. Stalin agrees but progress is very slow as Stalin does not wish Americans on Soviet territory.
23 June	Two weeks after the Anglo-American landings in France, the Soviet summer Belorussian offensive begins. Two marshals of the Soviet Union command: Vasilevsky to the north of the sector and Zhukov to the south. The Germans are prepared to defend the Ukraine, but the Red Army, now heavily outnumbering the Germans in men, tanks, guns and aircraft, strikes through Belorussia towards the Baltic. Vitebsk is surrounded and Hitler, in Bavaria and not realising the hopelessness of the situation, orders its defence.

4 July	Red Army takes Minsk, the capital of Belorussia, and a huge breach is opened, leaving the way to the Baltic states and East Prussia clear.
13 July	Vilna is taken.
14 July	The Soviet offensive in the Ukraine, after two days' artillery barrage and probing reconnaissance raids, starts with overwhelming air superiority. One surrounded group includes an SS division recruited from Galician Ukrainians.
25 July	The Vistula River is reached with elements of the Soviet-created Polish Army following.
	A 'Rada', the 'Committee of National Liberation', is set up as a Soviet-controlled Polish government and Lublin is declared the capital.
27 July	Lvov is entered after several days' fighting.
28 July	Brest-Litovsk falls after attempts to defend it by the Germans and the northern offensive reaches the Baltic coast near Riga, cutting off a large German army.
30 July	Mikolajcek, the head of the Polish government in London, arrives in Moscow, hoping to make some agreement with the Soviet Union in the belief that it needs his co-operation with the Polish underground.
1 August	The Finnish President resigns and is replaced by Marshal Mannerheim. He gets Sweden's promise of food supplies and is able to act independently of Germany. As the Red Army reaches the outskirts of Warsaw, the 35,000-strong Polish 'Home Army' rises against the German occupiers. Not under the control of the Soviet Union, they wish to take Warsaw themselves and not be liberated by, nor in the debt of, the Russians. The Soviet Union publicly declares that there is no rising, but if there is one, it is of a group friendly to the Germans, and in any case, that they are criminally wasting Polish lives.
7–8 August	Mikolajcek speaks to the Polish Committee and to Molotov. He is offered a place in their government and advised not to return to London but to stay with them and go to Warsaw. He refuses.
10 August	A bridgehead on the east bank of the Vistula goes on the defensive as the Red Army advance loses its momentum.
16 August	The Soviet Union tells Britain that it will not go to the help of the Polish Home Army and refuses Anglo–American aircraft permission to land in a supply-dropping mission.
20 August	The Red Army moves into Romania, whose army offers little resistance and leaves German units to fend for themselves.
21 August	At Dumbarton Oaks in the USA, there are Anglo–Soviet–American talks on the planning for the future United Nations.
23 August	The Romanian dictator Antonescu is overthrown and there is an immediate armistice with the Soviet Union. Upwards of 150,000 German troops are lost in the surrender.
4 September	Finland sues for peace and an armistice is signed. German troops are expelled after fighting.
7 September	Soviet troops, having crossed the southern Carparthian Mountains, are in Hungarian Transylvania. Hungarian troops begin to run away from the German lines.

8 September	The Soviet army enters Bulgaria, with which it is not at war (although Bulgaria is at war with Britain). Under these pressing circumstances Bulgaria declares war against Germany.
14 September	On the Baltic front an offensive starts, but after ten days it is halted after the German Army Group North has withdrawn from Estonia and is cut off in Kurland. The Stavka now changes the northern attack westwards.
21 September	Tito, the Yugoslav guerrilla leader, who has been in close co-operation with the British, flies to Moscow and meets Stalin, who promises him military help.
2 October	The last of the Home Army in Warsaw surrenders. The special SS police who have been given the task of putting the rising down, do so with terrible brutality.
6 October	Under Timoshenko Soviet troops, with Romanian allies, thrust into Hungary.
9 October	Churchill and Eden in Moscow. With Harriman, the US ambassador, they ask Stalin how long it will be before the Soviet Union declares war on Japan. Stalin agrees to US air bases in Siberia and this matter is raised again in 1945 at Yalta. A further Lend–Lease programme of assistance to the Soviet Union is agreed. They review the present military situation and describe how the Germans will be finally conquered. An agreement is reached on the control of the Balkans, with the Soviet Union dominating Bulgaria and Romania, Britain Greece, but Hungary and Yugoslavia being equally shared.
15 October	Horthy, the Hungarian dictator, attempts to make peace but he is arrested and taken to Germany. By the end of the month Soviet troops are just outside Budapest, which they gradually surround.
22 October	Soviet troops enter their first German territory, East Prussia.
14 November	The 'Committee for the Liberation of Russia' set up in Prague, with its armed forces under the nominal command of Vlasov.
December	A Hungarian provisional government is set up at Debrecen and declares war on Germany.
	Zhdanov is moved from Leningrad to Moscow to run Party affairs for Stalin.
2 December	General de Gaulle of newly liberated France, comes to Moscow. The meeting culminates in a Franco-Soviet accord.

1945

12 January	Konev, on the Ukrainian front, begins an offensive from the Vistula to the Oder Rivers. The attack is made at the earliest possible moment, to relieve some of the pressure on the Americans and British fighting in the Ardennes. Hitler, in the west, switches reserves from East Prussia to support the defences. Konev's men are soon racing to the Oder River.
14 January	Rokossovsky's offensive starts north into East Prussia, where Hitler has weakened his forces.
19 January	Rokossovsky's men reach the Baltic, east of Danzig. The Germans here,

now called Army Group Kurland, are cut off and stay there until the end of the war.

23 January   Konev's Ukrainian front reaches and crosses the Oder River.

February   The Japanese approach the Soviet ambassador with proposals for peace with America. This approach is not reported to the USA.

3 February   German forces withdraw from Warsaw.

4–11 February   The heads of the Allied governments, the Great Powers, including Stalin, Roosevelt and Churchill meet at Yalta in the Crimea. Stalin agrees to end the Russo-Japanese Neutrality Pact of 1941 and declare war on Japan two or three months after Germany's surrender, provided 'The Mongolian People's Republic is maintained; the 1904 gains by Japan against Tsarist Russia are returned, including Sakhalin, Dairen to be internationalised; the Soviet Union to have a naval base at Port Arthur and the railways to be brought back to Sino-Russian control; the Kurile islands to be given to the Soviet Union.'

8 February   Konev moves into Lower Silesia. His men draw level with the Belorussian front troops of Zhukov in Pomerania. Breslau is surrounded, and the Germans in it fight on.

10 February   Rokossovsky's offensive in north-east Germany halts, worn out and short of ammunition.

11 February   The last surviving German troops try to leave Budapest and most of them are killed.

5 March   A German offensive is mounted in southern Hungary and Yugoslavia and for ten days it advances until the troops and ammunition are exhausted.

16 March   The Soviets counter-attack in southern Hungary, nearly cutting off part of the German army, which escapes and is followed into Austria.

25 March   Soviet and US forces meet on the Elbe River.

28 March   Gdynia and, two days later, Danzig (Gdansk) are taken with large numbers of prisoners and 45 submarines. The surviving garrisons, with a mass of refugees, move into the estuary of the Vistula River, where they hold out until after the war.

5 April   Molotov renounces the Neutrality Pact with Japan. Japan assumes this to be the beginning of the agreed 12-month notice of the ending of the pact.

6 April   An assault on the city of Königsberg starts. Resistance is fanatical and fighting goes on for six days, followed by scenes of terrible atrocities and revenge by the Red Army men.

13 April   Vienna is occupied after seven days' street fighting.

15 April   Zhukov starts his final assault towards Berlin. When the Soviet armies reach the city, from north, east and south, they have to fight every yard of the way.

29 April   The German army in Italy surrenders to the British.

30 April   As Soviet troops reach the centre of Berlin, Hitler kills himself in his bunker-HQ.

1 May   The first negotiations for a cease-fire start in Berlin.

2 May   All fighting in Berlin stops.

7 May	Unconditional surrender is signed by the Germans with the Anglo–Americans.
	The Russian ROA, 'National Liberation Army', the army under Vlasov created by the Germans, takes Prague from German SS troops.
9 May	A second surrender document, ratifying the first, is signed in Berlin.
June	In Poland a Government of National Unity is set up. Stalin assumes the rank of Generalissimo, confirming his status as victor of the Great Patriotic War.
1–13 July	A Sino-Soviet conference in Moscow confirms the terms of the Yalta agreement. China receives a pledge from Stalin that any Soviet troops would be withdrawn from Chinese territory three months after Japan's surrender and that the Soviet Union would give the Chinese nationalist government military support. This seems to repudiate support for the Chinese communists.
17 July–2 August	The Potsdam Conference, attended by Stalin, Truman and Churchill (whose place is taken by Attlee after the British elections).
	The Oder–Neisse Line is agreed as the western frontier of Poland.
	Truman asks Stalin formally to co-operate in joint action against Japan.
6 August	The first atomic bomb is dropped on Japan at Hiroshima. The Soviet Union is not consulted.
8 August	Soviet Union declares war against Japan.
9 August	The Red Army under Marshal Vasilevsky attacks in Manchuria and meets only weak resistance.
10 August	The Chinese communist army commander, Chu Teh, orders his men to accept the Japanese surrender and to move into Manchuria to meet and work with the Soviet army. Chiang Kai-shek's order to the communist army to remain in place is ignored.
12 August	Soviet forces land in Korea.
14 August	Japan offers to surrender. The USSR's official line is that Japan's surrender is caused by the Soviet Union's decisive contribution to victory, not the atomic bombs.
20 August	The Japanese army in Kwantung is defeated.
2 September	The Japanese surrender ceremony is held on the US battleship *Missouri* with the Soviet General K.N. Derevyanko present.
	Soviet losses in this campaign are put officially at 8,219 dead against 80,000 Japanese.
	Stalin proposes General Vasilevsky as an equal commander in Tokyo to the US General MacArthur. This is not accepted: there is to be no four-power control of Japan. However, Vasilevsky has command of Manchuria and North Korea, to whom Japanese forces north of the 38th parallel of latitude are ordered to surrender. In Manchuria the Soviet Union begins to remove industrial units and to control the railways. Chinese communists of Manchurian origin (and some who had been in the Soviet Union since the 1930s) occupy the land.
	A conference of Foreign Ministers in London ends in deadlock over Balkan issues.

9 November	Chinese communists block the entry of nationalist Chinese troops to Manchuria, while Soviet troops control the ports of entry.
15 December	At a Foreign Ministers' conference in Moscow, including Marshall from the USA and Bevin from Britain, Molotov obtains agreement that both Soviet and American forces will withdraw from China. Korea is not to be reunified immediately, but there will be a trusteeship of the USSR in the north and America in the south, with a future government based on 'democratic' parties. However, there was to be no part for the Soviet Union to play in Japan. Khrushchev is appointed First Secretary of the Ukrainian Party.

1946

January	250,000 Soviet occupation troops move into North Korea, Kim Il Sung, a former Communist Party secretary in Manchuria, is sent there.
16 January– 5 February	A Soviet–American conference on Korea in Seoul ends without decisions.
21 January	All Japanese industrial developments in Manchuria, described as the property of the Japanese army, are deemed booty of war by the Soviet Union.
February	Stalin announces the 4th Five Year Industrialisation Plan. He says that in 15 years the Soviet Union will produce 500 million tonnes of coal, 60 million tonnes of steel and 60 million tonnes of oil, perhaps outstripping the USA. In fact all these long-term targets are achieved (with the initial help of two million German prisoners of war and the industrial plant shipped as reparations from Germany and Manchuria).
13 February	Nationalist China accepts the independent status of Outer Mongolia (the Mongolian People's Republic) and establishes diplomatic relations with it.
5 March	Churchill's Iron Curtain speech at Fulton Missouri. Stalin tells the US ambassador that he demands a base in the Turkish Dardanelles.
20 March	A second Soviet–American conference on Korea ends in failure with accusations that the Americans have blocked Korean unity.
May	The Foreign Ministers' conference on Germany having assumed the 1932 level of production as the norm (unattainable under the conditions of 1946) and basing reparations on this, the USA finds it unjust and declines to make further shipments of goods or machinery to the Soviets.
31 May	After demonstrations in universities and cities of China, Soviet troops finally leave Manchuria. At this time many of the Russians living there in exile after the Civil War, especially in Harbin, are made Soviet citizens and many returned to the Soviet Union. The British and US occupation zones of Germany are merged into one economic unit, while the French zone remains separate, pending their claims on the Saar. This makes a powerful economic unit in West Germany, dividing the country effectively into East and West Germany. The USSR, with post-war occupation forces in Iran, takes steps to annex Iranian Azerbaijan and to integrate

it into the Soviet Azerbaijan Republic. Iran appeals to the United Nations and the Soviet troops are withdrawn.

August   Beginning of the 'Zhdanovschchina' in Leningrad, purging the Party that survived the siege.

2 August   Vlasov and his associates are hanged in Moscow.

December   Construction of the first Soviet nuclear reactor.

1947

5 January   The US State Department demands that Dairen becomes a free port according to the 1945 agreement. The Soviet Union replies that since the war with Japan (in the sense of a peace treaty) has not ended, Dairen is still in their hands.

February   Peace treaties with Bulgaria, Finland, Hungary, Italy, Romania are signed.

March–April   Foreign Ministers' conference in Moscow (Molotov, Bevin for Britain and Marshall of the USA) to prepare a peace treaty with Germany.

12 March   US President Truman responds to Soviet moves in Iran and Turkey with a message formulating the 'Truman Doctrine': the US policy to support 'free peoples to work out their own destinies their own ways'. US military assistance to Turkey and Greece follows. The Truman Doctrine is accepted by US Congress in April.

June   Aid is offered to all Europe under the 'Marshall Plan' of the US Secretary of State; Stalin refuses it. The Czechoslovak coalition government (with its communist Premier Gottwald) decides to accept it.

September   Zhdanov denounces both the Truman Doctrine and the Marshall Plan as the 'twin forks' of US imperialist policy. He claims the support of the people's democracies and also other freedom-loving people, including what was to become known as the Third World.

October   Cominform established at a Warsaw conference, but at it the Yugoslav leader Tito rejects Moscow control and claims each nation's right to its own 'road to socialism'.

16 December   Currency reform is announced in the USSR, rendering all existing banknotes useless but exchangeable, ten for one new rouble in cash, with varying exchanges for amounts held, legally, in banks. The aim is to wipe out the profits of wartime speculators.

1948

January   A United Nations Special Commission visits Korea, but the USSR does not take part, although the delegate for the Ukraine (a full member of the UN) has been nominated to the commission.

13 January   Mikhoels, the Jewish actor and leader, is killed in Minsk; the traffic accident has been arranged by the MGB (the Ministry of State Security).

February	A fully communist government takes over in Czechoslovakia after claims that Beneš was going to form a government without communists. Although there are riots, the communist leader Gottwald forms a new coalition government, including the liberal Jan Masaryk. There is a purge of officials and academics. Masaryk dies. This is either suicide or murder, but the facts are concealed.

The joint Allied Control Commission in Berlin ceases to function. |
March	In Berlin the Soviet commander walks out of the four-power military control council.
April	Travel restrictions are imposed by Russians between their zone and the Allied zones of West Germany.
28 June	Cominform, at its first meeting, expels Yugoslavia, after Stalin has failed to obtain their submission.
June	The Soviets refuse further collaboration with the Berlin four-power control council.

Berlin blockade: Berlin, lying within the Soviet occupation zone of Germany and divided into four sectors, each controlled by one of the Allies, is seen as an obstruction to Soviet control of their zone. They try to isolate the city by land, closing the roads and railways from the western zones, which meant that food and fuel supplies are cut off. The Western Allies respond with a massive airlift of fuel, food and other supplies. The blockade and the airlift last nearly a year. |
31 July–7 August	Stalin gives public support to Lysenko's biological theories at a session of the Academy of Agricultural Science.
31 August	Death of Zhdanov, the powerful Secretary of the Central Committee and leader of the Leningrad Party, at the age of 52. His death is followed by the arrest and execution of many of his associates, with thousands sent to camps. This is the 'Leningrad Purge'.
10 October	The first Soviet long-range guided missile is launched. During 1948 there are revolts in forced labour camps, of which there are not yet full details, notably in Vorkuta where prisoners of field officer rank rise and are only subdued by the use of bomber aircraft.

≡ 1949 ≡

5–10 January	The Academy of Sciences condemns 'Western idolatry', forcing scientists to turn away from research conducted outside the USSR.

'Anti-Cosmopolitan' campaigns are launched; these are effectively anti-Semitic. |
| 25 January | Comecon set up in Moscow. |
| March | Vyshinsky becomes Foreign Minister.

Treaty with Korea. |
4 April	NATO, the North Atlantic Treaty Organisation, is formed.
12 May	The Berlin blockade lifted.
May	A communist government takes over in Hungary.

25 September Tass announces the testing of the first Soviet atomic bomb.

1 October The Communist People's Republic of China is formed.

November Soviet Control Commmission in Berlin is constituted.

Marshal Rokossovsky appointed Supreme Commander in Poland. He holds this post until 1956.

December On Stalin's seventieth birthday there are major public celebrations. Foreign communist leaders visit Moscow, including Mao Zedong.

1950

10 January The Soviet delegation to the United Nations objects to nationalist China rather than the People's Republic being seated at the United Nations. In protest the Soviet Union boycotts the United Nations for the next six months.

14 February Treaty of friendship with China. Stalin attends Mao Zedong's reception in its honour.

Stalin's letter on linguistics, attacking Marr, a theorist of language evolution. This signals attacks on large areas of academic research, in sociology, archaeology and ethnology.

25 June Outbreak of Korean War. This conflict between the Koreans, with Chinese participation, against the USA and her allies lasts until July 1954, with the Soviet Union keeping itself out of direct involvement.

7 July The United Nations Security Council, which the USSR is boycotting over the issue of China and so cannot veto, votes to establish a United Nations military command in Korea.

During 1950 there is a wave of executions in the Gulag camps.

1951

5th Five Year Plan

The camps on Sakhalin break into revolt.

1952

10 March The Soviet Union sends a diplomatic note to the US, proposing a peace treaty with Germany, with all Germany becoming a neutral area. The US does not accept this.

5–15 October 19th Party Congress. Stalin's paper on 'Economic problems of Socialism in the USSR' is put forward. The term 'Bolshevik' is dropped from the Party's title and the Politburo is renamed the Central Committee Praesidium. The possibility of 'peaceful co-existence' with capitalist countries is expressed.

1953

13 January	The 'Doctors' Plot': nine Kremlin doctors, seven of whom are Jewish, are arrested, accused of espionage for a US Jewish organisation and of murdering Party leaders, including Zhdanov. Confessions are obtained (although two of the doctors die during the investigation).
5 March	After a heart attack, Stalin dies. A specialist doctor, with the Doctors' Plot in mind, hesitates to examine him.
	A conference of Politburo members and the Council of Ministers is held. Malenkov takes over his posts as its Chairman, or Premier, and Party Secretary, Beria retaining control of the security services and Bulganin taking over the armed forces. A week later Khrushchev is moved from the Party Secretaryship for Moscow and appointed to the Party Secretariat.
14 March	Malenkov is relieved of his functions in the Party Secretariat.
April	The arrest of the doctors is condemned in the Press as having been irregular and unlawful. *Pravda* attacks MGB men who had caused dissension among 'people of different nationalities'. This is the end of the anti-Semitic campaign of Stalin's last years.
17 June	Riots in Berlin put down by Soviet tanks.
July	Beria, suspected by the other leaders of trying to take over power from them, is arrested in the Kremlin on orders signed by Voroshilov. At a signal from Malenkov, soldiers led by Zhukov seize Beria and take him away to the headquarters of the Moscow military district, while Khrushchev, Bulganin and Molotov reveal the extent of Beria's ambitions to the other Party leaders.
	Under Serov the MVD, the Ministry of Internal Affairs, is neutralised; new troops are put on guard at the Kremlin and all senior MVD men in Moscow and throughout the Soviet Union are detained.
27 July	An armistice is signed in Korea.
9 August	Malenkov makes the first of several speeches calling for consumerism: an increase in the production and consumption of goods and food, a decrease in military expenditure and an increase in the money in the hands of the people. He turns against the Stalinist doctrine that heavy industry has priority. To the Supreme Soviet he states that people have the right to demand consumer goods of a high quality.
20 August	The first Soviet hydrogen bomb test is announced.
September	Khrushchev is elected First Secretary of the Party Central Committee.
December	Execution of Beria and other leading MVD officers announced publicly.
	The second Russian hydrogen bomb test is carried out at a great altitude, showing that Russia now has the most powerful missile in the world.

1954

25 January–18 February	At a Four Powers conference in Berlin of Britain, France, the US and USSR, Molotov proposes a peace treaty with Germany with both states, East and West, signing as equals (thus ensuring the recognition of two Germanies). The conference ends without a decision.

22 January	In contrast to Malenkov's consumerism, Khrushchev proposes to the Praesidium to improve the economy through the Virgin Lands campaign, using fallow land for increased grain production.

In Kazakhstan there are protests about this policy because it will also lead to the use of traditional and necessary grazing land, and the extra work involved will mean the importation of more Russians.

Khrushchev also argues that the need to use fallow land should take priority over the improvement of existing agricultural resources. He appeals directly to the Komsomols to carry out this policy.

March	The Central Committee resolves that 32 million acres (13 million hectares) be ploughed up for the Virgin Lands campaign and that maize alone should be planted there.

Russia helps to negotiate the treaty at Panmunjon to end the Korean War.

April	Soviet Union joins UNESCO and the International Labour Organisation (ILO).
26 April–15 June	A conference on East Asia with Britain and the Soviet Union co-chairing, with representatives from France, China, the US and the Indo-China states, agrees to elections in both North and South Korea and, after the French evacuation of Indo-China, to the setting up of North and South Vietnam.
5 June	The Virgin Lands target is raised to 74 million acres (30 million hectares).
27 June	The first nuclear power station is put in operation at Obninsk, near Moscow.
21 July	The partition of Vietnam into north and south republics is agreed. The French leave Indo-China.
12 October	Khrushchev and Bulganin visit Beijing. A friendship agreement is signed.
22 November	Vyshinsky dies in New York.
December	Viktor Abakumov, who had been Minister of Internal Security 1947–51 and had succeeded Zhdanov in the purge of Leningrad, is put on trial with other security men on charges of corrupt behaviour. The case reveals scandals of the Stalinist period. All the accused are found guilty and executed.

1955

8 February	Malenkov is dismissed as premier on charges of mismanagement of industry and agriculture, and Bulganin takes his post.
18–27 April	Bandung Conference: 29 states of Asia and Africa (including communist China, but excluding the USSR) meet at Bandung in Indonesia. Dissatisfied with the quarrels of the USSR and USA, the conference attempts to make the 'Third World' a force in international politics.
14 May	The Warsaw Pact, a military alliance between the USSR, Bulgaria, Czechoslovakia, East Germany, Hungary, Poland and Romania, is

signed. It is a response to the inclusion of West Germany in the North Atlantic Treaty Organisation.

27 May–
2 June
Bulganin and Khrushchev visit Yugoslavia, seeking reconciliation with Tito.

18–23 July   Geneva Summit meeting: Bulganin, Eisenhower, Eden and Faure.

27 July   USSR agrees peace with Austria and ends its military occupation.

August   There is a better harvest – but this is on traditional lands: the fallow lands suffer from a drought!

September   Adenauer, Chancellor of West Germany, visits Moscow: there is agreement on the recognition of West Germany through diplomatic relations.

November–
December
Khrushchev and Bulganin visit South-East Asia.

1956

January   The port of Porkkala is returned to Finland.

14–25
February
20th Party Congress. The most important session excludes the Press and features Khrushchev's speech attacking Stalin and the Cult of Personality and revealing for the first time details of the purges.

March   Riots in Tblisi, Georgia.

April   Bulganin and Khrushchev in Britain.

June   Food riots in Poznan, Poland.

Peoples, including Kurds, Turks and the Islamic Kemshin Armenians, are exonerated of charges of treason during the war.

2 June   Shepilov succeeds Molotov as Foreign Minister.

July   Karelo-Finnish SSR is reduced to the status of an autonomous republic, bringing the total of republics in the Soviet Union down from 16 to 15.

In the Virgin Lands campaign, 74 million acres (30 million hectares) are cultivated. While this is successful in neglected arable land, in the virgin lands there are severe problems of erosion.

11 September   The Crimean Tatars are exonerated of war crimes by the Supreme Soviet Praesidium.

21 October   Gomulka is appointed Polish Party Secretary in spite of Russian protests and a visit by Khrushchev.

23 October   Riots in Budapest, the capital of Hungary, against the communist regime.

24 October   Imre Nagy becomes premier of Hungary and promises reforms, including elections, and a break with the military treaty with Russia. This causes Khrushchev to take firm action to protect Russian interests.

4 November   Khrushchev sends in Russian tank forces to crush the Hungarian revolt. Imre Nagy is later shot, in 1958, without an open trial. He is publicly rehabilitated in 1989.

Russian student groups organise meetings and distribute leaflets condemning Soviet intervention in Hungary. Many of the protesting students are arrested, expelled from the university or sent to detention camps.

1957

January	Chou En-lai in Moscow, Warsaw and Budapest.
16 February	Gromyko replaces Shepilov as Minister for Foreign Affairs.
March	Khrushchev makes new economic proposals, reducing the functions of Gosplan, decentralising economic planning and introducing new local economic councils (Sovnarkhoz).
April	Directives to decentralise the economy.
May	Sixty central industrial ministries are abolished in Moscow and Local Economic Councils ('Sovnarkhozes') set up, in the hope that local interests will produce more effective planning.
June	There is a plot to depose Khrushchev by leading Stalinists in the Politburo, including Molotov, Kaganovich, Bulganin and Voroshilov. They claim that he has undermined the reputation of the Party internationally and put Malenkov forward as leader. However, the army and the KGB do not support them and Khrushchev counters with a meeting of the Party Central Committee, which backs him. None of the factional groups is expelled from the Party, in contrast to the practices of Stalinist times.
29 June	Kaganovich, Malenkov, Molotov and Shepilov are removed from the Praesidium and Central Committee.
	The Cominform (which had replaced the Comintern) is abolished.
4 October	Sputnik I, the world's first artificial satellite, is launched. This causes considerable consternation in the West, the first American satellite not being launched until 1958.
	Boris Pasternak's novel *Dr Zhivago* is published abroad, first in Italy, having been rejected by Soviet publishing houses.
	Khrushchev visits China, signing agreements on aid and nuclear cooperation.
26 October	Zhukov is removed from the Central Committee and his post of Minister of Defence while on a visit to Yugoslavia. He is accused of withdrawing the army from Party control and of a 'cult of personality'. He is also perhaps felt to have political ambitions and to object to Khrushchev amassing power. He is replaced by Malinovsky, a senior officer with no political weight.
7 November	Fortieth anniversary of the October Revolution. Conference of Communist Party leaders of the world, including Mao Zedong but not Tito, in Moscow.

1958

January	The decision to reduce the Soviet armed forces by 300,000 men as an economy move meets with resistance from senior officers.
26 February	Machine Tractor Station (MTS) reorganisation: the tractor stations are dissolved and their machinery sold to the kolkhozes.
26 March	Khrushchev is appointed chairman of the Council of Ministers, while Bulganin is relegated to the chairman of the State Bank, having been accused of taking part in the previous year's attempt to oust Khrushchev. The 6th Five Year Plan (1956–60) is dropped since its targets are seen to be over-optimistic and a new Seven Year Plan (1959–65) is instituted with the aim of improving standards of living.
May	Russian credit to Yugoslavia is cancelled in retaliation for Tito's alignment with the Third World and with the West.
	Russia makes loans to support the economy of the West African state of Guinea, which has had all French aid cut off. One totally inappropriate item is said to have consisted of an entire airport and all necessary equipment, including the standard snow plough for use in the (Russian) winter.
24–27 August	Race riots in Grozny: deported Chechens and Inguish want to return home after banishment.
September	Bulganin and Voroshilov expelled from the Praesidium. Record grain harvest, although meat production is not as high as planned. Oblasts are ordered to double their meat production.
23 October	The Pasternak affair: he is awarded the Nobel Prize for Literature for his novel *Dr Zhivago*: in the Soviet Union he is attacked by the Writers' Union and the Komsomol. Condemned by mass meetings, he is obliged to write a letter recanting the novel.
November	Educational reforms are introduced, adding practical training to secondary schools' curriculum. The earlier intention to increase the compulsory seven-year schooling to ten years is dropped and an eight-year system introduced. Post-school training is increased and the number of correspondence or evening students increased to exceed the full-timers.
	Serov, head of the KGB, is demoted to run the GRU (Army intelligence) on the pretext of the Belgian queen's crown (stolen during the war) having been found in his possession. This is followed by the retirement of many long-serving KGB officials.
December	By the end of the year most communal farm machinery and tractor stations have been closed, larger farms having their own. This leaves the large number of average or smaller farms ill-equipped, with ill-maintained machinery and unable to achieve their targets.

1959

January	Khrushchev and Gromyko visit China. After this Sino–Soviet relations deteriorate.
	21st Party Congress adopts the Seven Year Plan. The 6th Five Year Plan was an admitted failure.

New Party leaders, Kozlov, Kosygin, Polyansky and Suslov are promoted.

A new *History of the Communist Party of the Soviet Union* published to replace Stalin's version, which had been removed from the Party reading list in 1956.

February	British Prime Minister Macmillan visits Moscow.
May	Khrushchev visits Albania, attempting to avoid a threatened rift.
June	Sino-Soviet atomic agreement is rescinded by the USSR.
July	American exhibition in Moscow visited by Vice-President Nixon: in a demonstration house Nixon and Khrushchev hold the 'kitchen debate', in which Khrushchev promises that Soviet Russia will 'teach America a lesson' and that they 'will bury you all'.
September	Russian rocket Lunik II lands on the moon.

The Chinese express anger at the Russian failure to support them in their claim for Indian territory.

Khrushchev visits the USA, staying with President Eisenhower. He holds a press conference, visits farms in Iowa and steel works in Pittsburgh.

1960

January	The Supreme Soviet cuts the establishment of the army and navy from 3,600,000 to 2,400,000. This is half the 1953 strength and there are consequently numbers of disgruntled prematurely retired officers who add to the growing lack of support for Khrushchev in the forces. It is expected that this demobilisation will include 250,000 officers, some of them generals and admirals.
February	Khrushchev visits India, has meetings with Nehru, visits the Bhilhai steel works, being funded by Russia, and signs agreements on economic and cultural co-operation.

Mikoyan visits Cuba.

March	Khrushchev visits de Gaulle in Paris.
April	A shake-up in the military high command removes opponents of Khrushchev's policies, puts Konev in command of Warsaw Pact forces and retires old friends of Stalin, such as Timoshenko.
1 May	The American U2 reconnaisance aircraft piloted by Gary Powers is shot down near Sverdlovsk. This results in formal protests and the cancellation of a summit meeting with Eisenhower in Paris. At first Khrushchev reports the event to the Supreme Soviet without saying Powers had been captured. He thus traps the US State Department into making easily disprovable statements denying the flight's purpose.
May	Kozlov elected to the Secretariat of the Central Committee.

Voroshilov replaced by Brezhnev as Chairman of the Praesidium of the Supreme Soviet.

	Marshal Sacharev appointed Chief of the General Staff.
30 May	Death of the novelist and poet Pasternak.
July	Economic and technical aid to China stopped; Soviet experts recalled.
	US plane shot down over the Barents Sea.
September	Khrushchev walks out of a UN General Assembly meeting, losing his temper and interrupting a Western delegate by banging with his shoe on the desk.
October	A missile at the Tura Tam test range blows up on the launch pad and kills the Chief Marshal of Artillery, Nedelin, and perhaps 300 other officers and scientists.
December	Cuban delegation visits Moscow.
9 December	Volga power works opened.

1961

January	M. A. Olshansky, a follower of Lysenko, appointed Minister of Agriculture.
25 January	The aircrew of the US plane shot down in 1960 released.
12 April	Yuri Gagarin orbits the world in the spaceship Vostok.
May	A 'Ukrainian Workers' and Peasants' Union' is uncovered; its leaders are tried and condemned for anti-Soviet activity in planning to set up a separate Ukrainian socialist state.
June	Khrushchev and President J.F. Kennedy meet in Vienna.
29 July	The Supreme Soviet revises the penal code and introduces the death penalty by shooting for those convicted of currency speculation.
August	Russia demands from USA, Britain and France peace treaties with the two Germanies.
6–7 August	Titov's space flight.
13 August	The Berlin Wall is erected, cutting off West Berlin. It is built as a result of the Western Allies' refusal to sign the two treaties.
	Khrushchev, in response to America's increased military budget and the Berlin crisis, cancels further cuts in the armed forces.
	The Soviet Union resumes nuclear testing.
	Albania breaks off relations with Russia.
September	The Belgrade Conference: 35 Mediterranean and Afro-Asian countries meet and agree on the principles of Bandung and declare 'non-alignment'. This conference is an embarrassment to the Russians, since the dissident communist leader of Yugoslavia, Marshal Tito, is the host.
	Kwame Nkrumah, the President of Ghana, tours the Soviet bloc after the Belgrade Conference.
17–31 October	22nd Party Congress.
	The Seven Year Plan is replaced with the 7th Five Year Plan (1961–65).

Khrushchev speaks both of increasing consumer satisfaction and of holding traditional budgetary policies.

30 October   Stalin's body is removed from the Lenin Memorial in Red Square.

1962

March   Khrushchev criticises Soviet agriculture.

June   Comecon meeting in Berlin.

Food prices are increased. In Novocherkassk there are riots in protest.

September   The Cuban missile crisis. Soviet guided anti-aircraft missiles are sent to Cuba, but President Kennedy warns that he will not tolerate any such weapons in Cuba.

October   Kennedy orders a blockade of Cuba and puts the US forces on alert. Russian troops are equally placed on alert. Soviet ships are halted outside the blockaded area. After messages between the two leaders, the weapons are returned to Russia.

November   The reorganisation of the Soviet Union's administrative apparatus starts.

Solzhenitsyn's *One Day in the Life of Ivan Denisovich* is published in *Novy Mir*, possibly on the instructions of Khrushchev.

1963

June   Brezhnev becomes Secretary of the Central Committee.

14 June   Khrushchev is attacked in the Chinese Press as 'the Great Revisionist' and in a letter to the Communist Party of the Soviet Union (CPSU).

16 June   Valentina Tereshkova becomes the first woman to travel in outer space.

5–19 July   Sino–Soviet talks in Moscow show a further deterioration in their relations. Co-operation between the two countries is almost at an end.

At an international conference in Tanganyika President Nyerere warns of a second scramble for Africa in the form of Sino–Soviet rivalry.

5 August   'Détente': an agreement to ban the testing of nuclear weapons in the atmosphere is signed between Russia, USA and Britain.

31 August   The Moscow–Washington 'hot-line' installed.

The very poor harvest following bad weather leads to food shortages and Russia is obliged to import grain from Canada and the USA, bringing disrepute to Khrushchev's agricultural policies.

November   There are provocative Sino-Soviet 'border incidents' between herdsmen and frontier guards.

The USSR offers to establish for Somalia an army of 10,000 men, and an air force in 1964.

1964

A revolution in Zanzibar puts Sheikh Karume's Afro-Shirazi Party in power: Russia supports this group, even though its Marxist elements are soon discarded.

May–June   Khrushchev visits Egypt and Scandinavia.

July   Mikoyan replaces Brezhnev as Chairman of the Praesidium of the Supreme Soviet.

September   Khrushchev decides to increase consumer production.

13–14 October   While Khrushchev is on holiday at the Black Sea, meetings of the Politburo, Praesidium and Central Committee agree to dismiss him. He is retired quietly with a pension.

Khrushchev is replaced by Brezhnev as First Secretary and Kosygin as Chairman of the Council of Ministers (Premier).

November   Party reorganisation takes place.

1965

February   Kosygin visits Paris.

March   The astronaut Leonev becomes the first person to walk in space.

A new agricultural plan to expand production by increasing investment, lowering delivery quotas, cancelling Kolkhoz debts, and awarding higher prices and higher wages.

International Communist Conference in Moscow.

4 July   Brezhnev demands rearmament, citing increased defence expenditure in the USA.

28 August   The Volga Germans are exonerated of treachery during the war.

September   Daniel and Sinyavsky 'secret' writers of parodies of Soviet life, little known but read abroad, are arrested.

December   Podgorny succeeds Mikoyan as Chairman of the Praesidium of the Supreme Soviet.

Nyerere, sensitive to international feelings, maintains his Third World non-alignment but says, 'I gather that even the suits I wear have been adduced as evidence of pernicious Chinese influence.'

1966

3–11 January   USSR mediates at Tashkent between India and Pakistan.

USSR–Mongolian Treaty of Friendship.

10–14 February   Daniel and Sinyavsky trial results in sentences of five and seven years but gives a bad impression of Soviet justice and censorship throughout the world.

March	US–Soviet agreement on cultural and technical exchanges.
March–April	23rd Party Congress. The Politburo is reintroduced, replacing the Central Committee Praesidium and bringing in younger men.
20 June–July	De Gaulle visits Moscow and a Soviet-French communiqué is issued which reduces East–West tension, heightened during the Vietnam War, by promising co-operation in several areas.

1967

April	Svetlana Alliluyeva, Stalin's daughter, refuses to return from abroad.
June	The Praesidium of the Supreme Soviet removes the accusations of treason against the Soviet Kurds, Turks and Muslim Armenians made during the war.
September	The Crimean Tatars are exonerated from charges of wartime treason.

1968

	'Prague Spring'. The reforming government of Dubček in Czechoslovakia introduces democratisation.
21 April	Crimean Tatars celebrating in Uzbekistan are dispersed by police action.
21 August	The Soviet Union and Warsaw Pact allies invade Czechoslovakia. Dubček and the Central Committee are replaced with hardliners led by Husák.
October	Spaceship Soyuz launched.
December	The Tu–144 supersonic airliner makes its maiden flight.

1969

16 January	The first space station is put into orbit.
March	A border clash between Soviet and Chinese troops, fighting over an island on the River Ussuri.
	A military coup in Somalia, led by General Mohammed Siad Barre, who proclaims a Marxist state.
16 May	Venus 5 spacecraft makes a landing on the planet Venus.
September	Kosygin meets Chou En-lai to open border negotiations.
November–December	Preliminary Strategic Arms Limitation Talks (SALT) held in Helsinki.
December	The Soviet budget allows for a 5.9 per cent increase on defence for the coming year.

1970

March	USSR–Czechoslovak treaty of friendship.
	Extension of Russo-Finnish treaty.
July	Treaty of friendship, co-operation and mutual assistance signed with Romania.
11 August	Treaty between USSR and West Germany, signed by Chancellor Brandt and Brezhnev.
October	Solzhenitsyn is awarded the Nobel Prize for Literature.

1971

February	Details of the 9th Five Year Plan call for greatly increased production of consumer rather than producer goods.
April	24th Party Congress emphasises the need for a new European security settlement.
	US President Nixon gives figures for US–USSR relative missile strengths at the end of 1970:

	US	USSR
ICBMs	1,054	1,440
Submarines launched	656	350

July	Ninety Soviet diplomats and other officials are ordered to leave Britain on grounds involving espionage.
	Zhores Medvedev papers published in Britain, revealing his experiences and those of his brother Roy in Soviet psychiatric hospitals.
11 September	Death of Khrushchev.
October	Kosygin announces that the emigration of Jews in the past eight months of the year has exceeded the emigration of the past 20 years.
December	Brezhnev visits France, meets President Pompidou and signs a joint declaration of co-operation between France and the USSR.

1972

January	Suppression of samizdat journals in Moscow and Ukraine after large-scale police searches.
May	Riots in Kaunas, Lithuania, in support of greater religious and political freedom. A 20-year-old worker, Romas Kalenta, burns himself alive in protest against persecution of the Church.

22 May	Visit of President Nixon, signing the first SALT anti-ballistic missile treaty, interim agreement on offensive missiles and establishing a US–USSR Commercial Commission. This is the first-ever visit of a US President to the USSR.
	Berbera in Somalia is made a Soviet military base and more military aid is given to the country.

1973

February	A report from the London School of Economics claims that there are one million prisoners in 1,000 camps, and that 10,000 of them are political prisoners.
May	Brezhnev visits Federal Republic of Germany, signing cultural and economic agreements.
June	Brezhnev visits USA, signing agreements on the prevention of nuclear war and on trade promotion. He make a TV broadcast to the US nation.
	The Tu-144 airliner crashes at the Paris air show.
July	International Lenin Peace Prize presented to Brezhnev.
October	The supply of natural gas by pipeline to West Germany begins.

1974

	Brezhnev agrees to a golf course near Moscow (in 1989 this proposal was renewed).
February	Demonstrations in Moscow and Tallinn by Volga Germans wanting to leave Russia and Estonia.
	Solzhenitsyn expelled from USSR after publication of *The Gulag Archipelago*.
July	Nixon's second visit to the USSR; agreements on nuclear arms control signed.
November	President Ford meets Brezhnev in Vladivostok.
	The Somali army reaches 22,000 with equipment and jet fighters from Russia.
	The Ethiopian Emperor Haile Selassie is overthrown by a coup and his US military support is withdrawn.

1975

January	Soviets decide not to ratify USSR-US trade agreement of 1972.
February	Meeting in Moscow of Comecon and EEC Secretariats.

15–21 July	A joint Soviet–American space flight, involving Soyuz 19 and Apollo, is carried out.
1 August	Thirty-two European heads of state, with Canada and the United States, hold a meeting with Brezhnev at Helsinki. The final act of the conference is signed, confirming the post-1945 frontiers, giving permanence to newly shaped countries, such as Poland and East Germany. In exchange, the Soviet Union agrees to the recognition of basic human rights. A result of this in the Soviet Union is the setting up of dissident 'Helsinki groups' to monitor the behaviour of Soviet authorities.
December	The Nobel Peace Price is awarded to the Soviet scientist Sakharov.

1976

	Mengistu Haile Mariam, having emerged as the leader of the Dergue, the Ethiopian ruling group, makes declarations of Marxism and concludes an arms deal with the USSR.
February	25th Party Congress. Brezhnev reports shortcomings in agriculture and light industry.
	An open letter protesting against conditions in the Soviet Union is sent to the congress by dissidents.
	The 10th Five Year Plan is announced. The production of consumer goods promised by the 9th Plan is not fulfilled. This plan again calls for an emphasis on consumer goods.
	It is announced that the 1975 grain harvest was the worst for ten years; total grain imports from the USA, July 1975 to January 1976, have been 13 million tonnes.
28 May	The Treaty on Underground Nuclear Explosions is signed between the USA and USSR.

1977

16 June	Brezhnev made Chairman of the Praesidium of Supreme Soviet, nominal head of state.
September	Hunger strike by the inmates of Perm prison camps.
7 October	Fourth (since 1917) constitution adopted.
	Somalia and Ethiopia come to war over Eritrea, whose ownership they dispute: two Soviet-armed states in conflict. Forced to take sides, Russia chooses Ethiopia as its ally.

1978

January	Gromyko protests against the possible introduction of the neutron bomb.
February	Soviet nationals are expelled from Canada for involvement in espionage.
June–August	The trial and sentencing of the dissidents Orlov, Scharansky and Ginsburg. This arouses strong reactions in the USA.
August	China and Japan sign a treaty of peace and friendship. The Soviet Union protests against this.

1979

January	In the USA there is anger when it is disclosed that 20 MiG-23 fighters have been delivered to Cuba in the previous year.
	Viktor Korchnoi, the chess grandmaster living in Switzerland, is deprived of Soviet citizenship, under a law endorsed in December 1978.
18 July	SALT II (the Soviet–American Treaty on the Limitation of Strategic Arms) is signed by Brezhnev and President Carter in Vienna.
	In Cambodia the Khmer Rouge are ousted and replaced by Soviet-backed Vietnam.
24 December	Afghanistan invaded. By 1988 Soviet casualities will be 13,000 dead and 35,000 wounded.

1980

January	Sakharov exiled to Gorky after protesting openly against the invasion of Afghanistan.
February	The American CIA claims that the Soviet defence budget must increase from 11 per cent of the GNP to 15 per cent by 1985.
August	After strikes in Polish industrial centres, the independent trade union Solidarity is formed.
October	Negotiations on normalisation of relations with China are suspended due to the invasion of Afghanistan.
October–December	Kosygin resigns, and dies shortly afterwards.

1981

24 February–3 March	26th Party Congress. Guidelines for the next Five Year Plan are affirmed.
April	The US lifts the embargo on grain sales to the USSR.
July	China protests over the Soviet occupation of the Wakhan salient in Afghanistan on their mutual border.

December	Leningrad Writers' Union monthly journal *Aurora* has an issue devoted to Brezhnev's 75th birthday containing a satire on a man resembling him.

1982

25 January	Suslov dies.
22 February	*Pravda* makes indirect comments on Brezhnev's daughter Galina and 'Boris the Gypsy', her blackmarketeer circus performer lover.
9 November	Manager of the major store Gastronom No.1 arrested and charged with fraud; he is a friend of Galina Brezhnev; he is sentenced on 25 November 1983 and shot in July 1984.
10 November	The death of Brezhnev.
12 November	Andropov is elected General Secretary of the Central Committee of the CPSU.

1983

January	Andropov is elected Chairman of the Supreme Soviet Praesidium.
1 September	A South Korean airliner, having strayed off course, is shot down by Soviet fighters, killing 269 people.

1984

9 February	The death of Yuri Andropov.
13 February	Konstantin Chernenko is elected General Secretary and President of the Praesidium.
	Sharaf Rashidov removed from post of Party Secretary of Uzbekistan after 24 years. This is part of the uncovering of the Uzbekistan corruption scandal.
1 October	The Lena to the Pacific coast section of the Trans–Baikal–Amur railway is opened.

1985

10 March	Chernenko dies.
April	Mikhail Gorbachev is elected General Secretary of the Central Committee of the Communist Party.

2 July	Gromyko is elected Chairman of the Praesidium of the Supreme Soviet, head of state.
6 August	The Soviet Union announces a unilateral moratorium on all nuclear explosions.
September	Ryzhkov succeeds Tikhonov as premier.

1986

24 February–6 April	27th Party Congress. Mikhail Gorbachev stresses the need for radical change after the stagnation of the Brezhnev years. He calls for a restructuring ('perestroika') of Soviet society. The Party adopts his line and follows his call for a greater openness ('glasnost') in public dealings. Perestroika and glasnost become words frequently used in reporting and debating current Soviet problems.
26 April	Chernobyl: the atomic power station explodes.
18 August	The 1985 ban on nuclear explosions is extended to 1987.
22 September	29 lb (13 kg) of gold from the British cruiser *Edinburgh*, sunk in 1942, during World War II, is recovered by a British diving team. The gold, payment for wartime munitions, is divided between Britain and the USSR.
2 October	The remaining Chernobyl atomic reactor is buried under a security mound of metal and concrete.
December	In Kazakhstan there are seven deaths in a students' nationalist protest demonstration.

1987

12 February	140 dissidents, accused of anti-Soviet statements or actions, are pardoned.
26 February	An underground nuclear test is carried out, ending the unilateral moratorium.
March	Muslim riots in Tajikistan.
10–11 March	A Soviet–US meeting is held in Moscow on the future of Angola and the Cuban presence there.
18 March	A US nuclear test in Nevada is observed by a Soviet team as part of an experiment in the international monitoring of such tests.
28 March–1 April	Margaret Thatcher, the British Prime Minister, visits the Soviet Union.
29–30 June	The Supreme Soviet approves the restructuring of the national economy, with laws on state enterprises and on procedures for suing officials who infringe citizens' rights.

July	Crimean Tatars protest in Red Square, Moscow, against their continued exile.

1988

27–28 February	Twenty-six Armenians killed by Azeris at Sumgait, near Baku, in an outbreak of racial violence. This signals the resurgence of old antagonisms which the Soviet system had thought buried.
	Nikolai Bukharin (shot after trial in March 1938) rehabilitated by a commission set up to study the trials.
15 April	The withdrawal of Soviet troops from Afghanistan begins.
21 May	The first announcement by Tass of the Nagorny Karabakh (autonomous region cut from Armenia by Stalin in 1923) dispute.
26 May	Law on co-operatives gives impulse to private enterprise. The CP Central Committee publishes 'theses' or platform for a meeting on 28 June. This gives a blueprint for greatest social changes since 1917, as a step towards a market economy.
28 May	Hints appear in the Soviet press that the Soviet Union, not the Nazis, was responsible for the Katyn massacre of 4,000 Poles.
29 May–2 June	Reagan–Gorbachev summit in Moscow.
30 May	Boris Yeltsin, ex-CP chief in Moscow, calls for the removal of Yegor Ligachev, Party No. 2.
3 June	Sakharov endorses perestroika.
4 June	Moscow demonstrators chant (among others things) 'Down with KGB'.
5–17 June	1,000th anniversary of Russian Christianity celebrated.
9 June	Igor Muradian, Armenian activist, says that Party leaders of Armenia and Azerbaijan have decreed that the Armenian enclave of Nagorny Karabakh, in Azerbaijan, cannot be handed over by Azerbaijan to Armenia, but might be raised to 'autonomous republic'.
10 June	*Pravda* admits the Party's loss of control in Nagorny Karabakh. There is a two-day general strike, then recently appointed (May) Armenian Party chief Suren Arutyunyan speaks to a crowd of 300,000 in Erevan, assuring them that the Armenian Soviet would back demands for a return of Nagorny Karabakh to Armenia.
11 June	In Moscow reports are confirmed that an Azeri policeman was killed in an anti-Armenian fight in Baku, Azerbaijan's capital.
13 June	Gorbachev opens dialogue with the Vatican, breaking years of hostility.
	Lev Kamenev and Grigory Zinoviev, executed in August 1936, have their sentences annulled by the Soviet Supreme Court (according to *Izvestia*), so too were the sentences of Karl Radek (executed after a trial in 1937) and Yuri Pyatakov (who died in a labour camp during a ten-year sentence).
	A Moscow 'beauty queen' crowned: a 16-year-old Komsomol member, another break with tradition.

28 June– 1 July	19th Party Conference (the first conference, held between Party Congresses, since 1941). The conference is mostly taken up by a discussion of perestroika.
1 September	Strikes over increased food prices in Poland end with the legalization of the hitherto banned trade union movement Solidarity.
28 October	In Prague 5,000 people demonstrate on the anniversary of Czech independence (1918), which the police break up with violence.
November	The Hungarian Communist Party announces the introduction of a multi-party system.
	The names 'Brezhnev' and 'Chernenko' are removed from towns and institutions, being linked with the period of stagnation.
30 November	Yuri Churbanov, son-in-law of Brezhnev, found guilty of taking bribes and abuse of power while Deputy Interior Minister and sentenced (30 December) to 12 years' hard labour in a camp. Two former Deputy Interior Ministers, Tashtemir Kakhramanov and Khaidar Yakhyayev (in office 1964–79), are released. The investigator of the case stated in February 1989 that the trial had shown the accused as petty criminals and had covered up the real extent of the bribe-taking and had blunted the struggle against organised crime.
7 December	Gorbachev's speech to the United Nations General Assembly includes a promise to cut Soviet forces in Europe by 500,000 as part of the MBFR (Mutual Balanced Force Reduction) talks.
	Marshal Sergei Akhromeyev, the head of the armed forces, (coincidentally?) resigned but later publicly justifies the reduction both politically and militarily.
	An earthquake destroys part of northern Armenia at 11.41 am. Of a population of three million, half a million are homeless. The centre of the earthquake, at Spitak, killed 11,000 of its 22,000 inhabitants.

1989

10 January	Gorbachev addressed the Central Committee of the Party, meeting to draw up its list of candidates for the congress elections in March, and tells them that they have 'no God-given right to rule', but must earn their position in 'the political vanguard of society'.
18 January	Gorbachev announced that the Soviet Union's military budget will be cut by 14.2 per cent, the personnel by 12 per cent. This will involve 240,000 men from Eastern Europe starting in April and 200,000 from Asia, in particular 75,000 from Mongolia and 60,000 from the frontiers of Afghanistan, Iran and Turkey. 10,000 tanks would leave Europe and all aircraft would leave Mongolia.
January	The conservative, official daily paper *Pravda* accuses the pro-glasnost weekly magazine of the intelligentsia, *Ogonyok*, of distorting history and setting itself up as the judge of the country's cultural, political and moral life.
	Estonia's parliament votes (204 for, 50 against and 6 abstaining) to enforce the use of the national language.
	Tajikistan is reported to have had anti-Russian and anti-Uzbek riots.

February	Shevardnadze, Foreign Minister, visits China: the first since 1959.
21 February	Vaclav Havel, the Czech dissident playwright, is sentenced to 9 months imprisonment for subversion. The sentence is later reduced and he is released in May.
9 April	In Tblisi, Georgia, troops use gas and clubs to attack a protest meeting, killing 20.
23 April	Supporters of the radical grouping 'Democratic Union' are arrested at a demonstration in Moscow.
25 May	Gorbachev is elected Chairman of the Supreme Soviet of the USSR.
10 July	Coal miners go on strike in Mezhdurechensk, western Siberia. This is followed by strikes in the Donbas.
July	Strikes by Russian workers in Estonia, protesting against discriminatory laws. There are links with the 'United Front of Workers', a recently formed body backed by Ligachev.
19 July	General Jaruzelski is elected President of Poland. In August he invites Solidarity to form a government.
24 July	In Georgia, crowds of 20,000 in Tbilisi shout 'Down with the Russian Empire!'
30 July	An unofficial opposition, the 'inter-regional group', is formed by over 200 Soviet deputies, with Yeltsin as leader and including Sakharov.
16 August	A draft law published, giving workers the right to strike.
21 September	At Semipalatinsk in Kazakhstan, interracial riots leave three dead.
22 September	At Yaroslavl the RSFSR Congress votes for future elections to be by straightforward constituencies and without the supremacy of the Party.
2 October	The Supreme Soviet imposes a ban on all strikes in key industries.
26 October	Miners in the Arctic city of Vorkuta walk out on strike, claiming that the promised improvements had not reached them.
4 November	Members of the Bulgarian opposition demonstrate in Sofia. Todor Zhikov is replaced by Peter Mladenow.
17 November	Czechoslovaks hold anti-government demonstrations. These are broken up with police brutality.
24 November	Mass demonstrations lead to the resignations of the Czech party leader, Milos Jakos.
29 November	Direct rule in Nagorny Karabakh, the Armenian enclave, is ended and it returns to Azerbaijani administration.
1 December	President Gorbachev meets Pope John Paul II in the Vatican, the first-ever encounter between the leader of the world's 800 million Catholics and the head of an officially atheist super-power.
17 December	Rioting in the Romanian provincial city of Timisoara is brutally suppressed by the army and Securitate (political police). More than 600 are killed.
21 December	Nicolae Ceaucescu's appearance in Bucharest is greeted with derision. He and his wife Elena flee, but are captured. The National Salvation Front take over.
25 December	The Ceaucescus are tried and shot.

28 December Alexander Dubcek becomes Chairman of the Czech parliament and the dissident playwright, Vaclav Havel, of Civic Forum, is elected President of Czechoslovakia.

1990

5 January Azerbaijani Muslims demonstrate at the Iranian frontier, calling for the opening of the border dividing them from their fellow Azeris in Iran.

6 January In the Aberbaijan capital, Baku, there are demonstrations calling for the return of their control of Nagorny Karabakh. 25 Armenians are killed in later riots.

7 January Renewed rioting and fighting in Georgia between Ossetians and Georgian nationalists.

15 January Algirdas Brazaukas elected president of Lithuania by a majority (228 to 4) of the republic's Supreme Soviet.

8 February In Odessa at a large demonstration Ukrainian members of the nationalist Rukh Party call for political change.

9 February Gorbachev, at a meeting with US Secretary of State, James Baker, agrees to destroy 'a significant part' of Soviet chemical weapons and offers further arms reductions.

In the Tajik capital, Dushambe, rioters attempt to storm the local police headquarters. At least 22 are killed.

13 February The Soviet Communist Party Central Committee issues its revised policies, including guarantees of human rights, with a high court to protect them, emphasis on the production of consumer goods and the development of a market economy. The nation's government should be based on an electoral system allowing political parties, abandoning the monopoly of the Communist Party, and instituting a presidential head of state, responsible to the Congress of People's Deputies but with powers to ensure the functioning of the state. On the federation of nations within the Soviet Union there should be 'unity in diversity' and attempts at secession should be opposed.

25 February Elections are held in Lithuania, Moldavia, Tajikistan, Kirghizia.

In the Belorussian capital, Minsk, a Popular Front rally of 150,000 people demands extra funds from Moscow to help overcome the results of the 1986 Chernobyl disaster. 100,000 people are still to be relocated.

28 February The Congress of Deputies passes a new law to redefine rights to own property and land. Peasants may choose to be in Kolkhozes or to receive their own allotment of land.

March In Donets, in the Ukraine, coal miners come out on strike. They claim that their action is not affected by the ban of October 1989, because it is for political, not economic, purposes. They call for full democracy in the Communist Party. In the Ukraine, though the miners are believed to have strong links with Russia they are beginning to support the Rukh Party.

3 March There are anti-Mesketian riots in Uzbekistan, Uzbeks attacking the camps where refugee Mesketians are housed.

4 March	Elections in the RSFSR, Ukraine and Belorussia. In the RSFSR alone there are 6,700 candidates contesting 1,068 seats.
6 March	The Congress of Deputies passes a further law on property, allowing ownership of assets and shares in enterprises, and also allowing these to be passed on to heirs. This is intended to provide the ground for a new market economy.
9 March	The Georgian parliament declares its sovreignty.
11 March	Lithuania declares itself independent after 124 delegates to its new parliament voted unanimously in favour. They also voted to change the republic's name by dropping the words 'Soviet Socialist'. Because of the declaration the Soviet army starts rounding up 'draft dodgers'.
13 March	1,800 out of 2,000 delegates to the Congress of Deputies vote to alter the constitution by removing the Communist Party's supremacy and instituting an executive presidency.
14 March	The Congress votes to appoint Gorbachev as President of the Soviet Union. He is the sole candidate, but only 60 per cent vote for him; of the remainder 495 hard line conservatives vote against and 426 abstain. Anatoly Lukyanov, one of eight candidates, with only 54 per cent of the votes, is elected to succeed Gorbachev as head of the Congress.
	The Congress also passes a resolution, with a large majority, that the Lithuanian declaration of independence has no legal force.
18 March	Soviet troops in Lithuania show their strength in open manoeuvres, and mount extra guards on the Lithuanian nuclear power plant.
20 March	Romanian nationalists attack a demonstration by Transylvanian Hungarians. Two people are killed.
21 March	The Alliance for Germany, backed by the West German Christian Democrat Party, wins the East German elections, beating the Social Democrats.
22 March	Gorbachev orders a show of military strength in Lithuania.
23 March	All foreign diplomats are ordered out of Lithuania.
8 April	In Hungary the Democratic Forum wins 165 seats forming a coalition. The communists hold only 33 seats.
19 April	The Soviet Union starts a blockade of all imports of fuel and power to Lithuania.
5 May	At the annual May Day parade Gorbachev and the Politburo are booed off the rostrum by demonstrators.
9 May	The Estonian SSR changes its name to the Estonian Republic and reinstates its pre-war constitution. Russian workers demonstrate in Tallinn.
26 May	The National Salvation Front in Romania gains two-thirds of the votes. There are protests that the party contains many old-guard communists.
30 May	Boris Yeltsin is elected President of the RSFSR and declares Russian law to have priority over Soviet Union law.
31 May	President Gorbachev meets President Bush in Washington, mainly to discuss German reunification and NATO.
2 June	Ethnic riots among the minority Uzbeks in the Kirghiz republic leave nearly fifty dead.

8 June	The Warsaw Pact decides to become a mainly political body. Hungary declares it wishes to leave the Pact.
	The RSFSR assembly makes a declaration of sovereignty within the USSR.
10 June	Civic Forum wins the Czechoslovak elections, with the communists gaining 13 per cent of the vote.
	In Bulgarian elections the Socialist Party (formerly communist) has a majority and forms a government. The Union of Democratic Forces (UDF) refuses to join in a coalition.
11 June	The Soviet and West German Foreign Ministers meet at Brest in Belorussia to discuss German reunification.
13 June	The Central Committee announce over 130,000 resignations from the Communist Party in the previous six months.
19 June	The newly formed Russian (RSFSR) Communist Party opens its Party Congress with 3,000 delegates in Moscow.
20 June	The Georgian parliament starts a study of measures for economic and political independence.
	The Uzbek parliament in Tashkent makes a declaration of sovreignty.
22 June	Ivan Polozkov, an orthodox communist, is elected head of the new Russian (RSFSR) Communist Party, with 1017 votes against the radicals' 848.
	Vladimir Ivashko resigns as President of the Ukraine, handing over to the conservative Stanislav Gurenko.
1 July	Albanians demonstrate against the Communist Party leader Ramiz Alia.
	East Germany switches to West German currency as part of a move to a market economy and reunification. A Soviet offer to put the disputed Kurile islands under United Nations trusteeship is rejected by Japan.
	The 28th Party Congress opens in Moscow. Gorbachev attacks Ryzhkov's move towards reforming the economy by raising prices.
	The Kosovo parliament declares their territory separate from Yugoslavia. The Slovene parliament also declares all Slovene laws have priority over Yugoslav laws.
2–3 July	150 Albanians take refuge in foreign embassies.
4 July	Shevardnadze states that the end of the Cold War would save the Soviet Union 250 billion roubles over the next five years.
	The Central Committee gives the Party's income as 2.7 billion roubles with profits from newspaper and magazine publishing of 4 billion.
4 July	Gorbachev is elected by 3,166 votes to 1,046 to a commission to make new Party rules.
5 July	The 300 military delegates to the Party Congress, under Marshal Dmitri Yazov, support an attack on the foreign policy of 'giving in' and the depoliticization of the army.
	A new Estonian police force replaces the militia, and Soviet troops prevent a meeting to commemorate Estonian dead 1918–1945, claiming it is a covert pro-Nazi rally.
6 July	A NATO summit agrees to a peace declaration with Warsaw Pact countries.

The Albanian Communist Party agrees to allow refugees in foreign embassies to leave the country.

The Bulgarian president, Peter Mladenov, resigns after charges of bringing in the tanks to crush the December 1989 demonstrations.

8 July Boris Yeltsin offers Lithuania a treaty of co-operation with the RSFSR.

9 July Lithuania agrees to hold talks with Nikolai Ryzhkov and the Soviet blockade of fuel and power is lifted.

The Congress approves a new post of Deputy General Secretary, and makes all leaders of the republics members of the Politburo.

11 July Miners strike in the Donbas and Kuzbass, calling for the government's resignation and the removal of the Party from industry, the army, education and all other bodies.

Gorbachev is re-elected as General Secretary by a two-thirds majority. He rejects conservative suggestions of slowing down perestroika. Vladimir Ivashko, former Ukrainian President and regarded as a centrist, defeats Ligachev for the post of Deputy General Secretary.

12 July Boris Yeltsin resigns from the Soviet Communist Party which has rejected his radical proposals for reform (changing the party's name to Democratic Socialist, allowing factions within the party, calling for a popularly supported economic programme and for the party to drop its role in the army, KGB and all other bodies).

13 July The mayors of Moscow and Leningrad, elected in 1989 on a pro-Yeltsin platform, resign from the party.

Some 5,000 refugee Albanians are shipped to Italy.

14 July As the Congress closes, 25 delegates from the 'Democratic Platform' announce plans for the formation of a new party, and resign from the Communist Party.

A new Politburo is elected containing no government minister other than Gorbachev and his Deputy Vladimir Ivashko. Not included are Shevardnadze, Vadim Medvedev, Marshal Yazov, KGB head Vladimir Kryuchkov, nor Alexandra Biryukova (its only woman). Yegor Ligachev, defeated, retires to Siberia.

15 July The Mongolian Democratic Association say they will boycott elections, unless constitutional changes are made, claiming that the nomads are out of touch and cannot be influenced by the urban Democrats.

In Poland Solidarity claims that the old Party 'Nomenklatura' has taken advantage of its position by taking over privatised industries at advantageous terms.

16 July The Ukrainian parliament declares sovreignty, claiming the right to its own armed forces, banking system, its own foreign policy and the primacy of its laws.

The West German Chancellor Helmut Kohl and Gorbachev agree on terms for German reunification with safeguards for Soviet security interests. It is agreed that East Germany shall be included in NATO.

ENCYCLOPEDIA

Aeroflot

The Soviet airline set up in 1928, as part of the 1923 Five Year Plan, under the name of Dobroflot but restructured in 1932 under its present title. By 1935 its services spanned the whole of the USSR. At the end of World War II, after a relatively slow beginning, it expanded with aircraft based on the Douglas DC3, the Lisunov Li–2. It is now the world's largest airline, carrying an estimated 15 per cent of all passenger traffic.

In the 1950s the airline had a generation of turbo-prop and turbo-jet aircraft, of which the TU–104 carrying 100 passengers with a range of 1,900 miles (3,000 km), was the main one. The next most effective long-range aircraft was the TU–114 with a range of 5,600 miles (9,000 km). In 1973 the TU–144, a supersonic plane resembling the Anglo-French Concorde, was exhibited at the Paris Air Show, where it crashed. It later went into service on internal flights in the USSR, but was withdrawn in 1977.

By 1980 Aeroflot was serving all the major cities of Europe, Africa, the Middle East and South and South-East Asia, including a direct flight to Havana from Moscow. The most common Aeroflot plane now is the Il–62, carrying up to 180 passengers, and the Il–86, in service since 1977, capable of carrying 350 passengers.

Afghanistan

Russian Aid and Diplomacy under Khrushchev In the nineteenth century Afghanistan was the buffer state between the expanding Russian Empire in Asia and the British Empire in India with its interests in Persia. Afghanistan's frontier with British India (the 'North-West Frontier') which ran along the mountains south of the Hindu Kush, ignoring the tribal and clan boundaries, became the Pakistan frontier in 1947 when that nation was born. The Russian frontier lay mainly along the Oxus River to the Pamirs; it was established at the end of the nineteenth century and confirmed when the Soviets took over the Kingdom of Bokhara, Afghanistan's last independent northern neighbour, in 1920.

After the death of Stalin, the Soviet Union took a fresh look at the world outside and, in particular, their neighbour Afghanistan. The Bandung Conference had shown the Great Powers that the smaller nations of the Third World could, united, have more muscle than had been appreciated. Afghanistan was of obvious interest: a long-standing quarrel with Pakistan arising from the Afghan claim to the whole tribal area had resulted in the closure of that frontier to Afghan trade. Russia offered and encouraged an alterative route and sent a large trade mission to Kabul. At this time the USA was also offering aid to Afghanistan through agricultural development (the vast and ambitious 'Helmand Valley Authority'). The Russians, in direct competition, built grain silos, which housed the American-donated grain, and also constructed new roads in and out of the capital Kabul.

In 1955, to show their sincere friendship, Bulganin and Khrushchev paid a state visit to Afghanistan (countered shortly afterwards by a visit from the American Vice-President Richard Nixon). Russia then stepped up its involvement and new projects included the huge Salang Tunnel, through the Hindu Kush, which allowed trade to move north and south all the year round. This was followed by a military-aid pro-gramme by which the Afghan defence forces were re-equipped and given jet fighters.

The Russians made little move to exercise direct political influence at this stage and were content to deal with the dictatorial Daoud Shah, uncle of the king and prime minister from 1953 to 1963. But the political climate among the educated Afghans moved steadily away from traditional conservative Muslim and tribal ways to more democratic liberal and international ideas. Women were encouraged to appear in public without the veil and religious leaders protesting against this were jailed. As part of his strengthening of the Afghan central government, Daoud Shah used troops to collect taxes and enforce his rule.

From Russia's point of view, this development of a strong and friendly government in its neighbour was most satisfactory. American influence was weakened by the massive Russian programmes and the Khrushchev policy of trade and aid with little attempt at political infiltration seemed to have paid off.

1963–79 By the mid-Sixties Afghanistan had changed enormously. Tourists from all the world visited Kabul and the social contrasts between the city and the mountain villages increased. The small pro-Russian Marxist parties began to divide into urban and rural factions, but both remote from day-to-day life. In July 1973 the Parcham urban faction, with Daoud Shah, carried out a coup expelling the king. But when Daoud seemed to turn against the Parcham in April 1978, they liquidated him with their Soviet-acquired military power. A Democratic Republic of Afghanistan was proclaimed. But the Parcham were not in touch with the country and local uprisings broke out. The rural Khalq faction disputed power and the Soviets found their ally in danger of civil war.

1979–88 In late December 1979 Soviet armed forces moved into Afghanistan. They killed the Parcham leader and put the Khalq in power as the most likely faction to gain widespread popular support. But rather than settling matters, the invasion roused the whole country. Resistance forces, labelled generally Mujahideen appeared and were supplied with arms from US and Arab sources through Pakistan and Iran; sometimes for anti-Soviet motives, sometimes for patriotic Afghan motives and sometimes for the support of Islam. Their increasingly sophisticated weapons denied the Soviets any chance of success.

In 1986 a more moderate leader was found in the Parcham, Dr Najibullah, and the Soviet Union under Gorbachev began to find a way out. Not only was the war unwinnable, it was having a negative effect in the USSR. In eight years over 13,000 Soviet soldiers had been killed. Soviet conscripts from Central Asia (usually in the ranks without technical skills) were not sent to Afghanistan, regarded as unreliable against fellow-Muslims, which increased the proportion of ethnically Russian casualties and the dislike of the war within the USSR. Returning soldiers reported against the war's aims and its conditions. There was also evidence of drug abuse among returning soldiers.

On 8 February 1988 Gorbachev announced that Soviet troops would begin to withdraw on 15 May. In April at Geneva, Afghanistan and Pakistan signed agreements to cease interference in each other's lands, to help refugees and to co-operate with the withdrawal of Soviet troops. This was followed by guarantees by the USSR and the USA to respect these commitments. The Soviet troops withdrew on the planned timetable and Afghanistan since then has settled in to its own civil war.

Agriculture

The Background During the 1905 revolution there were uprisings among the peasantry and, after the revolution was suppressed, reforms which enabled peasants to buy and sell land removed more than two million households from the landless communes that hired out their labour. This was particularly marked in the rich black earth country of west Russia, the Ukraine and north Caucasus. Stolypin said that the government was placing its wager 'not on the needy and the drunken but on the sturdy and strong'. While these reforms did create a class of strong peasants (kulaks), they also led to increasing bitterness among the remainder. This was fertile ground for the revolutionary doctrines of the various socialist parties contending for future power in Russia at the time.

The Socialist Revolutionaries (SRs) were in direct succession to the nineteenth-century radical Narodniks and above all were the champions of the peasants. They believed that socialism would develop naturally in the countryside through the activities of the peasant communes. Followers of Marx, such as Plekhanov and, even more so, Lenin, were totally opposed to such a notion, realising that it would be necessary to create large-scale agricultural units to supply a socialist economy. There was also a powerful bias against the peasantry in the Bolshevik Party where they were believed to be a naturally reactionary force and a breeding ground for capitalism. But no party could afford to ignore them. They represented 80 per cent of the population and contributed 50 per cent of the national income.

During World War I the agricultural sector was affected more drastically than the industrial. The best manpower had gone to the front and replacements for worn-out agricultural machinery and implements were unobtainable. Food production had slumped and the combination of hunger in the cities and the conduct of the war revived all the forces that had erupted in 1905. When the revolution took place there were sporadic seizures of landlords' land by peasants in various parts of the country, despite exhortations by the Provisional Government to await the decision of the Constituent Assembly.

The 1st All-Russian Congress of Soviets in June 1917 had an SR majority and although their agrarian policy was very similar to the Bolsheviks (in fact Lenin later adopted it for the Bolsheviks), there was a significant difference: the SRs backed the Provisional Government in telling the peasants to wait for the Constituent Assembly before expropriating land, while Lenin backed their actions and further added that large estates should be transformed into model farms run by local soviets. But this argument was interrupted by the success of the October Revolution and all that this brought in its train.

The 1917 October Revolution Lenin realised that the vital issues to the peasants, the vast mass of the population, were the war and the land. At the 2nd All-Russian Congress of Soviets on 26 October, the Decree on Land was submitted and passed unanimously; this declared all private property in land abolished, and called for all land, private, State and Church to be handed over to rural district land committees. The small holdings of working peasants and Cossacks were exempted.

This was certainly one of Lenin's most ingenious political moves. It had the effect of making the Bolsheviks popular while preparing the ground for the division of the SRs.

The split was widened when Kolegaev, a prominent Left SR, was appointed People's Commissar for Agriculture. On 18 January the 3rd Congress of Soviets approved a draft law on the Socialisation of Land, promulgated on the 57th anniversary of Tsar Alexander's decree emancipating the serfs.

One of its clauses stressed the object of a socialist agricultural programme as follows: to develop the collective system of agriculture, as being more economic in respect both of labour and of production, at the expense of individual holdings, in order to bring about the transition to a socialist economy.

During the next four or five months a massive redistribution of land took place throughout most of European Russia. But, except in areas where the power of the soviets was firmly established, the distribution of land was often haphazard; in some places peaceful, in others leading to violence and destruction of property and equipment. It has been calculated that of the seized land 86 per cent went to the peasants, 11 per cent to the State, and 3 per cent to collectives. Owing to the strength of the SRs in the local land committees, the well-off peasants probably did better from the transfer than the poor peasants.

The harvest of 1917 was a poor one, largely because of the war, and by January 1918 the food shortages in the cities were becoming acute. At a meeting of the Petrograd Soviet Lenin proposed the searching of all storage areas where grain might be being hidden and the immediate shooting of speculators.

War Communism (1918–20) The People's Commissar for Supply organised armed bands of men to go out into the villages to offer goods to the peasants in exchange for grain or, where that proved unproductive, to take it by force. Neither expedient proved effective. The peasants would not give up grain without goods and the goods offered were of little interest to them. This attitude and the menacing approach of the Civil War led to the decree of the 18 June setting up the Committees of Poor Peasants. Membership of these was open to anyone in the rural community. Their purpose was to extract grain from the kulaks and the rich. Lenin regarded this as a vital step in the progress of the revolution. It meant the beginning of the true socialist revolution in the countryside in which the poor peasants, led by the industrial proleteriat, took their decisive action against the bourgeois in the shape of the kulaks. It also signalled the first step in what was to become known as War Communism.

The result of all these measures was that peasants hid their grain and refused to sow more than would feed their families. With the end of the Civil War by the autumn of 1920, it was apparent that there had been an appalling decline in agricultural production. The redistribution of land had led to the virtual elimination of the large estates but the natural unit for agriculture had now become the peasant small holding: a plot of up to 10 acres (25 hectares) cultivated by the labour of a peasant family owning a horse. This unit represented 86 per cent of all holdings, while the collective, the desired socialist solution, had everywhere met with almost total failure.

The area of sown land in Russia had declined from 260 million acres (105 million hectares) in 1913 to 185 million acres (75 million hectares) in 1920 and the grain harvest of 80 million tonnes in 1913 had dropped to less than 50 in 1920. What was worse, the small peasant holdings not only produced less, they consumed more, and even if they produced a surplus it was more difficult and expensive to collect. The 8th Congress of Soviets recognised that the real problem for Soviet agricultural policy was not to find the means of collecting crops but to find an effective way of increasing production. This led directly to the New Economic Policy (NEP).

NEP (1921–27) At the 10th Party Congress in March 1921 Lenin announced a series of measures aimed at encouraging the production of surpluses. These consisted of a tax in kind based on a percentage of crops harvested, calculated to favour the middle and poor peasants, and a freedom to trade surpluses in the market place. A fund was promised to provide agricultural equipment and consumer goods. Almost immediately the area of sown land in some provinces increased by up to 15 per cent, though it was offset by decreases elsewhere. Much more seriously, a severe drought affected the harvests of 1920 and 1921. The State had to find large quantities of relief supplies to which were added considerable quantities from abroad. Hoover's American Relief Administration (ARA) was a major force in famine relief.

In 1922 there was a massive agricultural campaign, including an agricultural exhibition held in Moscow, which was rewarded by an excellent harvest. The effects of the NEP were considerable and lasted for almost the next ten years. The peasant, and in particular the well-off and energetic peasant, was given the chance of treating his holding as his own, of employing hired labour on it if he so wished and of selling its produce where he wished. Essentially his obligation to the State was that of a taxpayer. Lenin continued to say that the ideal socialist development was large-scale agriculture but did little in practice to bring it about. So little, indeed that by 1927 98.3 per cent of all land was in the hands of individuals and 1.7 per cent in the hands of collectives or State farms.

The agricultural policies of the NEP were criticised like the rest of its arrangements. First, on ideological grounds, particularly by the left, including Trotsky and Kamenev, and secondly by industrial workers who felt that they were being discriminated against. Much debate went on about these issues but that was normal during the 1920s in the country and by 1925 the sown area had increased to 260 million acres (104 million hectares) and the grain harvest had climbed from 50 million tonnes to 72 million. The NEP could be seen to be working.

Collectivisation (1927–36) By 1927 Stalin believed that 'The Soviet regime was walking on two unequal legs, the socialist sector in towns and the private sector in villages and that this could no longer go indefinitely.' The idea of collectivisation was not a new one and in fact Stalin was taking the left-wing policies of Trotsky and Zinoviev to their logical conclusions. The Five Year Plan was not officially promulgated until April 1929, but many of the measures contained in it were already being put into effect.

Soviet agricultural policy had as its main thrust the herding of peasants into collectives. They either went to voluntary collectives, such as the Kolkhoz, working on a co-operative basis with the peasants sharing the profits from the produce which now had to be sold to the government, or joined a Sovkhoz which, as a State farm, paid a wage. The inhabitants of the Kolkhoz were permitted an acre or less of land on which they were allowed to keep a cow, a pig, four sheep, rabbits and poultry.

Since, as we have seen, not more than 2 per cent of land was collectivised in 1927, drastic measures, plainly, would have to be taken in order to meet the targets set out by the Party.

The collectivisation policy was aimed at the whole peasant population but it was now being proposed that the land belonging to the kulaks should be expropriated and the owners expelled from the community. Kulaks were defined by Sovnarkom as peasants who: hired permanent workers; owned an industrial enterprise, a flour mill for example; hired out agricultural machinery; had any member of their family involved in usury.

Stalin claimed that the kulaks represented 5 per cent of the population, though 3 per cent is a more generally accepted estimate.

Pravda published an article entitled 'Neither terror nor dekulakisation, but a socialist offensive on NEP lines'. This was in June 1929. By December Stalin had ceased to pretend. 'Now we are able to carry on a determined offensive against the kulaks, eliminate them as a class. It is an integral part of the formation and development of collective farms. Consequently it is ridiculous and foolish to discourse at length on dekulakisation. When the head is off, one does not mourn for the hair.' Action against them started almost immediately, though official instructions were only issued in February of the next year. There are no official figures as to the number of households dekulakised but about one million seem to have been affected, a total of at least 4.5 million people. Their fate depended upon what category they came into. The 'actively hostile' were handed over to the OGPU and sent to forced labour camps, while their families were deported to distant regions, Siberia or the Far East. The second category 'the most economically potent' were deported outside the region of their residence. The final group, those with little land and a minimum of capital equipment, was to be allowed to remain in the region but was to be given the worst of the land.

It is of course true that in the Caucasus and the Ukraine richer peasants did own a disproportionate percentage of the land compared to other parts of the country, and that more of them had joined the White armies in the Civil War than their poorer neighbours. However the basic reason for the assault on the kulaks was the belief, not confined to Stalin, that they were 'a petit bourgeois class of aspiring capitalists who were hostile to the socialist revolution'. As a class they paid for their beliefs and attitudes under Stalin.

Deprivation was not confined to the kulaks. In the winter of 1930–31 collectivisation and confiscation were being employed against the whole spectrum of peasants of the Ukraine and, by 1933, in Siberia. Livestock was compulsorily purchased, though frequently the peasants slaughtered their beasts before this could happen. In Kazakhstan there was a disastrous decline in the sheep population leading quite directly to a decline of Kazhaks themselves, as many as 20 per cent dying of famine. Another method used to persuade peasants to join collectives was the imposition of arbitrary demands for grain. Failure to meet these was punished by fines, confiscation of property and even imprisonment. The human cost of collectivisation was high. The estimated death toll, between 1930 and 1937, was 11 million, added to which another 3.5 million died later in camps. Of these deaths 5 million were in the Ukraine, one million in the north Caucasus and another million in the Kazakhstan disaster.

Agriculture (1936–41) Collectivisation was more or less complete by 1936 and the pattern of collective institutions remained more or less the same from the time of the Kolkhoz Congress until after the death of Stalin. In 1937 there were nearly a quarter of a million Kolkhozes and 4,000 Sovkhozes. In the the Kolkhoz the peasants grew grain and industrial crops, cotton, etc., but the supply of meat and vegetables came almost entirely from their private holdings, and the same applied to fruit, eggs and poultry.

Collectives 1928–37

	1928	1932	1937
Households collectivised (%)	1.7	61.5	93.0
Sown area collectivised (%)	2.3	77.7	99.1
No. of Kolkhozes (000s)	33.3	210.6	242.5
No. of Sovkhozes (000s)	1.4	4.3	4.0
No. of MTSs (000s)	–	2.4	5.8

Adapted from Munting, *The Economic Development of the USSR* (1982)

Payment for collective work was not good, and Kolkhozes had to pay for the services provided by the Machine Tractor Stations (MTSs) which provided agricultural machinery and also exercised political control over the collectives. The constant problem therefore was to exert pressure on the peasants to work for the collective when it was in their interests to work for themselves. In 1939 an edict was made defining the number of hours to be worked for the Kolkhoz, but enforcing it was not easy – particularly when industrial prices rose more sharply than agricultural incomes, the so-called 'Scissors Effect'.

The Sovkhoz, although it had more access to capital goods than the Kolkhoz and had a fully paid staff of workers, did very little better in production terms. But the harvest of 1937, at 87 million tonnes, was the best since the Revolution.

The harvests declined sharply for the next two years. But in 1939, at the outbreak of World War II, there was a record harvest of 95 million tonnes, of which procurements for the State amounted to 36 million tonnes. It might be said that Stalin had won his battle against the peasants, a contest which, according to Roosevelt, he compared to the terrible experience of war against the Germans.

It has been said that the survival of the peasantry from 1930 onwards was due to the toleration by the government of private food growing. With 3.5 per cent of the sown area, this produced 45 per cent of all agricultural output, including 71 per cent of milk, 70 per cent of meat and 43 per cent of wool. Non-collectivised agriculture has been called, appropriately, the 'giant dwarf'.

The introduction of compulsory work units on the Kolkhozes further increased peasant grievances and led to a further decline in their standard of living. Vast and ill-conceived plans, like Stalin's dream of growing cotton in the Ukraine, and huge plantings of a supposed rubber-bearing plant, the *kok-sagyz*, did little to increase agricultural production at a critical time for the USSR.

World War II (1941–45) Soviet agriculture was hit almost immediately by the rapid advances made by the German army in the summer of 1941. Much of the best agricultural land in the Ukraine and north Caucasus was lost to the goverment and it has been estimated that by the end of November 1941 38 per cent of grain production, 84 per cent of sugar and 60 per cent of pig production were held by the invading Germans. Unlike the industrial capacity, much of which was removed to the east, good agricultural land could only by made up for by increased production off worse land. By herculean efforts, this was achieved, though by the end of 1942 the Nazi occupation of the north Caucasus and the Don area had deprived the country of almost all its first-rate grain-growing areas. The grain harvest in 1942 was reduced to 30 million tonnes.

The invading Nazi forces used the Kolkhozes to supply their forces and, particularly in the Ukraine, they were at first welcomed by the peasants who had every reason to dislike their own regime. But the brutality of many of the occupying units soon turned the peasants against them and drove the more adventurous members into joining the partisan units.

Total food rationing was introduced in July 1941, and as the war went on the share of the free market in supplying foodstuffs and other products increased, until in 1945 it was more than 45 per cent.

1946–53 Announcing the 4th Five Year Plan in 1946, the Central Committee spelt out the situation in the Soviet Union. There were 25 million people homeless, 1,700 towns and 70,000 villages destroyed and because of the terrible casualties, estimated at 20,000,000, there was an acute shortage of agricultural labour. Despite this the plan called for a huge increase in agricultural production. Stalin was determined to regain complete control over the Kolkhozes and to tax them as onerously as in the 1930s to make them pay for the reconstruction of the country's economy. Like the 1st Five Year Plan, if one can ignore the ruthlessness of its execution, it was a brilliant success.

A Council of Kolkhoz Affairs was established to ensure strict observance of the Kolkhoz statute. Procurement prices of crops were not increased but taxes were. In 1948 there was a drought and, partly as a result of this, Stalin announced plans for the 'great transformation of nature'. To deal with future shortages of water, vast belts of forest shelter trees were to be planted, canals were planned and irrigation schemes announced. The trees refused to grow but the cost was taken from the Kolkhoz's income. A new system of crop rotation was introduced by direct command of the Commissariat for Agriculture without regard for local conditions.

Kolkhozes growing cotton or other industrial crops or those near to large towns with a ready market for their privately grown produce did quite well, notwithstanding. But the more remote collectives did very badly. For some products, such as potatoes, the payments were less than the cost of production. At the same time many Kolkhozes were amalgamated to form larger units. In 1950 there were 250,000, by 1952 this had been reduced to 97,000.

In 1952 the 6th Five Year Plan was announced which called for increases of 40 per cent in grain production, 80 per cent in meat and 50 per cent in milk. However the death of Stalin early in 1953 and the subsequent struggle for power among his succesors meant that it was never put into effect.

The Khrushchev Revolution 1953–54 In the power struggle after the death of Stalin, Khrushchev had emerged as a powerful figure and in 1954 he was put in charge of agriculture.

Khrushchev's first moves were directed at improving the lot of the Kolkhozes. He had been deeply involved in the agricultural field under Stalin and, coming from a peasant background himself, was totally committed to improving their lot. The following measures were introduced immediately: the State was to pay transport costs of procured produce; debts of the Kolkhozes were to be written off; MTS charges were to be fixed and not based on a percentage of the harvest; work minima for members were to be decided by the Kolkhoz itself; peasants could consume more of their own produce from private plots or, if they wished, sell it in the market-place; compulsory procurement prices were to be increased and there was to be an increase in State investment.

The Virgin Lands Programme (1954–58) In addition to the above reforms, in January 1954 Khrushchev first proposed the Virgin Lands programme, an attempt to solve at a stroke the perennial problem of the Soviet Union: feeding itself. There seemed to be an absolute limit to increasing yield by more intensive cultivation of the existing sown area, so logic demanded an increase in the absolute amount of land under cultivation, by ploughing up virgin untilled land, hitherto only used for grazing.

Khrushchev also wished to shift the production of grain into the Virgin Lands so as to allow the cultivation of fodder, in the shape of maize, in the more naturally fertile areas of the Ukraine and the Caucasus. The areas chosen were in northern Kazakhstan, the southern part of Siberia and in the south-east of European Russia. Between 1953–56 cultivated land was increased by 87 million acres (35 million hectares). In 1954 the harvest was excellent but in 1955 there was a drought. In 1956 there was another good harvest. Meanwhile in January 1955 Khrushchev had got the Central Committee to agree to a concentration on maize, increasing it from 9 to 69 million acres (3.5 to 28 million hectares).

He also continued the policy of amalgamating Kolkhozes or turning them into State farms. By the end of his period in office, in 1965, they had been reduced to 36,000 from 125,000 in 1950. There were also reforms of the pricing structures and in February 1958 the MTSs were abolished and their equipment sold to the Kolkhozes. There were also moves to restrict the amount of private land available to the Kolkhozes and the food they could sell in the market. This was in the year following Khrushchev's success in fighting off the attempt of the old guard, Molotov, Kaganovich, etc., to unseat him.

1958–64 Khrushchev's agricultural reforms suffered from major faults. Shutting down the MTSs and selling their equipment to the Kolkhozes and forcing them to rely more on their collective income and less on the earnings from their private plots was neither successful nor popular. The Kolkhozes had to pay for the equipment which meant they had less to invest.

The new Territorial Production Administrations he set up were inefficient and the price structure had become chaotic. His intensive maize production was not a success and led to the extensive slaughtering of cattle, both through grain shortages and a desire to increase short-term meat production.

Finally, the great Virgin Lands scheme was a disappointment, the hoped-for huge increases in grain production were short lived, due to the nature of the soil and the climate in the chosen areas, and also to the quality of labour and management available. In 1963, the year of the 21st Party Congress, Khrushchev had come to the conclusion that increasing agricultural production by the extensive method (i.e. ploughing up more land) had to be succeeded by the intensive method (i.e. the use of fertilisers). He, therefore, called for the expansion of agro-chemical production, at one time suggesting a requirement of 100 million tonnes by 1970. His efforts to fight off his critics were in no way assisted by the fact that large quantities of grain had to be imported from the West. In October 1964 Khrushchev was dismissed from office.

Agricultural Output 1958–65 (1958 = 100)

	Total	Crops	Livestock
1958	100	100	100
1959	110.4	95	108
1960	103	99.4	107
1961	106	101	112
1962	107	101	115
1963	99	92	108
1964	113	119	106
1965	114	107	123

Brezhnev and his successors (1965–85) When Brezhnev and Kosygin succeeded Khrushchev, they set about reversing many of his agricultural reforms. Restrictions which he had placed on the private plots were relaxed and procurement prices were raised. Kolkhoz prices for agricultural machinery were reduced and Motshevich, who had been fired by Khrushchev, was brought back as Minister of Agriculture, while the Territorial Production Administrations were reduced to purely local functions. Under the dual leadership, soon to be reduced to Brezhnev on his own, agricultural production once more increased. Indeed Brezhnev, in his speech introducing the Food Programme in May 1982, was able to claim an increase in gross agricultural production of 50 per cent. What he did not say was that these achievements had been effected by considerable and growing increases in food subsidies – necessary in order to keep consumer prices at an artificially low level – and by a continual increase in the percentage of investment going into agriculture. While the share of national income from agriculture was in continual decline, there was the rising cost and embarrassment of grain imports from the West, more specifically from the US.

This situation, though not remarked on in the speech, was prominent in the minds of the Politburo and was brought sharply into focus by the American grain embargo in January 1980. The fact that, under pressure from American farmers, President Reagan dropped the policy in April 1981 did not lessen its effect on the USSR.

The Food Programme was launched in May 1982 with the avowed intention of making the Soviet Union self-sufficient in its food and fodder requirements. It indicated a considerable body of support for agricultural reform in the Politburo already.

The Food Programme, when it finally appeared, contained more rhetoric than novelty. In many ways it appeared to be a continuation of the policies adopted in the 1970s. These included increased procurement prices and additional subsidies for unprofitable farms. However, behind the scenes there were other forces at work, indicated by the fact that from 1980 onwards there had been a slight but continuing decline in the percentage of investment in agriculture. But Brezhnev was not the man to make decisive strategic moves and in March 1985 his policies were overturned by Gorbachev.

Gorbachev (1985–   ) Mikhail Gorbachev's background fits him almost uniquely to deal with the agricultural problems of the USSR. He is a qualified agro-economist and after 20 years working in Party organisations in Stavropol took charge of the Agricultural Department of the Central Committee in 1978 and obtained a full seat

Grain Production and Net Imports (million tonnes)

	Production	Net imports	All grain	Imports from USA	Net imports as % of domestic production
1970	186.8	−7.2	180	n/a	n/a
1971	181.2	1.4	182	2.9	0.8
1972	168.2	21.0	189	13.7	12.5
1973	222.5	5.2	227	7.9	2.3
1974	195.7	0.4	196	2.3	0.2
1975	140.1	25.4	165	13.9	18.1
1976	223.8	7.7	230	7.4	3.4
1977	195.7	16.8	213	12.5	8.6
1978	237.4	12.8	250	11.2	5.4
1979	179.2	30.2	209	15.2	16.9
1980	189.2	34.3	224	8.0	18.1
1981	160.0	45.5	206	15.4	28.4
1982	180.0	40.3	220	6.2*	22.4
1983	190.0	33.9	224	14.1*	17.8
1984	170.0	45.0	215	18.3*	26.5
1985	178.0	30.0	–	–	16.9
1986	210.0	26.0	–	–	12.4
1987	211.3	30.0	–	–	14.2
1988	195.0	41.0	–	–	21.0
1989	209.0	41.0	–	–	19.6

* Wheat and maize only

on the Politburo only two years later. He has made several statements concerning agriculture. In September 1985 at Tselinograd (the town named after the Virgin Lands programme) he said 'The problem of providing the population with foodstuffs has not been completely solved. The demand exceeds the supply'. For this he blamed the growth of cash incomes compared to food production. 'Meat is sold in our stores at prices that are only one-third to one-half the cost of production. At present this disparity is covered by state subsidies amounting to 20 billion roubles a year.'

At the 27th Party Congress, Ryzhkov, Chairman of the Council of Ministers, suggested that capital investment in the agro-industrial complex would grow at a mere 22 per cent compared to the overall growth of the economy of 36 per cent. A further move in the direction of shifting investment away from this sector. Gorbachev himself continually emphasised 'we must face up to real problems'. Some hint of how this might be done came in a speech he made to the Supreme Soviet concerning the 1986 plan for agriculture in which he noted the introduction of methods such as cost accounting, self-financing and self-recoupment to be introduced in all collective and State farms. The farms will be given more autonomy, he added, but concluded, 'As in previous years, the state will subsidise the output of staple products.'

The removal or drastic reduction of subsidies, which would mean substantial rises in the price of food to the consumer, is a nettle that he has not as yet quite dared to grasp. A problem that is not unique to the USSR.

AIDS

Until 1989 the disease AIDS was dismissed as a phenomenon of the capitalist world and non-Soviet citizens were accused of being its carriers. In October 1985 the *Literary Gazette* claimed that AIDS had been created by Western scientists working on germ warfare, but AIDS had already been detected in the USSR in 1978. However by September 1987 AIDS was no longer presented as a Western problem, millions of copies of an informative booklet were issued and a programme to train 2,000 specialist physicians was announced. In February 1989 *Pravda* and *Trud* reported an emergency meeting of the Ministry of Health stating that there were 150 people known to be infected in the USSR and that by the year 2000 there could be 15 million carriers and hundreds of thousands dying or dead. In fact, by the end of 1988 there were already over 700 HIV-positive cases. In one Caucasus town 27 infants had been found infected from unsterilised syringes. With homosexuality illegal, and therefore kept hidden, and with 40,000 intravenous drug users in Moscow alone, the task of containing the infection is clearly formidable.

Air Force

In 1917 there were over 2,000 aircraft in Russian military service. After the collapse of 1917 and the Brest-Litovsk Treaty in 1918, much of this strength had been destroyed. Furthermore, the Bolshevik leaders had no experience in air warfare and regarded the plane as some sort of middle-class luxury, despite the substantial air force they had inherited from the Tsarist army. The German advances of 1918 and the Civil War reduced the surviving planes to just over 300 by the end of that year.

The Red Air Force, set up in May 1918, short of fuel, lubricants and spare parts, played a limited role in the fighting against Denikin and Wrangel. The air force and its supporting industry, for the reasons given, were in decline, despite the existence of design teams of high quality, such as that started by Zhukovski and carried on by Tupolev. In the 1920s planes were bought from abroad, but the Soviet–German Trade Agreement of 1921 was used as a cover for the manufacture of German planes in the Soviet Union and, after the 1922 Treaty of Rapallo, the secret training of German aircrew at the Lipetsk Air School. New engineers and designers were produced from the Zhukovski Academy, the most distinguished being Ilyushin in 1926, Yakovel in 1931 and Mikoyan in 1936. Between 1923 and 1940 over 6,000 pilots were trained by the Air Force Academy at Kacha in the Crimea, where there was good flying weather all the year round and also a centre for glider training.

In 1924, as Trotsky's control of the armed forces was removed, the command of the Red Air Force was given to Baranov with the German-speaking Latvian Alksnis as his deputy. Stalin became dissatisfied with the results of Soviet aircraft design and designers were subjected to continual surveillance by the NKVD – some teams having to continue their work while interned. By 1938 the air force's frontline strength was assessed by the Germans at over 6,000 aircraft (Soviet figures were deliberately obfuscated).

In 1933 Baranov died in an air crash and was succeeded by Alksnis, who, because of his sympathy with the military ideas of Tukhachevsky, was arrested on 23 November 1937 and shot on 28 October 1938. This was part of Stalin's purge of the military, and the senior Red Air Force command also went to their deaths.

The Spanish Civil War gave the Red Air Force an opportunity for combat experience and the first 18 Il–15 fighters were shipped to Cartagena on 13 October 1936. Probably up to 1,500 planes were sent to Spain and up to 770 aircrew served for some time during 1936 to 1938. The Soviet aircraft outmatched the first German aircraft they met, giving the Republicans air superiority until the Messerschmitt Bf109 altered the balance in mid-1937.

Bluykher's defence of the eastern frontiers against Japanese incursions from 1931 on provided another opportunity to exercise the Red Air Force. Some 400 aircraft and

40 instructors went to China in 1937. On 20 May 1939 a series of air battles against the Japanese air force started in northern Manchuria, continuing until 16 September. Accurate figures are unavailable from either side, but Soviet losses of 202 and Japanese of 162 planes are likely. General Zhukov's ground offensive was accompainied by the, then, massive air support of 200 bombers covered by 300 fighters.

The Red Air Force were world pioneers in the use of parachute troops, the first demonstration was in August 1931 when 19 men were dropped to seize a landing area for troop-carrying planes. By 1935 there was an entire airborne brigade. Although by the time of the German invasion in 1941 there were at least three fully equipped and trained brigades, and the framework of three airborne corps, paratroops were not used until early in 1942 as part of the Soviet counter-offensive, but the results were disappointing and Stalin ordered their employment as infantry.

The next wartime use of the air force after the Manchurian campaign was against Finland in 1939, where 900 aircraft were opposed by less than 100 Finnish machines. In three and a half months, Soviet losses were heavy, over 800 to the Finns' loss of 70.

World War II In 1941 the Red Air Force was large but obsolete and its poor showing in Finland led the Germans to rate it very poorly. When they attacked, the slow heavy Russian bombers were shot down in large numbers by the Bf109 fighters and the powerful German anti-aircraft artillery. The purges of air force commanders, and the extraordinary detention of Tupolev on the charge that he had given the Germans the design of the Bf109 further led the Germans to underestimate the Red Air Force and the Soviet aircraft industry.

On the first day of the German attack 1,800 Soviet aircraft were destroyed, mostly sitting on their airfields. The Red Air Force was no longer in a state to attack or defend, but the loss was not so much of aircrew as of obsolete aircraft. When the rapid German advance began to leave its base airfields far behind, their aircraft began to encounter new and improved aircraft, including British Hurricane and American P-40 fighters, but especially the new Yak-1 fighter and the ground-attack Il-2 Stormovik. Equipping aircraft with cannon and rockets improved their firepower, but heavy or long-range bombers were lacking. Nor did the Red Air Force at this time have more than the rudimentary use of radar. Between January and May 1942 an encircled German army had to be supplied by air and the Red Air Force took the opportunity to revenge itself, destroying 262 Junkers transport planes and their aircrews and showing that the Bf109 did not necessarily control the skies.

The battle of Stalingrad repeated the Red Air Force's experience of dealing with a surrounded German army and in ten weeks the Germans lost 488 planes attempting to drop supplies.

The Soviets developed three women's air regiments in 1941, two of bombers and one of fighters, as well as employing women pilots individually in other units, both combat and transport. Lidya Litvyak was a fighter ace with 12 victories before she was shot down at the age of 22.

In 1943 aircraft production was re-established and the Red Air Force increased its size to 8,300, twice that of the Germans. Part of this was the supply of aircraft from the USA and Britain (some 20,000 during the whole war). At the Battle of Kursk, the German Luftwaffe was to have swept the sky clear for the army's advance, but the Red Air Force withstood this and attacked the German air bases, while harassing the assembling troops. On the day of the German attack, 5 July the Soviets sent in a wave of ground-attack planes but these were countered by a prepared massive force of Messerschmitt and Focke-Wulf fighters, shooting the Red Air Force down in hundreds, claiming over 600 in two days. But the Germans found the pace difficult to maintain and the Soviets continued to attack the German Panzers with Stormoviks en masse. When the counter-attack began on 12 July, huge air reserves had been brought in and the Soviet armour rolled forward. The Luftwaffe's command of the sky had been only local and temporary.

Post-war By the end of the war the Red Air Force had expanded hugely, the aircraft factories turning out over 40,000 machines in 1944, giving an active frontline strength of 18,000. But the post-war period saw most of these planes as obsolete; the jet plane had appeared and the early German types were captured at the end of the war in 1945 and tested in Russia. On May Day 1947 two groups of 50 Yak–15 and MiG–9 jet fighters flew over Moscow. The first jet bomber, the Il–28, was shown in 1950. In the Korean War the Russian-built MiG–15, flown by Chinese pilots, met and showed its superiority to the American F–51 – but was mastered by the F–86 Sabre. The Superior MiG–17 appeared at the end of the war. From now on, Western military analysts would look anxiously at new Soviet aircraft developments.

Khrushchev appreciated that Soviet air power required advanced weapons research and development, particularly in rocket development and in space. He successfully conducted an aspect of the Cold War by demonstrating each May Day progressively greater rocketry, giving weight to the USSR's world position. Khrushchev seemed to indicate that the Soviet Union would move away from long-range bombers to rocketry. However in 1954 a Moscow air display showed new big bombers and in 1955 the turbo-prop Tu–20 (called 'Bear' by NATO) was seen. It could clearly deliver an attack on North America, flying over the Pole and back. In the 1970s and 1980s 'Bear' was followed by 'Bison', 'Backfire', 'Blinder' and 'Badger' bombers. The MiG–25 ('Foxbat') outclassed all other combat aircraft on its appearance in 1970; it has been developed as a high-altitude, all-weather interceptor and reconnaissance plane.

Experience in Afghanistan showed the development of frontal air attack units, with helicopters and ground-attack, rocket-firing aircraft.

While the Strategic Rocket Forces launch the space vehicles, the cosmonauts are generally air force men and this is seen as part of their professional future.

Albania

Population: *c*. 3,000,000 Area: 11,099 sq miles (28,748 sq km)
Capital: Tirana.

The 'People's Socialist Republic' is the least-developed country in the Balkans. Its economy is largely agricultural, with some mining. Seventy per cent of the population is Muslim, though all places of worship were closed in 1976.

Before World War II Albania was ruled by the self-crowned King Zog and from 1939–44 was occupied by Italy. Local communists, aided by the Yugoslav partisans, formed the National Liberation Front, which established a goverment without opposing parties in November 1944 under the leadership of Enver Hoxha.

In 1948 Hoxha broke off relations with Tito and moved closer to the USSR. This came to an abrupt end after Khrushchev's denunciation of Stalin at the 20th Party Congress in 1961. Hoxha turning to the Chinese and Mao Zedong, deeply at odds with the USSR, was pleased to find a sympathetic communist ally in Europe. China supplied more than 700 million dollars worth of aid, including economic and military advisers. By the late 1970s China was set on improving relations with the West, and in 1978 withdrew its aid to Albania and its civilian and military mission, leaving Albania even more isolated. Hoxha died in 1982 and was replaced by Ramiz Alia but the party still strongly resisted any of the ideological changes that were beginning to make themselves felt in other communist states. On the economic front, a system of wages by result has been introduced in some areas, while in diplomatic circles there is talk of the possibility of reopening relations with both Moscow and Washington. The dramatic events in Eastern Europe of the last months of 1989 had some effect on the country and there were protest meetings. For events in 1990 see the Chronology.

Anarcho-Communists

A small group in 1917 deriving from the nineteenth-century anarchists, particularly from Bakunin. They were openly against any parliamentary system. Although they were briefly allied with the Bolsheviks in order to achieve a revolution and played an important role in the fighting both in the 1917 October Revolution and in the anti-Denikin warfare in the Ukraine, 1919, they underestimated the Bolsheviks and were eliminated as enemies.

Leading personalities among them were Bleikhman and Volin. Probably the best known was the veteran Kropotkin who returned from exile in 1917, but his association with the Provisional Government isolated him from his fellow anarchists.

Apparat

The Party machine, the organisation of professional Party workers and office-holders, controlling all levels of Soviet life.

Apparatchik

Colloquial (and often derogatory) term for a Party or government official.

American Relief Administration (ARA)

An agency, directed by Herbert Hoover, providing help for famine victims after World War I, particularly in Russia.

Architecture

The most significant architectural movement of pre-revolutionary Russia was art nouveau, of which the most noted practitioner was F O Shekhtel, one of whose villa designs is now the Gorky Museum.

In the immediate aftermath of the Revolution there was little possibility of major architectural work. Commemorative buildings, such as the Lenin Mausoleum and the Monument to the Victims of the Revolution in Petrograd, were designed by architects established before the Revolution, such as Shchusev and Rudnyov. With the increased prosperity of the NEP, and under the sympathetic eye of Lunacharsky, the more avant-garde architects, such as Barkhin and Melnikov, were given a chance and the style they chose was constructivism, based on the theories of painters such as Rodchenko. By the late 1920s constructivism was beginning to be looked on with suspicion because of its formal elements, and the huge projects, industrial and administrative, being built in the 1930s were all of the neo-classical kind favoured by Stalin and the Party. There were such vast projects as the Mosvka (Moscow Hotel) and the unbuilt Palace of the Soviets, which was to have been 1,220 feet (400 m) high surmounted by a 305-foot (100-m) statue of Lenin (cancelled for fear that the figure of Lenin might be covered by low cloud in inauspicious weather). One great sucess for Soviet architecture is the Moscow Metro, magnificent by comparison with the London Underground or New York Subway.

After World War II the main task was reconstruction, carried out with exemplary concentration while the construction of huge wedding cakes, such as the Hotel Ukrainia in Moscow, went on. There is little indication that the loosening of censorship under Khrushchev and more recently under Gorbachev has made a great deal of difference to architecture in the USSR. Buildings take a long time to plan and construct.

Armed Forces

Not all armed forces of the Soviet Union come under the Ministry of Defence (see **Red Army**). There are the border guards of the KGB and the internal security troops of the MVD, both fully armed for action.

The border guards, with ships, tanks, helicopters and light aircraft, cover the whole frontier of the USSR and are the soldiers with green lapel tabs the tourist sees at airports.

Other KGB troops are the Kremlin guards, marked by royal blue tabs, and those at sensitive sites throughout the Soviet Union, such as nuclear weapon stores or communications centres.

The internal troops of the MVD (with dull brick-red lapels) are the descendants of the Cheka's armed force and have the duty of guarding labour camps, maintaining civil order in the country or, during war, policing the rear of the fighting lines and holding prisoners of war.

The armed forces under the Ministry of Defence are the army (formerly the Red Army), the air force and the navy (see entries on each of these). There is also a special feature of the Soviet Union: the Strategic Rocket Forces, which were formed soon after the end of World War II when captured German technicians were made to develop rocketry. With nuclear warheads, these became a high priority in Soviet budgeting. The setback of 1960, when many of its senior staff were killed by an experimental rocket, was overcome and the service has been responsible for the launching of the many Soviet space vehicles.

Armeni

The Armenians, a people living in both Turkey and Russia. In the 1880s a group of Armenians in Russia organised the anti-Russian revolutionary federation party 'Dashnak', which was the leading political force there in 1905.

Armenian Soviet Socialist Republic ('Hayastan')

Population: 3,400,000 (90% Armenian)
Area: 11,306 sq miles (29,290 sq km)   Capital: Erevan

After years of persecution of Christian Armenians by the Ottoman Empire, following the killing of many leaders and intellectuals, and their enforced removal from the Turkish border areas in April 1915 during the war with Russia, Armenians wanted safety within the Soviet Union. The dominant political group were the Dashnaks ('Dashnaktsutiun', the Armenian Federation).

In 1918, with the collapse of the Russian Empire, an Armenian Republic emerged, strongly influenced by the power of the Turkish army nearby. Under the terms of the Treaty of Brest-Litovsk, Turkey took the province of Kars from Russian Armenia and was awarded control of Batum.

Turkish troops of the Ottoman Empire occupied much of Armenia and Georgia and in mid-1918 German troops also advanced into Georgia. In December 1917 the soviets in Petrograd acknowledged the right of Armenians to self-determination in a 'Decree on Turkish Armenia' which would have made a state including much of the territory taken in Turkey by the Tsarist armies. Turkey forced the Transcaucasus to declare independence as the Transcaucasian Federation on 22 April 1918. Turkish troops and Azerbaijani Musavets took over Baku in September 1918, which resulted in the massacre of some 30,000 Armenians. As World War I ended, British troops arrived in Baku and Batum. In Baku the British declared the area their 'government general' and forced first the Azerbaijani and then the White troops out.

The Turks, by a treaty of 11 May 1920, recognised a Soviet Republic of Armenia, under Dashnak control, and the Allied Powers also recognised it. In 1920 the Western Allies signed the Treaty of Sèvres with the Turkish Ottoman Empire, ending its rule outside Asia Minor and giving the new Armenian republic parts of Turkey. However the new ruler of Turkey, Kemal Atatürk, refused to accept the treaty and in September he attacked the Armenians. In a two-month campaign 200,000 Armenians were killed. Following the peace treaty of Alexandropol between Turkey and the Dashnak government of Armenia, land, including Erevan, was yielded to Turkey and Armenia would actually have become a protectorate of Turkey. However the Red Army pre-empted this, moving into the territory, declaring it, on 29 November 1920, a Soviet republic.

Armenia was made part of the 'Transcaucasian Federal Republic' of the USSR in 1922. When this was abolished in 1936, Armenia became one of the USSR's constituent republics.

From November 1920 the Armenian Christian Church (the oldest established State Church in Christendom, founded in AD300), found itself at once freed from the tyranny of the Russian Orthodox Church but faced with the declared atheism of the State, nationalising its schools and libraries. The Armenians were inured to persecution and survived even the general purges of 1936. During World War II the Church made sure that its patriotism was evident. The influence of the Armenian Church in the Middle East and in the USA has undoubtedly modified the Soviet State's attitude and ensured a policy of co-existence.

In 1988 Nagorny Karabakh, the (Christian) Armenian enclave in (Muslim) Azerbaijan, was the cause of ethnic riots in both republics. As a result the Party heads of both Armenia and Azerbaijan were dismissed. Some 80,000 Azeri refugees left Armenia and 14,000 Armenians left Azerbaijan. There were strikes, riots and as a result curfews imposed. The leader of the Krunk, the group urging the return of Nagorny Karabakh to Armenia, Musa Manucharoy, was arrested (for bribery and embezzlement as head of a building firm).

On 7 December 1988 an earthquake shattered Erevan and Leninakhan. As a result, the 1989 election issues in Armenia were dominated by Nagorny Karabakh and the effects of the earthquake (linked with demands to close a nuclear power station). In protest against Armenian claims on Nagorny Karabakh, Azerbaijan blockaded Armenia in 1989, preventing the railways from carrying goods to Armenia.

Because of the violence in the republic, in reaction to the earthquake and the threat of Azerbaijani attacks, the 1990 elections to the republic's new parliament were postponed.

Art, plastic and graphic

Twentieth-century art came to Russia with the movement known as The World of Art – the title came from the movement's magazine published in 1898. The movement, whose credo was essentially Art for Art's Sake, had a number of important painters, most notably Bakst and Benois. They became best known for their theatrical and costume design for the ballets of Diaghilev, who had been a co-founder of the movement. The real significance of the movement lies in the degree to which the rest of Europe was made aware of Russian art. Most of this group left to live in Western Europe and America, but in Russia itself before the 1917 October Revolution the neo-primitivist movement led by Larionov and Goncharova was becoming important. In 1910 this group, known as the Knave of Diamonds Group held two major exhibitions of their work in Moscow and included paintings by Malevich and Kandinsky. The movement split and Larionov's group held two major exhibitions, the Donkey's Tale in 1912 and Target in 1913. The other splinter, led by Konchalovsky, promoted such important artists as Altman and Marc Chagall. Larionov went on to develop a version of cubism called rayonism, while Malevich showed at the Last Futurist Exhibition of Pictures several paintings done in accordance with his theory of suprematism.

After the October Revolution, Narkompros (People's Commissariat for Enlightenment) headed by Lunacharsky set up a new range of art schools, such as Svomas (Free State Art Studios). For the first time avant-garde artists felt that they no longer needed to shock. For the new Commissariat for Popular Culture, Kandinsky ran museums and art galleries in Moscow, Talin in Petrograd and Malevich in Vitebsk. At the same time there were other movements, such as constructivism, afoot. Led by Rodchenko this declared that easel painting was a useless activity and proposed that artists should now be concerned only with industrial design. In 1922 there was a significant exhibition by the Association of Artists of Revoutionary Russia which called for a style of heroic realism.

After the dissolution of Narkompros and the decree by the Central Committee in 1932 on the Reconstruction of Literary and Art Organisations, socialist realism took over from heroic realism as the officially approved style. Abstract art virtually disappeared, Kandinsky left Russia with Gabo, and of the others some, like Malevich, had died, others had ceased exhibiting. But there was not the same savage persecution of artists as was meted out to writers. Rodchenko went on painting abstracts in his studio in the 1940s. Officially approved painters, like Avilov and Brodsky, continued to paint portraits, events of the Civil War and scenes on the collective farms. The same thing happened during World War II with Gerasimov painting subjects like *Mother of a Partisan*. After the Khrushchev revolution there was a loosening of constraints, though Khrushchev himself had harsh things to say to painters interested in abstraction in his well-known visit to an exhibition in 1962. Since then there has been a considerable degree of freedom for all types of experimentation, and exhibitions are beginning, in the age of glasnost, to be held in the West.

Some of the better-known artists exhibiting in the USSR and the West are two graduates of the Repin Institute of Leningrad, Valerie Lukka and Viacheslav Mikhailov, both born in 1945, and both working in mixed media with an emphasis on acrylic. Gleb Bogomolov (b. 1933) one of the leaders of the non-conformist art movement has never studied art formally, but is highly thought of by the Establishment. His work has been bought for the State Russian Museum in Leningrad. Dmitri Plavinski (b. 1937) is probably the most cosmopolitan artist in Russia. He studied at the Regional College of Art in Moscow and has had several exhibitions in the USA, Western Europe and the USSR.

Artel

The prototype of the collective farm organisation, in which only the land and other means of production were socialised, unlike the earlier type of commune in which everything was held in common and the surplus of products was delivered to the local soviets in exchange for goods needed by the commune. Distribution of the cultivated produce was allotted in proportion to the work performed by the members. By 1920 there were more than 8,000 artels holding more than 2 million acres (810,000 hectares).

Ataman

A Cossack military leader, sometimes called 'Hetman'. (See also **Cossacks**)

Azerbaijan Soviet Socialist Republic

Population: 6,800,000 (78% Azerbaijani, 8% Russian and 8% Armenian).
Area: 33,436 sq miles (86,621 sq km)   Capital: Baku
Includes Nakhichevan Autonomous Soviet Socialist Republic (population 278,000, capital Nakhichevan) and Nagorny Karabakh Autonomous Region (population 177,000, capital Stepanakert) an Armenian enclave whose history still causes dispute. Until 1813, when part of it was ceded to the Tsar, Azerbaijan (meaning the land of the Azeri people) was all in Persia. In 1917 all the Transcaucasus came under the influence of nationalist revolutionaries, Georgian Mensheviks, Armenian Dashnaks and Azerbaijani Musavets, the Muslim Democratic Party, a group not unlike their contemporary Young Turks who were taking over the Ottoman Empire. Baku, an industrial oil town with a large Russian population, was in the hands of a revolutionary government from October with a Musavet majority. The Musavets, moving politically away from the left, withdrew from this government, leaving it in Bolshevik hands in November 1917 and establishing their 'Transcaucasian Commissariat'.

In March 1918 Baku was the scene of ethnic riots, Azeris killing Armenians. At that time, as the Russians came to terms with the Central Powers at Brest-Litovsk, Turkish power grew in Azerbaijan, encouraging the formation of a separate Transcausasian alliance. There was a proclamation of Azerbaijan independence in May and Turkish troops advanced towards Baku. In August 1918 British forces landed at Baku ostensibly to defend the area against the Turks, but also to protect the oil fields. They left in September, with a local anti-Bolshevik administration in charge. The Musavet Party in Baku made an alliance with the Turks, seen by them as allies, but regarded as enemies by the Armenians and Georgians: this resulted in a massacre of some 30,000 Armenians and 26 Bolshevik 'commissars', the leaders of the earlier attempt at control of the area, who were taken from Baku and shot. Anastasy Mikoyan was a survivor of these events in which British complicity was assumed.

Another British contingent arrived at Baku in November 1918 as World War I ended, being met by an Azerbaijan Musavet government which they could not recognise unless it admitted to being a part of Russia. In December a coalition government for Azerbaijan in Baku was accepted by the British, who also had outposts at Batum and Tiflis.

On 28 April 1920 Soviet troops entered Baku and with little opposition took control of Armenia. There was an Armenian army of 40,000, equipped by the British and Americans, deployed in Nagorny Karabakh, the Armenian enclave in Azerbaijan, around which the bulk of the Azeri Musavetist army of 20,000 with Turkish and German arms was stationed. In mediating with Turkey that year the Soviet government accepted the compromise of a previous agreement on a separate status for Nagorny Karabakh with a largely Armenian people, recognising the ethnic difference but also the economic reality of its situation.

Azerbaijan entered the USSR as the Autonomous Soviet Socialist Republic on 31 December 1922. It includes the autonomous territories of Nakhichevan, which is surrounded by Armenian territory, and Nagorny Karabakh. Today a further 5,000,000 Azeris, using the common Turkic Azeri language and also following the Muslim Shia faith, live over the frontier in Iran. In 1945 the Soviets, who had occupied northern Iran during the war, attempted to integrate all the Azeri area into the Soviet Union by supporting a local puppet communist government, but were forced out under Anglo–American pressure which contributed to the beginnings of the Cold War. Many Azeris are leading figures in modern Iran and there is a growing interest in Islamic fundamentalism in Azerbaijan. In July 1989 the Speaker of the Iranian Parliament, Ali Hashemi Rafsanjani, visited Baku and, speaking at a mosque, promised help in promoting their religion. In January 1990 numbers of Azeri Muslims demonstrated on the frontier with Iran, some swimming over the dividing river, demanding that the border be opened between them and their cousins. This had the effect of causing anxiety both to the Soviet Union and to Iran, neither welcoming a larger nationalist Azerbaijan republic.

Nagorny Karabakh This enclave, 75 per cent (Christian) Armenians in (Muslim) Azerbaijan, has been the cause of riots in both republics. On 28 February 1988 there was a massacre in Sumgait, where 26 Armenians and six Azerbaijanis died. The Party lost control in Nagorny Karabakh and as a result the Party heads of both Armenia and Azerbaijan were dismissed. When, in November 1988, a young Azeri was sentenced to death by a Moscow court for his part in the Sumgait murders, and thousands of Azeris protested, a curfew was imposed in Baku (with 200,000 Armenian inhabitants). In Kirovabad and other towns there was a 'pogrom' of Armenians; 2,000 Armenian women and children were taken out of Nakhichevan and Kirovabad by lorry and helicopter. That month 80,000 Azeris left Armenia, while 14,000 Armenians left Azerbaijan. In Baku the army cleared the main square where demonstrators had carried red Turkish and green Islamic flags and were said to have burned Christian Armenian crosses.

In January 1989, the parliament of Nagorny Karabakh was suspended, bringing it under direct Moscow control, with the intention of it remaining part of Azerbaijan. In August, 150,000 Azeri workers demonstrated in Baku demanding that Nagorny Karabakh be kept in Azerbaijan, hoisting the flag of the 1918–20 Azerbaijan Republic. At the same time, workers in Nagorny Karabakh added to the chaos with strikes against Azeri rule.

In January 1990 there were further riots in Baku, attacking Armenians and demanding the return of Nagorny Karabakh to Azerbaijan's administration. On 19 January, after 60 Armenians had been killed, the Soviet military intervened toughly and, from official figures, 147 people were killed. As a result, the elections to the republic's parliament were postponed.

Azeri

The people of Azerbaijan. The socialist-nationalist Musavet ('Equality') Party was founded among the Azeri in 1911.

B

Babi Yar

In Kiev during the 1941–43 Nazi German execution squads slaughtered over 150,000 men, women and children and threw them into a ravine, Babi Yar, near the city. Most of the victims were Jews. Yevtushenko's poem of that name (1962) was central to action against anti-Semitism in the Soviet Union.

Baikal–Amur Magistral railway

The direct, northerly route to the Pacific ports, avoiding the Trans-Siberian railway's detour around Lake Baikal, was completed in 1979 to Komsomolsk-on-Amur.

Ballet

After the departure of Diaghilev to the West, the great classical tradition in Russian ballet continued. There were contemporary pieces with themes arising out of the Revolution, such as Glière's *The Red Poppy* in 1927 and *The Age of Gold* in 1930 with music by Stravinsky. After World War II the great ballerina Ulanova created a sensation with Prokofiev's *Cinderella*. Then in 1956 there was *Spartacus* by Khachaturian. Both the Bolshoi and the Kirov ballet toured the West and a new crop of great artists, including Nureyev, Makarova and Baryshnikov, left their companies and found fame in the international ballet world.

Baltic States

Estonia, Latvia and Lithuania (1917–80) Tsarist Russia obtained control of the peoples and lands of the Baltic coast, formerly subject to the Swedes and once the estates of German barons, by the end of the eighteenth century. These countries differed from the rest of the Empire in their religious, linguistic and economic development. The Lutheran and Roman Catholic Churches dominated, the languages were distinct from the slavic Russian and their tradition of craft, industry and trade with the rest of Europe had developed a *bourgeoisie* unlike any other part of the Russian Empire. Railways and industry were developed earlier than in other parts and illiteracy was rare by the beginning of the twentieth century.

The 1905 revolution saw as much unrest in Baltic cities as any other part of the Empire and, although many of the leaders were exiled, a new generation of political leaders was generated by the new Duma.

The collapse of the Russian Empire in March 1917 left Lithuania and half of Latvia under German military occupation. In February 1918 Lithuania and Estonia declared independence. Latvia, with a strong working-class movement having sympathies with the Bolsheviks on the one hand and Baltic German nationalists supported by Freikorps (bands of German soldiers fighting for the old landowners) on the other, did not declare independence until November 1918. The three republics signed treaties with the Soviet Union in 1920. Poland, however, as a result of its war with the Soviets, took and kept the ancient cathedral city of Vilnius (Wilno to the Poles) and left the new republic of Lithuania to make do with Kaunas as capital. For their part, the Lithuanians held the largely German city of Memel (Klaipeda) in 1923, which gave Hitler an excuse for expanding his Greater Germany in 1939. Latvian soldiers (the Latvian Rifles) provided the Bolsheviks with their best unit of professional soldiers in 1917–18, but Latvia preferred independence, and an attempt at a communist coup in 1924 failed, resulting in the Communist Party there being made illegal.

During the next 20 years each republic, under economic pressure from within and under the shadows of their neighbours, Hitler's Germany and Stalin's Russia, became politically authoritarian and failed to gain other allies. Hitler demanded and took Memel from Lithuania in March 1939 and met no effective protest from the rest of the world. When the Molotov–Ribbentrop pact was signed on 23 August 1939, a secret protocol assigned Latvia and Estonia to the Soviet sphere of influence and part of Lithuania to Germany's. On 2 October 1939 a 'mutual assistance pact' was signed, allowing Red Army bases in Estonia. In June 1940, when Hitler's troops moved into France in the west, Soviet troops occupied the Baltic states completely. Senior Soviet officials were sent to ensure control, Zhdanov to Estonia and Vyshinsky to Latvia. Demonstrations called for 'People's Assemblies' and in July elections were held with massive turnouts and huge majorities of 95 per cent and more being claimed. The new governments adopted new soviet socialist constitutions and applied to join the Soviet Union. These requests were, not surprisingly, granted in August 1940. Integration with the Soviet system was rapid and determined; by mid-1941 it is estimated that 10 per cent of the Latvian population had been deported.

The German invasion of the Soviet Union on 22 June 1941 saw the rapid occupation of Lithuania; Nazi forces penetrated into most of Latvia by August and Estonia was taken by October. At first some inhabitants greeted the Germans as liberators and a few set out to re-establish independent republics. A provisional government in Lithuania welcomed the Germans, but it was soon disbanded; the Nazi intention was to make the Baltic states into part of Greater Germany, deporting the Balts and replacing them with German settlers. The area was then called 'Ostland' and given an administration headed by compliant and racially acceptable local people. Workers were drafted to fill vacancies in German industry and ex-soldiers and new conscripts were formed into 'Defence' battalions: as support, rather than combat units, they were therefore given the secondary and unpleasant duties of controlling the civilian populations behind the German front lines. The SS formed divisions from the Baltic states. In 1944, when the tide of war had turned against the Nazis, many of these recruits began to desert and hide in the woods.

The Jewish communities suffered terribly. Of an estimated 250,000, only 10,000 survived the German extermination camps. Nazi brutality led to the formation of resistance groups. In 1944 Estonian groups had contacts, via Finland and Sweden, with London, but, in general, armed resistance was on a small scale. Partisans were more likely to be escaped Jews or communists helped by others infiltrated or parachuted from Soviet Russia.

From January 1944 the Red Army began to retake the territory, finally bottling up German forces in Courland from October 1944 until the final surrender in 1945. The Baltic soviet republics were re-established but controlled from Moscow with a degree of mistrust. Some who had hidden in the woods were joined by others who hated or were hated by the new regimes. There were Russian and German deserters among them and for eight years – until 1952 – there were groups, some as large as 800, hiding, raiding and robbing. An individual might only stay or survive in the forests for a couple of years or less, and therefore in all probably 100,000 in Lithuania, 40,000 in Latvia and 30,000 in Estonia took to guerrilla activity at some time or other. A central organisation was attempted: in 1947 there was a 17-day officer training course and news sheets were distributed until 1951. The Soviets tried to counter these groups sometimes by offering amnesties and at other times, in contrast, by sending in MVD special task divisions. There was little tangible help from Western intelligence agencies, although a few parachute drops of men and materials were made. Guerrilla casualties in Lithuania are estimated at between 20,000 and 50,000.

In 1948 the MVD and MGB had over 70,000 men with eight regular army divisions engaged against guerrilla activity in Lithuania. There were few pitched battles, for the guerrillas' aim was to disrupt Soviet administration and to unnerve the MVD units by small surprise raids.

Soviet rule re-established the republics' Supreme Soviets and ensured a Secretariat loyal to the Soviet Union in each; often they were either Russians or local citizens who had spent the war in Russia, in this way Mikhail Suslov arrived in 1944 to run a special Soviet Union Communist Party Bureau. Collectivisation of farming was enforced again and deportation to the interior of the Soviet Union was carried out for tens of thousands of suspected kulaks in 1949. In Estonia the native party was purged and replaced by what were called 'Yestonians'.

Lithuania was mainly Roman Catholic and the Church was associated with the opposition to the Soviets. In Estonia and Latvia the prevalent Lutheran Church had not the same grip on the people and did not represent an equal threat. The minor Protestant Churches were ordered to join the USSR's Baptist League. The remnants of the Jewish communities never reformed.

With the 'thaw' and after Stalin's death, there was a re-emergence of national identities throughout the Soviet Union and particularly in the Baltic republics with their comparatively advanced economies. Roman Catholic bishops were consecrated in Latvia and Lithuania in the 1960s. A Union of Fighters for Political Freedom, led by naval officers, was crushed in Estonia in 1969.

However 'Russification' continued, partly through the immigration of Russian officials and skilled workers, often moving there with priority in housing over local workers. In 1978 a directive throughout the USSR affected the Baltic states: the use of the Russian language was extended from nursery school to university. Just as a similar drive to promote the language in the 1890s under the Tsarist Empire had resulted in an increase in nationalist consciousness, so did this. (See also **Estonia**, **Latvia** and **Lithuania** for post-1980)

Banking

The Soviet Union's Central Bank, 'Gosbank', is now part of the banking system set up in 1987, which in 1989 was still not functioning. There are specialised banks dealing with housing, agriculture and industry and, now, 60 commercial banks (28 set up by co-operatives and 32 by State organisations). The Banking Law of 1 April 1989 will make the State pay interest on its loans to cover the budget deficit. The public's savings accounts are reckoned to be 300 billion roubles; from this the government appropriates what it needs, 63 billion in 1988, to cover its expenditure, adding this to the published deficit while the true annual deficit is about 100 billion roubles or 11 per cent of GNP.

Internationally, the Soviet Union has been hampered by the 1918 Soviet refusal to recognise debts incurred by any previous government. There are, for example, the $192.6 million lent by the US to the 1917 pre-Bolshevik Provisional Government and another $75 million worth of Tsarist Russian bonds held by US citizens. There have been discussions for years on how to clear these debts before the Soviet Union can enter the international markets and raise money through bonds.

Basmachi
'Bandit' or 'robber' in the Uzbeki language. Anti-Bolshevik partisans in Central Asia who were not finally suppressed until 1926.

Belorussian Soviet Socialist Republic
Population: 10,141,000
Area: 80,300 sq miles (208,031 sq km)   Capital: Minsk

1917–45 Also known as 'White Russia', a land taken into the Russian Empire in the eighteenth century, and, like the Ukraine, speaking a language closely allied to the Russian language and under Polish and Roman Catholic influence. In World War I the Germans advanced into Belorussia, which became a battleground and a place of famine. The Tsarist military headquarters, Stavka, was in Mogilev and hundreds of thousands of soldiers were stationed in the territory. The February 1917 revolution was greeted there with relief, and with hope for peace.

In March 1917 Belorussian nationalists, socialists and other politicians gathered in Minsk and by 5 August had formed a Rada (a council) with a largely Socialist Revolutionary policy, hoping to become something like an autonomous republic under the Petrograd Provisional Government. After the Bolshevik Revolution in October, however, a trainload of troops was sent to Minsk and a Bolshevik *coup d'état* took place. The Rada acquiesced and Bolshevik rule was established on 15 November.

But the war with Germany continued and by the time of the treaty of Brest-Litovsk in March 1918, a large part of the land, including Minsk, was in German hands. The nationalists in the Rada saw the opportunity for independence and met on 25 March to declare a national republic. But when the Germans left, the Bolsheviks reoccupied Minsk and their Central Committee decided on 23 December to establish a Belorussian Soviet Socialist Republic.

In March 1919 Polish armies under Pilsudski advanced into Lithuania, the Ukraine and Belorussia. They proclaimed Belorussia part of Poland and both the nationalists of the Rada and the Bolsheviks were forced to flee. It was not until 11 July 1920 that the Red Army retook Minsk from the Poles. On 19 July, by a treaty, parts of Belorussia were handed over to Lithuania and finally, under the Treaty of Riga signed on 18 March 1921, a large area was given to Poland.

The reduced Belorussian SSR (areas around Mogilev, Vitebsk and to the south were added to it in 1924 and 1926) was in economic chaos and peasant risings were ferociously put down by the Cheka. The NEP was enthusiastically accepted and for a time Belorussia flourished. In 1929 Stalin began the programme of collectivisation. By 1 January 1930 one in five of the 165,000 Belorussian farms had been collectivised and the pace was increased. In common with the rest of the USSR, there were riots in reaction to the demands and repression by the GPU, with numbers of peasants or kulaks sent to labour camps. In particular, the Belorussian nationalists were a primary target together with the organisers of Belorussian schools and education. In the summer of 1933 the Party announced the discovery of a 'Belorussian National Centre' controlled from Poland, implicating nationalists freed from Poland as traitors.

On 17 September 1939 the Red Army marched into Poland, countering the German invasion from the west. The Belorussian SSR was enlarged with territory taken from Poland and, in October, from Lithuania. The NKVD came with the army and arrested all who had been Polish officials. The purges of suspects continued up to June 1941 when the Germans invaded.

Belorussia was overrun in three weeks. The Nazis had plans for Eastern Europe and some Belorussian land was given to east Prussia and some to the Ukraine. The remaining territory was earmarked as land for future German settlement: 75 per cent of the present inhabitants were to be expelled or killed and the remainder to be assimilated as Germans. A General Commissar, Wilhelm Kube, was appointed in

July. The large Jewish population, three quarters of a million, was rounded up for extermination. Younger people were shipped to Germany as forced labour. A puppet government was set up under a former officer of Wrangel's army, Ivan Ermachenko, but it had no popular support.

The Soviet response was partisan warfare, infiltrating thousands into the forest areas behind the German lines. Sabotage of the Germans resulted in savage reprisals which in turn added to the hatred of the Germans. Kube was killed by a bomb in his bed, put there by the Belorussian girl he used as servant and bedmate. Terror was again answered by resistance and Soviet partisans by Belorussian nationalists recruited by the Germans. In mid-1942 the capital, Minsk, was controlled by partisans and by the end of 1943 over half of Belorussia was in the hands of 300,000 partisans.

By the war's end in 1945, Belorussia was wrecked. Approaching 1,300,000 had been killed and still the NKVD sought traitors or suspected collaborators among the survivors. From 1946 to 1948 all managers and Party officials were examined and any hint of 'cosmopolitanism' or Western ideas led to dismissal or the labour camp. New senior officials in the Belorussian Party were all Russian. Stalin's concept of 'linguistics' was that languages other than Russian were marginal and would die out.

By agreement with the Allies at the 1945 Yalta Conference, the borders of Belorussia were extended to include the land that Poland had taken in the 1920s. To demonstrate the constitutional freedom of Soviet republics and eligibility for entry to the United Nations, Belorussia and the Ukraine were proposed for independent entry as nations. They took their seats on 30 April 1945.

Black Hundreds
The general name for the groups who roused popular feelings by demonstrations of loyalty to the Tsar and the Church, and hatred of Jews, socialists and intellectuals. They were small shopkeepers, tradesmen, priests and minor officials drawn to extremism by the turmoil and class fears of 1905. In the Duma, the 'Union of the Russian People' led by Purishkevich represented these extremists. They organised riots and pogroms against their enemies and were unofficially encouraged by the police and openly thanked by the Tsar. They were an object of hatred, though they ceased to play any role, in 1917.

Bolshevik
The Majority. The faction led by Lenin at the Russian Social Democrat Congress in 1903 which obtained a narrow majority over Martov and those in favour of a broad-based movement. Lenin wanted an élite centralised party of professional revolutionaries and so arranged that the congress voted out affiliated groups, such as the Jewish Bund. The Bolsheviks termed their opponents Menshevik (the minority) and the name remained with them. The split had become irreversible by the February 1917 revolution. (See also **Communist Party**)

The leading figures in 1917 were Lenin, Kamenev, Lunacharsky, Zinoviev and Trotsky (who had sided with neither Bolshevik or Menshevik until his return to Russia in May 1917).

Bolshoi Theatre
The State Academic Bolshoi Theatre of the USSR. The Bolshoi was built in 1824, to replace the Petrovsky Theatre, for the performance of opera and ballet. The period from 1870 represents the great flowering of ballet and opera in Russia and the Bolshoi saw productions of Tchaikovsky's *Swan Lake, Eugen Onegin* and *The Queen of Spades*. Operas by Mussorgsky and Rimsky Korsakov were also performed there, as well as works by Western composers. During the upheavals of the Revolution and the Civil War, Lenin made special arrangements to keep the theatre open. After the Revolution, works of a specifically ideological nature were performed, such as Zolotaev's *The*

Decembrists in 1925 and Prokofiev's *Love of Three Oranges* in 1927, while at the same time the company continued to perform the classical repertoire both in opera and ballet. Since World War II the same policy has been followed. Some of the better-known post-war works are Prokofiev's *War and Peace* and Khachaturian's *Spartacus*. The company has followed a consistent policy of touring all over the world.

Borotbists
The name of the Ukrainian SR nationalists in 1918–20.

Brest-Litovsk Treaty
The peace agreement signed in March 1918 between the Bolshevik government and the Central Powers, the German and the Austro–Hungarian Empires. Determined to end a futile war (in their eyes), the Bolsheviks tried to negotiate, but were forced to accept the Central Powers' terms. Trotsky's revolutionary attitude of 'Neither peace nor war' did not strengthen Russia's bargaining position and Germany forced the acceptance of Polish, Georgian, Lithuanian, Latvian, Estonian and Ukrainian independence. It was signed by Sokolnikov, because major Bolshevik figures would not risk putting their name to it. There were supplements to the treaty signed with Bulgaria, Romania and Turkey. Russia surrendered Kars, Ardahan and Batum to Turkey. The Left SR voted against the treaty and resigned from Sovnarkom. The treaty was invalidated after the 1918 Allied victory, when different territorial terms were imposed on the Central Powers.

Brezhnev Doctrine
The policy outlined in an article in *Pravda* in September 1968 and now generally called the 'Brezhnev Doctrine'. Moscow had the right to intervene with force in its satellite states when they deviated from the Soviet version of socialism. The prime examples were the invasion of Hungary in 1956 and the overturn, the month before the article, of the Czechoslovak government.

The doctrine was abandoned when Mikhail Gorbachev stated in March 1989 that 'each ruling Communist Party solves tasks in accordance with its historical conditions and national values, and works out its policies in a sovereign fashion'. In 1989 a Soviet spokesman referred to the new policy towards satellites as the 'Sinatra Policy': 'They do it their way'.

Bulgaria
Population: 8,948,388 Area: 42,823 sq miles (110,912 sq km)
Capital: Sofia
In 1941 Bulgaria, a largely agricultural country with a constitutional monarchy under King Boris III, found itself allied with Nazi Germany. In 1944, as German resistance crumbled, Soviet forces occupied the country and the Fatherland Front, including communists, Social Democrats, agrarians and others, formed a government. In November 1945 the Fatherland Front, of whom 277 out of 364 were communists, won the election under their leader Dimitrov (the hero of the 1933 Reichstag fire trial in Nazi Germany, who had lived in Russia since then). He was succeeded by Vulko Chervenkov who took a very strong Stalinist line and dominated the Party until 1954, when Todor Zhivkov became First Secretary.

Under the New Economic Mechanism instituted in 1976 there was a considerable improvement in the economic situation, foreign investment was encouraged and joint ventures established with Western multinationals like Shell and Occidental. The majority of export trade is with the USSR but the country has had great success with exports of its wine to the EEC, particularly the UK. But the general economic situation has not really improved, particularly as far as the availability of consumer goods is concerned. Bulgaria's reputation has not been improved by the expulsion of a large

Turkish element in the population, more than 300,000 strong. The influence of Moscow has always been very strong and the general liberalisation in economic and social relations has caused the Party to accept change. On 4 November 1989 members of Eco-glasnost led huge street demonstrations against the government and Todor Zhivkov was forced to resign. He was replaced by Peter Mladenow, but popular demonstrations were suppressed in December. For events since December 1989 see the Chronology.

Bund

A socialist movement of Jewish workers in Imperial Russia, founded in 1897. The Bund developed skills in smuggling illegal persons and materials in and out of Russia, faced with the repression of Tsarist days. The Bund supported the Mensheviks from 1906 and, in the attention it paid to improving wages and working conditions, seemed to follow bourgeois goals and so separated itself from the orthodox Marxists. In 1920 the majority joined the Communist Party, but a minority, which continued separately until suppressed, carried on operating in isolation in the old Jewish settlements far from Moscow and sent delegates to the 2nd Social Democratic Congress. The Bund was dissolved in 1921 when a Jewish section of the Party was formed.

C

Cadets see Kadets.

Cadres

The most important or key members of an organisation at various levels, who, if selected for indoctrination, will form opinion throughout the organisation. The use of cadres has been an essential part of Communist Party tactics in social control.

Calendar

Russia officially maintained the Julian Calendar long after Western Europe had changed to the Gregorian calculation. Thus by the twentieth century Russian dates in the Julian Calendar were 13 days earlier than elsewhere. The October 1917 Revolution on 25 October (Julian) is now celebrated on 6 November (Gregorian). On 1 February 1918 the Gregorian Calendar was adopted.

Camps

In 1918, under the guidance of Lenin and Trotsky, camps were set up to hold, as a preventive measure against potential enemies of the new state, old bourgeois politicians, non-Bolshevik Social Democrats, SRs, anarchists or the rebels of Kronstadt, and, as early as 1919, for the corrective treatment of all offenders against the regime's decrees. There were soon tens of thousands of prisoners in the camps, many of which were sited on the islands of the White Sea. It was the prisoners' labour that built the White Sea Canal, completed in 1931–33.

In 1934 the system was organised by the NKVD under Gulag (the Chief Administration of Corrective Labour Camps and settlements) which at its peak had 10 million prisoners at work. These camps were sited in inhospitable areas in Siberia and the Arctic. The NKVD in this respect resembled the SS in Nazi Germany, controlling a vast industrial empire, becoming a major element in the Soviet economy. After its workers had built the White Sea–Baltic Canal, they built the Moscow–Volga Canal (1932–37), started the Baikal–Amur railway in 1934 and were responsible for one in ten of the electrical power stations. Whole towns in remote parts of the USSR were built by the NKVD. The Gulag system had, like the rest of Soviet society, a plan to fulfil and it achieved its high output targets by offering adequate food rations only to those teams that achieved the norm set for them. By thus establishing a common motivation for groups, the Gulag reduced the risk of mutiny by prisoners.

The collectivisation programme increased the number of camps and changed the character of the inmates. With the purges of the mid-1930s, to the old guard and the peasants were added city dwellers, the highly educated, Party officials and army officers.

The increasing supply of prisoners was largely due to these purges, but it was the purge ordered by Stalin in 1936, without the Party's authority, and carried out by Yezhov, that brought in prisoners by the million.

There were camps of various levels of intensity, from the katorga, hard labour camps from which few prisoners ever came out alive, to the camps such as the one where Tupolev and his aircraft design team lived and carried on their work.

The world knows of the camps through the novel authorised for publication by Khrushchev, *One Day in the Life of Ivan Denisovich* (1962) and *The Gulag Archipelago* (1973–75), both by Solzhenitsyn.

Central Committee see **Political Structure**.

Central Committee Secretariat see **Political Structure**.

Central Executive Committee
Elected at the 1st Congress of the Soviets of Workers' and Soldiers' Deputies in July 1917, being the inner 'cabinet' for the congress' delegated executive powers. In 1922 similar committees were formed in the republics of the USSR. The 1936 constitution passed this role to the Supreme Soviet (see **Political Structure**).

Cheka see **Political Police**.

Chernobyl
The atomic power station near Kiev which exploded on 26 April 1986. During tests of its functions, the graphite core in Unit 4 of the station caught fire and burnt for ten days. Nine tonnes of the fuel went into the fall-out cloud, one tonne of which fell back on the site and the rest was distributed westward over Europe by the winds. Increased levels of radiation were recorded in most of Europe. Some 120 miles (200 km) away in Belorussia, there were seriously affected areas three years later.

The USSR was condemned for the delay in admitting to the disaster and for its slow response in dealing with it. A Soviet press conference on 21 August 1986 blamed human error and disregard of safety rules; six managers were given jail sentences. Thirty-one of the staff were killed in the explosion and one man in fighting the fire, over 200 suffered from acute radiation sickness. A 30-mile (50 km) exclusion zone was created around Chernobyl and 135,000 people were evacuated from 100 villages within it. Mutations of vegetation have been observed and some seeds, apparently resisting the heavy radiation, have been noted for possible use in contaminated land.

The need for electricity in the area meant that, in 1988, Units 1, 2 and 3 were recommissioned, but the reactor type 'RBMK' (of which 15 were built) is now being closed down and no new ones built. Unit 4 was buried in a mountain of concrete.

Chervonets
A gold coin, the first Soviet hard currency, of 3, 5 or 10 chervonets denomination. In circulation 1922–47.

Cinema

There was a flourishing film industry in Russia under the Tsars, starting with the 1908 production *Cossacks of the Don*, made by Pathé. By 1910 there were 15 companies making pictures, many of them historical subjects and some of real artistic merit, such as Meyerhold's *Dorian Gray* made in 1915.

The October 1917 Revolution caused many of the veteran film directors and technicians to flee to the West, and the harsh conditions during the Civil War made cinema production and exhibition difficult. In 1919 the industry was nationalised, and Lenin, who was a great believer in the cinema as a propaganda tool, put it in the hands of the State Department of Education, with his wife Krupskaya in charge. During the Civil War, Agit Trains, as they were called, complete with projection equipment, were sent out to deliver the political message to the country, and also to shoot fresh footage. Eisenstein, his future cameraman, Tisse, and Vertov all learnt their craft on these trains. By 1921 the economic crisis had closed all but ten of the cinemas in Moscow and production was down to almost nothing. With the semi-capitalist NEP policies introduced later that year, production again expanded, from 11 films in 1921 to 157 in 1924.

The Sovkino Trust was set up in 1925 to control and co-ordinate production and distribution in the USSR, though ideological decisions still lay with the Education Department. At first there was little experimentation with new techniques but the Politburo decision in 1925 for non-intervention by the State in matters of artistic style led to a period of great creative excitement in the industry.

High points in this period, the last years of silent cinema, were Eisenstein's *Strike* and the *Battleship Potemkim*, Pudovkin's *Storm over Asia*, and Vertov's *A Sixth of the World*. But this period of freedom soon came to an end under Stalin and at the All-Union Party Conference on the cinema in March 1928 it was stated that 'the basic criterion for evaluating the art qualities of a film is that ... it can be understood by millions'.

The sympathetic Sovkino was replaced by the authoritarian Soyuzkino, headed by Boris Shumyatsky. The result was a period of sterility for the cinema. However following Shumyatsky's visit to Hollywood, production was enormously increased and musicals, such as *Moscow Laughs* by Alexandrov, and literary adaptations, such as Mark Donskoy's production of Gorky's Trilogy, were produced. Several actors made a good living playing Lenin and Stalin in 'personality cult' pictures like *The Man with the Gun*.

Eisenstein suffered under the new regime. His *October, Ten Days That Shook the World* was criticised for formalism (that is, too great a concentration on style and the use of abstract elements) and he was only allowed to direct *Alexander Nevsky* after he had made a public recantation of his errors.

During World War II the Soviet cinema was almost entirely concerned with heroic documentaries, like Varlamov's *Stalingrad*. The high point of feature-film production was Eisenstein's *Ivan the Terrible*, shown in 1945. After the war the censorship on film production was, if anything, tightened. Yutkevitch's *Light over Russia* was banned in 1947 and the second part of *Ivan the Terrible* was not finally shown until 1958. Many of the films made in this period were straightforward anti-Western propaganda, but there were notable exceptions, such as Ptushko's *The Stone Flower* and Pudovkin's *Vasili's Return*.

In the more liberal atmosphere that followed the death of Stalin, a much greater variety of subjects was allowed to be dealt with by the cinema. Such films as Kalatozov's *The Cranes are Flying* in 1957 and Heifitz's *The Lady with the Dog* in 1960 would have been impossible before Khrushchev, and new talents like Andrei Tarkovsky were also emerging. But the fall of Khrushchev once again imposed limits on the arts. And although self-expression was easier than in the Stalin era, many pictures, like Tarkovsky's *Andrei Rublov*, were held back from distribution for ideological reasons.

Tarkovsky seems to be the outstanding talent to have emerged since the war and his recent death has been a great loss for world cinema.

There are now 43 film studios in the USSR and feature output is roughly 140 films per year.

Cities
Below is a table of the cities of the USSR by population size. It is an interesting comment on the structure of Soviet society that only four of them exceed two million.

Population	(million residents)		
Moscow	8.9	Tbilisi	1.2
Leningrad	5.0	Erevan	1.2
Kiev	2.6	Odessa	1.2
Tashkent	2.2	Omsk	1.2
Baku	1.8	Alma Ata	1.1
Kharkov	1.6	Kazan	1.1
Minsk	1.6	Donetsk	1.1
Gorky	1.4	Perm	1.1
Novosibirsk	1.4	Ufa	1.1
Sverdlovsk	1.4	Chelyabinsk	1.1
Kuibyshev	1.3	Rostov-on-Don	1.0
Dnepropetrovsk	1.2		

Civil War
The Civil War in Russia, 1918–20, was a complex affair consisting of a number of separate campaigns against the Bolsheviks, not co-ordinated by any central command on the White or anti-Bolshevik side, and taking place over a vast area.

After the Bolshevik revolution's success in Petrograd, Moscow and elsewhere in October 1917, a number of local anti-Bolshevik 'Provisional Governments' were set up. In January 1918, although the war against Germany was still in progress, the Bolsheviks set out to take control of these bodies, and the Civil War began.

The Red Army, under its Commissar for War Trotsky, took Kiev in the Ukraine and caused the collapse of the Don Cossack government. Then the White Volunteer army formed by two Tsarist generals Kornilov and Denikin was pushed back into the Kuban.

The war with Germany, however, continued and the German armies resumed their attacks in February 1918, obliging the Bolsheviks to accept the terms of the Brest-Litovsk Treaty. This allowed anti-Bolshevik forces to act under German protection. General Mannerheim crushed the Reds in Finland, the Ukraine formed an independent government under the German puppet General Skoropadsky, and while German troops reached Rostov in May, their Turkish allies moved into the south Caucasian territories of Armenia and Azerbaijan. The Don Cossacks rose again, the Volunteer Army returned from the steppes, and in the Far East another Tsarist general Semenov, with Japanese backing, began anti-Bolshevik operations on the Manchurian border.

In May 1918 the 40,000-man Czech Legion, formed by Masaryk with the assistance of the Allies, was spread out over 5,000 miles (8,000 km) of the Trans-Siberian railway. It was making its slow way eastwards out of Russia, when the Allied High Command ordered it to rejoin the war against Germany. In self defence against local soviets, it revolted and became a powerful anti-Bolshevik force in the centre of Russia. Its presence permitted the formation of new non-Bolshevik governments in Samara and further east in Omsk. The threat of its advance was the direct cause of the killing of Tsar Nicholas and his family. (See also **Czech Legion**)

To protect their own interest in Russia and to try and check the further expansion of their German enemies, the Western Allies decided to intervene. The British landed troops in the north at Murmansk and Archangel, where they supported the Russian General Miller, and in the Caspian area where they supported the regime of Chaikovsky, blocked the Turkish advance and encouraged a nationalist Azerbaijan government in Baku. They also conducted a general blockade of Russia in the Baltic from October 1919 to January 1920. Some 40,000 British troops were involved. In August 1918 10,000 US troops and a much larger Japanese contingent landed at Vladivostok.

The arrival of the Allied forces gave impetus to the Whites and in the south the Volunteer Army took the Black Sea naval base of Novorossiisk, although the Red Army consolidated its hold on the centre by taking Kazan in October. That month the White Admiral Kolchak seized power in Omsk and had himself declared Supreme Ruler of the Russias. In January 1919 the French landed 30,000 troops in Odessa, on the Ukrainian coast of the Black Sea, and the peasant army of Makhno, fighting against Skoropadsky and his German-backed forces, benefited from their intervention. The war with Germany had ended in November 1918 with victory for the Western Allies and in March 1919 they decided to pull out of Russia. That March, Kolchak's offensive westwards from the Urals faltered and was followed by Red Army counter-attacks. In May, Denikin opened offensives in the south and south-east fronts, taking Kharkov in June and Poltava in the Ukraine in July. While the Red Army retreated in the south, they continued to advance against Kolchak.

The White armed forces of southern Russia (the joint armies of the Cossacks and the Volunteer Army) under Denikin continued their offensives, taking Kiev and Odessa in August, Kursk in September and Orel in October. This was the peak of White success. On the Baltic, General Yudenich advanced towards Petrograd and then was halted by the superior force of the Red Guards and the Red Army, with Trotsky himself engaged in the fighting. The Red Army also counter-attacked at Orel.

In November Kolchak was forced to evacuate Omsk and came under the protection of the Czech Legion. Antagonised by the Whites' brutality under Kolchak's leadership, they handed him over to a revolutionary government in Irkutsk in January 1920, which executed him, and the power of the Whites east of the Urals was at an end.

In the north, the White rule of Murmansk ended with the departure of the British forces and the Red Army took the town in March 1920.

In January 1920, Baron Wrangel, a dashing cavalry leader, took command of the White forces in the south, but the retreats continued and the Red Army soon entered Kiev, the capital of Ukraine. However the new Polish republic, on behalf of the Ukrainian separatists, retook the city and in April 1920 the Bolsheviks found themselves at war with an invading Poland. Neither the Poles nor the Bolsheviks were able to put together strong enough armies to inflict a decisive defeat on the other. The Red Army, brilliantly led by Tukhachevsky, pushed back the Poles to the gates of Warsaw. This was a tactical error, over-extending its lines of communication, carried out at Lenin's urging, and against Trotsky's advice. The Poles, helped by French military advisers, launched a savage counter-attack, defeated the Red Army and drove it back into its own territory. There was disagreement, perhaps amounting to disloyalty, among the Bolsheviks at this time, and blame has been attached to Stalin and Budyenny for failing to support the Warsaw front. International arbitration brought an armistice, and the advancing Poles were required to withdraw to the 'Curzon Line', a proposed frontier named after the British foreign secretary. The outcome of the Russo–Polish war was that the Poles, by the Treaty of Riga in 1921, were able to claim land in Lithuania, Belorussia and the Ukraine.

In June Wrangel, benefiting from the diversion of Red Army troops to the Russo–Polish war, broke out of the Crimea. But with the full strength of the Red Army turned against him, he was driven back into the Crimea in October and forced to evacuate all his men from Russia in November 1920. The Civil War was ended, though the Japanese had 60,000 troops in the Maritime provinces until 1922 and occupied Sakhalin until 1925.

The Russian Civil War was not fought on broad fronts with the trench and tank warfare of World War I, but in a much more fluid series of campaigns. These were often more like raiding parties following railway routes, with the armoured train taking the part of the tank. Cavalry played an important part in the battles but the plane played a very minor role. The greatest Red Army leader in terms of inspiration and organisation was undoubtedly Trotsky, but in the field, the cavalryman Budyenny was outstanding (just as the most successful White general was the cavalryman Wrangel). Peasant armies played a part, notably those of the Ukrainian Makhno and the Red Army's Chapayev.

The effect of the fighting was catastrophic: harvests were spoiled or not collected, and food often rotted unable to be moved from country to town. There was famine and the Bolshevik's immediate answer was the emergency measures of 'war communism' (i.e. the seizure of crops, often using the most brutal methods). The use of terror tactics was justified by White atrocities which, in turn, justified the growth and the powers of the Cheka, the political police. This led within a few years to the setting up of the centralised and repressive regime which became the main feature of Stalinism. A generation brutalised by World War I followed by the Civil War was more easily able to accept the horrors of the great purges of the 1930s, and by extension also to stand up to the rigours of World War II.

Cold War
The term used in 1947 by the US statesman Bernard Baruch to describe the rivalry between the USSR and its allies and the USA and the Western nations. (See also **Détente** and **Iron Curtain**)

Collectivisation
The Communist Party in 1929 ordered the amalgamation of individual peasant holdings into collective farms. (See also **Agriculture** and **Kolkhoz**)

Comecon
Council for Mutal Economic Assistance, founded in 1949 with the USSR, Bulgaria, Czechoslovakia, Poland and Romania as members. Albania ceased to be part of it in 1961, but East Germany (1950), Mongolia (1962) and Cuba (1972) joined later. Comecon acts a a clearing house for problems of trade and industrial development for its members. A mutual recognition pact was signed with the EEC in June 1988.

Cominform
The Communist Information Bureau founded by Zhdanov and Malenkov in 1947, with its offices in Belgrade, to co-ordinate the Communist Parties of the world. It replaced the Comintern, dissolved in 1943. The break with Yugoslavia in 1948 caused its move to Romania. It was dissolved in 1956.

Comintern
The Communist International founded in 1919 to establish the leadership of communism in world socialism. This was the Third International, breaking from the non-revolutionary Second (formed in 1889), which had collapsed with World War I. The Comintern was formed when expectations of world revolution were high. Outside the Soviet Union it was much feared, but it followed events rather than led them. Stalin ordered the Comintern to pursue objectives in the Soviet Union's interest rather than for the furtherance of a truly international movement. The 1934 Congress, which

urged a Popular Front of socialists against Italian and German fascism, was the last occasion when the Comintern was effective. The treaties between Stalin and Hitler in 1939 brought disillusion to supporters throughout the world. The Comintern was dissolved in 1943, partly because its functioning had ceased and partly as a token of goodwill to the Soviet's American and British allies.

The Comintern Congresses:

1st	2–6 March	1919 Moscow
2nd	19 July–26 August	1920 Moscow and Petrograd
3rd	22 June–12 July	1921 Moscow: 'United Front'
4th	5 November–5 December	1922 Moscow
5th	17 June–8 July	1924 Moscow
6th	17 July–1 September	1928 Moscow: 'Ultra Left faction'
7th	25 July–20 August	1935 Moscow: 'Popular Front'

(See also **International**.)

Commissar

The head of a 'Commission', the title used by the heads of government departments set up by the February 1917 Provisional Government and the regional governors they appointed, and used by the succeeding Bolshevik rulers. 'People's Commissars' were the heads of ministries (and became known as ministers from 1946). Military Commissars were Party officials attached to supervise army commanders.

Communications

Rail Railway construction began in Russia with the St Petersburg–Moscow line, completed in 1851. The most famous railway, the continent-spanning Trans-Siberian, was started at both the east and western ends in 1891. By 1914 the Russian rail system was the second largest in the world, although 5-foot gauge is found now only in the Soviet Union and Finland. But World War I devastated the railways in the west and the Civil War left 60 per cent of the locomotives out of action.

The Civil War, from 1918 to 1921, was largely a railway war for, with no developed road or canal transport system, railways were the main means of moving food, materials and people in Russia. The evacuation of the Czechoslovak Legion along the Trans-Siberian railway and the campaigns in the Ukraine and the Donbas, with the rival cavalry sweeping the country on either side of the tracks, typified the war.

The expansion of Bolshevism through Russia, Siberia and into Central Asia relied on the railway network. Special Agit trains brought the messages of the Revolution to the people and taught the lessons of Party doctrine.

The pattern of railway expansion and development, started under the Tsars, continued under Stalin, the most notable being the Turksib railway, opened in 1933. In Manchuria, control of the railway leading to the Pacific and Vladivostok became a cause of conflict with China, and later of war with Japan.

In World War II the German invaders found only a rudimentary road system compared to the autobahn network they had created. The war resulted in the destruction of railways and the consequent need for road transport. Heavy-duty trucks were a major element in Anglo–American supplies during the war. But after the war railway reconstruction, both rebuilding and upgrading, were given a high priority. Steam locomotives were replaced gradually with diesel and now steam is used only for shunting or local traffic. Electrification has been carried out on major lines and new lines have been opened in Kazakhstan while the Baikal–Amur extension was opened in 1976–77. The Soviet Union now has one-eighth of all the world's rail mileage.

Roads Russian roads have always had a bad reputation and no government has ever given them a high priority. The severity of the Russian winter provided a hard surface for vehicles, though destructive of conventionally made roads, but the spring thaw often meant the rebuilding of the roads among oceans of mud. Long-haul transport is either by rail or water; roads are planned for short-haul only and there is therefore no national motorway network. Inter-city roads are usually two-lane, expecting a low traffic density, and only one-third of the ten million miles (16 million km) of rural roads are paved.

Waterways Until 1917 inland water transport was largely on the Volga, Dvina, Don, Ob and Yenisei rivers. Winters freeze much of these and their use is therefore seasonal. In 1918 all river fleets were nationalised and extensive linking canals began to be built. The first of the major projects was the White Sea Canal, carried out with prisoners' labour and completed in 1931–33. This was followed by the Moscow–Volga Canal (1932–37) and the Volga–Don Canal in 1952. Waterborne traffic is substantial but carries only one-twentieth of all freight movement. The Soviet Union has taken pride in its development of large hydrofoil vessels for passengers on main routes.

Urban transport Private ownership of cars has not reached the scale of Western countries and cities rely on passenger bus, tramway and trolley bus services. The Moscow Metro, built in the 1930s, is one of the world's most efficient and extensive underground city railways. There are also underground railways in Baku, Kharkov, Kiev, Leningrad, Tashkent and Tblisi.

Communist Party
In 1917 this was the Bolshevik part of the Social Democrats (RSDLP) and effectively a separate party; in 1918 Lenin urged the Bolsheviks to rename themselves the 'Russian Communist Party (Bolshevik)'; in 1925 this became the 'All-Union Communist Party (Bolshevik)' or CPSU(B). The term 'Bolshevik' was officially dropped only in 1952.

Compromisers
SRs and Mensheviks who would have gone into a coalition with the Kadets or the Provisional Government in 1917.

Constitution
On 10 July 1918 the Russian Federal Socialist Republic, at the 5th All-Russian Congress of Soviets, adopted a constitution which laid down the 'Dictatorship of the Proletariat' as the basic instrument for enforcing the rule of the Revolution. This was replaced in 1924 by a federal constitution which provided for the constituent republics of the USSR, and in theory allowing them to decide whether they wanted self-determination or join the USSR.

In 1936 Stalin presented the Soviet Union with a new model. Although largely drafted by Bukharin and Radek before their arrest, it became known as the 'Stalin Constitution'. The constitution instituted the elections of delegates by all citizens rather than by nomination from within the local branch of the Party. It created a Supreme Soviet with one chamber elected by a direct one-man one-vote system in equally-sized electoral districts, and a second chamber made up of representatives from the different nationalities in the Union. The delegates were now not necessarily Communist Party members.

It confirmed a federation of Soviet republics, with the Union government in Moscow controlling matters of defence and foreign policy. All-Union Commissariats (later Ministries) dominated parallel Commissariats in the republics, but the republics had their own jurisdiction in some fields (such as primary education). It was a healthy decentralised democracy on paper. But while it set a liberal framework, in reality the Politburo or the NKVD could override anything they saw as an obstacle. The purges were already beginning and, in effect, decentralisation was out of the question.

After 40 years, the principles of the 1936 constitution were polished up again with the new constitution adopted on 7 October 1977. It confirmed the role of the Communist Party as the principal force in Soviet society and added statements on the rights of the citizen. This constitution was amended as a result of the 19th Party Conference, 'Implementing and Promoting Perestroika' in June–July 1988. From this conference's amendments came the Congress of People's Deputies which came into being in 1989. (See also **Political Structure** and **Law**)

Constitutional Democrats see **Kadets**.

Cossacks

The Cossack of legend, the fur-capped horseman, the flashing sabre, the wild dances to the music of the balalaika, is balanced by the image of the dark riders with lead-weighted whips slashing at demonstrating crowds in the city. They were people of south-west Russia descended from Tatar peoples and mixed with Slavs who had escaped serfdom. They lived in independent bands led by an 'Ataman'. In return for their military services, they were given land and privileges by the Russian rulers. Cossacks were used to repress risings against the State, but their very independence always made them a danger to central authority.

By the twentieth century the Cossacks were a mainstay of the Tsarist Empire. The Don Cossacks, with their capital city of Novocherkassk and land stretching to the Black Sea, had a thriving agricultural industry with corn, vines and tobacco. Settlements of Cossacks ran south of the Urals, through Orenburg and Omsk and along the border with China to the Amur. They guarded the Empire's frontier and provided it with soldiers.

In 1905 Cossacks played a major part in saving the Empire from revolution, but already there were signs of rebellion among them and there was an increasing number of incidents when Cossacks sided with workers rather than the authorities. In the Duma, Cossack representatives were largely liberals and began to call for more local self-government. The war of 1914 called 360,000 Cossacks to the army, but cavalry was no match for German machine guns, barbed wire and artillery barrages: Cossack casualties were heavy.

Called to put down revolution in Petrograd in 1917, Cossack regiments began to mutiny and their defection was a key to the Revolution. The Cossack communities elected their own Atamans and called Congresses in Petrograd in March and June 1917. In June, in Novocherkassk, the Don Cossacks' Krug, their ruling body, elected General Kaledin as their Ataman and a regional government was set up.

The Don Cossacks and Kaledin (1917) The July 1917 attempt by the Bolsheviks to take power in Petrograd was put down largely by Cossacks now loyal to the Provisional Government; there were few Bolsheviks among them at this time. But Kornilov's attempt to use Cossacks in his August move on Petrograd precipitated a split between the Kerensky government and the Don Cossacks, while more Cossack troops began to side with the Bolsheviks and Kerensky found his military support quietly slipping away.

Kaledin's authority in the Don was established and Cossack independence seemed to be a possibility as other Ural and Orenburg Cossack communities joined a 'South-East Union' of Cossacks. The example of the independent Rada of the Ukraine was to be followed. But in December 1917 Kornilov, Denikin, Alekseev and other generals came to the Don to build the Volunteer Army and Kaledin's moderation was swamped by the extremist Whites. The Cossacks did not flock to join the new army; many of them had had enough of war and had returned to their homes.

The Don Cossacks on their own (1918) When Red units appeared on the Don in January 1918, Kaledin called in vain for his people to fight against them. On 11 February 1918 Kaledin, in despair, committed suicide. On 25 February the Red Cossack Colonel Golubov led his men into the assembly building and dispersed the Krug. The Cossack communities of the Urals, Orenburg and Omsk were soon siding with the Bolshevik soviets.

Anarchy came to the Cossack country and partisan or bandit groups fought for their own survival. Kornilov's Volunteer Army, retreating to the Kuban, found the Cossacks there unhelpful, although by April 1918 the White army felt strong enough to attack the Red Army there (and it was in this fighting that Kornilov was killed). Denikin made sure that his soldiers treated the Cossacks with care and gradually he turned their opinion against the Bolsheviks. The Germans were advancing across the Ukraine and the Red Army was in retreat and foraging through Cossack land. As the Germans reached the Black Sea, Cossacks retook Novocherkassk and a new Krug was convened in May.

Krasnov's Cossacks in the Ukraine The new Ataman, General Krasnov, took dictatorial power, approached the Germans for help, made an alliance with the Skoropadsky government of the Ukraine, called back the Volunteer Army and raised a force of 40,000 Cossacks. By August 1918 the Red Army and the Bolsheviks were driven out. Krasnov encouraged a counter-Bolshevik terror and preached 'Don for the Don Cossacks'. The Ural Cossacks, too, rose against Bolshevik rule and killed everyone they suspected of being Red.

Krasnov's rule became unpopular with the substantial non-Cossack population and with his rivals in the Krug. The tide began to move against Krasnov as food shortages increased. In December 1918 whole regiments began to desert to the Red Army. In February 1919 Krasnov resigned. While Denikin advanced on the Kiev–Tsaritsyn line, Lenin's 'Cossack Department' in Moscow sent agitators into Cossack lands calling for peace. Denikin took Tsaritsyn in June and the Don Cossacks raided deep behind the Red Army lines and Orel was taken in October. However, the Red offensive restarted, retaking Orel and then sweeping the Whites into retreat. The Krug tried to disassociate itself from Denikin, but the prospects were poor. Denikin resigned and was succeeded by Wrangel. In 1920 there was another White resurgence, but Wrangel and his army were beaten back and fled from the Crimea that November. The Don and Kuban Cossacks sank back to banditry. The survivors were starving in a wrecked land, subject to searches by the Cheka looking for anti-revolutionaries or stores of food.

The end of Cossack power The Bolshevik government set out to destroy the Cossack privileges conferred by the Tsarist Empire and in 1929 the 15th Party Congress decreed that collectivisation of the Don and Kuban should be carried out within a year. The opposition to this brought hunger again in 1930 and there were armed risings which were put down ruthlessly. Some of the surviving Cossacks from these episodes took to the hills until the Germans came in 1941.

In 1941–45 many captured Russian soldiers, who agreed to put on German uniform, called themselves 'Cossack' to avoid the use of 'Russian', so that there was the illusion of a substantial pro-Nazi Cossack force on the German side.

Krasnov had gone to Germany where his anti-Semitism and nationalism made him a natural recruit for Hitler's New Order and he was nominated as head of a puppet Cossack state. The old man was rounded up with other Cossacks in Austria in 1945 and handed over to the Russians and, after a trial, was executed in January 1947.

Council of Nationalities see **Political Structure**.

Council of People's Commissars see **Sovnarkom** and **Political Structure**.

Crime
National crime figures have been collected but not published since 1933. The officially accepted story has been that 'organised crime' is only 'a form of criminal activity carried on in bourgeois countries, primarily the USA'. However in 1989 Major-General Anatoly Smirnov of the Interior Ministry announced figures for 1988, reflecting the changes over the previous year.

Premeditated murder	16,710	(an increase of 14% over the previous year)
Violent robberies	12,916	(an increase of 43%)
Break-ins/hold-ups	67,114	(an increase of 45%)

Total crimes had risen by 3.6 per cent over the year to nearly 1.9 million. Major cities like Moscow have high crime rates: drug addiction has increased as one result of the Afghanistan War; there are reckoned to be 4,500 prostitutes working in Moscow (although this too is against the officially recognised story).

Crimean Tatars
Muslim descendants of the Mongol and Turkic hordes who invaded eastern Europe from central Asia in the thirteenth century. In the fifteenth century the Crimean Tatars established an independent state. Their Khanate of the Crimea came under Ottoman rule in 1475, and passed in 1783 into the Russian Empire. Under Russian rule, the Tatar people were regarded as inferior and their lands were taken by Russian and Ukrainian settlers. By the start of the twentieth century they numbered less than 200,000.

The Crimean Autonomous Soviet Socialist republic was established in October 1921. After the German occupation of the Crimea in World War II, the Tatar population was accused of collaboration and treason. They were sent, under penal conditions, to Kazakhstan and Uzbekistan in 1944. The half million survivors were 'rehabilitated' in 1967 in a decree which referred to them as 'formerly resident in the Crimea'. The Crimean ASSR had been disbanded in 1946 and incorporated into the Ukrainian SSR and the land resettled. Crimean Tatars were able to make their first publicised protest only in 1987 in Moscow.

Curzon Line
The Polish–Soviet armistice line of 1920. In July 1920 the Polish armies were 125 miles (200 km) east of the 1919 frontier and the Allies demanded that they retire to a line proposed by the British Foreign Secretary Lord Curzon. This did not become the eastern frontier of the Polish republic, but was used by Stalin in 1939 to justify the extension of the Belorussian and Ukrainian republics westwards.

Czechoslovakia
Population: 15,500,000 Area: 49,370 sq miles (127,869 sq km)
Capital: Prague
Under Presidents Masaryk and Beneš, Czechoslovakia between the wars was a model democracy with a high standard of living. In 1938 Hitler demanded the border Sudeten lands which had a considerable German-speaking population, and added them to Germany with the agreement of the British and French at the Munich meeting that year. Then in 1939 Czechoslovakia was occupied by the Nazis and underwent the full

history of repression and exploitation experienced elsewhere in Europe. In 1944 the Red Army drove the Germans out of the country, although Prague, the capital, was liberated by the German-formed Vlasov army.

In March 1945 President Beneš, who had spent the war years in England, went to Moscow to negotiate setting up a government. Gottwald, the leader of the Czech Communist Party, insisted on 8 of the 25 cabinet posts, but in the elections in May 1946 the communists got only 38 per cent of the votes. Gottwald became Premier none the less and in 1948, in a skilfully executed bloodless coup, seized power.

Gottwald was succeeded by Zapotocky in 1953 and Novotny in 1957. The latter, under pressure for reform of the doctrinaire political and social thinking of the last 20 years, was removed from office in January 1968 and replaced by Alexander Dubček in the brief period of liberalisation known as the Prague Spring. The attempt at reform did not last. In August troops from the USSR, Bulgaria, Poland and East Germany moved into the country and Dubček and his committee were taken unceremoniously to Moscow. In April 1969 he was succeeded by Gustav Husák and subsequently expelled from the Party.

With a population of 15 million and a Party membership of a million and a half, virtually all industry is in State hands and more than 90 per cent of agriculture was either in collectives or State farms. Under Husák, Czechoslovakia has been the scene of considerable and vicious religious persecution.

On Friday 17 November 1989, inspired by the events in Hungary and East Germany, there was a massive anti-government demonstration in Prague. The crowd was mostly composed of students and the demonstrations were broken up by the police with some brutality. This caused fierce reactions throughout the country and mass demonstrations followed. On 24 November Milos Jakes, the Party leader, resigned, and on 30 November the Communist Party announced that it was giving up its leading role.

On 28 December Alexander Dubček was declared Chairman of the Parliament and on the 29th Vaclav Havel, the playwright recently released from prison and a prominent member of Civic Forum, the citizens' movement for democracy, was elected President. Multi-party general elections were announced, the last having been held in 1946. For events since December 1989 see the Chronology.

Czech Legion

Czechoslovak soldiers trying to leave Russia played an extraordinary role in the Civil War, making possible anti-Bolshevik risings in Siberia and being the indirect cause of the Tsar's death.

There had been large numbers of Czech and Slovak émigrés from the Austro-Hungarian Empire in Imperial Russia for centuries, the majority of them craftsmen, small businessmen or clerical workers. In World War I Russia recruited many of them into a 'Czech Brigade'. At the same time, in France, a special Czech unit of the French Foreign Legion was formed which became the 'Czech National Army'; there was a similar 'Legion' in Italy. These legions played an important part in the establishment of a new nation, created out of the wreckage of the Austro-Hungarian Empire at the Treaty of Versailles.

In Russia the Czech Legion became a significant military unit of about 40,000 men in the Provisional Government's army. It distinguished itself in Kerensky's July 1917 offensive against the Germans, growing to the strength of an army corps. The Provisional Government agreed that the Legion in Russia should now be regarded as officially part of the Czech national army. After the Bolshevik revolution, Masaryk, the present of the Czech National Council, affirmed that the Czech army would be neutral in the Civil War. He made an agreement with the new Bolshevik regime in the person of the People's Commissar for Nationalities, Joseph Stalin, that the legion should be brought out of Russia to join the rest of the Czech army. On 27 March 1918 the first Czech group began to leave by rail across Siberia to Vladivostok.

But on March 31 the Germans mounted a major offensive on their eastern front. The Allied governments first asked the Czechs to stay and fight, but then the Allied Supreme Commanders issued a further command to send them to France and ordered that all Czechs still to the west of Omsk should be re-routed via Murmansk and Archangel. However the Czechs, who were for the most part nationalists and revolutionaries themselves and had nothing to fear from the Russian Revolution, preferred to continue with their original evacuation plan through Vladivostok. The Soviet administration authorised this, although there were vain attempts to persuade them to join the Bolshevik cause.

When on 14 May there was a fight between some Hungarian ex-prisoners of war and soldiers of the legion, the local soviet arrested the Czech delegation who had come to them to protest about the incident. The Czech soldiers came armed, forced the release of the comrades and set up a provisional committee to run their affairs. Trotsky, as People's Commissar for War, ordered the Czechs to disarm. The provisional committee replied by affirming their support for the Russian Revolution, but saying that they chose to keep their arms – since the Soviet government had no power to guarantee their transport. The French Military Mission in fact supported Trotsky's decree, which he reinforced on 25 May with an order that any armed Czech found on the Penza–Omsk line was to be shot immediately.

Some of the Czechs were supporters of the Bolsheviks, more were followers of the older Czech independence movement and tended to side against the Red Army (one battalion of them fought with Denikin in the Ukraine), but the majority were more interested in their own survival and in returning to a new independent Czechoslovakia. They were well equipped, well trained and had high morale: they were one of the most effective fighting bodies in the world, when Red Army units tried to oppose them or disarm them, *they* replied by disarming the Soviet troops.

Using their military superiority, by early June the Czechs had taken control of almost the whole Trans-Siberian railway. When they seized Penza, the Socialist Revolutionaries persuaded them to move on into the provincial capital Samara (now Kuibyshev). The Czechs' success encouraged anti-Soviet groups. In Samara the Officers' Associations opened the prisons, while the Menshevik railwayman declared neutrality. The Bolshevik forces prepared to defend the town, but the Czechs took it on the night of 7–8 June 1918. The Socialist Revolutionaries declared a new government and began to celebrate. They fully expected the arrival of Allied interventionist forces – but these were nowhere near and had no plan to relieve them.

Czech-supported troops moved on to take Ekaterinburg on 25 July (their approach had alarmed the defenders who had immediately killed the Tsar and his family). The Czechs next took Simbirsk and, on 7 August, Kazan.

As the Czechs moved, they roused hopes among minority peoples, as well as landowners, of countering the Bolsheviks. On 8 September an all-party anti-Bolshevik conference declared an 'All-Russian Provisional Government'. But on 17 November a group of officers overthrew it and called on Admiral Kolchak to be 'Supreme Ruler of all Russia' and Commander-in-Chief of the armed forces. The Czechs protested, but the British and French Allies began sending supplies to Kolchak through Vladivostok by the railway.

The Czechs were disillusioned. World War I was over. They had fought for democracy for four years and were now tired. The Czechoslovak republic had been declared; it was time for them to go. In early 1919 the Czech Legion was withdrawn from fighting and was only used to guard the railway. Transport and supplies were insufficient and the Czechs could not move as a body, whereupon they effectively took over part of Siberia and used their civilian skills. A bank was opened by a colonel (formerly a Prague banker); a daily newspaper was printed at several stations on the railway; their companies bought and sold commodities. The Czechs prospered economically in the middle of a chaotic decaying world.

Kolchak was losing the battle against the Red Army. He was taken under Czech guard to Irkutsk, which was shortly after taken by the Bolsheviks and Kolchak was shot on 7 February 1920. The Czechs agreed to release the Imperial gold reserves which had come into their custody. On 1 March the last Czech train left there and the gold was handed over.

The Japanese were the Allied power patrolling from Lake Baikal to Vladivostok and although they halted this train at Chita to search for Bolsheviks, the Czechs made no objection: they were glad to be out of Russia and the evacuation went on from May to 30 December, when the Allies declared the operation ended. One of the ships used, the *Legia*, had been bought by the legion's own bank and became inland Czechoslovakia's first merchant ship.

D

Dacha
A holiday house, usually in the country or at the sea-side. For Soviet officials, it means a villa allocated to them, sometimes for life.

Dashnak
The anti-Russian 'revolutionary federation' party of the Armenians, founded in the 1880s and the leading party in 1905 and from 1917 to 1920.

Decembrists
Members of the anti-Tsarist revolt of 1825; the revolt failed, but the tradition of Decembrist conspiracy contributed to the 1905 risings.

Defence Council
A body founded at the beginning of December 1917 by the Sovnarkom, shortly after the Petrograd Soviet's MRC (Military Revolutionary Committee) was dissolved.

Defensists
Socialist politicians who agreed with World War I as 'Defence of the Fatherland'.

Democratic Union
A movement in 1988 styling itself as the opposition party, but unrecognised since political pluralism was not yet tolerated in the Soviet Union.

Détente
Relaxation of tension, the attempts to end the Cold War.

Directorate (Council of Five)
Kerensky's proposal for governing Russia after the Kornilov affair, and set up on 1 September 1917.

Dissidents
From the moment that the Bolsheviks took over the Revolution in October 1917 there were parties and groups in violent disagreement with them, and this continued until Stalin imposed his will on the Party. Opposition was not heard in the Soviet Union until after Stalin's death. The USSR refused to sign the 1948 Universal Declaration

of Human Rights made by the United Nations. However, the USSR did eventually sign the 1967 International Covenant on Economic, Social and Cultural Rights, though not until 1973. The Helsinki Conference, with its Final Act in August 1975, proclaimed 'respect for human rights and fundamental freedoms' and was signed by Leonid Brezhnev. Monitoring groups were set up in the USSR and were themselves the subject of some persecution, and the tolerance of dissent of any kind seemed frequently a function of the relationship of the Soviet Union with other powers.

Civil Rights groups in the Soviet Union have been very disparate, including independent trade unions, organisations seeking autonomy for national minorities, campaigners for religious freedom, and Jews wishing to emigrate. A popular tool of all these groups was the unofficial publication known as the samizdat (see **Samizdat**). For those who were tried for making their views known, punishments included expulsion from their unions (the Writers' Union for example), dismissal from employment, internal exile, imprisonment in forced labour camps or psychiatric hospitals, and in some cases (Solzhenitsyn for example), expulsion from the Soviet Union. Among the internationally known dissidents the most prominent were the writer Anatoly Kuznetsov, who came to Britain in 1967, Alexander Solzhenitsyn, expelled in 1974, Vladimir Bukovsky, a writer who was imprisoned in a psychiatric hospital and brought this abuse to world attention in 1971, Zhores Medvedev, a biologist and writer who came to Britain in 1973, his historian brother Roy, who was often threatened with arrest. Andrei Sakharov, the famous physicist, who was only released from internal exile in 1986 at Gorbachev's insistence, and Natan Scharansky, who spent a decade in the Gulag for campaigning about Jewish rights and left the USSR for the West in 1986.

Many dissidents from the Baltic Republics, Crimean Tatars and Ukrainian nationalists have been punished by imprisonment in labour camps and internal exile.

Although many millions of political prisoners were released during Khrushchev's period as General Secretary, he was responsible for reactivating religious persecution. Between 1960 and 1964 10,000 orthodox churches were closed. The Baptists were also severely persecuted, as were the Pentecostalists. He also attacked the observances and culture of Russian Jews.

The 1977 constitution, introduced under Brezhnev, was intended to spell out the majestic progress being made towards the perfect socialist state. Its preamble talks of guaranteeing 'personal rights and freedoms, including the freedom of conscience'. Freedom of speech is ensured, it says, by placing public buildings and streets at the disposal of the working people. It states that 'all power in the USSR belongs to the people' and confirms this in the now well-known Article 6, which states that 'The leading and guiding force of Soviet society ... is the Communist Party of the Soviet Union.'

But Article 6 was removed from the constitution in February 1990 and the Central Committee announced that 'The Soviet Communist Party does not claim a monopoly and is prepared for a political dialogue ... with everyone who favours the renewal of socialist society.' A series of revolutionary changes has been put forward. A new constitution is being devised and a jury system is to be introduced into Soviet courts. Bills guaranteeing the freedom of the press and of conscience are under preparation. Indeed, the freedoms supposedly guaranteed in the constitutions of 1936 and 1977 are now being translated into reality. It is probably true to say that for the first time since the Revolution there are no political prisoners left in the Soviet Union.

Duma

The elected legislative assemblies which resulted from the demands of the 1905 revolution. The electorate was to be of all adult men at first, but property qualifications were made. The first Duma met for 73 days in 1906, the second for 102 in 1907, but their liberal demands were unacceptable to the Tsar's government. With a more restricted electorate, a third Duma ran from 1907 to 1912 and supported the government's policies; but the fourth Duma, from 1912 grew critical of the Tsar's regime and of the war. When the Tsar abdicated in 1917, the Duma formed a provisional committee and asked Prince Lvov to form the Provisional Government.

E

Education

A full education for all has always been called for by the Party in the Soviet Union, but universal education for only eight years from the age of seven has been achieved. In the cities there are pre-school facilities, crèches and kindergartens for most children. The main school years are in schools with a centrally planned curriculum and with regular annual promotion of the pupils to the age of 15. There is general conformity throughout the USSR and in all republics priority has been given to the use of the Russian language.

Sixty per cent of children at the age of 15 continue with two years' general secondary education, leading to employment. Others go on to four years' specialised secondary schooling, leading to careers such as nursing or clerical work. There are also vocational and technical schools, specialising in practical training for industry. Apart from these there are special schools for the handicapped and for the selected few with outstanding talent.

Although the principle of equal opportunity for all is held, children in Moscow or Leningrad, for example, have greater chances of good schooling than those in remoter parts of the Union. Children from managerial and intellectual families also have greater chances of success. Partly to offset this, points are given for entry to higher education to children of workers and farmers, and to those who have already worked for two years in industry, or are seconded from the armed forces.

Higher education is run by a separate ministry. Entry is highly competitive and, once selected, high achievement is expected. Courses are normally for five years. Part-time courses are encouraged, for study while working is cheaper for the state. Full-time students, who pay no fees, are given grants while they study. Universities tend to be for pure sciences or the arts, but higher Professional Institutes, also leading to a 'Diplom', can have as much status. In recent years the Soviet Union's number of students in higher education has fallen and, in world terms, they have gone from ninth in students per 10,000 of population to twenty-third. This is partly due to the increase in other countries, but it also represents an economic retrenchment in the USSR.

Employment

Unemployment, it used to be claimed, disappeared from the Soviet Union in 1931 and was only a feature of the capitalist world. Under the constitution of 1977, Article 40, Soviet citizens have the rights to work: 'guaranteed employment and pay in accordance with the quantity and quality of their work, and not below the State-established minimum'.

With the openness of the Gorbachev era, official figures for 1984 revealed severe unemployment in some parts: Azerbaijan 27.6 per cent, Tajikistan 25.7, Uzbekistan 22.8, Turkmen SSR 18.8, Armenia 18 and Kirghizia 16.3. These are people capable of work, but not earning an official wage (thus housewives and small-holding farmers are included). Central Asia's high birth rate, the single-crop economy (cotton) in Uzbekistan and tighter management of enterprises are contributory factors. While there are areas with employment vacancies, such as Siberian industrial plants, the cut-back in the armed forces and the inevitable decline in the numbers of the bureaucracy will lead to colossal retraining programmes.

A social security system with payments for those left unemployed by the newly recognised market forces was still being contemplated in 1989.

Environment

In the building of new heavy industry and the expansion and mechanisation of farming under the Five Year Plans, little heed was paid to the long-term effects. Industry and agriculture have brought pollution to the steppes – an outcome quite unexpected in the 1930s or even in the 1950s. Combined with the heavy use of pesticides and chemical fertilisers to boost agricultural production (and now showing their poisonous results) the immense and rapid ploughing of land for the 'Virgin Lands' has brought erosion. Ecological disasters have taught the planners terrible lessons. It is reckoned that 20 per cent of Soviet citizens live in ecological disaster zones, that life expectancy in them is reduced by seven years and infant mortality is unacceptably high.

The coal-mining cities of the Kuzbass, in western Siberia, are among the most polluted in the world. Novokuznetsk's 700,000 inhabitants have over 800,000 tonnes of effluent poured back down on them from their metallurgical works. The demand for coal has led to vast acres of virgin land being stripped of soil and vegetation as near-surface coal is scooped out.

The Aral Sea has been used to irrigate the cotton of Uzbekistan. Since 1960 the sea has contracted by one-third and its level has dropped by 40 feet (12 m). A salt desert has been born from which poisonous salts blow over the surrounding country. Without urgent remedies the sea will disappear by the year 2010 and the desert will have grown to cover its area. In Aralsk, once a port on the sea but now with stranded fishing boats, infant mortality is now one in ten; typhoid has increased 29 times and hepatitis seven times.

The development of nuclear power had brought disasters before the Chernobyl explosion. It is said that in 1957, between Sverdlovsk and Chelyabinsk, a large area, about 580 sq miles (1,500 sq km), was severely contaminated after an explosion in a nuclear-waste dump, and at Shevchernenko in 1974 at atomic breeder leaked.

On 3 June 1989 the natural gas pipeline from western Siberia to the industrial centre of Ufa, built in 1985, leaked a cloud of gas. Two railway trains passing sparked an explosion and over 400 passengers were killed.

The Congress of Deputies set up a Commission on Ecology in 1989, led by Professor Yablokov, associated with the international Greenpeace organisation. An awareness of ecological dangers led to a protest against the building of a nuclear-waste storage site near the city of Kranoyarsk, which would take the waste from all Eastern Europe. No such protest would have been conceivable in previous years. In 1988 and 1989, ecological protests have led to the abandonment of a hydro-electrical scheme, a phosphate mine in Estonia, banning certain defoliants and attempts to save Lakes Baikal and Ladoga. Most important has been the decision to discontinue work on diverting the flow of Siberian rivers from north to south.

Espionage

The GRU (Glavnoye Razvedyvatelnoye Upravleniye, the Chief Intelligence Directorate of the General Staff) operates from 19 Znamensky Street, once the Moscow home of a Tsarist millionaire. It acquires military intelligence mainly through the legitimate operation of military attachés in embassies throughout the world.

Although it was founded by Trotsky in 1919 as the army's source of intelligence, distinct from the civil government's Cheka, the GRU is nowadays subordinate to the Cheka's descendant, the KGB. Its successes in running agents overseas have been the atomic energy spies, Klaus Fuchs in England and the Rosenbergs in the USA. The GRU also organised 'Gordon Lonsdale' in England to obtain naval secrets and Rudolf

Abel in America, whose career was acclaimed as a success in the USSR after he had been exchanged for the U2 pilot Gary Powers, but whose achievements are still a matter of puzzlement in the USA. However the defection of the GRU Colonel Penkovsky damaged the reputation of the organisation severely. Penkovsky, while on missions to Britain in 1960 and 1961, revealed details of the state of Soviet military preparedness which helped President Kennedy outface Khrushchev during the 1962 Cuban missile crisis. After returning to the USSR, Penkovsky was detected and shot.

The KGB now claims credit for all espionage success and has recently publicised the case of 'Glenn Souther', alias Mikhail Orlov, who, while serving in the US Navy under the full cover of American citizenship, had engineered espionage in the USA until 1986; fearing exposure he returned to the USSR, where he killed himself in depression at the age of 32. It is also proud of the exploits of the British Kim Philby, who retired and died in 1988 in Moscow as a KGB general. (See also **Political Police, KGB**)

Estonian Soviet Socialist Republic
Population: 1,557,000 (65% Estonian, 28% Russian, 5% Ukrainian and Belorussian)
Area: 17,413 sq miles (45,111 sq km)   Capital: Tallinn
For the earlier history of Estonia, see **Baltic States**. In November 1988 the Communist Party leader called for a reform programme. Its Supreme Soviet amended the Estonian constitution to give the republic the right to refuse All-Union laws. Estonia demanded that its own language replace Russian officially and claimed its own citizenship laws. A 'Popular Front' voiced these demands and more. They also proposed their own currency for 1990, the Korus, with its own international exchange rate. The Estonian Supreme Soviet has also recognised the right to private property; declared land, air, water, minerals, forests and natural resources to be the exclusive property of Estonia (the USSR previously claimed these as belonging to the whole Soviet Union); banks and major enterprises to be owned by Estonia (previously under the Union's jurisdiction). Later Indrek Toome, the Prime Minister, announced plans less dramatic than earlier proposals, but including a new form of income tax and the legalisation of forms of private enterprise, the return of collective and State farms to farmers and a control over immigration.

On 24 February 1989 Arnold Ruutel, the 'suave and diplomatic' President, raised the Estonian flag, blue, black and white, over the government building at Tallinn on the old Independence Day (1918). To counter the Popular Front, an 'International Movement', Yedinstvo, was formed to represent Russian interests. In August 1989 many Russians came out on strike in protest against discrimination.

In March 1989 the Popular Front candidates were elected to the All-Union Congress, but four of the successful candidates were of the Yedinstvo. In May a 'Baltic Assembly' of the Popular Fronts of Estonia, Latvia and Lithuania was held in Tallinn. It rejected a Moscow plan which would concede control over the production of food and consumer goods in the 15 Soviet republics, but retain control over energy and heavy industry. The deputies to the All-Union Congress agreed on a united stand. This congress met again in March 1990, with 499 delegates elected by over half a million Estonians. For events since March 1990 see the Chronology.

F

Fellow-travellers
Intellectuals who, although not communists, sympathised with the Party. A term (*poputchiki*) coined by Trotsky in 1925 and much used in the USA during the McCarthy period.

Finland

1905–20 The 1905 revolution regained for Finland some of the independence which it had lost at the end of the nineteenth century. It established, within the Tsarist Empire, its own legislature elected by both women and men. It was the first elected assembly in Europe to have both men and women delegates.

During World War I many Finns chose to be pro-German because this expressed their hostility to Russian rule. In January 1915 200 Finns went for military training in Germany; by May 1916 their numbers had reached 2,000 and they had formed the '27 Königliche Preussische Jäger' battalion, deployed on the eastern front near Riga.

In March 1917 Russian troops in Helsinki, as elsewhere, rose against their officers and the Provisional Government in Petrograd gave Finland self-government, with its legislature headed by a Social Democrat minister. But, in July 1917, the Provisional Government dissolved this legislature and elections in October 1917 gave the Social Democrats 92 seats (less than the 103 they had had in 1916) and the non-socialists 108. In November 1917, with the Bolsheviks in power in Petrograd, the new Finnish parliament decided to stand alone and Lenin recognised the independent Finnish state in December. This was followed by recognition in January 1918 by Germany, France and the Scandinavian nations.

In January 1918 Mannerheim, a Tsarist general of Swedish–Finnish family, started training a Finnish army at Vaasa, just as a left-wing revolt broke out in Helsinki. The Finnish government fled to Vaasa, but Mannerheim led a campaign (with some German help, in the form of their Finnish battalion of Jägers) against the rising and headed a victory parade in Helsinki in May 1918. The Soviets regarded this as a Finnish civil war and they accepted the Mannerheim reaction. In October 1920 Finland and Russia signed the peace of Dorpat.

1939–45 In October 1939, anticipating war with Germany, Stalin and Molotov demanded that Finnish territory in the Leningrad area be ceded for the defence of the Soviet Union. But the Soviet-Finnish talks broke down, since the Finnish parliament would not trust their emissaries to deal with the Soviets. In November, after declaring that Finland was threatening them, the Soviet Union bombed Helsinki and invaded Finland. Stalin set up a 'Finnish Democratic Republic' which, joined with the Karelian Autonomous Republic, would have become a 'Karelo–Finnish Soviet Republic' within the USSR.

Mannerheim assumed supreme command of the Finnish forces. The world looked on Finland with admiration, but without any ability to help. In December the USSR was expelled from the League of Nations without any nation voting in her support.

The Soviet 7th Army proved to be ill-trained and ill-equipped for a winter attack on the Finish defence positions and in January 1940 the Red Army commander, Meretskov, was removed from overall command of the Finnish war and replaced by Timoshenko. An attack on the 'Mannerheim Line', preceded by a heavy artillery barrage, allowed Soviet tank forces to sweep around the defences and drive back the Finnish troops. After Norway and Sweden had refused passage of a small Anglo-French force, on 12 March Finland stopped fighting against the Soviet Union and signed the treaty demanded in 1939, to which extra clauses were now added. The Finnish army lost 25,000 men killed, but the Red Army casualties were much greater, possibly 200,000, reflecting their appalling military miscalculation.

Following the German attack, on 25 June 1941, Finland declared war on the Soviet Union and her troops advanced to the old 1939 frontier on the Karelian isthmus and to the River Svir between Lakes Ladoga and Onega, where the line stayed until 1944. For, in spite of a strong German presence, the Finns only carried out military operations that were in their interest. Marshal Mannerheim would not take command of the German troops in Finland, since that would have reduced him, in effect, to merely one of Hitler's generals. In December Britain declared itself at war with Finland after long diplomatic attempts to persuade it not to align with Germany.

In February 1944 Finland began secret discussions on peace terms with the Soviet Union through its ambassador in Sweden, Kollontay. The war continued, however, and in June an attack drove the Finns back to their 1940 lines on the Karelian isthmus. In August the Finnish president resigned and was replaced by Marshal Mannerheim, who got Sweden's promise of food supplies. Thus able to act independently of Germany, Finland sued for peace and an armistice was signed in September 1944, and after some fighting, German troops were expelled. Mannerheim declared war on Germany in March 1945 and, his work completed, resigned as president a year later. In February 1947 Finland signed a peace treaty with the Soviet Union and its independence was assured.

Finland Station

The Petrograd station in the north of the city at which Lenin and his companions arrived in April 1917. (See also **Sealed Train**)

Five Year Plans

The idea of planning was fundamental to socialist thinking but it was Lenin's observations of the wartime economies of the Western Powers that led to the adoption of similar measures in Russia during the period of War Communism though of course they went much further and included the elimination of markets and the nationalisation of industries. In agriculture, it included the detested methods of requisition and confiscation of grain crops.

However the NEP did not dismantle the basic structures of State planning organisation introduced after the Revolution. They were: the VSNKh, Supreme Council of the National Economy, established in December 1917; the VTsIK, All-Russian Central Executive Committee; Gosplan, the Committee for a General State Plan established on 22 February 1921.

Under VSNKh were local organisations, called Sovnarkhozes and Glavki, or Central Administrations, who looked after nationalised enterprises. The boundaries of their authority were not always entirely clear and varied with time and circumstances.

The reason for the five year period of the plan was that it fitted quite neatly the cycle of construction for major works, such as power stations, rail links and canals. In agriculture it helped to average out the variations caused by climate.

In the event the plans' length varied according to economic and ideological circumstances and rarely fitted a precise five-year span. Revisions and updating were a normal occurrence.

The Plans

1st: April 1929 The plan called for a 250 per cent increase of investment in the economy. It assumed no crop failures, and a growth in foreign trade and credits. The real situation was quite different. Agriculture was being ruthlessly collectivised, and the kulaks, the most efficient agricultural producers, were being wiped out. This led to the appalling famine of 1933. On the international scene, the Wall Street crash signalled the beginning of world-wide recession. In the circumsances, the achievements of the plan were remarkable, and in many cases the targets, particularly on the industrial front, were substantially exceeded.

2nd: February 1934 This plan called for more realistic growth rates than the first but it still asked for a doubling of industrial production, which was achieved. Agricultural output was well below the target, as were all sections of consumer goods' production. There were some impressive construction achievements: the Magnitogorsk and Stalinsk steel works were built, and the Dnieper Dam was completed.

3rd This plan was prepared in 1937–38 in the period of the Great Purge. It called for an increase in industrial output of more than 90 per cent, but increased defence expenditure and the removal of many of the better managers by the purge left most of the targets unfulfilled. Output was also affected by the Finnish war of 1939–40, and in June 1941 the Nazi invasion put the entire economy on an emergency footing.

4th This covered the years 1945–50 and was therefore largely concerned, initially, with reconstruction of the shattered economy. Huge efforts were made but the results achieved were, by Soviet standards, modest. Industrial production, for instance, using 100 as an index for 1940, was 173 by 1950. Overall production reached pre-war levels for producer goods in 1948 and for consumer goods in 1951. Agricultural production, particularly the grain harvest, did not reach 1940 levels until 1952.

5th The new plan covering 1951–55 was supposed to begin in 1951 but was finally presented to the 19th Party Congress in October 1952. It called for an increase in industrial production of 70 per cent, and large increases in agricultural production, though no provision was made for increases in farm prices. The plan had only been in operation for less than a year when Stalin died.

6th The 1955 plans was prepared with great thoroughness. Nikita Khrushchev who had replaced Stalin as General Secretary had divided Gosplan (State Committee on Planning) into two parts: one for current, the other for long-term planning. The plan, passed by the 20th Party Congress, famous for Khrushchev's denunciation of Stalin, called for large increases in industrial output, including the creation of a third metallurgical base in Kazakhstan and Siberia, for the production of pig iron. However, this plan had been in existence for only a year when it was decided, on 20 December 1956, that a revision was required. This coincided with Khrushchev's battle for survival against his rivals Molotov, Malenkov and Kaganovich.

7th This was essentially a revised 6th, and covered the years of 1959–65. It called for an increase in industrial production of 80 per cent on 1958, which was achieved, but the output of consumer goods was well below the set target, and the grain harvest, planned for 180 million, was less than 120 million tonnes, despite the enormous areas of new planting in the Virgin Lands campaign. In part, this was caused by Khrushchev's confused attempts to reorganize the structure of agriculture, but also by the continuing growth of bureaucracy and muddle.

8th The plan covering the years 1966–70 was adopted by the September 1965 Plenum of the Central Committee. It called for an increase of industrial output over the whole period of 50 per cent, and in agriculture of 21 per cent. During the period of plan the integrated power grid of the USSR was completed.

9th Ratified in 1971, and covering the years 1971–75, it had as its proclaimed main drive the improvement of living standards within the USSR. After only four years it was announced that national income had increased by 24 per cent, industrial output by 33 per cent, and agricultural by 15 per cent. One of the main projects completed during the plan was the Baikal railway line. During this period there was a very large increase in defence spending.

10th This plan covered the period 1976–80 and, partly as a result of high oil prices caused by the OPEC price squeeze, the economy was doing well. Anyway it was enough for Brezhnev to postpone the intended measures of reform which had been planned to increase the efficiency of industry. Industrial output was scheduled to rise by 36 per cent, and that of consumer goods by an unheard of 32 per cent, even agriculture was planned to increase by 24 per cent. The targets were not achieved, and defence spending had increased to some 11 per cent of the GNP by the end of the period.

G

General Army Committee
The central committee after soldiers formed their own committees, or soviets, in February 1917.

Geographic Features
The USSR's territory covers one-sixth of the land surface of the globe – 8.6 million square miles (22.4 million square km).

Occupying one-half of Europe and one-third of Asia and having 11 of the world's 24 time zones, the Soviet Union stretches for 3,000 miles (5,000 km) from north to south, and 6,000 miles (10,000 km) from east to west.

The total length of the USSR's land and sea borders is over 37,000 miles (60,000 km).

Seas The USSR is washed in the north by the Arctic Ocean, with the Barents, White, Kara, Laptev, East Siberian and Chukchi Seas; in the south by the Black and Caspian Seas; in the east by the Pacific Ocean, with the Bering Sea, the Sea of Okhotsk and the Sea of Japan; and in the west by the Baltic Sea.

Name	Area	
	thousand sq miles	sq km
Bering Sea	889	2,304
Sea of Okhotsk	614	1,590
Barents Sea	542	1,405
Sea of Japan	378	978
East Siberian Sea	361	936
Kara Sea	341	883
Laptev Sea	251	650
Chukchi Sea	225	582
Black Sea	159	413
Baltic Sea	149	386
White Sea	35	90
Sea of Azov	15	38

Mountains Stretching for 1,200 miles (2,000 km) from north to south, the Ural mountains separate the European part of the USSR from the Asian. In the south there are the Carpathian and Caucasian mountains, and in the east the Pamirs, Tien Shan, Altai, Sayan, Sikhote-Alin and Kamchatka mountains.

In the Kamchatka Peninsula there are 30 or so active volcanoes. The highest is the Klyuchevskaya Sopka, a cone-shaped mountain over three miles (five km) high.

Name	Location	Height	
		m	ft
Communism Peak	Pamirs	7,495	24,590
Victory Peak	Tien Shan	7,439	24,406
Lenin Peak	Tien Shan	7,134	23,405
Khan-Tengri Peak	Tien Shan	6,995	22,949
Revolution Peak	Pamirs	6,974	22,880
Moscow Peak	Pamirs	6,785	22,260
Karl Marx Peak	Pamirs	6,726	22,067
Frunze Peak	Pamirs	5,790	18,996
Mount Elbrus	Greater Caucasus	5,642	18,510
Mount Kazbek	Greater Caucasus	5,033	16,512

Rivers There are more than 100,000 large rivers in the USSR. The main rivers in the European part have their sources in the middle of the East European Plain and flow in different directions to seas. The Dnieper empties into the Black Sea; the Don into the Sea of Azov; the Western Dvina into the Baltic Sea; the Northern Dvina into the White Sea, and the Pechora into the Barents Sea.

Europe's biggest river, the Volga, flows into the Caspian Sea. This is the main water transport artery of the USSR. Almost half of all cargo carried by river is transported along the Volga and its tributaries.

The main Siberian rivers – the Ob, the Yenisei and the Lena – flow from south to north.

The Amur in the Far East flows into the Pacific Ocean.

Central Asian rivers, the largest of which are the Amu Darya and Syr Darya, do not reach the open sea.

Name	Length	
	miles	km
Ob*	3,360	5,410
Amur*	2,742	4,416
Lena	2,732	4,400
Yenisei*	2,541	4,092
Volga	2,193	3,531
Syr Darya*	1,857	2,991
Amu Darya*	1,615	2,600
Kolyma	1,560	2,513
Ural	1,508	2,428
Dnieper	1,367	2,201

* With tributaries.

Lakes The USSR has about three million lakes with an area of more than one-third of a square mile (one square km).

The biggest portion of the Caspian Sea, the world's largest lake, lies in the USSR.

There are big lakes – the Aral Sea and the Balkhash – in the semi-desert and desert zone of the south. In the north-west are Lakes Ladoga, Onega, Peipus and Ilman.

In the mountainous regions of the country, where rocks prevented the flow of rivers or where there were hollows, mountain lakes came into being. The biggest is Lake Baikal. It is the world's deepest freshwater lake – 5,250 feet (1,600 m). Although in area Lake Baikal is much smaller than the Baltic Sea, the volume of its water exceeds that of the latter. Other big mountain lakes are Issyk-Kul in Kirghizia and Sevan in Armenia.

About a thousand artificial reservoirs have been formed in the country, among them are the Bratsk and Irkutsk on the Angara River, the Krasnoyarsk on the Yenisei River, the Kuibyshev and Volgograd on the Volga River, and the Bukhtarma on the Irtysh River.

Name	Area	
	sq miles	sq km
Caspian Sea	143,206	371,000
Aral Sea	25,476	66,000
Lake Baikal	12,159	31,500
Lake Ladoga	7,102	18,400
Lake Balkhash	7,025	18,200
Lake Onega	3,709	9,610
Lake Issyk-Kul	2,424	6,280

Climate Climate of the country is varied. The northern shores, washed by the Arctic Ocean, have a severe Arctic climate. In the south, on the southern coast of the Crimea and in the Central Asian valleys, the climate is dry subtropical, and humid subtropical along the Caucasian Black Sea coast. A moderate continental climate prevails on the greater portion of the country's territory.

The mean temperature in January in the west is slightly below 0°C (32°F) and in the Lena River basin in Eastern Siberia it is −40°C (−40°F). The Northern Hemisphere's Pole of Cole is located near the settlement of Oimyakon on Yakutia (North-Eastern Siberia), where the mean temperature in January is −50°C (−58°F), but can go down to as far as −72°C (−98°F). In Central Asia it is hot and dry. The mean temperature in July in its plains is 30°C (86°F), and rises to 50°C (122°F).

Minerals The USSR ranks first in the world in deposits of coal, iron ores, manganese, natural gas, apatites and asbestos.

The prospected iron ore deposits exceed 40 per cent of the world's total. The greater part is located in the Krivoi Rog and Kursk basins in the European part of the Soviet Union. Rich iron ore deposits are concentrated in the Urals, in Kazakhstan and in Eastern Siberia.

Manganese ores lie mainly in Georgia and in the Ukraine; non-ferrous metal ores in Kazakhstan and in the Urals.

The Soviet Union possesses more than half the world's deposits of phosphorites and two-thirds of potassium salts. The Ural mountains are rich in emeralds, rubies, malachite, jasper and other precious and semi-precious stones. Gold and diamonds are also mined in the country.

The USSR also possesses considerable **fuel resources**. The main deposits of oil and natural gas are situated in Western Siberia, along the Volga, and in the Urals, the Caucasus and Central Asia. Coal deposits are concentrated in the Ukraine, Kazakhstan, Western Siberia and Yakutia, and combustible shales in the country's western regions.

Georgian Soviet Socialist Republic

Population: 5,298,000 (69% Georgian, 5% Azerbaijani, 7% Russian)
Area: 26,911 sq miles (69,718 sq km)   Capital: Tbilisi (population: 1,211,000)
The Georgian SSR includes:
Abkhaz ASSR, population, 536,000; area 3,320 sq miles (8,600 sq km); capital Sukhumi;
Adzhar Autonomous SSR, population 386,000; area 1,158 sq miles (3,000 sq km); capital Batumi;
South Ossetian Autonomous Region, population 99,000; area 1,505 sq miles (3,900 sq km); capital Tskhinvali.
Georgian nationalism developed strongly in the nineteenth century. Among Georgian political groups, the so-called Third Group (Mesami Dasi), the first of the Marxist radical groups, was formed in 1892, and joined by the young Stalin. Georgian politics in the early twentieth century was dominated by the Social Democrats, largely Menshevik.

In 1917, Menshevik revolutionaries proclaimed a republic, though first Turkish and then German troops moved in, prompting the Western Allies to intervene. After the Treaty of Brest-Litovsk, the Georgian Soviet Democratic Republic was proclaimed on 26 May 1918, and recognised by Germany, Turkey and by the Moscow Soviet in August; 22 nations recognised independent Georgia. A treaty was signed between the Soviet Union and Georgia in May 1920 agreeing on the borders between the countries; then on 25 February 1921, the Red Army, headed by Ordzhonikidze, marched in and Georgia became a Soviet Socialist Republic. It was joined to the Transcaucasian Federation in 1922, until that was abolished in 1936, when Georgia became one of the USSR's constituent republics.

Georgians have played a leading role in the Soviet Union, Stalin, Ordzhonikidze and Beria being particularly famous. After Stalin's death, the Party was purged and Vasily Mzhavanadze took over as Party Secretary until he was removed and replaced by the head of Georgian Internal Security, Eduard Shevardnadze in 1972. A further purge took place, aimed at curbing Georgia's reputation for unorthodox free-wheeling trading methods throughout the Soviet Union. The February–April 1973 meeting of the Georgian Communist Party was devoted to exposing 'nationalist deviations': there had been anti-Russian riots in 1956 and in 1978 there were further demonstrations against the official use of Russian as a language equal to Georgian.

The Georgian Church was incorporated into the Russian Orthodox Church when Georgia was taken into the Empire, but it declared its independence in 1917, although the Orthodox Church would not recognise this until 1943.

Georgian language (a distinct language of the Caucasus) and culture have retained independence and vigour and it has its own tradition of poetry, music and dance.

Georgia, with a large Russian population, is not as fervently nationalist as other republics, partly because of its fear of its neighbours Armenia and Azerbaijan. However, in common with other Soviet republics, there have been nationalist movements. A recent one is called 'Ilya Chavchavadze' (after a nineteenth-century poet and patriot, a Saint of the Georgian Orthodox Church). In 1989 a 'Popular Front' put forward candidates for the People's Congress; its radical leader, Zviad Gamsakhuria, having previously been jailed for his views on nationalism. The Rustaveli Society is a further nationalist group represented in the Congress.

In November 1988 a 200,000-strong rally insisted on an end to 'russification' and called for Georgia's withdrawal from the Soviet Union. On 25 February 1989 (on its 'Independence Day') a meeting of 15,000 in Tbilisi demanded independence for Georgia. More serious events began in April. In Sukhumi, the Abkhazi capital, there were riots as Abkhazis called for secession from Georgia and the establishment of an Abkhazian republic within the USSR. Then, on 9 April, after demonstrations in Tbilisi by about 10,000 calling for greater Georgian autonomy, 19 Georgians, including 12 women, were killed and hundreds injured by Soviet troops imposing order on demonstrators in the city. It was admitted that tear gas and CS gas were used, but video film showed troops moving into the gas and hitting out with shovels and clubs. As a result, Shevardnadze flew to Tbilisi, a curfew was imposed and arrests of over 400 people were made.

In July there were more ethnic clashes between Georgians and Abkhazians, Georgians calling for the abolition of the Abkhazi region and its absorption into Georgia. In Sukhumi, riots between Abkhazians and Georgians broke out over quarrels about the quota of each group to be given admission to a proposed new university there, and 16 people were killed. Similarly, in the Ossetian Region there have been demonstrations, some in favour of leaving Georgia and joining with the North Ossetians in the RSFSR.

German Democratic Republic (GDR)

Population: 16,664,000

Area: 41,768 sq miles (108,207 sq km)　　　Capital: East Berlin

The Allies agreed on occupation zones of conquered Germany in 1945. With the realignment of the Polish frontiers, absorbing what had been part of Prussia, the Soviet Zone took in the land to the west of the River Oder and included Berlin, controlled by all the Allies. West Germany grew out of the American, British and French Zones, while the GDR was established in 1949 from the Soviet Zone. Berlin became a contentious issue and the attempt in 1948–49 to blockade it from the West led to the massive Berlin Airlift. The next crisis came when the Soviet Union sought to have the Western Zones of Berlin incorporated in the demilitarised free city: no agreement was reached and in 1961 the Western Zones were sealed off when Soviet and East German troops put up the Berlin Wall around them. This, with stricter border controls between the two Germanies, made the Iron Curtain concept a reality.

Effective political power lay with the communist Socialist Unity Party (SED), controlling a national front of other parties which have withered since 1949, leaving the GDR as a one-party state. The GDR has been the most economically successful of the Eastern bloc countries, although in common with others in the bloc, there have been constant shortages of consumer goods.

One reason for the strict border controls has been to prevent a drain of skilled workers from the GDR to the West. However, on 2 May, 1989, Hungary, which with Poland was in the forefront of the pro-democracy movement in Eastern Europe, tore down the Iron Curtain on its borders with Austria and allowed East German workers to cross into Austria and thence to the West. Honecker's government protested strongly but to no avail and finally a ban was imposed forbidding travel into Hungary.

By now, more general protest meetings, inspired by the movements for perestroika and glasnost in the Soviet Union and in Poland, had started, centred on the city of Leipzig. A political movement linked to the evangelical church, New Forum, came into existence, while a new exodus of citizens began through the West German Embassy in Prague. The government reacted by ordering the border to be closed. On 9 October there were mass demonstrations leading to arrests and beatings by the hated security police, the Stasi. This led to further demonstrations and on 18 October Erich Honecker was replaced by Egon Krenz (Honecker, accused of corruption, was to be tried for high treason when his health permitted). On 31 October the Czech border was reopened, and on 9 November the newly appointed Politburo declared that the Berlin Wall, the hated symbol of division, would be opened and free passage would be allowed for all East Berliners. Much of the wall has now been demolished and pieces are being sold off as souvenirs.

Egon Krenz was replaced by Hans Modrow, a man more acceptable to the people for being out of favour with Honecker. German reunification is the biggest single issue in Europe at the moment. The Alliance For Germany, a party associated with the West German Christian Democrats, had a clear victory in the March elections. For events since March 1990 see the Chronology.

Germans in the USSR

German settler-farmers of the seventeenth century became a recognised part of Russian society. They were grouped in an autonomous republic on the lower Volga from 1924 until 1941, when they were rounded up as potential traitors and sent east, to Kazakhstan and Siberia. There are now estimated to be 1,800,000 people described as German in the Soviet Union, over half in Kazakhstan, with other substantial groups in Kirghizia and Tajikistan. There is no provision for German-language education, and the proportion of German speakers has been on the decline for years. However an 'All-Union Society of Germans' has called for a rebirth of the German Autonomous Republic, claiming that emigration to West Germany would otherwise increase. In 1988 74,000 left the Soviet Union (most to West Germany which has a constitutional requirement to accept them).

Glasnost

The practice of 'openness' and honesty about official matters and Soviet history, associated with perestroika in the 1980s.

Glaviskusstvo

The Central Directorate for Artistic Affairs.

Glavlit

The Soviet Censorship Office established in 1922: all publications were passed through this body for approval until the advent of glasnost.

Gorkom
Gorodskoy Komitet, the Party committee of a town or city.

Gosagroprom
The All-Union Ministry of Agriculture.

Gosbank
The State bank.

Gosizdat
The State publishing house.

Goskino
The State cinema industry.

Gosplan
The State Planning Commission, founded on 22 February 1921, which produced the first Five Year Plan. From then on Gosplan was directly controlled by the Party. (See also **Five Year Plans**)

GPU see **Political Police**.

Great Purge see **Yezhovshchina** and **Purges**.

GRU
The Intelligence Department of the Military General Staff. (See also **Political Police** and **Espionage**)

Gubernia
A Tsarist administrative territory, a province. The term was replaced by oblast or kray in 1929.

Gulag
The Chief Administration of Labour Camps, a function of the KGB whose name became familiar through Solzhenitsyn. (See also **Camps**)

GUM
The Gosudarstvenny Universalny Magazin, the large department store in Red Square, Moscow.

Head of State see **President**.

Helsinki Accord
The Human Rights Final Agreement signed in Helsinki in 1975.

Helsinki Groups
Formed in 1976 and 1977 in several parts of the USSR to monitor the effects of the Helsinki Accord, often to further the rights of would-be emigrants, Germans, Jews and, to a lesser extent, Armenians, and to urge disarmament. They operated through small meetings and the distribution of samizdats. The groups were subjected to close police surveillance and their members often imprisoned, put under restriction orders or subjected to psychiatric treatment. (See also **Dissidents**)

Hetman see **Ataman**, and **Cossacks**.

Hungary
Population: 10,658,000   Area: 35,919 sq miles (93,030 sq km)   Capital: Budapest
After World War I there was a short-lived communist regime set up by Bela Kun, who later died in the Soviet purges. This was followed by a right-wing regime under Admiral Horthy, who allied himself with Nazi Germany. Hungary was occupied by the German army in March 1944 and liberated by the Red Army in April 1945. In October 1945 free elections were held in which the communists, led by Rakosi, only obtained 17 per cent of the votes. The largest party, the Smallholders' Party under Bela Kovacs, was soon put under attack by the communists who arrested him on trumped-up charges. By June 1948 Rakosi and his Soviet masters had imposed a one-party system on the country. Agriculture was gradually collectivised and most of industry nationalised.

In 1953, under Khrushchev's influence, Rakosi was replaced by Imre Nagy, who proceeded to introduce more liberal economic and social measures. In early 1955 Rakosi returned to power and removed Nagy from the Party and reimposed strict controls. This led to a popular uprising in October 1956 during which some of the hated Secret Police (AVH) were lynched. Soviet troops intervened and there was fierce fighting; tanks and armoured personnel carriers against lightly armed freedom fighters. The outcome was never in doubt. Imry Nagy was arrested by a trick, tried and executed in June 1958. He has since been rehabilitated and indeed given a proper burial.

In November 1956 Janos Kádár was appointed Party leader and from 1962 onwards instituted social and economic reforms. Since 1968 the 'New Economic Mechanism' has allowed more decentralised decision making than other Eastern bloc countries, restoring a degree of capitalism into small enterprises, such as bars, cafés, small holdings.

Perestroika reached Hungary in November 1988 when the Communist Party, without any massive pressure from outside, announced that it planned to move to a multi-party system. Janos Kádár had already been removed from office and replaced by Karoly Grosz. In the spring of 1989 the Party, which was shedding confidence as a result of losing arguments with reforming elements, was prepared to admit that it might well lose power.

In the elections in 1945 the communists got only 17 per cent of the vote, compared to the Smallholders' 57 per cent. In the elections in March 1990, the leading contenders for power were the Alliance of Free Democrats and the Democratic Forum. Both parties are in favour of a market-type economy, but the Free Democrats want to move more quickly in this direction. For the outcome and subsequent events see the Chronology.

I

Industry

Before the Revolution Russia has always been a country rich in natural resources, coal, iron, gold and oil. Under Witte, the Minister of Finance from 1892–1904, great strides were made in exploiting them in order to build an industrial base. There was direct State investment in the railway network and encouragement for foreign investment in mining, chemicals and textiles, while Russian industry was protected by high tariff walls. The growth of the economy under Witte was over 5 per cent per annum and by 1913 Russia was the fifth largest industrial producer in the world.

The outbreak of war in 1914 caused almost total dislocation of the economy and this, with military defeat, produced the revolutionary situation which had first surfaced in 1905 and was then to be exploited by Lenin and the Bolsheviks.

Following the October 1917 Revolution, an immediate but confused policy of nationalisation was embarked upon which included the land, larger factories and the banks. In December, the Supreme Economic Council (VSNKh) was created. In 1918 Civil War broke out.

War Communism The newly established government, fighting for its life, brought in a series of draconian measures which came to be known as War Communism. They included total nationalisation of industry, the outlawing of trade and the virtual exclusion of money from the economy. Industrial production fell by 70 per cent, coal production by nearly 80 per cent and agriculture by 40 per cent. There was a serious famine. Grain was seized from the peasants by force and there were riots in the countryside and the towns. The climax was a mutiny by the sailors of Kronstadt in March 1921. The government had to act to save the Revolution.

The New Economic Policy (NEP) Despite the nationalisation of all factories employing more than five people and the banning of private trade, the urban population obtained as much as 70 per cent of grain, and as much as 66 per cent of all consumer goods through private channels at this time.

In February 1921, at the 10th Party Congress, and partly in response to the Kronstadt rebellion, measures were introduced to substitute taxes for requisitions of grain, while other harsh measures taken against the peasants under War Communism were dropped. The number of collective farms declined quite sharply and, shortly after, the reintroduction of private trading and manufacturing on a small scale was begun.

Monetary reforms were introduced, including a new unit of currency, the chervonets, to deal with the collapse of the rouble, but it was not until 1923 that the budget was balanced. The inheritance of private property was allowed in order to encourage business people to invest rather than spending their profits. In October 1921 Lenin said 'By attempting to go straight to Communism we suffered an economic defeat by the spring of 1921 worse than any defeat at the hands of Kolchak, Denikin and Pilsudski.' Though at other times he claimed that War Communism was simply a policy produced by an emergency situation.

Over the next two years private trade and manufacturing were actively encouraged, and private credit organisations were allowed to exist. Lenin talked of using the NEP and its active constituents, the Nepmen, as they were called, to help the growth of socialism by teaching 'communists how to become business men'.

On ideological and emotional grounds this was a dangerous policy and, as can be seen in the cartoons of the time, Nepman was portrayed as greedy, vulgar and, ominously, as Jewish. They were blamed for rising prices and attacked as capitalist leeches.

After Lenin's death in January 1924, there was a sudden shift in policy. The Nepman's life style, often lavish and accompanied by the opening of casinos, race tracks, expensive food shops and hotels, made many Bolsheviks wonder what the Revolution had been for. Many businesses were closed, the banks reduced credit to the private sector from 42 million roubles to 17 million in one year and swingeing increases in taxation indicated a general feeling of hostility to the NEP.

But in 1925 the NEP became, at least in part, a marker in the power struggle within the Party leadership. The left wing, led by Trotsky, Zinoviev and Kamenev, was opposed to a right wing led by Bukharin, Rykov and Tomsky, with whom Stalin's group had formed a temporary alliance. The left were totally opposed to NEP and proclaimed that it was the path back to capitalism. Bukharin and the right were just as committed to communist doctrines but believed that gradualism was necessary. 'Grow rich with the peasant' was his battle cry. Stalin accepted Bukharin's ideas in order to defeat the left.

Meanwhile, with Bukharin's enthusiastic support, NEP was once again in favour and 1925 saw the full flowering of the policies. Taxes were reduced once more, and bank credits were increased by 200 per cent during the year.

Industrial output 1913–25

Product	1913	1921	1925	1925 as % of 1913
Coal[1]	29.1	9.5	16.5	57
Oil[1]	9.2	3.8	7.1	77
Peat[1]	1.7	2.0	2.7	159
Pig iron[1]	4.2	0.1	1.3	31
Steel[1]	4.2	0.2	1.9	45
Rolled steel[1]	3.5	0.2	1.4	40
Cement[1]	1.5	0.06	0.9	60
Paper[1]	0.2	–	0.2	107
Sugar[1]	1.3	0.05	1.1	85
Fish[1]	1.0	0.3	0.7	70
Electricity[2]	1,975	520	2,925	150

1. Million tonnes 2. Million kWh
Adapted from Munting, *The Economic Development of the USSR* (1982)

This brief but brilliant period was already being threatened by Stalin's speeches at the 15th Party Congress in December 1927, after the final defeat of the left, in which he declared that the right underestimated the dangers of the NEP to the State.

The poor grain collections of that year led Stalin to re-introduce War Communism methods of grain collection in Siberia. From then on attacks on Nepmen were stepped up. Businesses were closed down. They were forbidden to hold public office and many were driven from State housing. Shock brigades were formed to seize goods from any suspected of making money by illegal trading activities and even street traders were driven from the streets again.

The attack on the 'new bourgeoisie' heralded by Stalin's speeches at the 15th Party Congress were almost complete and in December 1929 the Right Deviationists made a public confession of their errors.

An American visitor to Moscow in December 1929 recorded 'On the streets the shops seemed to have disappeared. Gone was the open market. Gone were the Nepmen'.

In March 1930 Stalin's article 'Dizzy with Success' signalled the end of the whirl-wind campaign against NEP and reined in the extreme reaction of those Party officials who were closing street markets all over the USSR. But, thenceforward, private trade was confined to the margins of the economy.

The 1st and 2nd Five Year Plans

	1st Five Year Plan 1929		2nd Five Year Plan 1934		
	plan	outcome	plan	revised plan	outcome
National income[1]	24.4	49.7	45.5	100.2	96.3
Gross industrial production[2]					
industrial goods	6.0	18.1	23.1	45.5	55.2
consumer goods	12.3	25.1	20.2	47.2	40.3
Workers in State employment (millions)	11.3	15.8	22.9	28.9	27.0

[1] and [2] thousand million roubles at 1926–27 prices
Adapted from Munting, *The Economic Development of the USSR* (1982)

1934–39 The 2nd Five Year Plan, approved in January 1934, called for a 250 per cent increase in investment over the first and 52 per cent of this was to be in industry. This enormous investment in industry meant that by 1937 nearly 80 per cent of industrial production was taking place in either new or completely refurbished factories and workshops. Growth was dependent on a huge increase in the input of both labour and capital, not on the more efficient use of resources.

Because of the huge new labour force recruited from agriculture and the shortage of consumer goods, there was a considerable degree of inflation. This was not absorbed by income tax – only 3.5 per cent at the time – but by the sale of State bonds to the public. They paid 10 per cent interest but had no redemption date. Businesses paid a turnover tax, which was the main source of State income, and a profits tax.

World War II The 3rd Five Year Plan was affected both by the Great Purge of 1937 and also by war preparations. Defence expenditure jumped from 3.5 per cent of the budget in 1933 to 18.6 in 1937. Although Soviet defences were unprepared for the German assault in 1941, there had been a great deal of preparation for conflict. Tractor factories had been built with an eye to conversion to tank production, and some industrial complexes had been moved for strategic advantage, to Stalingrad for example. A comparison between Soviet and German wartime production demonstrates that although German industrial production was considerably higher than in the USSR, the number of weapons manufactured – tanks, military aircraft and guns – was considerably less. The USSR, like the UK, was far more committed to a total war economy. The effects of the war were shattering on the economy, towns and villages were destroyed on a massive scale, more than half the steel-making capacity was lost, also 50 per cent of electrical generating and 60 per cent of coal output. In addition, there had been a huge loss of population, something like 20 million dead, which represented a sizeable proportion of the industrial and agricultural work force.

Post-War reconstruction The 4th Five Year Plan, 1946–50, aimed at an increase of industrial output of nearly 50 per cent, seeking to achieve in five years the increase planned for ten before the war. In general, targets were met except in consumer goods. Despite the state of Russia's economy, Stalin would not accept the offer of Marshall Aid from America and instead insisted on large-scale reparations from the defeated Germany and its allies, including those parts of Europe under its domination. Rationing was ended in December 1947 and subsidies to heavy industry in 1948. To benefit the consumer there was a policy of price reduction in industry. An attempt to emphasise the importance of the consumer at the expense of heavy industry was brought to a halt when Voznesensky, the head of Gosplan, was tried and executed for suggesting just this.

The Khrushchev Reforms When Stalin died in 1953, Khrushchev showed interest in increasing the supply of consumer goods but was more concerned, because of his background, in the agricultural sector.

Economic indicators 1950–64

	1950	1958	1963	1964
National income (index)	100	229	311	339
Gross industrial production				
industrial goods	100	263	487	475
consumer goods	100	225	320	332

Adapted from Munting, *The Economic Development of the USSR* (1982)

Nevertheless, between 1953 and 1958 there was an increase in the GNP of 6.7 per cent. In 1957 Khrushchev made a dramatic industrial reform with the introduction of regional economic councils, or Sovnarkhozes, which were to take the place of the ministries. It was also decided to abandon the 6th Five Year Plan and introduce a Seven Year Plan, starting in 1959. The targets were optimistic and Khrushchev made a confident prediction that the economy would overtake the UK and West Germany by 1965 and the USA by 1970. In fact, although industrial production was on target, consumer goods were well below and agriculture achieved a 15 per cent rather than a 70 per cent increase. At the same time, the USSR was funding military expenditure at 12 per cent of GNP and a space programme whose achievements, although impressive, were eating up valuable resources. In 1963 the long-term planning body, VSNKh, reappeared, but after Khrushchev's downfall in the following year, the Sovnarkhozes were closed down and the ministries were restored to their old function.

The Brezhnev era Under Brezhnev, as Party Secretary with Kosygin as Prime Minister, reforms were introduced which were intended to give more autonomy to industry and instil a more commercial attitude, as many be seen from the accompanying table.

Economic indicators 1965–75, 8th and 9th Five Year Plans

	1970 (1965 = 100)		1975 (1970 = 100)	
	Plan	Real	Plan	Real
National income	140	141	138.6	127.5
Gross industrial production				
industrial goods	149–152	151	146.3	145.4
consumer goods	143–146	149	148.6	137.4
Agricultural production	125	121.4	121.7	101.8
Labour productivity				
industry	130	132	138.8	133.8
construction	125	122	137	128.5
collective farms	–	136	138	107
State farms	–	138	138	102
Real income per capita	130	133	130.8	123.9

Adapted from Munting, *The Economic Development of the USSR* (1982)

Although the 8th Plan met most of its targets, bar agriculture and construction, the 9th was well below planned output, particularly serious in that for the first time in the history of the USSR consumer goods were given a higher priority than producer goods. Despite the reforms, the bureaucracy were reluctant to give up their control of the economy.

Under both the 9th and 10th Five Year Plans, 1970–80, there was a considerable emphasis on investing in Siberian resources, which in turn led to further investment in infrastructure, gas-pipe lines, roads and railways. The Soviet Union is one of the very few countries currently investing heavily in rail transport. Oil has become more important than coal as an energy source but the actual output of both has declined. There is a large nuclear power programme, though how viable this will prove after the Chernobyl disaster is unpredictable. Despite the investment in Siberia and the east, the major industrial power is still in the west, in the Ukraine and, significantly now for the USSR, in the Baltic states. Estonia is the most industrially developed republic in the USSR.

To tackle the demand for consumer goods, deals have been made with companies in the west, like the Fiat plant at Togliattigrad which was producing more than a million private cars a year in 1978. The chemical industry, also in collaboration with Western companies, has vastly expanded, more than six times between 1960 and 1980.

Perestroika and plans for the future In his book *Perestroika*, Mikhail Gorbachev says 'Many things are unusual in our country now: self financed factories and plants, encouragement of individual enterprises in small scale production and trade, and closure of non-paying plants and factories operating at a loss.' This represents far more than a continuation of the changes introduced under Brezhnev: it is more reminiscent of the policies introduced under Lenin's NEP programme of the 1920s. It is a high-risk economic strategy and, although initially greeted with huge enthusiasm, it has now run into difficulties. Promises of improved conditions for groups of workers, miners and others, have not been kept and there have been extensive strikes. Troubles with the nationalities have caused disruption in the rail system leading to shortages at the workplace and in the shops. More important, the supply of consumer goods seems to be getting worse rather than better. A recent statement in the Congress of Deputies announced a budget deficit of 120 billion roubles. The Soviet Union has enormous resources but there must be some danger that the relaxation of the old controls may plunge its economy into the same state as some of the Third World countries, such as Brazil.

In 1990 the system of taxes will be altered to fit the changes in society; a powerful central bank will begin operation and businesses which are habitually loss-making will be forced out. In the next two years, the large loss-making Kolkhozes will be closed and private farms encouraged in their stead. During this period, the foreign exchange currency auction will be well-established, as will commodity auctions and the foundations of the first Soviet Stock Exchange.

By 1995, if the plans progress, there should be a market regulated by interest rates and credit controls and there could be a partially convertible rouble. There would then be a balanced consumer market with true competition. Eventually, the country may have the fruits of perestroika.

International

The international association of socialist parties founded to co-ordinate their policies. The First International was founded by Marx in 1864; the Second International was established in 1889. The Third or Communist International split from this and became the Moscow-centred Comintern, while the Second continued for a few years as an association of moderate socialist parties. In 1936 a number of small radical parties formed, under Trotsky in exile, a Fourth International which never amounted to an effective body outside its committees.

The International is celebrated in the song often heard at socialist gatherings, the *Internationale*.

International Trade

Stalin's 'Socialism in One Country' policy effectively meant that the USSR was to rely on its internal market to achieve its economic aims. There has always been a resistance to becoming involved in the international market-place, subject as it is to unpredictable forces. This was increased after World War II by the extension of the Russian hegemony into Eastern Europe and formalised by the founding of Comecon in 1949. Essentially a free trade area, though tilted quite strongly in favour of the USSR, it has the major advantage of trading within the entirely artificial 'credit rouble' currency area.

The main exports to the West are primary products, oil and ores, though there is a growing trade in industrial products, such as the Lada car, and scientific instruments. The main imports consist of the sophisticated technological products not available in the USSR and needed to develop its own industry. Food, particularly grain, is also imported when the harvests are poor. In general, the overall position is not dissimilar to what it was in the time of the Tsars, though under the new policy of glasnost a trade deficit of 50 billion roubles was recently revealed.

Intervention

The intervention of the Allied forces in the Russian Civil War, 1918–20 or 1925 in the east. (See also **Civil War**)

The Western Allies first landed at Murmansk, Archangel, Odessa and Batum to secure communications with the anti-Bolshevik governments and to dislodge the Germans and the Turks from their gains as a result of the collapse of Russian armies and the Treaty of Brest-Litovsk.

Britain sent 40,000 troops, to the northern ports, the Caspian Sea and some along the Trans-Siberian railway. They conducted a blockade of Russia from October 1919 to January 1920 and provided supplies to Denikin, including some tanks.

France had 30,000 troops, mainly based at Odessa, concentrating on the Crimea and southern Ukraine. A military mission helped the Poles against the Soviet Russians.

Greece had 30,000 men in areas of Turkish control. This led to war with Turkey. Under Kemal Atatürk's revived nationalism, the Greeks suffered severe defeats.

The USA provided some 10,000 soldiers who worked beside British and Japanese forces.

Japan, keen on exploiting the collapse of Tsarist Russia, had 60,000 troops in the Maritime Province until 1922 and on Sakhalin Island until 1925.

Iron Curtain

A phrase used by Winston Churchill in a speech at Fulton, USA, on 5 March 1946, to describe the political and military barrier dividing East and West Europe: 'From Stettin on the Baltic to Trieste on the Adriatic, an iron curtain has descended across Europe.' Earlier, in 1945, Churchill had referred to an 'iron fence' being put about Bucharest by the Soviets. (See also **Cold War**)

J

Jews in the Soviet Union

The Jews of the USSR are a nationality without a home republic. They have settled in eastern Europe since before the first century AD. In the seventh and eighth centuries they settled among the Turkic Khazars between the Black and Caspian Seas on the trade routes from the East to Byzantium, so successfully that the Khazars adopted the Jewish faith. In the fourteenth century Jews settled widely in Poland, moving into Lithuania and the Ukraine, their skills as craftsmen and traders being welcomed. However, often forbidden to own land, they became associated with the ruling classes as their financiers and tax-collectors, and correspondingly hated. In the mid-seventeenth century Cossack and Muscovite insurgents killed hundreds of thousands of Jews as an expression of their hatred of oppression by their rulers.

The fortunes of the Jewish people in Russia see-sawed through the nineteenth century, moving between encouragement and suppression. A period of officially organised persecution started with the assassination of Tsar Alexander II in 1871 and continued until 1917. Brutal pogroms became an accepted part of their life and drove many Jews into revolutionary activities and many into emigration to western Europe, America and Palestine. Pogroms were not only officially encouraged, but through the so-called Black Hundreds officially carried out.

In 1917 many of the revolutionary leaders were Jewish, some experienced in conspiracy through the Bund and some trained in radical thinking by their alienation from bourgeois society. They included Martov, the Menshevik leader, Trotsky, Sverdlov, Kaganovich, Radek, Zinoviev and Kamenev. In the course of the Civil War more massacres took place as Ukrainian nationalists, Cossacks and others took advantage of the situation to revenge themselves. The Bolshevik regime, too, found that Jews could be an enemy, for many were properous capitalists. The propagada against exploiters of the NEP often depicted the villainous Nepmen with grotesquely 'Semitic' features. Stalin undoubtedly employed anti-Semitic tactics in his campaigns against Trotsky and then against Zinoviev and Kamenev.

In 1928 it was announced that a territory would be set aside for Jews in the Far East and a Jewish Autonomous Province was proclaimed in May 1934. Few settled there, but the Jewish Centre of Birobidzhan remains as an autonomous region in the RSFSR.

There are several Jewish communities in the USSR. The best known are the Ashkenazi Jews living in the Baltic states, Belorussia, Ukraine and Moldavia and Russia; these are the people who suffered directly from the anti-Semitism of the Nazis and of the later anti-Zionist campaigns; many are actively religious and Zionist and many were the early Bund members and socialists. The Oriental Jewish communities are the long-standing groups of Georgia (some 50,000), Bokhara (about 100,000 Persian-speakers who settled centuries ago along the 'silk road' from China to the West), and the Mountain Jews of Daghestan in the Caucasus (some 20,000 speaking a Persian dialect called Tat). Jews total between two and three million on a broad count, but officially there are 1,800,000 in the Soviet Union.

The synagogue was the centre of Jewish life, but after the decree of 23 January 1918 the soviets began closing them and suppressing Jewish culture. There was a further campaign in 1927–28 and the Jewish Commissar for Foreign Affairs was removed by Stalin during his dealings with Nazi Germany in 1939.

The Jewish people fought willingly and well for the Soviet Union in the 1941–45 war. On the other hand, in the occupied areas of the Ukraine, Belorussia, the Baltic states and in the RSFSR, Jews were the target of Nazi extermination teams, often abetted by anti-Soviet local inhabitants who reverted easily to anti-Semitism. One of the great tragedies of the war was the failure of the Soviet authorities to realise the intensity of Nazi anti-Semitism and to evacuate or at least to warn the Jews of their danger. The mass killing of Jews in Kiev was the subject of Yevtushenko's poem *Babi Yar* (1962). In the German-occupied areas all synagogues were destroyed and few rebuilt after liberation.

The post-war era saw a new wave of anti-Semitism. Although during the war Jewish citizens had been encouraged to maintain a high profile as evidence of patriotism, Stalin saw their fund-raising ability from America as evidence of the infiltration of American anti-Soviet ideas. In 1948 the famous actor and leading member of the Jewish Anti-Fascist Committee, Solomon Mikhoels, who had had great success in fund-raising, was killed in a traffic accident arranged by the KGB, possibly on the instructions of Zhdanov. The peak of Stalin's pathological fear of Jews came with the 'Doctors' Plot' in 1953, exposed only by Stalin's death. After that, it seemed that life for Jews in the Soviet Union might become secure.

On 12 February 1989 the first Jewish Cultural Centre was opened in the presence of Edgar Bronfman, President of the World Jewish Council, and Elie Wiesel, the 1986 Nobel Peace Prize winner. The centre is dedicated to Solomon Mikhoels.

The number of synagogues has been variously reported from 100 to as few as 60. Official Soviet figures put the numbers who attend synagogues as very low (and point out that in general religious attendance is higher in rural areas and that 98 per cent of Jews are city dwellers). However in Tbilisi, Georgia, in the mountains of the Caucasus and in Bokhara, Uzbekistan, synagogue attendance is admitted to reach 20 per cent of the registered Jewish population. Soviet law and order demands that every 'Church' have a head, so the rabbi of the Moscow synagogue is usually quoted as the official voice of the Jewish religion.

While Soviet relations with the state of Israel were fairly good until June 1967, the Six-Day War altered matters. Soviet friendship with the Arab Middle East produced official hostility to Zionism and in 1968 the issue of visas for Soviet Jews wishing to go to Israel began to be restricted. Jews organised demonstrations and sit-ins, circulated appeals within and outside the USSR, especially to the USA, and provided a stream of information to the foreign Press. To counter this, the KGB harassed, suppressed or arrested protesting groups. Harsh penalties were imposed on a group that attempted to hijack a plane in 1970.

Emigration has been at an average of 50,000 a year, particularly reducing the surviving Baltic Jews and the Georgians. After 1970 the numbers were cut and in 1987 about 8,000 emigrated, with an increase in 1988 to nearly 20,000. A core of 9,000 remains with permits refused year after year on the grounds that they have knowledge of State secrets. The *causes célèbres* have been of the intellectuals from the old Russian communities.

A paradox has often been that some applicants for visas to emigrate to Israel have little feeling for Zionism, but strong feelings for the freedom of Western democracy. Also, emigration itself can lead to terrible frustration: working to build Israel is not the same as enjoying the fruits of American democracy. (See also **Dissidents**)

July Days

On 3 July 1917 soldiers, sailors from Kronstadt and workers, in all over 30,000, demonstrated in Petrograd against the war, low wages and to show their detestation of the Provisional Government. They had been called out by activists of the Petrograd Soviet to overthrow it with the slogan 'All Power to the Soviets'. The Bolshevik leadership did not appear and some of the march was led by the Left Socialist Revolutionary Maria Spiridonova. Although there were rank-and-file Bolsheviks marching, Lenin and the Bolshevik leadership thought it premature. Trotsky tried in vain to stop them, but the workers were dispersed by troops loyal to the Provisional Government. Troops and workers who followed the first wave found there was no general rising and the day ended in disorder. Bolshevik leaders, including Zinoviev and Lenin, went into hiding, Lenin taking refuge in Finland. The next day, after further disorders, the Provisional Government issued warrants for the arrest of the Bolsheviks, partly on the grounds of their supposed support of Germany.

On 9 July Prince Lvov resigned and Kerensky became Prime Minister. On 12 July the Provisional Government reintroduced capital punishment and courts martial for the army at the demand of Kornilov. The immediate result of the July Days was a hardening of the government's attitude to the left.

K

Kadets

'Constitutional Democrats'; first named the Liberation Party, founded in Stuttgart in 1902; renamed the Kadets in 1905. A middle-class liberal party which would have fought World War I against Germany to the end. In their eyes the 1905 revolution had successfully transformed Russia. They saw a democratic parliamentary future ahead, with liberal capitalist economic policies. They opposed the October 1917 revolutionaries and were outlawed by the Bolsheviks at the end of 1917, particularly for their support of anti-Soviet activity in southern Russia.

Leading personalities of the Kadets were Prince Lvov (Chairman of the 'Union of Zemstvos and Towns' and head of the Provisional Government, February to July 1917), Prince Trubetskoy, Konovalov, Maklakov and on their left Nekrasov and right Milyukov (a minister in Lvov's Provisional Government) and Kokoshkin.

KGB see Political Police.

Kazakh Soviet Socialist Republic

Population: 16,200,000 (36% Kazakh, 41% Russian, 6% Ukrainian; also Vighurs, Germans and Koreans)

Area: 1,064,980 sq miles (2,759,016 sq km), including 880 sq miles (2,280 sq km) transferred from Uzbekistan in 1971

Capital: Alma Ata

An enormous area, rich in pasture and minerals, taken into Imperial Russia late in the nineteenth century and colonised with Russians. Russians at that time called the Kazakhs 'Kirghiz' (to distinguish them from 'Cossacks') and they called the Kirghiz 'Kara-Kirghiz'. The 1916 wartime decree extending conscription to all peoples, when previously the subject peoples of the Empire had not been included, led to the July 1916 revolt of the Kazakhs. It was put down with the loss of 150,000 local people, some killed by the punitive force sent there and some by the Russian colonists, many thousands of whom were also killed.

The February 1917 revolution unleashed a Kazakh nationalist movement, the 'Alash Orda' which threatened to throw the new Russians out. There were three Kazakh Conferences, in April, July and December, but they attracted no outside support. The Kolchak government claimed power, but by the end of 1919 Moscow-equipped troops were gaining control.

On 10 July 1919 Lenin signed a decree creating a 'Kirghiz Revolutionary Committee' and, with Red Army help, liquidated all its nationalist opponents. These events combined to force large numbers of Kirghiz to move into Chinese territory. A 'Kirghiz' Autonomous SSR was formed on 26 August 1920. The republic became the Kazakh ASSR in 1925 and on 5 December 1936 it became a full Soviet Socialist Republic within the USSR.

Kazakh Bolsheviks were very rare and many Kazakhs moved with their herds away from the new power, into Chinese Turkestan or Afghanistan. The depredations of Russian settlers, the White army and Red Commissars caused famine and about one millions deaths in 1921–22.

One of the most dramatic developments under Soviet rule was the completion of the 'Turksib' railway, started in 1913 but completed with the Five Year Plan in 1930, linking the industries of Tashkent with the Trans-Siberian railway through Orenburg.

'Russification' and collectivisation ran into serious difficulties in the 1930s and Kaganovich was sent there in 1932 to clear up the situation. As a result, nomadic peoples, once they joined the collective system, were officially allowed to own flocks of sheep, goats, horses and camels. Official 'collectivisation' was not completed until 1937. Purges took a great toll of all Kazakh leaders. World War II evacuated (or deported) large numbers of Germans, Jews, Chechens, etc. to Kazakhstan. The resentment against this influx caused continual unrest and in 1954 Ponomarenko was sent as Party First Secretary from Moscow. Brezhnev was also there as Second Secretary and then First Secretary 1955–56.

Khrushchev's 1954 policy of ploughing the 'Virgin Lands' for grain production was most vigorously followed in Kazakhstan. Some 62 million acres (25 million hectares) of the 104 million acres (42 million hectares) ploughed between 1954 and 1960 were in Kazakhstan. Intensive ploughing has now threatened the land with erosion.

Riots in 1986 in Alma Ata foreshadowed a growing nationalist sentiment against immigrant labour to the oil fields. In 1989 oil-workers' caravans were burnt by Kazakh rioters. In September 1989 there were inter-racial riots at Semipalatinsk; shortly afterwards a political movement there demanded the end of nuclear testing. In recognition of the growth of nationalism, the Kazahk language was given status as the official language of the republic.

Kirghiz Soviet Socialist Republic

Population (1988): 4,208,000 (48% Kirghiz, 26% Russian, 12% Uzbek, with other
    peoples, including Ukrainians, Germans, Tatars and Kazakhs
Area: 76,642 sq miles (198,554 sq km)   Capital: Frunze

Tsarist Russia encouraged Russian immigration into the Kirghiz area, the Khanate of Kokand. The practice continued under Soviet rule, the very capital being renamed after a Russian.

The Kirghiz, known then as 'Kara-Kirghiz' (while the Kazakhs were called 'Kirghiz' by the Russians), were included in the Turkestan Autonomous Soviet Socialist Republic (ASSR) controlled from Tashkent until 1924 when, still part of the RSFSR, it was made the Kara-Kirghiz Autonomous Province. In 1925 this became the Kirghiz ASSR and on 5 December 1936 the Kirghiz SSR was made a full Union Republic.

Attempts by the Kirghiz to establish their national identity started with the commandant of the Kokand garrison rallying forces to oppose the Red Army in 1919; these became the Basmachis. The revolt ended with the killing of Enver Pasha in 1922 and the Basmachis fought only as small local bands until 1929, when they gained strength in opposition to land collectivisation.

Soviet economic policy required the traditional nomads to settle, with the result that their herds of cattle, sheep and goats declined catastrophically. A group of Kirghiz Communists, 'the Thirty', presented the Party with a list of criticisms, principally against the import of Russian officials. They were removed from all posts, expelled from the Party and some exiled. Any survivors were later victims of the purges.

Kolkhoz

Producers' co-operatives formed by combining the land of formerly independent peasants, or from confiscated estate lands. They were the main instrument used by Stalin in his mass collectivisation programme begun in 1929 which took the percentage of collectivised peasant households from 1.7 per cent in 1928 to 90 per cent in 1936.

The Kolkhoz Congress of 1935 defined it as a 'A voluntary co-operative whose members had pooled their means of production in order to produce in common. Members ran their own affairs, and elected their management committee.' However, in practice, this democratic element was curtailed by having to obey instructions from the local Party organisation. Payment of members depended upon the trudoni (workday units) worked by each man. At this stage, roughly two-thirds of the produce went to the State either in direct procurements or in payment to the machine tractor stations. Payments in cash to the members were dependent upon prices paid by the government, usually low, and were subject to taxes, insurance, etc.

The congress gave legal recognition to the right of the Kolkhoz household to hold and farm a private plot, limited to approximately $1\frac{1}{4}$ acres (0.5 hectare), on which they could keep a cow, a pig and four sheep. Some of this produce could be sold in the market-place. In practice, as much as 60 per cent of all Soviet meat and vegetable produce has traditionally come from this private-sector agriculture from the time of the 1917 Revolution.

The number and size of the Kolkhozes grew steadily throughout the time of Stalin and reached a peak of 125,000 units in 1950. By 1965 it had declined to 36,000, partly by amalgamation but also by conversion to Sovkhozes. (See also **Agriculture**)

Komsomol

The 'All-Union Leninist Youth Organisation' founded in 1918. It now covers the 18 to 28 year olds. Apart from intensive political education, the Komsomol are called on to act as responsible citizens and are sometimes used as an auxiliary force, patrolling special occasions, Enrolment is voluntary, but membership, which was over 40 million in the 1980s, can lead to Party membership and the possibility of a career through the Party. Younger children are members of the 'Pioneers', a politically oriented organisation not unlike the Scouts in other countries.

Kornilov Affair

General Kornilov, appointed Commander-in-Chief of the army in place of Brusilov in July 1917 by Kerensky and greeted as a hero and saviour by many, had insisted on an end to Kerensky's wasteful offensive against the Germans. In August he demanded extra powers to control the anarchic situation after the 'July Days'. On 27–29 August troops moving towards Petrograd were observed and suspected by Kerensky of being part of a *coup d'état*. The reason for the moves remains obscure, but Kerensky ordered the arrest of Kornilov and other generals. Kornilov claimed he was acting in the defence of the Russian people with no political ambition. As Kornilov's cavalry approached Petrograd, people began to see the Red Guards as their defence against a military counter-revolution. But Kornilov submitted to arrest and, with other generals, he was moved to a barracks in Bykhov. Their detention lasted from September to the beginning of December, when Kornilov and his fellow officers made their escape and went south to join the new anti-Bolshevik Whites and Kornilov himself was killed the next year.

The effect of the affair was to remove army support from the Provisional Government and to open the way for the October 1917 Revolution.

KPK

Commission of Party Control, set up in 1934, replacing the Central Control Commission (TsKK). In 1952 it was reorganised under the Party Central Committee.

Kremlin

The term for the main fortress of a Russian city. The Moscow Kremlin, built in the fifteenth century and added to continuously since then, with a cathedral and a mid-nineteenth-century palace, has been the seat of government since 1918. The Red Square is on one side of the Kremlin.

Kresty Prison

The St Petersburg prison used, for example, for the Kronstadt sailors taken in the July Days.

Kronstadt

The fortified city on an island 20 miles (30 km) west of Leningrad which was the principal base of the Tsarist Baltic fleet. In 1917 there were some 80,000 people there, consisting of sailors, garrison soldiers (mostly artillerymen), officials and artisans. There were several minor mutinies during World War I and in February 1917, hearing the news of the Petrograd revolution, the sailors seized and shot 80 hated officers and policemen. The sailors, in the hands of a Soviet of Military Deputies, supported the Socialist Revolutionaries (SRs), the Mensheviks and the Provisional Government. Gradually the balance of political grouping in the soviet moved from right to left. While the right wing of the Provisional Government was never represented there, at the start there were only 11 Bolsheviks among the 280 Deputies, but by August there were 96. Kronstadt remained an independent community, had its own newspaper and managed to help feed itself with its socialised kitchen gardens then and during the hard years to come.

After the failure of the June 1917 offensive, the sailors became hostile to the government and on 3 July 12,000 sailors, with working men and women, landed at Petrograd to join in what had initially been a Bolshevik-inspired demonstration. The march turned into chaos and the Kronstadt men returned dispirited and alienated from Petrograd. In their frustration with the July Days, some Petrograd soldiers even believed that the Kronstadt sailors were in the pay of enemy Germany.

The Kronstadt community's dislike of and lack of trust in Kerensky grew and it became a major force in the October 1917 Revolution. On 25 October 1917, at the call of the Petrograd Military Revolutionary Committee, some 5,000 sailors and soldiers landed in the city, occupied key posts and stormed the Winter Palace, the seat of the Provisional Government. A further 3,000 were landed in the next four days. Kronstadt became the October Revolution's major source of troops, ammunition and even food.

Dzerzhinsky ordered Kronstadt's prisons to be used for prisoners of the Revolution and Lenin ordered hoarders and saboteurs to be sent there. Loyal and secure as it was, Kronstadt was not a Bolshevik town. 'All Power to the Soviets' was their slogan and they accepted in their ruling coalition Bolshevik, Menshevik and SRs of the left.

Between 14 and 20 June 1918, the Menshevik and Right SRs were expelled from the Kronstadt Soviet (as they were from all Russian soviets after the Mirbach assassination. Its multi-party democracy faded, and about 300 officers were summarily executed.

In June 1919 the advance of General Yudenich's north-western White army forced the evacuation of over 16,000 women and children. In the panic the mainland fortress of Krasnaia Gorka, part of the Kronstadt garrison, mutinied and defected. It was recaptured on 16 June and a purge began on Kronstadt and hundreds of the garrison were shot after brief courts martial. The Bolshevik Party grew in numbers and took firm control.

By January 1921 Kronstadt still had 50,000 inhabitants and was regarded as a loyal stronghold of the regime. It was organised and well fed. Petrograd in contrast was starving. On 27 February a delegation of Kronstadt sailors visited the city and returned to report the failure of the Bolshevik rule and to demand a non-party conference. The next day the sailors of the battleship *Petropavlovsk* passed a resolution calling for free elections of new soviets, freedom of speech, the liberation of all socialist political prisoners, equal rations for all and full rights for land-holding peasants and small industrialists who were not employers. On 1 March Kalinin, the nominal head of state, went to the island to appeal to the sailors, and to warn them. The outcome was a mass meeting which elected a non-Bolshevik Revolutionary Committee. Kronstadt was at once blockaded.

On 8 March an attempt to take the island failed and Tukhachevsky and Kamenev mobilised a force of upwards of 50,000 men which, on 17–18 March, under heavy machine-gun and artillery covering fire, went over the ice to enter the fortress. Some 8,000 sailors escaped to Finland, thousands of others were drafted to other naval units or labour camps and hundreds rounded up and shot. It was the end of Kronstadt as a revolutionary force.

Krug

A Cossack council, similar to a soviet or rada, many of which were formed in the emergencies of 1917–19.

Kulak

Literally 'fist', used for a wealthy peasant. They were encouraged by the New Economic Policy from 1921, to the fury of old-guard Bolsheviks, but with the encouragement of Stalin who saw this as part of building 'Socialism in One Country' and Bukharin, who wanted their integration into the economy as the only element which was producing a surplus. However with the programme of collectivisation they again became objects of enmity and many were sent to camps or executed as their lands were taken over. (See also **Collectivisation**)

Kursk, Battle of

The biggest tank battle in the history of warfare took place in and around Kursk, a town in central Russia, south-west of Moscow, from 5 July to 23 August 1943.

By the winter of 1942 the German forces had formed a salient around Kursk and consolidated their positions. To regain the initiative, Hitler had decided on a massive offensive in the summer of 1943 on the central front, using the salient as a springboard. The offensive was codenamed Operation Citadel and the German forces earmarked for it were the Ninth and Second Armies of Army Group Centre, commanded by Field Marshal von Kluge, the Fourth Panzer Army and the Battle Task Force of Army Group South, commanded by Field Marshal von Manstein. The German forces consisted of 900,000 men, 10,000 guns, 2,700 tanks, including the latest Tiger and Panther models, and the new Ferdinand self-propelled guns: nearly all the tanks available. Among the 2,000 aircraft were the powerful Focke-Wulf 190 fighters.

The Russian armies were under the overall command of Marshals Zhukov and Vasilevsky, though naturally all important decisions were cleared with Stalin as Commander-in-Chief.

Von Kluge's forces in the north face of the salient were opposed by Marshal Rokossovsky's Central Front armies, while von Manstein's forces in the south were confronted by General Vatutin's units.

The total Russian forces consisted of 1,300,000 men, 20,000 guns, 3,600 tanks and self-propelled guns and 2,800 aircraft. The armour consisted of the latest versions of the T34s, and SU medium and the heavy KV tanks. The aircraft included Yak–9 and La–7 fighters and Il–10 ground attack planes.

At the Battle of Kursk, the German Luftwaffe was to have swept the sky clear for the army's advance, but the Red Air Force withstood this and attacked the German air bases, while harassing the assembling troops. On the day of the German attack, 5 July, the Soviets sent in a wave of ground-attack planes but these were countered by a prepared massive force of Messerschmitt and Focke-Wulf fighters, shooting the Red Air Force down in hundreds, claiming over 600 in two days. But the Germans found the pace difficult to maintain and the Soviets continued to attack the German Panzers with Il-10 planes in mass. By the time of the start of the counter-attack on 12 July, huge air reserves had been brought in and the Soviet armour rolled forward. The Luftwaffe's command of the sky had been only local and temporary.

Von Kluge's Second and Ninth Armies launched a powerful offensive in the north face of the salient on 5 July, but only succeeded in creating a limited wedge between the Russian armies. The Ninth Army lost two-thirds of its tanks and had to switch to a defensive role. On the southern face von Manstein made more progress, advances up to 22 miles (35 km) were achieved quite rapidly and heavy casualities were inflicted on Vatutin's forces, but Stalin agreed under pressure to allow Rotmistrov's Fifth Guards Tank Army, consisting of 800 T34s, to go to his rescue.

From 9 to 12 July in the area around Prokhorovka, a huge tank engagement took place. More than 1,500 tanks and self-propelled guns were in action and the close infighting was not to the advantage of the German Tigers and Ferdinands, which were faced with the Russian anti-tank artillery, their ground-attack aircraft and the massive blasts from their 'Katyusha' rocket launchers. Over 350 tanks and 10,000 of von Manstein's Fourth Panzer Army were lost and his advance halted.

The force of the German advance was spent and now General Vatutin's armies from the Voronezh front and Konev's men from the steppe front strongly counter-attacked and drove them back to their start line. This attack was followed by Generals Sokolovski and Popov who attacked on the Orel front and penetrated it to a depth of 16 miles (25 km). The Russian offensive then developed on a broad front and included Marshal Rokossovsky's Centre Front forces; by 16 July the Germans were forced to desert their Orel base.

By 3 August a further counter-offensive was developed by Marshal Malinovski's unit. German forces, amounting to 18 divisions, including four Panzer divisions, were forced to retreat and the First Tank and Sixth Guards armies together covered 62 miles (100 km) and took the town of Bogodukov. By 11 August, Voronezh front forces under General Vatutin had cut the Kharkov–Poltava Road. The Germans counter-attacked but without success. By 22 August Kharkov had been cleared of enemy forces and the whole southern wing of the German forces was threatened, thus allowing the Russians to go over to a general offensive. This allowed them later in the year to liberate the left flank of the Ukraine and reach the Dnieper.

The Russians were much assisted by the action of partisans in the rear of the German armies who destroyed locomotives and derailed military trains in large numbers. Their activities obliged the Luftwaffe to keep its supply and repair bases far behind, in Poland, letting the Russians obtain air supremacy.

Kursk was the last major German offensive of the Russo-German war and the beginning of the end for the Wehrmacht as a triumphant military machine. (See also **World War II**)

L

Labour Camps see **Camps**.

Latvian Soviet Socialist Republic
Population: 2,673,000 (54% Latvian, 33% Russian, 8% Belorussian and Ukrainian)
Area: 24,695 sq miles (63,977 sq km)   Capital: Riga
For the earlier history of Latvia, see **Baltic States**. The most Russianised of the three Baltic states, in November 1988 its Supreme Soviet decided not to push for full autonomy on the Estonian line. However in March 1989 a demonstration by independent groups outside Party headquarters was broken up savagely by the militia. In

the election to the All-Union Congress, the Popular Front candidates and their allies took 26 of the 30 seats. The Prime Minister was among the defeated candidates, although the Party Secretary, Janis Vagris, was elected as a Deputy. The largest majority went to the nationalist leader and another large vote to Yuri Dobelius.

The population's split is exemplified by the two extremist groups, the LNNK (National Independence Movement of Latvia) claiming the illegality of the Soviet take-over in 1939 and the opposing Russian organisation 'Interfront', strong among the immigrant workers.

For events since December 1989 see the Chronology.

Latvian Rifles

The First Latvian Rifle Regiment was formed during World War I, in 1915, when the battle front was in that territory. From this, two battalions of former Tsarist soldiers were formed as a locally employed force by the Provisional Government. They held part of Latvia against German occupation in 1917 and prevented a German advance on Petrograd. A number of them were the Smolny Institute guard in the October 1917 Revolution and many joined the Red Army.

Law

Background The system of law established in the Soviet Union after the October Revolution was meant to be based ideally on the doctrines of Marx and Engels. This held that law in a communist state when first established should (1) eliminate the political power of the bourgeoisie and (2) educate the citizens in the disciplined pattern of behaviour necessary for the operation of a socialist state. It was held that the police, the army, courts and hence lawyers would prove unnecessary and would, like the state, wither away.

These ideas were enshrined in the First Constitution of the RSFSR on 10 July 1918. This document issued a few decrees: depriving private individuals of the ownership of land, banks, insurance companies, merchant fleets and large-scale industries. It also secularised marriage and divorce.

People's Courts were set up without professional staff to operate them. Judges, appointed from a panel of responsible citizens, were directed to use Russian Imperial laws, except where they had been revoked, or where they conflicted with the revolutionary conscience of the judge.

Political offenders were judged by revolutionary tribunals or were arrested and imprisoned, perhaps shot, by the security police – the Cheka. This was justified by Lenin as a temporary expedient and the tribunals were officially abolished in 1922, after the end of the Civil War, though the activities of the Cheka were continued by the special or administrative boards of the NKVD. Thus emergency measures became institutionalised and became the mechanism of the Terror in the 1930s.

In 1922 a three-tier system of courts was established. The lowest was the People's Court. This had a full-time judge and two lay judges, selected from a local panel, and dealt with minor civil and criminal cases. The Provincial Court, with three professional judges, heard more serious civil and criminal cases and also dealt with the offences against the security of the State.

The Supreme Court's function was to hear appeals from other courts and to deal with vital matters affecting the State. Codes of law specifically dealt with criminal, civil, family, land and labour matters. Essentially it was a Roman law system, as found in most European countries.

The formation of the USSR in December 1922 made little difference to the situation, in that the republics, although conforming in general terms to the RSFSR's code of practice, had local variations of their own. The first federal Constitution, adopted in

1924, put military and transport matters (vital to State security) under the aegis of the Supreme Court.

In 1936 the second Constitution, drafted by Bukharin, strengthened the power of central government by transferring to it the power to enact codes of law to replace those existing in the republics.

Characteristics Soviet law is based upon the premise that the legislature is supreme over the executive and the judiciary. In theory the only source of law is the full legislature but in practice laws were mostly enacted by an elected committee (the Praesidium), often backed by the Party and usually carrying the signature of the General Secretary. The 1936 Constitution specifically reinforced the power of the legislature, but in effect the executive, essentially dominated by Stalin, soon reigned supreme.

After Stalin's death in 1957 the Constitution was amended to restore rights to the individual republics and to prevent courts meting out punishments that were not prescribed by the appropriate code. This was intended to prevent a return to the extra legal aspects of Stalin's rule.

The election of judges has always been controlled by the Party, quite openly in the case of the People's or Provincial Courts through the local soviet, and through the one (Party-approved) candidate system for the Supreme Court.

Labour Law. Strikes were declared unthinkable in 1928, as being an action taken against the workers' own state. During World War II absence from work for longer than 20 minutes was a punishable offence.

Land Law. By the Land Code of 1922 all land belonged to the State for its use, though small private plots of land or dwellings could be passed on to descendants.

Civil Rights. The rights of the individual were limited to such actions as might strengthen socialism. Any statements made by individuals evoking hostility to authority could be punished as a crime against the State.

Investigative Procedure. This is broadly similar to the French system, which emphasises investigation before the trial, though the investigating official is not, as in France, a magistrate but an official attached to the office of the prosecutor. Until 1985 the defendant had no right to an attorney before the trial. Most of the interrogation of witnesses during the trial is carried out by the judge rather than the prosecutor or the attorney for the defence.

Many changes have been proposed under perestroika, particularly concerning the rights of inheritance, but none has yet become law.

League of Nations
The international body formed after World War I which the USSR regarded as a capitalist–imperialist body. The USSR joined it in 1934 but left it at the end of 1939 on being condemned for the invasion of Finland.

Left Deviationists
The name given by Stalinists to those led from 1918 by Bukharin and from 1923 by Trotsky who believed in world revolution, opposed the New Economic Plan and the attempt to build socialism in one country.

Lend–Lease
Supplies given to the USSR during World War II by America on credit terms. After the war the USSR refused to make the token payments that the USA demanded.

Lenin Prizes
Prizes on the model of Nobel Prizes given annually from 1925 to outstanding scientists, artists and others. Thirty prizes are awarded every two years. While many winners

have been merit-worthy, the prize has frequently been awarded to politicians. Leonid Brezhnev awarded himself the prize and the hardline Ukrainian Vladimir Shcherbitsky, who was dropped from the Politburo in 1989, was given the prize in 1982.

Leningrad Affair

The purge of 1950. To honour the heroism of the people of Leningrad after the World War II siege, a suggestion was made that the capital of the RSFSR be moved there from Moscow. Stalin, always uneasy about the Party in Leningrad, thought this might be a challenge to his national power through a 'Leningrad Faction'. When Andrei Zdhanov, Leningrad's wartime leader, died in 1948 he sent Malenkov there on the pretext of investigating the election of city officials. The new mayor, Popov, and his precedessor, Kuznetsov, were accused of plotting to set up a separate Russian Communist Party, tried by a special tribunal and shot in September 1950. At least 200 others who had been prominent in Leningrad's siege were also taken and shot. This was one of the episodes exposed by Khrushchev at the 20th Party Congress.

Liberals

The party in the Duma particularly associated with the zemstvo (local, elected assemblies with limited administrative powers) and the large bureaucratic class who strove for constitutional change and political liberty.

Literature

Literature has been a major feature of Russian and soviet culture. Reference to the major authors will be found in the Biographies of this volume. See also **Writers' Union**.

Lithuanian Soviet Socialist Republic

Population: 3,682,000 (80% Lithuanian, 9% Russian, 7% Polish and 2% Belorussian)
Area: 26,173 sq miles (67,806 sq km)   Capital: Vilnius

For the earlier history of Lithuania, see **Baltic States**. On 23 October 1988 Cardinal Vincentas Sladkevicius celebrated mass at Vilnius Cathedral, newly opened after over 30 years' use as an exhibition gallery. Vilnius had been regained from Poland by Lithuania as a result of boundary changes made by the Soviet Union after World War II. Kaunus, the former capital, is now the second city, with a population of 450,000.

Sajudis, the Lithuanian 'Movement to Support Perestroika', had held its inaugural congress on 22 October and 200,000 people assembled, singing patriotic songs, waving the old Lithuanian flag of yellow, green and red and chanting '*Lietuva, Lietuva*' (Lithuania, Lithuania). On 28 September 1988 10,000 had turned out and been faced by riot police acting under the orders of the Party Secretary: the next month he was replaced by Algirdas Brazauskas. Sajudis has one and a half million names on its petitions urging total sovereignty.

A more extreme nationalist group, the Lithuanian Freedom League, demanded full independence at the rally, but the Sajudis, committed to working with the Party, stopped short of secession from the USSR, preferring a looser federation with economic independence for each republic. Lithuania, however, feels less threatened by Russification than the other two Baltic states.

In March 1989 Sajudis won a clear majority of the 39 seats in Congress, both Brazauskas and his deputy being elected, while the sitting President and Prime Minister were defeated. The Sajudis chairman, Vytautas Landisbergis, was also elected.

The government under Brazauskas has agreed to consider reopening the University of Kaunas (closed by Stalin in 1950).

In November 1989, the Lithuanian Supreme Court passed a bill enabling a referendum on matters of vital public interest to be held at the request of either half the republic's Parliament or 10 per cent (300,000) of its citizens. This was seen in Moscow as a step towards secession.

In elections to its new Congress in March 1990, Vytautas Landisbergis defeated the leader of the break-away Communist Party, Algirdas Brazauskas, for the post of chairman by 91 votes to 42 and Sajudis obtained two-thirds of the seats. Although the head of Gosplan warned that the USSR might demand the repayment of seven billion roubles, on 11 March the Congress declared its independence, by 124 votes to nil. The USSR Congress of Deputies immediately vetoed this declaration. For events since March 1990 see the Chronology.

M

Marinsky Palace
The office of the Provisional Government in Petrograd until it moved to the Winter Palace in August 1917.

Marshall Plan
The US Secretary of State, General Marshall, proposed on 5 June 1947 American aid for post-war European recovery. Under Anglo–French leadership, plans were made which led, in 1948, to a $17,000,000,000 programme and the creation of the Organisation for European Economic Co-operation. The Soviet Union suspected the terms meant the economic dominance of the West and refused offers to take part, adding to the growing East-West split in Europe. It was the Yugoslav acceptance of Marshall Aid terms that led to the break with the Soviet Union.

Marxism in Russia
Marx never carried out a detailed study of conditions in Russia but, in general, he and Engels seemed to have believed that it was the absence of private property in Russian villages that was the obvious basis for the form of tyrannical government in the country. The 'Populist' view, held by the Narodniks and their heirs, the Socialist Revolutionaries, was that the commune formed the basis for a special kind of Russian socialism. This idea had been entirely rejected by the Group for the Liberation of Labour, founded in Geneva in 1883 by Plekhanov, Axelrod, Lev Deutsch and others. Marx's views on this matter were not entirely clear, though he seemed to favour the SR view. To avoid difficulties he said that his predictions were based on an analysis of fully capitalist societies.

Both Engels and Marx really seemed to have held to the conviction that whatever form it took, what Russia really needed, and would certainly have, was a revolution.

Plekhanov and his group believed that capitalism was a stage through which Russia would have to pass before a revolution would be possible. Whereas Lenin, who had been converted to Marxism while at university in Kazan, had quite early come to the view that capitalism existed in the Russian village because of the exploitation of poor peasants by richer ones. This being the case, there was no necessity for Russia to pass through a more complete capitalist phase of development. This was all spelled out in *What is to be Done?*, published in 1902, which includes Lenin's call for the awakening of revolutionary consciousness in the masses by trained professional revolutionary leaders. Lenin's subsequent writings have formed a canon which is the basis of so called Marxism–Leninism.

Maximalists
A splinter group of the Socialist Revolutionaries. They believed in terrorism in political action, and many were arrested and executed when they attempted to kill Stolypin,

the Minister of the Interior, in 1907. They were usually identified as being near to the Bolsheviks, with whom they collaborated in 1917, but were later persecuted as enemies and the party ceased to exist by 1920.

Mensheviks

The non-Leninist 'minority' faction of the Social Democrats in 1903, but later they were the majority of Social Democrats. They were divided into: Internationalists against World War I on the principle that it was not in the people's interest and agreeing with the Bolsheviks on many issues); the Right who took part in the Petrograd Soviet and in Lvov's Provisional Government from May 1917; and the Defensists (supporting the war patriotically and thus to the right of most Mensheviks).

Prominent among the Mensheviks were: Internationalists: Martov, Sukhanov (a journalist who had left the Socialist Revolutionaries and joined Martov in 1917); Right: Chkheidze (the Chairman of the Petrograd Soviet), Dan, Tsereteli (both prominent in the Petrograd Soviet, the latter taking a post in Lvov's Provisional Government from May 1917); Defensists: Plekhanov, Deutsch, Vera Zasulich and Breido.

The Mensheviks formed a separate party in August 1917. They included followers of Trotsky, who led the Internationalist wing. The party was suppressed in 1922 and survivors figured in a show trial in 1930.

Metropol Hotel

The temporary seat of the Bolshevik government in Moscow in 1918.

MGB see **Political Police**.

Military Revolutionary Committee (MRC)

An ad-hoc committee set up by the Petrograd Soviet on 12 October 1917 to control troop movements. It was dissolved on 18 December, having been superseded by the Defence Council under the Sovnarkom.

Militia

The civil police, so-called in preference to the term police which had been made unpopular by their support of Tsarist rule, from February 1917, under the MVD (Ministry of Internal Affairs) and under the immediate control of the local soviet.

Minerals see **Geographical Features**.

Moldavian Soviet Socialist Republic

Population: 4,190,000 (64% of the inhabitants speak Romanian, 14% are Ukrainian, 13% Russian and the remaining 9% are a mixture of Jews, Germans, Bulgarians and Turkic Christian Gagauzians)
Area: 13,912 sq miles (36,041 sq km)   Capital: Kishinev
A full Soviet republic since 1944, previously part of 'Bessarabia', Moldavia was a disputed Romanian-speaking area on the edge of the Russian Empire which, as with the Baltic states, was included in the secret protocols of the Russo-German pact of 1939 as part of the Soviet sphere of influence.

There was a small Moldavian Autonomous Soviet Republic within the Ukrainian SSR, but modern Moldavia was annexed and added to it by the Soviet Union on 2 August 1940, though when Romania joined Hitler's 1941 invasion, it was made part of Germany and there were mass deportations.

Since its formation, Soviet policy in Moldavia has worked to distinguish it from its Romanian neighbour and to emphasise its historical authenticity. Russian Cyrillic script has been imposed on the Moldavian language, which is a dialect of Romanian.

In 1988 the small 'Democratic Movement in Support of Perestroika', led by Yuri

Rozhka, was accused of stirring up ethnic tension and merely imitating movements in the Baltic states. It also called for 'relatinisation' of the script used for the Moldavian language.

Among other recent movements are the Green Movement, which argues against insensitive central planning from Moscow, the Alexei Mateyvich Movement (named after a Moldavian author) demanding the deportation of 'non-Moldavian undesirables', the League of Students whose pro-perestroika meeting in November 1988 was savagely broken up. This was followed by another meeting at which 6,000 or more demanded the rewriting of Moldavian history, the revision of the alphabet and the return of university buildings from government use. The Moldavian Popular Front, formed in May 1989 under the auspices of the Writers' Union, aroused a contrasting pro-Russian Yedinstvo International Movement, urging the retention of the Russian language and Cyrillic script.

In January 1989 the authorities gave way to the growing pressure and recommended that Moldavian be made the official State language and that consideration be given to using the Latin alphabet. In September this was put into effect. To add to national demands, the 140,000 Gagauze are asking for autonomous status.

There was violent rioting in November, 1989, followed by more riots demanding the release of other nationalist protesters. As a result of the disturbances, the old Party Secretary was replaced with a younger, Moldavian man.

Monarchists
The Duma party who supported direct rule by the Tsar, led by such as Shulgin (who left Russia an 1918 but patriotically returned in 1945 and was sent to a camp).

Mongolia
The plateau region in east Central Asia which was the original home of the Mongols, whose thirteenth-century empire reshaped Asia and eastern Europe. After the decline of the Mongol khanates, the area became subject to the Chinese Empire. In the nineteenth century the Russians moved in as Chinese central power decayed, and Mongolia and Manchuria became regarded as part of Russia's rightful sphere of influence.

In the turmoil of the Russian Revolution, an area administered by the Tsarist Empire, but abandoned by officials, was declared the People's Republic of Tannu Tuva. The territory of Mongolia, after Baron Ungern-Sternberg had used it as a base for his own imperial ambitions, was established as the People's Republic of Mongolia under Soviet protection in July 1921. The religious city of Urga was renamed Ulan Bator and became the capital.

When the Japanese penetrated beyond Manchuria in 1938, there was a brief clash, but in 1939 another confrontation resulted in an undeclared six-week war. The Red Army were superior to the Japanese with the result that the Japanese gained a respect for the Soviets which added to their determination to stay out of the 1941–45 war; it also provided the Soviet Union with an experienced army that would come to the rescue of the nation in the winter of 1941–42.

The post-war agreements included holding a plebiscite which confirmed the country's independence as 'Outer Mongolia', and a series of Sino-Soviet treaties have maintained this. Tannu Tuva (from being one of the postage-stamp collector's joys) because an autonomous region in 1944 and an autonomous republic in the RSFSR in 1961.

Mongolia has remained firmly under Soviet control and although the nomads have been formally collectivised, the country is still thinly populated (1,900,000 people in 600,000 sq. miles/1,554,404 sq km) with nomad cattle men and with little industry. However, in March 1990, crowds in Ulan Bator demonstrated, demanding the resignation of the Party. A revised Communist Party, the Mongolian People's

Revolutionary Party, was formed, but other groups, including the Mongolian Democratic Party, have emerged and elections have been promised.

In 1989 the Soviet Union began withdrawing its troops from Mongolia, aiming to have the bulk of the army out during 1990. For subsequent events see the Chronology.

Moscow Tribune

A group formed in 1988 by intellectuals, among them Andrei Sakharov, to urge radical political reform in the USSR.

MRC see **Military Revolutionary Committee**

MTS (Machine Tractor Stations)

These units had no land of their own to farm. Their purpose was to service the Kolkhozes with tractors and other machinery. Devised by A M Markevich, manager of a state farm near Odessa in 1927 who perished in the purges, they were under the jurisdiction of the Commissariat of Agriculture and were normally divided into a number of tractor brigades. At their peak in 1954, there were nearly 9000 MTSs employing an average of 3,000 each.

Until 1934, each MTS had a political departent which served to keep watch over the orthodoxy of the Kolkhozes it serviced, but these were then abolished. In 1958 Khrushchev abolished the MTSs and ordered the Kolkhozes to purchase their equipment. It was a part of his policy to make the Kolkhoz more self-reliant and therefore productive. (See also **Agriculture**)

Musavet

The socialist-nationalist political party of 'Equality' founded in Azerbaijan in 1911.

Music

In 1907 a festival of Russian Music and Art was staged by Sergei Diaghilev in Paris. He was a brilliant impresario and in 1909 he put on a production of Borodin's *Prince Igor* in which the dancers attracted as much attention as the singers. Over the next four years he scored an incredible success with his ballet company, for which he commissioned works by Stravinsky, such as *Firebird, Petrushka* and *Rite of Spring*. He also introduced the sensational dancer Vaslev Nijinsky in Claude Debussy's *Après-midi d'un Faune*. Largely through Diaghilev's efforts, Russian music and ballet had achieved an international reputation.

The October 1917 Revolution and Civil War at first produced chaotic conditions for Russian music, with no fuel for concert halls and no money to pay the salaries of staff at the conservatories. But under the policies of the NEP and the flexible and imaginative guidance of Lunacharsky, Commissar of Public Education, there seemed to be a real future for freedom and imaginative experimentation in music. The Association for Contemporary Music, set up in 1923 by Miaskovsky, Belayev and Lamm, encouraged all this. But by 1932 Lunarcharsky was gone, the association was dissolved and the Union of Soviet Composers was established with a requirement that music must have a socialist content, and be expressed in a mode readily understood by the masses. Thus the works of Schoenberg, Hindemith and Strauss were banished. This step effectively cut Russian music off from the developments that were taking place in the rest of the world, and led to a certain provincialism of which Prokofiev had warned before he went to America.

During the years of repression under Stalin and his cultural henchman Zdhanov, there were conventional composers such as Kabalevsky, Shebalin and Miaskovsky who were content to turn out approved works, but all the major talents – Prokofiev, Shostakovich and Khachaturian had difficulties with the authorities. Prokofiev had returned to Russia in 1933 but although his *Love of Three Oranges* was tremendously popular, his *Cantata for the Twentieth Anniversary of the October Revolution* was not performed until 1966. His successes, like the score for *Alexander Nevsky* and the *Second Violin Concerto* were undoubtedly more accessible musically.

Shostakovich, by no means a rebel, was attacked in *Pravda* a few days after Stalin had seen a performance of his opera *Lady Macbeth of Mtsensk*. Khachaturian had fewer problems in that his naturally folk-based musical language was in little danger of being attacked for formal elements.

After Stalin's death, the loosening of political control of the arts made an enormous difference to the musical world. Khrushchev himself said in a speech in 1963, 'We stand for melodious music with content, music that stirs people and gives rise to strong feelings, and we are against cacophony.' It was clear that the Soviet Union was no place for dodecaphony or serialism. There are contemporary composers in the Soviet Union now who are more in touch with the musical idioms of the West, such as Shchedrin, whose *Second Symphony* was enormously popular. In Moscow avant-garde composers, such as Denisov and Volkonsky, are highly thought of critically, but little of their music is played in the West.

MVD
Ministry of Internal Affairs, controlling the ordinary police. (See also **Political Police**)

N

Narkomfin
The People's Commissariat of Finance.

Narkomindel
The People's Commissariat for Foreign Affairs.

Narkomnats
The People's Commissariat for Nationalities.

Narkomprod
The People's Commissariat of Food Supply.

Narkomvnutorg
The People's Commissariat of Domestic Trade.

Narodnaya Volya
'The People's Will', a revolutionary group formed in 1879, believing in violent means to seize power, and the killing of senior officials. It was responsible for the assassination of Tsar Alexander II in 1881. Lenin's elder brother was a member and his section attempted the murder of Tsar Alexander III. Members mostly joined the Socialist Revolutionaries, but some joined the Social Democrats.

Narodnik
'Men of the People' (see also **Narodnaya Volya**), the name used from the 1870s for socialists who appealed directly to the people and hoped for a peasant revolution, rather than the orthodox Marxist expectation of a capitalist–industrialist transitional phase. In 1874 some 2,000 young men and women throughout Russia put on peasant clothes and went to live among them, hoping, in vain, to start a political move towards

democracy; but they were seen as a threat to established society and arrested by the police. Some Narodniks then turned to terrorism and succeeded in 1881 in killing Tsar Alexander II. Other parties such as the Socialist Revolutionaries, Trudovik and Narodnye Sotsialisty (People's Socialists) continued Narodnik policies, but more radical elements turned to Marxism and founded the Social Democrats.

A veteran Narodnik leader, Nikolai Chaikovsky, returned to Russia in 1917, opposing the Bolsheviks and headed a government in Archangel until 1919.

National Bolsheviks
A non-communist party supporting Bolshevism after 1917 in the belief that it was the best solution for the nation's problems.

Naval Academy
On Vasilevsky Island in Petrograd, the building used by the All-Russian Congress of Soviets in June 1917.

Navy
The disastrous performance of the Imperial Navy in the 1904–05 war with Japan and its indifferent effect in either the Baltic or the Black Sea in World War I was balanced by the reputation the sailors gained as revolutionary activists, in 1917, taking control of the fleet base of Kronstadt on the Baltic, and their fighting role in the October Revolution and the following Civil War. In 1922 a decision was taken to rebuild the navy, but serious recruitment of naval cadets, from the ranks of the Komsomols, began only in 1927. The navy had then in commission: 3 battleships; 2 cruisers, including the *Aurora*; 10 destroyers; 19 submarines, all survivors of World War I.

Between 1927 and 1941 there was a considerable shipbuilding programme. Voroshilov, as Stalin's Commissar for Defence, planned for a deep-sea fleet policy and, as well as 18 cruisers, four battleships were laid down, but never completed.

The military purges, in which Stalin liquidated senior officers in fear that they might rise against him, started in the navy in July 1937 when the fleet commander was arrested and shot. The top command was almost totally eliminated in the next year.

World War II saw part of the navy idle in the Pacific, part taken or destroyed in the Baltic and the remainder fighting desperate coastal actions in the Black Sea and the Arctic. In spite of the urgency of bringing munitions from Britain and America through the German blockade, the escort of convoys was almost totally done by the Western Allies, the Soviet navy being unable to help. The most successful naval work was on inland waters, the Caspian, the Don and Volga Rivers and on Lake Ladoga, where supplies were taken to the beleaguered city of Leningrad.

The Soviet Navy (Voyenno-Morskoy Flot, VMF) in 1945 comprised about 220 warships, many of them obsolete and confined to coastal operations. Post-war expansion increased the navy to 1,400 ships, including 630 warships by 1962. Under Admiral Gorshkov, commander of the navy from 1956, its growth continued and by the mid-1980s this strength was approximately doubled. The navy was transformed from a coastal into a 'blue water' force.

The Soviet Navy has four fleets: northern, based at Severmosk; Baltic at Baltiysk; Black Sea at Sevastopol; and the Pacific at Vladivostok. There is also a Caspian flotilla based on Baku.

The most striking development of the Soviet navy has been in submarines. Diesel-electric-engined submarines were converted to carry and fire long-range missiles in the early 1950s and in 1960 nuclear-powered submarines began to be built. In 1973 submarines carrying missiles with a maximum range of 4,200 miles (6,700 km) came into operation, capable of reaching targets in any part of the USA; several of these were kept permanently deployed in the North Atlantic and North Pacific. With the more sophisticated submarines introduced in 1978, there were also the highly accurate

MIRV (multiple independently targeted re-entry vehicle) missiles. In 1984 the first of a new class of 13,600-tonne submarines was launched, capable of carrying 16 long-range missiles and of staying hidden under the polar ice-cap for long periods.

With all its northern seaports liable to become ice-bound, the Soviet Navy places great reliance on ice-breakers. The world's first nuclear-powered ship was the *Lenin* (1960), a 16,000-tonne merchant ship capable of breaking through the Arctic ice 12 feet (4 m) thick. The *Lenin* however, disappeared (perhaps the result of an accident with her reactors) in 1967.

The Soviet Navy no longer sends submarine patrols close to the US Atlantic seaboard and is sending fewer surface ships on world ocean cruises. This may be because the USSR has better weapon technology which does not require standing patrols; because Western navies have responded with more aggressive counter-patrols, and because of budgetary restraints. A big fleet was no longer necessary when submarines with intercontinental missiles could hit America without leaving port. Under Gorbachev new economies were introduced and the world role of the Soviet fleet allowed to diminish.

After the rapid expansion of the 1960s and 1970s, Red Navy ships are now plagued with mechanical faults. In October 1986 a 'Yankee' class submarine (a class of 10,500-tonne missile-carrying boats, built in 1963–68, with two nuclear reactors for power) ran into difficulties. Nuclear disaster was averted by a crew member who, in shutting down the power plant, was himself entombed in the reactor compartment. By 1989 the total of nuclear-powered submarines lost was six. On 7 April a 9,700-tonne 'Mike' class hunter-killer was the sixth of these, losing 42 from its crew of 80 as it sank off Norway. On 26 June 1989, a 1960s-built 'Echo' class nuclear-powered submarine broke down and was taken in tow to Murmansk; this happened again in July to an 'Alfa' class.

New Economic Policy (NEP)

Economic policies introduced by Lenin in 1921 when the harsh measures of War Communism had alienated the peasants and failed to achieve the necessary industrial production in the country. Monetary reforms were introduced and the inheritance of private property was allowed. Private trade and manufacturing were actively encouraged, and those involved became known as Nepmen. Lenin talked of using the New Economic Policy to 'teach communists how to be good business men'. The peasants were encouraged to produce surpluses by paying their taxes in goods, and being allowed to sell in the market-place. Essentially their relationship to the State was as taxpayer only. The policy was so effective that by 1927 less than 2 per cent of the land was in the hands of collective or State farms. Although the policies continued after Lenin's death in 1924, there was always opposition from the left of the Party and from the public who resented the Nepmen. Stalin's speeches at the 15th Party Congress in 1927 sounded the death knell to NEP. (See also **Agriculture**)

Nepman

The denigratory term used for those who took advantage of and profited from the New Economic Policy.

Newspapers

Pravda (*Truth*) The leading Soviet newspaper with a circulation of 9,700,000 in 1989 and the official organ of the Central Committee of the CPSU. Founded by Lenin in 1912, and edited by him, with Maxim Gorky as literary editor, until 1914. The paper was hounded by the Tsarist government and during the Revolution its offices were destroyed by military cadets.

Pravda is essentially an organ of information and education, reporting on scientific, economic and cultural topics. It contains no sensational or scandalous news items and is concerned to stress and interpret the Party line; stories concerning international relations are, in general, left to *Isvestia* which is the official Soviet government newspaper. *Pravda* carries a staff of more than 100 full-time correspondents. The editorial staff is headed by a board approved by the Central Committee of the Party.

Pravda was first published as a daily in St Petersburg by the Party in 1913. Appearing in various forms, it settled into publication from Moscow from 3 March 1918.

On 18 October 1989 its editor, Victor Afanasyev, was removed after 13 years in the post, and replaced by Ivan Frolov of *Komsomolskaya Pravda*. *Pravda* had been criticised for tendentious coverage of nationalist movements and a crude attempt to smear Boris Yeltsin. Frolov was faced with a drop in circulation from 10 million to an estimated 5.5 million.

Isvestia (*The News*) The first issue came out on 28 February 1917. Now published by the Praesidium of the Supreme Soviet and thus under the strong influence of the new Congress of People's Deputies, its illustrated Sunday supplement is *Nedelya*, first issued in 1960. The circulation was 10 million in 1989.

On 2 January 1989 it published two pages of advertising – the first-ever Soviet daily to do so: a full page for a French industrial concern and a second with advertisements for Soviet, West German and Belgian companies and a bank. *Isvestia* is trying to attract readers with human-interest stories rather than the traditional issue of official communiqués.

Krasnya Zveda (*Red Star*) The daily paper of the Ministry of Defence, first issued on 1 January 1924.

Literaturnaya Gazeta (*Literary Gazette*) The weekly paper of the Writers' Union, from 1929, now with a circulation of 3 million. Its political pronouncements were until recently the voice of the Party's ideology specialists.

Moskovskiye Novostni (*Moscow News*) A weekly published in Moscow by Tass since 1930, directed at a foreign audience. At present it is published in seven languages with a total circulation, throughout the world, of a million.

Trud (*Labour*) The official organ of the trade unions with a circulation of nearly 20 million in 1989. It has shown little urge to move with the times and a projection for 1990 suggests a drop to 17 million.

Argumenty I Fakty (*Arguments and Facts*) Edited by Vladislav Starkov. A popular weekly with a circulation which has risen to 22 million, the biggest-selling weekly in the USSR. First published in 1979 from a basement on the outskirts of Moscow, it retains the appearance of an underground bulletin. It is the organ of what was originally a strict Party-based ideological group, but under glasnost it has found a hungry market. It gives *facts* without the traditional verbal padding of the official Press. It prints scoops and reveals scandals. *Argumenty I Fakty* went too far in publishing a poll which suggested that opposition figures, such as Sakharov, might be more popular than Gorbachev; the remarkable thing is that the editor survived the Government's fury. It is suggested that its circulation could reach 30 millions in 1990, if enough newsprint were to be allotted.

Komsomolskaya Pravda (*The Komsomol's 'Pravda'*) The communist youth organisation paper. As with other official papers, it suffers under glasnost and is losing circulation from an estimated 17 million in 1989 to a probably 13 in 1990.

NKGB see **Political Police**.

NKVD see **Political Police**.

Nomenklatura

The list of posts in the Party and State appointment to which requires higher Party approval. Those on the list are likely to be re-elected to their posts or promoted to similar or higher positions in other parts of the USSR. Under Brezhnev there were perhaps over two million people on the nomenklatura constituting a new, secure social class.

Nuclear power

The first nuclear-generated electricity in the world came from Obninsk, near Moscow, in 1954. In the 1970s the USSR began a nuclear-energy programme and in the 10th Five Year Plan, 1976–80, installed capacity was to be expanded from 5.5 to 19.4 million kilowatts. Volgodorsk, on the Don–Volga Canal, was opened in the Five Year Plan as a centre to manufacture equipment for nuclear power stations. Nuclear power stations in the Soviet Union are of two types, graphite-water and water-moderated.

Operational nuclear energy stations by 1984 were:

1,000 megawatt or more
Leningrad (2 stations)
Chernobyl (where the reactor exploded in 1986)
Kursk

Less than 1,000 megawatts
Beloyarsk (3 stations, in the Urals)
Troitsk (in the Urals)
Bilibino (in the north of the Far East)
Rovno
Dmitrograd
Obninsk
Shevchenko (east of the Caspian)
Metsamor
Novovoronezh (4 stations)

The nuclear energy station at Razda, in Armenia, was closed down as a safety measure after the December 1988 earthquake. Semipalatinsk in Kazakhstan is a nuclear-weapon testing site.

Nuclear weapons see Armed Forces.

O

Obkom

The Communist Party committee of an oblast.

Oblast

A province or region. After 1929 the term replaced *Gubernia* for an administrative unit. There are also nine autonomous oblasts in the USSR, including Nagorny Karabakh in Azerbaijan.

Octobrists

A political party founded in 1905 to ensure the success of the Duma and the continance of the Tsarist regime. It represented large commercial interests, supported the Tsar's

1905 manifesto and it was a majority party in the third and fourth Dumas. In 1915 it suggested a coalition to the Kadets in order to form an effective war-government, and in 1916 it was in a conspiracy with senior army officers to overthrow the Tsar. In March 1917 it joined with the Kadets in Prince Lvov's Provisional Government. Leading personalities were Guchkov (a minister in Lvov's Provisional Government), Rodzianko (President of the fourth Duma) and Savich.

OGPU see **Political Police**.

Okhrana see **Political Police**.

Orgburo
The Organisational Bureau of the Central Committee, a key group with the Secretariat, Stalin joined it in 1920; it drafted the 1922 constitution.

OVIR
The MVD (see **Political Police**) department of visas which arranges emigration or private foreign trips.

P

Pamyat (Memory)
An anti-Semitic, Russian nationalist group, often opposed to the Soviet republics' calling for greater autonomy.

Partisans
There had been a tradition of irregular fighting bands, in parts of Russia, especially among the Cossacks of the south who remembered their eighteenth-century rising under Emelyan Pugachev. The origins of the Red Army lie in part in these, so in World War II it was natural when civilians or soldiers found themselves overrun by the rapid advance of the Germans to consider forming guerrilla units. Early Red Army thinking had included Tukhachevsky's 'Doctrine of Proletarian War', which was hostile to centralised control and made use of partisans. When the tide of the 1941 German advance had swept over whole regions and armies, there were left behind arms and men waiting to rise again. At first, loot and pillage were their main activities and all contact with the army was lost. The Nazis added to the impetus to go underground with their savagery and exploitation of all local resources. However, the institutions that survived, such as collective farms, became the focus for anti-Nazi resistance movements. The terrain was an important element in determining where partisan groups thrived; neither the cold northern front nor the open plains of the Ukraine offered cover, while the forests and marshes of Belorussia and the mountains of the Caucasus and the Crimea were well suited.

A partisan headquarters was set up in Moscow in 1942 to direct units and to try to organise radio contact and parachute drops, which became an effective part of Soviet strategy from 1943. The partisans developed different roles. In areas near the fighting lines they became the Red Army's advance guard, most markedly at the Battle of Kursk where they destroyed the German lines of communication and created their own, by building bridges and providing in effect a corridor for the Red Army's advance. Around Bryansk the forests held major units who could sweep an area behind the German lines, denying them control. The Germans in 1943 estimated 80,000 partisans in Belorussia, while in the Ukraine there were 220,000. As the Red Army advanced, partisans lost their function and were either incorporated into the army or deployed as security forces behind the lines.

To counter the partisans, who were subject to Hitler's merciless decree to shoot them on sight, mass hunts were organised, but with little success in the forests. Around Briansk anti-Soviet civilians were armed and encouraged to attack the partisans. This had some success, but the bands themselves took to banditry for their own, rather than the German, good. Another approach was to use prisoners who volunteered for the work, usually Lithuanian, Ukrainian or Tatar, but they, as soon as they saw the winning side, often deserted the German cause.

Parallel to the Soviet partisans were the national groups who formed up, with Soviet encouragement, in Hungary, Romania and Bulgaria and paved the way for Soviet take-over. The same would have been true of Tito's partisans in Yugoslavia, but their victory bred a sense of self-reliant achivement and led to Yugoslavia's independent attitude to Russia. In Poland the 'Home Army' grew from a coalition of small groups, but it was never acceptable to Moscow and led to the tragedy of their 1944 rising in Warsaw.

Party Congresses

Parallel to the Supreme Soviet, the Communist Party of the Soviet Union has as its supreme body the Party Congress which meets only rarely to discuss its Central Committee's report, the new Five Year Plan and changes in the Party rules and programme. It elects the Central Committee which discusses policy proposals and decisions. Party Congresses were held at irregular intervals, but since 1971 they have been held every fifth year.

Between the congresses, Party Conferences have been held which have a similar attendance but are not customarily used for vital policy decisions.

1st March 1898, held in Minsk, attended only by nine, announced the formation of the 'Russian Social Democrat Labour Party'.

2nd July 1903, held in secret in Belgium, then moved to London; it led to the Menshevik/Bolshevik division.

3rd April 1905, held by the Bolsheviks in London while the Mensheviks held their congress in Geneva.

4th April 1906, the 'Unity Congress', in Stockholm, there was a Menshevik majority.

5th May 1907, in London, with a small Bolshevik majority.

6th January 1912, in Prague, the Bolsheviks here constituted themselves a separate party, finally splitting with the Mensheviks and electing a Central Committee. Lenin, Ordzhonikidze, Sverdlov, Zinoviev and (in his absence) Stalin were the leading members. They became the 'Russian Social Democratic Labour Party (Bolshevik)'.

7th (Extraordinary) Congress, 6–8 March 1918, dominated by the problems of the Brest-Litovsk Treaty, the majority voting for Lenin's argument for its necessity and a minority for the 'Left Communist' call for a revolutionary war. The Party's name was altered to the 'Russian Communist Party (Bolsheviks)'.

8th 18–23 March 1919, meeting under the threat of intervention and immediately after the founding of the Communist International, questions of attitudes to the peasantry and of the building of the Red Army were discussed. Stalin obtained control of the Orgburo.

9th March 1920, in Moscow, Lenin announcing his ten- or twenty-year programme for the electrification of the country. A faction labelled 'Democratic-Centralists' advocating collective management was rejected.

10th 8–16 March 1921, announced the NEP and was interrupted by the Kronstadt mutiny. The Secretariat included Molotov.

11th 17 March–2 April 1922, the newly elected Central Committee voted to establish the post of General Secretary to run the Secretariat, to which Stalin was appointed. Frunze and others put forward 'The Doctrine of Proletarian War', formulated by Tukhachevsky, which advocated a decentralised and territorially raised army with no supreme command and reliance on a trained and armed people, fighting as partisans.

12th April 1923, Lenin being ill, Zinoviev gave the general report (Stalin had suggested Trotsky, who had declined). Stalin reassured the Party that there was no leadership split and expanded the Politburo, bringing in his nominees.

13th May 1924, Krupskaya handed Lenin's 'Testament' to Stalin who put it to a committee, an edited version was issued. Zinoviev demanded Trotsky's recantation of his 'permanent revolution'.

14th April 1925, 'Socialism in One Country'. The Leningrad delegation, under Zinoviev's influence and holding to ideals of world revolution, voted against Stalin's report and Zinoviev himself attacked it in public the following December. The new Central Committee was expanded from 51 to 63 with fewer opponents of Stalin.

15th 1927, preceded by 'discussion sheets' in *Pravda*, its resolutions were carried by a rehearsed group of Stalinists who drowned with shouting any attempt at opposition. The Five Year Plan was ratified, to expand heavy industry. The term 'Thermidorean' was used to describe the Trotskyite opposition.

16th 1930, the 1st Five Year Plan and its modifications were the main item. The slogan 'Fulfil the Five Year Plan in Four Years' was used to urge the Party to economic success.

17th January–February 1934, 'The Congress of the Victors': the authority of the Party and its leader Stalin was unquestioned.

18th March 1939, 2,035 delegates, but only 59 of those at the 17th attended; 1,108 of its 1,966 delegates had been arrested. The congress is to restore the Party after the Yezhovshchina through promotion to the many vacancies.

19th October 1952, after a 13-year break, a new Central Committee elected. Malenkov gave the Central Committee Report and Khrushchev put forward the new Party statutes; among changes, dropping the 'B' for Bolshevik from the Party name. The 6th Five Year Plan was announced which called for increases in food production. Stalin proposed that the Politburo be replaced with a new 'Praesidium', but this was only a manoeuvre to unsettle the top members of the Party.

20th 1956, marked by the 'secret speech' of Khrushchev, in which he revealed to the Party for the first time the 'illegal' activities and excesses of Stalin.

21st 1959, called to launch the Seven Year Plan.

22nd 1961, in which Khrushchev failed to get support for his educational reforms and to check the use of resources by heavy industry, in spite of the congress treating him with the greatest respect. A new Party programme was announced which would further the 'withering away of the State'. Shelepin made further disclosures of Stalin's misdeeds; it was outspokenly anti-Stalinist and as a result his embalmed body was removed from Red Square.

23rd 1966, organised by Suslov, but Brezhnev survived the power struggles and was formally appointed Party General Secretary.

24th 1971, emphasised the need for a new European security settlement and ruled that congresses should be held at five-year intervals.

25th February 1976, dominated by Brezhnev. The 10th Five Year Plan was announced, turning away again from consumer goods.

26th March 1981, organised by Chernenko, revised the system of leadership.

27th 1986; the Reforming Congress, a new edition of the Party programme, laying down the principles of perestroika. This was followed in 1988 by a specially convened 19th Party Conference (one had not been held since 1966). The Central Committee's report was used as a basis for debate, and not as heretofore simply to be accepted. It passed resolutions on perestroika and to ensure that Deputies had power and responsibility and on the greater independence of regions.

28th July 1990, brought forward from 1991. See Chronology.

Perestroika

'Restructuring'. The process of restructuring society and the State, dismantling the 'command-and-administer' system, following the 27th Party Congress.

Pioneers

The national organisation for 10 to 15 year olds. (See also **Komsomol**)

Planned Economy

A planned or 'command' economy is one in which the main drive is not consumer demand or choice, as in a market economy, but a plan drawn up by government in which the national resources are allocated in accord with political and social policies.

As early as December 1917 there were schemes for economic development, such as the plan to increase steel production using iron ore from the Urals and coal from the Kuznetsk basin. At the first meeting of the Council of Sovnarkhoz, an outline plan for the economy of the whole country was discussed. The Civil War soon put paid to this kind of global thinking but practical plans for the supply of fuel, metals, cotton, etc, were put into operation. No doubt an important link was established in the minds of the planners during the period of War Communism between the idea of planning and the use of coercion. At the 9th Party Congress in 1920, the preparation of an overall plan covering the whole country was adopted as official Party doctrine, and in December, with Lenin's blessing, a plan for the electrification of the RSFSR was presented. It was to carry out this plan that Gosplan was created. A similar plan to organise the metal industry was produced in 1923. In the same year Ivan Killinikov, an engineer and chairman of Gosplan's industrial section, put forward a plan which covered most of industry by which output was to increase by 182 per cent. The targets were reached, though from a very low start point, but the investment needed was vastly in excess of that planned.

Similar plans were prepared for transport and agriculture. The agricultural plan was devised by the economist Kondratiev, a member of the SR Party.

In 1925 Gosplan started work on the first fully comprehensive Five Year Plan, the final version of which was not accepted until May 1929.

Party resolutions concerning the plan were very firm on the need to expand defence and the socialist sector, that part of the economy in full public ownership, but were moderate concerning agriculture and on the balance between producer and consumer goods in industry. Of the major authors of the plan, the best known is S G Strumilin. Like most of the planners of this time, he disappeared in the purges of the 1930s.

The 1929 Plan called for extremely high growth rates in all areas of the economy, but especially in industry and agriculture. However by the time the plan was fully in operation, Stalin had effectively assumed power and his notion of planning was very different from the economists.

Stalin said 'We need a plan that will ensure a systematic preponderance of the socialist sector of our national economy over the capitalist sector. For a five year plan in which this was forgotten would not be a five year plan but a five year imbecility.' Considering that in 1928 approximately 75 per cent of industrial production and only 2 per cent of agricultural production came from collective or State farms, Kolkhozes or Sovkhozes, it was obvious that huge changes would have to be made to satisfy Stalin's ideals.

There was nothing cautious about his thinking and nothing humanitarian either. He had determined that the industrial sector would be funded by agriculture. Since the peasants would not co-operate, this meant that they would be forcibly collectivised, including the ruthless destruction of the kulaks. In the industrial sector he was not interested in the careful balancing of resources, or the gradual evolution of labour productivity by training schemes. He believed in the vast heroic gesture. Huge construction projects were embarked upon, all to be carried out by team leaders inspired by the white heat of socialist fervour. Ideas of carefully sustained growth he formally denounced as 'bourgeois deviationism'. He said 'We bring tremendous changes to every aspect of human life ... we penetrate the forces of nature and human relations in society.'

The planners had allowed for minimum and maximum versions of their goals, but Stalin was only interested in the latter. In almost all areas of the economy, the plan called for at least a 100 per cent increase in output, in some vital sectors, such as tractors, it called for output to increase by a factor of 50. The actual results, in so far as they can be realistically determined, were uneven. Producer goods achieved 127 per cent of target, consumer goods reached only 80 per cent, and agriculture was the most disappointing sector of all. Agricultural products in 1932 reached only 57 per cent of target.

However, even using the most pessimistic Western evaluation, an annual rate of growth of at least 10 per cent per annum was realised which, even considering the low starting base, was an impressive achievement whatever one may feel about the human cost. (See also **Five Year Plans** and **Industry**)

Pogrom
'Destruction'. In the Russian Empire attacks on Jews became officially condoned and mob assaults were common in the nineteenth and twentieth centuries.

Poland
Population: 36,745,000
Area: 120,725 sq miles (312,677 sq km)   Capital: Warsaw (Population: 1,641,000)
The ancient Kingdom of Poland had been shared among the Prussian, Austrian and Russian Empires in 1795. Russian Poland was fought over in World War I and its territory taken from the Empire under the Treaty of Brest-Litovsk. A republic of Poland was founded in November 1918 and guaranteed by the Treaty of Versailles. The new republic and Soviet Russia were engaged in war in 1919 as Polish troops, with French military advisers, attacked the Ukraine. The Red Army counter-attacked and was gaining the upper hand when, in August 1920, it was defeated outside Warsaw. Poland consolidated its victory with territorial gains, taking Vilnius (Wilno) from Lithuania and parts of the Ukraine and Belorussia.

In 1939 Poland was caught between Stalin and Hitler, hated and despised by both. When in March Stalin proposed a conference to discuss ways to stop Hitler, Poland refused for fear of provoking Hitler. In August Stalin, ignoring Poland as a power, signed a treaty with Germany in which spheres of influence were secretly included, dividing Poland on the Vistula and giving back to the Soviet Union those parts of the Ukraine and Belorussia lost in 1920. Assured that the Soviet Union would not interfere, on 1 September, Germany invaded Poland.

On 17 September the Red Army moved into Poland, taking the agreed parts of the Ukraine and Belorussia, 78,000 square miles (202,073 sq km) of land and over 12,000,000 people. Between 180,000 and 250,000 Polish soldiers surrendered to the Red Army. Most were sent east for detention. Soldiers found in civilian dress were arrested and sentenced to hard labour; from these were later recruited a new Polish army. Estimates of the numbers removed vary from a half million to one and a half million. Of 15,000 army officers arrested, 4,000 were shot in 1940.

Some of the Polish government escaped and formed a government in exile in London. In April 1943 Stalin broke off diplomatic relations with this government in protest at its accusations that army officers had been massacred in Katyn Forest. Later that year, at the Allied conference in Teheran, the Soviet Union was promised that its borders would be at least those of June 1941, and that Poland would not have any part of the Ukraine or Belorussia. The 'Curzon Line' was suggested as a border, westwards towards the Oder River.

In 1944, when the Red Army advanced over the Vistula, followed by units of the Soviet-created Polish army, Molotov asserted that the people of all Belorussia and the Ukraine had chosen to join the USSR and that the Poles must agree with the Soviet Union on new frontiers. He also attacked the anti-Soviet tone of statements by Polish generals and leaders of the underground. In July the Soviet Union set up a 'Rada', a 'Committee of National Liberation', in Lublin. Mikolajcek, the head of the Polish government in London, flew to Moscow, hoping to make some agreement with the Soviet Union in the belief that they needed his co-operation with the Polish underground. There was already a large non-communist underground army in Poland organised from London and commanded by General Komorovski, known as the Home Army.

On 1 August, as the Red Army reached the outskirts of Warsaw, the 35,000 strong Polish Home Army rose against the German occupiers. They wished to take Warsaw themselves and not be liberated by, nor in the debt of, the Russians. But the Soviets declared that there was no true rising and that it was of a group friendly to the Germans, and a waste of Polish lives. On 2 October the last of the Home Army in Warsaw surrendered. The rising was put down with terrible brutality. Mikolajcek went back to London.

In January 1945 the Russians entered Warsaw, set up a Government of National Unity, including Mikolajcek's Peasant Party. In June Poland signed a treaty agreeing to the new borders, thus moving the country west into Germany and causing large deportations of Germans. But Russian pressure led to an election in 1947 which put the communist–socialist alliance in power and drove Mikolajcek out of Poland. A constitution in 1952 modelled the country on Soviet lines.

Internal unrest persisted and, after riots in Poznan in 1956, forced the government to realease Cardinal Wyszynski from arrest and return Gomulka, who had been expelled in 1948, to the secretaryship of the Party. Gomulka was removed in 1970 in the face of popular unrest, but it was not until 1980, when food shortages brought industrial workers out on strike, that substantial change appeared.

The independent trade union movement, Solidarity, led by Lech Walesa made public demands, which at first were answered by martial law, but this was lifted in 1983. The economic difficulties of Poland persisted and Solidarity, encouraged by international support, particularly from the Vatican headed by a Polish-born Pope, edged towards open, multi-party elections in 1989. Solidarity won a majority and formed Poland's first non-communist government since 1947. For events since December 1989 see the Chronology.

Police

The term became tainted by association with the repressive Tsarist police and was dropped after February 1917. The civil police are the militia. (See also **Political Police**)

Politburo see **Political Structure**.

Political Parties

Main political groups prior to 1905

Liberals
Narodnik
Trudoviks

Parties and other political groups by 1917

The Left
Anarcho-Communists
Social Democrats (Mensheviks, Bolsheviks, also in Latvia, the Ukraine and Russian Poland)
Socialist Revolutionary (SR), founded in the 1890s from Narodnik groups:
  Left SRs (formed by Kamkov and Maria Spiridonova in 1917)
  Centre-Left
  Centre-Right
  Socialist Populist (Trudoviks)
  SR–Maximalists
The Centre
Kadets (Constitutional Democrats)
People's Socialists
Progressives
Octobrists
The Right
Monarchists
The Union of the Russian People

Political Police

Pre-Revolution, the Okhrana After the assassination of Tsar Alexander II in 1881, the rising number of active anti-monarchist terrorist groups caused the Russian government to strengthen the national gendarmerie by setting up a department for 'the protection of public security and order': the Okhrana. The Okhrana relied on a mass of paid informers and on fear. They had a reputation for beating confessions out of suspects, or simply arranging for their murder. Elements of the Okhrana continued to work up to 1920 for the various 'White' governments in Russia.

1917–22 Cheka Even the most liberal of revolutionaries had the lesson of the Paris Commune in their minds, for in 1871 when the Commune took over Paris, they killed one officer, but when the officers retook Paris, over 30,000 communards were executed. They feared any counter-revolution. From the start of the Revolution, to protect the Bolsheviks against subversion and to combat the Okhrana, Lenin employed Felix Dzerzhinsky, whom he had known in exile, to organise a political intelligence unit which became the 'Special Commission for the Struggle against Counter-Revolution and Sabotage' or Cheka. It was unusual among secret police organisations in being directly responsible to the centre of government and not to a Ministry of the Interior, as with the Okhrana.

In March 1918 the Cheka transferred its headquarters to Moscow, where political action was becoming centred in the course of the Civil War. In November its powers were modified by representatives from the Commissars for Justice and Internal Affairs, for up to then its 'Red Terror' had been administered by three-man tribunals responsible to no higher authority. In 1917 Dzerzhinsky had had no more than 100 operatives, but by 1921 there were probably 30,000. He employed informers and guards, often from nationalities whose cultural differences would make them indifferent to their prisoners.

1919 GRU To counterbalance the Cheka's power, Trotsky, as Commissar for the Army, set up a Department of the Red Army General Staff, the 'Chief Intelligence Administration' or GRU. Its first chief was General Jan Berzin, later executed in the 1937 purge. In 1921 the Cheka opened a foreign department, INO, which in its turn watched over Trotsky's GRU.

1922–34 GPU/OGPU In February 1922 the Cheka was abolished and replaced by the GPU (State Political Administration), which was brought under the control traditional for political police of the People's Commissariat for Internal Affairs (known as the NKVD), with Dzerzhinsky as head of both. The GPU was renamed the OGPU (Unified GPU) in November 1923.

Dzerzhinsky died in 1926 and was succeeded by Menzhinsky. He found that the Russian spy networks overseas had collapsed, starting with the arrest of their agents in Prague in 1926 and in Poland and Switzerland in 1927. Menzhinsky at once appointed Genrikh Grigorevich Yagoda as assistant chief of the NKVD's General Section for Terror and Diversion, SMERSH. Yagoda supervised the creation of new overseas networks, this time ensuring that they were supervised by a reliable Soviet resident.

1934–43 NKVD In 1934 the OGPU was abolished and its functions fully absorbed into the NKVD. The power of the NKVD grew and it developed para-military forces, including armoured units, capable of crushing any sign of resistance.

Labour camps had been set up as early as 1919 for the corrective treatment of offenders. In 1934 the system was organised by the NKVD under Gulag (the Chief Administration of Corrective Labour Camps and settlements). (See also **Camps**)

After the assassination of Kirov in December 1934, Stalin immediately decreed that the NKVD could carry out sentences of imprisonment or death as soon as their tribunal had judged a person guilty.

In 1936 Stalin ordered Yagoda's arrest and he confessed to poisoning Kuibyshev, Menzhinsky (thus taking over his post as head of the NKVD), Maxim Gorky and Gorky's son Maxim Peshkov: he was shot in the Lubyanka. His successor, Yezhov, had been since 1933 a member of the Party Purge Commission; in two years he raised the intensity of the purge to a peak, even purging the staff of the NKVD itself, before being removed himself (he vanished from Soviet history without trace). He was replaced in 1938 by Stalin's fellow Georgian Lavrenti Beria, the People's Commissar in the NKVD, who halted the policy of mass arrests.

1943–46 NKGB The reorganised People's Commissariat for State Security under Beria, the NKGB being responsible for seeking out the unreliable elements, while the NKVD continued to administer the camps.

1946–53 MGB The NKVD was replaced in name by the MVD when all 'People's Commissariats' were replaced by ministries, hence NKVD became MVD. But the MGB, Ministry of State Security, existed from 1946 to 1953. Beria remained in control of the State Security organs until shortly after Stalin's death in 1953 and then he too was shot.

1954– KGB In 1954 the MVD and MGB were reorganised, the former taking responsibility for all criminal matters and the latter becoming the KGB, the Committee of State Security, restricted to State security. The Prosecutor General, who had been subject to the authority of the NKVD, was confirmed as being in charge of all law enforcement in the USSR and being accountable to the Central Committee of the Party, with, under his authority, the prosecutors of republics, oblasts, towns and raions. The Special Boards, which had been able to pass sentence on cases presented by the NKVD and MGB, were abolished. This was followed in February 1955 by a change of personalities in the Supreme Court.

From its headquarters in the palatial building on Dzerzhinsky Square, the KGB controls an immense organisation, including the 23,000 uniformed border guards and, with the MVD, the internal troops, both part of the armed forces, but not under the Ministry of Defence. Although its latest chairman has given time to public relations, including a film explaining the work of the KGB, the Congress of Deputies in 1989 was unable to get figures on its budget.

The chairmen of the Committee of State Security, the KGB, since Beria's elimination, have been:

1954–58	Serov
1958–61	Shelepin
1961–67	Semichastny
1967–82	Andropov
1982–88	Chebrikov
1988–	Kryuchkov

Political Structure

Up to 1988 all voters elected their district soviets and their republic Supreme Soviets. They also voted for the USSR's Supreme Soviet: the All-Union Supreme Soviet of the USSR. This had two chambers, the Soviet of the Union of about 750 members, one for every 300,000 electors and, to provide a regional balance, the Soviet of the Nationalities of about 630, with 32 delegates from each republic, 11 from each autonomous republic and one from each autonomous area.

The delegates, elected every four years, were not necessarily Party members, nor were they necessarily of the nationality they represented; they were screened, however, by the Party-appointed electoral commissions and presented on an approved list. These bodies met for a few days twice a year to pass major items of legislation, but they appointed commissions to study proposals for legislation and, to carry on their functions throughout the year. They also elected the Praesidium of the Supreme Soviet. This Praesidium (meaning a standing administrative committee) consisted of about 40 people elected by the Supreme Soviet to run the affairs of the nation; it included the chairmen of the 15 Soviet republics, with senior Party officials and others who might also be members of the republics' soviets. Its chairman was the nominal head of state.

Parallel to the Supreme Soviet, the Communist Party of the Soviet Union has as its supreme decision-making body the Party Congress. It appoints the Central Committee of the Communist Party, also its Praesidium and Secretariat. The Central Committee functions between the Party Congresses, carrying out its decisions. From 1917 to 1934 it acted as the Party's parliament. In 1957, under Khrushchev, it became a decisive body, ending the assumption that only the small group in the Politburo held final power. It was the Central Committee that provided the majority that voted him out of power in 1964.

Its Secretariat of ten members was established after the 6th Party Congress and first headed by Y Sverdlov. In March 1919 a 'responsible secretary post was established and held by Molotov until 1922, when Stalin was appointed General Secretary. He

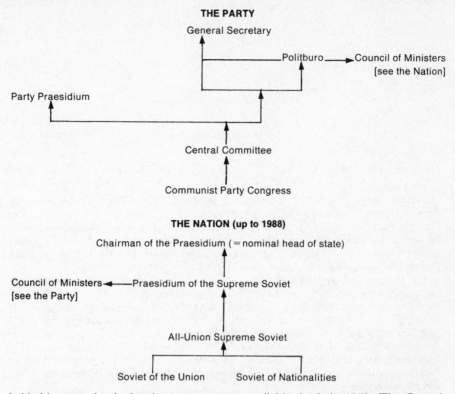

THE PARTY

General Secretary

Party Praesidium — Politburo ——▶ Council of Ministers
[see the Nation]

Central Committee

Communist Party Congress

THE NATION (up to 1988)

Chairman of the Praesidium (= nominal head of state)

Council of Ministers ◀—— Praesidium of the Supreme Soviet
[see the Party]

All-Union Supreme Soviet

Soviet of the Union   Soviet of Nationalities

held this post, developing its great powers, until his death in 1953. The Central Committee elects from its members the Politburo which is responsible for the running of the Party between plenary sessions of the Central Committee; it usually has 14 full and 8 'candidate members' who attend but have no voting right.

The Council of Ministers (originating in 1917 as Sovnarkom, the Council of People's Commissars) is appointed by the Politburo, or when it is not in session, by the Praesidium of the Supreme Soviet. Its members are the heads of ministries or departments running the nation, chairmen of key committees and heads of industries. The council has its own praesidium, composed of its leading ministers and the chairmen of the republics' Councils of Ministers. In theory the Council of Ministers implements the policies of the Supreme Soviet, and in practice it exercises its power by issuing decrees which have the force of law. The council usually meets only once or twice a year, hence its praesidium carries great weight, although its decisions are subject to the Politburo's scrutiny.

From 1988 the political–administrative structure of the nation was changed by the introduction of the Congress of People's Deputies, comprised of 2,250 deputies. One-third, 750, of the Congress seats were from the major all-Union public organisations (the Communist Party, Komsomol, trade unions, public committees, scientific academies, artists' unions, women's councils and so on). The Party itself has only 100 reserved seats – although Party members are likely to be in considerable numbers among the remaining 1,500 seats shared among the republics and regions. The Congress replaced the Party's rubber stamp, the Supreme Soviet.

Under the reformed constitution announced in 1988, from 26 March 1989 there were a variety of parliamentary candidates for the voter to choose from. Gorbachev ruled out 'multi-party' elections, and said that the Party would remain the 'huge

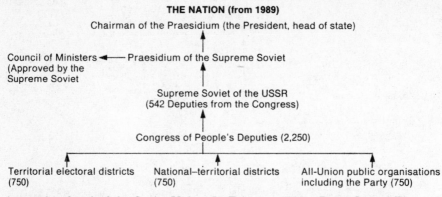

THE NATION (from 1989)

Chairman of the Praesidium (the President, head of state)

Council of Ministers ◄── Praesidium of the Supreme Soviet
(Approved by the
Supreme Soviet

Supreme Soviet of the USSR
(542 Deputies from the Congress)

Congress of People's Deputies (2,250)

Territorial electoral districts   National–territorial districts   All-Union public organisations
(750)   (750)   including the Party (750)

integrating force' of the Soviet Union. In February 1988 a Party Central Electoral Commission vetted the list of 8,300 candidates, producing a final short list for each of the republics' constituency seats. A quarter of the seats were single, unopposed candidates and many were contested by only two candidates, with a few having three or more candidates. In some, particularly in Lithuania, there were as many as eight. For the 750 seats for public organisations, there were 880 nominations.

The Congress of People's Deputies elected from its numbers a working parliament, still called the Supreme Soviet of the USSR (of two chambers, the Soviet of Nationalities – presided over by Rafik Nishanov – and the Soviet of the Union, with 271 Deputies each). One-fifth of the Supreme Soviet's 542 members stand down every 12 months and there are re-elections from the Congress Deputies. The Supreme Soviet chose its President, Mikhail Gorbachev, and Vice-President, Anatoly Lukyanov. The Supreme Soviet in 1989 set to debating an unprecedentedly heavy programme, from deciding its own rules of procedure to coping with the national demands of the constituent republics.

Population
The USSR gained land and people as a result of treaties made after World War II.

Territory	Sq miles (sq km)	Population (1945 estimated)
Lithuania ⎫ Latvia ⎬ Estonia ⎭	62,000 (160,622)	6,100,000
East Prussia	3,500 (9,067)	400,000
East Poland	68,000 (176,166)	10,000,000
Bessarabia & Bukovina	19,000 (49,223)	3,700,000
Moldavia	13,000 (33,679)	2,200,000
Carpathia	5,000 (12,953)	800,000
Karelia ⎫ Petsamo ⎭	20,000 (51,813)	500,000
Tanna Tuva	64,000 (165,803)	60,000
Kuriles & south Sakhalin Island	18,000 (46,632)	400,000
Total		24,160,000

The birth rate in the USSR has declined since 1950 from 26 per thousand to 18 in 1975. It is higher among non-Slav peoples. Russians now constitute less than 50 per cent of the population of the country.

Ethnic composition of the population (according to the 1979 census, thousands)			
Total	262,085	Yakuts	328
Russians	137,397	Komis	327
Ukrainians	42,347	Kabardins	322
Uzbeks	12,456	Kara-Kalpaks	303
Belorussians	9,463	Uigurs	211
Kazakhs	6,556	Gypsies	209
Tatars	6,317	Ingushes	186
Azerbaijanis	5,477	Gagauzes	173
Armenians	4,151	Hungarians	171
Georgians	3,571	Tuvinians	166
Moldavians	2,968	Northern ethnic groups	158
Tajiks	2,898	Komi-Permyaks	151
Lithuanians	2,851	Kalmyks	147
Turkmen	2,028	Karelians	138
Germans	1,936	Karachais	131
Kirghiz	1,906	Romanians	129
Jews	1,811	Kurds	116
Chuvashes	1,751	Adygeis	109
Ethnic groups of Daghestan	1,657	Turks	93
Letts	1,439	Abkhazians	91
Bashkirs	1,371	Finns	77
Mordvinians	1,192	Khakass	71
Poles	1,151	Balkars	66
Estonians	1,020	Altais	60
Chechens	756	Dungans	52
Udmurts	714	Circassians	46
Maris	622	Persians	31
Ossetians	542	Abazins	29
Koreans	389	Assyrians	25
Bulgarians	361	Tats	22
Buryats	353	Shortsy	16
Greeks	344	Other nationalities	136

Potsdam Conference

The conference of the Allied heads of state held shortly after the end of World War II in Europe, 17 July–2 August 1945. It was attended by Stalin, Truman and Churchill (whose place was taken during the conference by Attlee who had become British Prime Minister, defeating Churchill in a general election). Although there was deadlock over most subjects, particularly on the matter of political control in Soviet-occupied territories, Poland, Czechoslovakia and the Balkans, there was some agreement on the reparations each country could exact from their respective occupation zones in Germany. The Oder–Neisse Line was agreed as the western frontier of Poland. Truman told Stalin that the Allies had in their possession a bomb greater than anything used before. Stalin presumably thought this was some kind of bomb with a heavier load of explosive: he was not told it was the atomic bomb.

Truman asked Stalin formally to co-operate in joint action against Japan and the

Allies issued a final summons to Japan to surrender. From then on it was a race to see whether the Soviet troops could mount an offensive and gain a credible victory over Japan or whether the use of the atomic bombs would end the war before this.

Praesidium see **Political Structure**.

Pravda see **Newspapers**.

President

Until 1988 the head of state of the Soviet Union was, *nominally*, the Chairman of the Supreme Soviet. This was first Sverdlov until his death in 1919, and it was Kalinin in the war years from 1938 until his death in 1946. The *effective* head of state was the man who held the post of First Secretary or General Secretary of the Communist Party, a post first created by Stalin. Holders of this or equivalent posts have been:

Stalin	1927–1953	
Malenkov	1953–Feb 1955	
Bulganin	1955–1957	Head of government in concert with Khrushchev
Khrushchev	1955–Oct 1964	Head of Party, preferred the title of First Secretary
Brezhnev	1964–Nov 1982	Revived the post as 'General Secretary' 1966; also Chairman of the Praesidium of the Supreme Soviet
Andropov	1982–Feb 1984	
Chernenko	1984–Mar 1985	
Gorbachev	1985–	He became President of the Supreme Soviet in October 1988

The Chairman of the Praesidium of the Supreme Soviet has ranked as head of state in post-Stalin times:

1960–64	Brezhnev
1964–65	Mikoyan
1965–77	Podgorny
1977–82	Brezhnev
(the post was vacant from November 1982 until June 1983)	
1983–84	Andropov
1984–85	Chernenko
1985–88	Gromyko

Prime Minister

The 'Prime Minister' was the Chairman of the Council of People's Commissars (Sovnarkom) or 'Council of Ministers' from 1946, the body nominated by the Supreme Soviet as the government; post-holders to date:

1917–24	Lenin
1924–30	Rykov
1930–41	Molotov
1941–53	Stalin
1953–55	Malenkov
1955–58	Bulganin
1958–65	Khrushchev
1965–80	Kosygin
1985–	Ryzhkov

Progressives

A party in the 3rd and 4th Dumas representing landowners and the established middle classes, holding a political position between the liberal Kadets and the conservative Octobrists.

Progressive Bloc

1915–17, during World War I, the liberal centre of the 3rd and 4th Dumas, which was the overall majority, excepting the Social Democrats and Trudoviks on the left and the parties of the right, Monarchists and the Union of the Russian People, demanded that the Tsar have a government which would have the confidence of the people.

Provisional Government

The government formed by the Duma on the collapse of the Tsar's regime in February 1917. The Petrograd Soviet agreed to support the Duma's temporary committee headed by Prince Georgy Lvov, with the Kadet leader Milyukov as Minister of Foreign Affairs, the Octobrist Guchkov as Minister of War and the Socialist Revolutionary Kerensky as Minister of Justice. When the Soviet opposed the continuation of the war against Germany in May, Milyukov and Guchkov resigned, Kerensky became Minister of War and five more socialists came into the government. The Soviet mistrusted the Kadets and in July their pressure forced Prince Lvov to resign and Kerensky became premier of the Provisional Government.

Although the Provisional Government issued decrees on political and personal freedom, abolishing censorship and the existing police organisations, and promised elections to a new constituent assembly with universal suffrage, Kerensky tried to continue the war. The Petrograd Soviet, however, held greater power and from the July Days on, popular demonstrations and declarations centred on its activities rather than the Provisional Government. The army Commander-in-Chief Kornilov demanded firm action against the left, but in Petrograd factory workers, Kronstadt sailors and the Bolshevik Red Guards came out against such action and in defence of the Soviet. By October the Provisional Government had little control and the Bolsheviks seized their opportunity to overthrow it. Kerensky and the other ministers fled.

Purges

During the Revolution, and afterwards in the Civil War, terror was used as a conscious tool of policy by the Bolsheviks, admittedly to some extent in direct revenge for White terror tactics. Party purges were a different matter, intended to cleanse the Party of undesirable elements. Those purged simply lost their membership or Party posts. It was only later that purging implied imprisonment or killing. The first purge took place in 1921 after the 10th Party Congress. But in 1922 Lenin wrote 'We are living in a sea of illegality', and Stalin's ruthless treatment of the Party in Georgia made Lenin realise how dangerous Stalin's role as General Secretary could be. He could not have foreseen what was to come.

In the struggle for power after Lenin's death, it took Stalin six years of complex and vicious political manoeuverings to defeat his opponents of left and right. Trotsky was expelled to Turkey in January 1929 and his leading followers removed from the Party and exiled. The Right Opposition, led by Bukharin and Tomsky, were defeated in the Central Committee and both men were dismissed from their posts in April. Shortly after, they published recantations of their views. A second Party purge followed to weed out their supporters. In 1929 Stalin launched the collectivisation of land and the war against the kulaks. This climaxed in the famine in the Ukraine and Kazahkstan in which perhaps 5 or 6 million people died, and another 10 million kulaks were either mass deported in appalling conditions to Siberia or executed.

Stalin was imposing his will on the Party and the country, but there was opposition. In 1930 two members of the Central Committee circulated a memorandum criticising Stalin for his authoritarian attitudes. They were expelled from the Party and one of them, Lominadze, killed himself in 1935. Then, in 1932, Ryutin and some followers issued a platform specifically naming Stalin as 'the evil genius of the revolution' and calling for his removal. Stalin called for the death penalty but obtained little support. Kirov, Ordzhonikidze, Kuibyshev and Kossior are recorded as having spoken against him and he was supported only by Kaganovich. There seems, in fact, to have been a moderate bloc unwilling to use terror tactics against such respected members of the Party and many of Stalin's moves from 1932 until he launched the Great Terror in 1936 can only be understood in these terms.

In 1933 and 1934 a general purge of the Party was launched by the end of which nearly a million members had been expelled, and at the end of the year Ryutin was jailed.

In January 1934 the 17th Party Congress, the Congress of Victors, was held, at which Stalin proclaimed that, while at the last congress it had been necessary to finish off certain anti-Leninist groupings, now 'there is nothing to prove and, it seems, nobody to beat'. Of the 1,966 delegates to the Congress, 1,108 (nearly 60 per cent) were to die, and of the Central Committee elected then, 98 of the 139 members were to be shot during the peak years of the terror.

Stalin had already assembled his political supporters, such as Molotov, Orzhonikidze, Kirov, Kaganovich, Zhdanov, Khrushchev, Malenkov and Mikoyan. He now assembled his machine of repression. In April 1933 a new Central Purge Commission, with Yezhov and Shkiryotov, had been set up. This was followed by the Special Sector of the Central Committee headed by Poskrebyshev, and the State Security Committee with many of the same personnel. In July 1934 the OGPU was subsumed by the NKVD and Yagoda was put in charge of it.

The Murder of Kirov On 1 December 1934 Sergei Kirov, a member of the Politburo and Secretary of the Leningrad Party, left his office to attend a conference being held in a room in the same corridor. He was shot in the back by a young Party member, Leonid Nikolayev, and died almost immediately. Kirov was normally heavily guarded but on this occasion his chief bodyguard Borisov was nowhere to be found. The Party made an instant announcement claiming that the assassin was a supporter of Zinoviev and the Leftist elements in Leningrad. It now seems certain that the plot to kill Kirov was directed by Stalin through Yagoda, and that its purpose was to provide a basis for the total destruction of all opposition to his rule. Certainly everyone involved in the plot, including the NKVD men who killed Borisov in a faked car accident, were themselves disposed of: most of them immediately, all within a few years. Stalin himself went to Leningrad to conduct an enquiry into the killing and immediately issued a decree which became one of the legal planks for the conduct of the terror. It stated that:

1. Investigative agencies were to speed up the cases of those accused of acts of terror;
2. Judges were not to hold up execution of death sentences to consider the possibility of pardon because they would not be granted for these offences;
3. The NKVD were to carry out the death sentences immediately after the sentence was handed down.

There was an instant wave of arrests in Leningrad and Moscow. Declared to be counter-revolutionaries, the prisoners were quickly tried, sentenced to death and executed; many others were simply shot out of hand in the NKVD cellars. Throughout the country, thousands more people down on the NKVD lists as suspect were arrested.

In December 1935 Kamenev and Zinoviev were arrested and later in the month it was alleged that Nikolayev and some of the other accused were part of a Leningrad centre for terrorist activities. On 15 January Zinoviev, Kamenev and 17 others were brought to trial, accused of having given political encouragement to this group. They admitted moral responsibility for having encouraged opposition to the regime but denied any connections with the crime. Zinoviev was sentenced to ten years, and Kamenev to five years. The others were given similar sentences. This confession of moral responsibility was part of the process by which denials of responsibility by the accused for specific acts were devalued, and the outside world was led to believe that the charges were justified. Changes in Soviet law made at this time all seem to indicate preparation for the massive purge that was about to be unleashed. In June 1935 a decree was issued which provided a five-year exile for any adult member of a family one of whose number had fled abroad. All penalties, including the death penalty, were now extended down to 12 year olds.

The Show Trials Stalin now prepared to destroy the Zinoviev–Kamenev group and set out to obtain the confessions necessary for a public trial. Pressure was exerted on the accused sometimes by prolonged interrogations and deprivation of sleep accompanied by brutal bullying, sometimes by threatening their families, sometimes by straight torture or beatings by specially trained thugs, known as 'boxers'. But in the case of Zinoviev and Kamenev, although they were subjected to severe interrogation, the main reason for their agreeing to provide confessions to crimes, of which they were totally innocent, was Stalin's promise not to execute them or their followers, which he agreed would be given in the presence of the whole Politburo. In the end, it was given in front of a closed session consisting only of Stalin, Voroshilov and Yezhov. They were accused of having joined with a Trotskyite group, including Trotsky's son Sedov, for the purpose of assassinating Stalin and his close associates, Voroshilov, Kaganovich, Kirov and Zhdanov. At the trial, which was held in the little October Hall of the Trade Union House on 19 August 1936, the accused, with two exceptions, pleaded guilty. Vyshinsky in his speech for the prosecution talked of the Kirov murder in the following terms, 'These mad dogs of capitalism tried to tear limb from limb the best of the best of our Soviet land. They killed one of the men of the revolution who was most dear to us, that admirable and wonderful man, bright and joyous as the smile on his lips was always bright and joyous . . .' He ended by saying 'I demand that these dogs gone mad should be shot – every one of them.' The accused then made their pleas, most of them condemning themselves, some saying that they deserved to be shot as traitors. Kamenev was more dignified. 'No matter what my sentence will be, I, in advance consider it just.' The prisoners were taken back to prison and, despite Stalin's promises, immediately executed. According to reports, Zinoviev pleaded for his life when he realised that they had been tricked, whereas Kamenev went to his death maintaining his dignity.

The names of Bukharin and Rykov and Tomsky had been mentioned at the Zinoviev trial in connection with 'terrorist activities', and there is no question that Stalin was aiming the next major phase of the terror against them. But there was opposition to the idea of a trial on these grounds and instead Stalin turned on Yagoda who had been chief of the security police since 1934, accusing him of slackness. Yagoda joined others on trial in 1937 and was executed as a member of an 'anti-Soviet bloc of rightists'. In his place as head of the NKVD, Stalin appointed Yezhov in September 1938.

The Yezhovshchina In November there was a trial of Trotskyite saboteurs in Siberia, and in December another connected with sabotage on the railways. In January 1937 another group, of whom the main figures were Radek and Pyatakov, were tried and described as the Anti-Soviet Trotskyite Centre. Most of the accused were sentenced to death, Radek was given a ten-year jail sentence, but was later killed in prison by a criminal. In February 1937 Ordzhonikidze died under suspicious circumstances, whether murdered or forced to commit suicide it is not clear. He had resisted Stalin in the past and his elder brother had recently been shot after being tortured. At the February–March Plenum of the Central Committee, the direct attack on Bukharin and Rykov was made. Despite attempts by the remaining moderates, like Postyshev, to dissuade Stalin from proceeding with the purge, the two men were arrested at the meeting and removed to jail. In March Yezhov cleared the NKVD of all Yagoda's men, 3,000 are reported as being executed in the year. One of them, Chertok, who had interrogated Kamenev, jumped from his twelfth-floor flat rather than face interrogation.

Purge of the Red Army On 11 June 1937 Marshal Tukhachevsky and eight other senior army officers were tried and executed for 'breach of military duty and oath of allegiance, treason to their country, treason against the peoples of the USSR, treason against the workers and peasants Red Army'.

This revelation of treachery on the part of these eminent soldiers was as startling to the Russian people as it was to the world outside. There had been until then every sign that Stalin looked on the military with considerable favour.

Stalin's campaign started with the arrest of Dmitri Schmidt, an old veteran and commander of a Kiev tank unit in July 1936. He was accused of involvement in a Trotsky-inspired assassination attempt. In May 1947 Tukhachevsky and Gamarnik were both relieved of the office of Deputy Commissar of Defence and Tukhachevsky posted to the Volga military district.

The basis of the treason charge against the men surfaced in mid-May in the form of a dossier 'proving' that Tukhachevsky was preparing to betray his country's defence secrets to the German High Command. The documents were prepared with great care by Heydrich of the SD (Sicherheitsdienst, or SS intelligence) as part of a plot to destroy the High Command of the Red Army. The suggestion is that Stalin was fully aware of the origins of the material.

Tukhachevsky and the others were soon arrested and, after a purely formal trial, despite appeals to Stalin, shot, probably in the courtyard of the NKVD building in Dzerzhinsky Square.

Many explanations have been given for Stalin's actions against the army, including personal grudges. According to Trotsky, Tukhachevsky's attack on Warsaw in 1920 (leading to a severe defeat for the Red Army) was undermined by Stalin's attack on Lvov. The marshal had not hesitated to make his views known about this, which led to bad feelings between the two men.

Stalin, like all dictators, went in constant fear of a *coup d'état*, and although there is no proof that such a thing was ever contemplated by the accused men, Stalin may have genuinely believed it.

Following the execution of these dominant figures, the NKVD, at Stalin's behest, started on the wholesale slaughter of any 'dissident elements' in the Red Army. Soon after, 20 younger generals from the Moscow HQ were executed and the entire command of the Kremlin Military School was arrested. The campaign culminated in 1938 with the execution of Marshal Blyukher who had led the 1937 counter-attack against the Japanese in Manchuria. By the outbreak of World War II, the purge had accounted for 3 of the 5 marshals, 14 of the 16 army commanders, all 8 admirals, 60 of the 67 corps commanders, 136 of the 199 divisional commanders, 221 of the 397 brigade commanders. It has been estimated by Soviet sources that about half of the officer corps, perhaps 35,000 men, were shot.

As a result of this, the 1939–40 Finnish war was a disaster for Russia. Similarly the feeble response made to the German attack in 1941 can be directly attributed to lack of adequate preparation and poor leadership. The situation was only saved by the survival of two good generals, Zhukov and Timoshenko, and some excellent staff officers. Stalin's appointees, mostly part of his old Civil War group, such as Voroshilov and Budyenny, were often disastrous, and at best mediocrities. In 1940 German intelligence came to the conclusion that it would take the Red Army four years to recover from the effects of the purges and get back to its 1937 level of efficiency.

That the Red Army survived the assaults of the Wehrmacht and the Luftwaffe is remarkable, but perhaps even more so is that it survived the damage inflicted on it by the head of state. It may be that the unexpected result of the purge was to produce generals who were on average 20 years younger than their German opponents and that much more adaptable to new tactics.

The Provinces Now it was the turn of the provinces to feel the full effects of the Terror. Stalin's most trusted and most ruthless henchmen were sent to accomplish his intention, which was by now to crush any spark of resistance in the Party. Zhdanov took charge in Leningrad, where virtually the whole leadership, both political and industrial, was removed. Beria was sent to the Caucasus, Malenkov to Belorussia and Kaganovich to Smolensk. Khrushchev, Molotov and Yezhov were sent to the Ukraine to deal with what was described as the 'National Fascist Organisation' headed by the Party chairman there. Cn 30 August, alerted by Molotov's suggestion that a visit to Moscow would be in order, he shot himself and his wife. In January 1938 Khrushchev was appointed First Secretary of the Central Committee of the Ukrainian Party, replacing Kossior, who was arrested in April 1938, and proceeded to replace the entire Ukrainian Party structure. The purge proceeded at all levels and produced an atmosphere of fear that struck at the roots of political and social life. Denunciation was one weapon and there was a well-known case in Odessa of one man who denounced 230 people. Isaac Babel, the writer, who himself died in a camp in 1941, wrote 'Today a man only talks freely with his wife, at night, with the blankets pulled over his head.' One woman was sentenced to ten years for saying, after his arrest, that Tukhachevsky was handsome.

The Last Show Trial On 2 March 1938, the last great show trial took place in the October Hall. Bukharin, Rykov and Krestinsky were the most important Party figures, but there was also Yagoda, disgraced NKVD chief, Rakovsky and 20 others. They stood accused of spying, sabotage, of provoking a military attack on the USSR, of being responsible for the deaths of Kirov and Maxim Gorky. Bukharin was charged with plotting to seize power and kill Lenin and Stalin in 1918. Vyshinsky conducted the prosecution.

Krestinsky startled the court by withdrawing his confession but, after a night in the Lubyanka, once again adhered to it. Bukharin had agreed, threats having been made against his wife and young child, to pleading guilty to all charges, but he withdrew his confession before the trial started and only agreed after he had been severely interrogated, though not tortured. In court he defied Vyshinsky and denied all charges. Vyshinsky's final summing up produced his usual abusive rhetoric. Bukharin was that 'damnable cross of a fox and a swine'. The others 'must be shot like dirty dogs'. 'Our people are demanding one thing: crush the accursed reptiles'. Bukharin made a spirited defence of himself in his final speech; he denied the charges in detail, but agreed in general that he had degenerated into an enemy of socialism, and attacked Western commentators who suggested that the confessions were not voluntary. Aside from attempting to save his family, the only explanation for this confession, as for so many others, must be something like Koestler's in his *Darkness at Noon*; that loyalty to the Party and the historical necessity of its triumph overrode any values based on humanism. All the accused were found guilty, and, apart from three less important figures, sentenced to death.

The purge was not confined merely to the USSR; it spread its tentacles to foreign communists from Germany, Yugoslavia, Italy and Spain. The Polish Party was probably the worst affected, with 10,000 Poles in Moscow alone being shot at the time of the Bukharin trial.

In July two more important Party figures, Kossior and Eikhe, were arrested and disposed of after a brief trial and in August, just after the climax of the Terror, Yezhov was dismissed from the NKVD and Beria was appointed to take his place.

At the 18th Party Congress in March 1939, only 35 of the 1,827 delegates were left from the Victors' Congress of 1934: less than 2 per cent.

Body Count It has been estimated that at the time of the fall of Yezhov some 5 per cent of the population had been arrested, and that one of the reasons for his dismissal, and for the slowing down of the whole process of the purge, was that it was administratively impossible to keep up the supply of places in the prisons or the camps. The following are estimates for the population of the camps: in 1928, 30,000; in December 1938, 12,000,000.

Casualties During the whole period of Stalin's rule, and including deaths from the famine in 1932, the collectivisation of land and the massacre of the kulaks in 1929–30, and the Terror from 1934 onwards, the total must be of the order of 15 to 16 million. According to Robert Conquest, birth and death registration seems to have stopped in the Ukraine and north Caucasus during the Great Purge. Allowing for mortality and a declining birth rate, there was a 'population deficiency' of 15 million in the USSR between 1930 and 1937. The results of a census in 1937 were suppressed and the Census Board shot. The census of 1939 does not carry conviction, since Stalin announced the figures before the census had been completed, and no account was taken of deaths in the camps.

Current Russian figures show that in 1930–32, ten million peasants were deported to the Arctic, among them two million able-bodied young men, of whom at least a third died. In 1937–38, there were seven to eight million arrests and at least a million executions. In the course of recent investigations of the purges and the Terror in the USSR, the Kuropaty execution site (near Minsk in Belorussia) has been opened up. The number of bodies is estimated at 102,000 but it seems possible that the number at that place alone may approach 300,000.

R

Rabkrin (or RKI)
Raboche-krestianskaya Inspektya, the Commission of Workers' and Peasants' Inspection, established on 7 February 1920 under Stalin's control to monitor the working of the administrative apparatus. It functioned until 1934.

Rada

The Ukrainian term for council or soviet.

Raikom

The Party Committee of a raion.

Raion

An administrative district of an oblast.

Rapallo Treaty

The treaty ending the war between the two former Empires of Germany and Russia, signed in 1922, resuming diplomatic relations and renouncing all claims one against the other. One result of the treaty was the secret use of Russia by Germany to develop weapons and military tactics forbidden by the Treaty of Versailles.

Red Army

The army formed by Lenin in January 1918 from the Red Guards (see below). At first a volunteer army, conscription began during the Civil War. The name 'Red Army' was dropped after World War II in favour of 'Soviet Army'.

The war against Japan, which led to the 1905 revolution and the following years of repression by the army, saw the emergence of revolutionary tendencies even among Guards' regiments and signs of hesitancy in the Cossacks. The disasters of World War I, with hundreds of thousands of new recruits, ill-trained and poorly armed, smashed by German artillery, made prisoner by the thousand, or left wounded without help, led to the disintegration of the Tsarist army. By 1917 there were 15,000,000 men in the army. Casualties amounted to 3,000,000 dead or seriously wounded and 2,400,000 prisoners of the Germans and Austrians. In August 1915 conscription was extended to all males, with few exceptions, and by late 1916 mass draftings of men, some over 40 years old, were taking place, with resulting riots and desertions.

In 1917 Petrograd workers began to strike against their terrible conditions. There were 180,000 soldiers available to the authorities to control the city, and another 150,000 nearby. But many were untrained and many were recuperating wounded. Of these, perhaps only 12,000, including Cossack cavalry, could be counted as reliable. On 25 February the Tsar ordered the military commander to put an end to the disorders. The command forced the soldiers, and their officers, to take sides, and many sided against the Tsar rather than be used as the instrument of repression on their own kind. On 27 February the Volynskii Regiment paraded and refused to obey orders. They shot a captain and burst into the neighbouring barracks, where another regiment joined them. Soon 20,000 armed men were on the streets of Petrograd.

The great mutiny shook the Tsarist army. The Duma hoped the mutineers could control the army and Kerensky, then Minister for War, called on soldiers for support and to express their loyalty to the Duma. Most of the generals, too, preferred loyalty to Russia rather than to the Tsar. The army, in general, greeted the revolution but accepted the continuation of the war against Germany and the replacement of the Tsar by Alekseev as Commander-in-Chief.

'Order No.1' of the Petrograd Soviet (addressed to the Petrograd garrison) was issued on 1 March 1917. It decreed that soldiers' representatives should be chosen and report to the Duma, that the military were subordinated to the soviet, and that the Duma's orders should only be obeyed if not in conflict with the soviet's, that while discipline should be maintained, standing at attention and saluting were abolished and that elaborate Tsarist titles were to be abandoned in favour of 'Mr Captain'. The order reached the whole army and was greeted enthusiastically in the ranks, but it effectively destroyed the Tsarist army.

The October 1917 Revolution put the Petrograd Soviet into the Bolsheviks' hands. The remnants of the Stavka could not accept the new soviet's orders, and with no interest in continuing the war, the advance of the German army progressed steadily and met little resistance. The Bolsheviks needed an army if only to defend themselves against counter-revolution. Lenin issued a proclamation 'The Soviet Fatherland is in Danger' and on 23 February 1918 (now taken as the birth date of the Red Army) men flocked to enrol in the new army. In Petrograd 60,000 joined and 20,000 were sent straight to face the Germans. At the same time the Soviets began to make peace through negotiations at Brest-Litovsk, but appointed the Commissar for Foreign Affairs, Leon Trotsky, as Commissar for War. On 4 March 1918 he created a Higher Military Council (VVS) which drew up a plan for an army of 1,500,000 men. Lenin passed the instructions to Sverdlov's Central Executive Committee, the VTsIK, which on 29 March ordered compulsory military service.

1918–25 The new army was built out of the old. Old regular officers in the field, in headquarters and in the ministry became part of the Bolsheviks' army. They were invited, then ordered, to volunteer and in the year over 20,000 officers were enrolled. But they were called 'military specialists', since the concept of 'officer' had been banned. Political Commissars, trusted Bolsheviks, were appointed to every unit down to the regimental level, in conformity with the Provisional Government's practice (which derived from a similar usage in the early Napoleonic armies). The commissars led a Revolutionary Military Council (RMC) at each army headquarters, of which the military commander was a member, and the council conducted that army's campaign. The history of the Civil War on the Red Army's side was written by these commissars and they often depicted themselves as the generals. Many, of course, had no previous experience: Trotsky, Stalin, Frunze and Voroshilov being notable examples. Fewer cavalry officers had come over and their places as commanders were taken by sergeants, such as Budyenny.

By 1920 the Red Army had expanded to 5,500,000 men, of whom at least 48,000 were former Tsarist officers and 214,000 former non-commissioned officers. There had been defeats and chaotic routs, but in the long run it was gaining the upper hand in the Civil War over the Whites. By 1922 the Intervention was over and the last substantial White army, under Wrangel, had been driven out.

In 1922 Frunze put forward 'The Doctrine of Proletarian War' which emphasised mobility, the use of offensive strategies and guerrilla activity in a war which would liberate the workers of the world. Frunze and Tukhachevsky, with Voroshilov's support, put this to the 11th Party Congress. Trotsky opposed it and, with Lenin and other Bolsheviks, wanted to end the regular standing army and replace it with a militia (which would have been based on the urban worker and not the peasant guerrilla-cavalryman). In 1923 the Central Control Commission of the Party set up an enquiry which went against Trotsky and resulted in Frunze's appointment first as Chief of Staff in 1924 and, in January 1925, replacing Trotsky as Commissar for Military and Naval Affairs.

Frunze started on a programme of reform. By 1925 he had reduced the army from 5,500,000 to 562,000 and established a pattern of compulsory military service, a small regular army and a militia. Frunze had ousted Trotsky but he died, conveniently for Stalin, within the year and Voroshilov became Commissar and chairman of the RVS (as the VVS had become) of the USSR. The Red Army belonged to Stalin.

1925–37 Voroshilov was Frunze's heir. The Red Army had gained a corps of professional officers and a scheme to train them. The relationship between the army and the Party had been defined: while the politicisation of the soldiers decreased, the power of the Political Commissars was maintained. The 15th Party Congress, which formally expelled Trotsky, included in the 1st Five Year Plan a commitment to develop an economic base which would ensure the nation's defence.

In 1928 the Revolutionary Military Council gave Red Army commanders a rank and benefits they would retain into retirement and in 1935 officers were given new personal ranks, ranging from Lieutenant to Marshal. In the face of fascism and Nazism in Europe and the spread of war in the Far East, the standing army was increased by 1935 to 1,300,000, the RMC was abolished and replaced by a less powerful Military Council and a General Staff was created. In 1937 the army felt strong and free of the unpleasant purges in the Party and the rest of Soviet Russia.

1937–41 In April 1937 newspapers began to criticise the Red Army leadership, and Tukhachevsky cancelled a planned visit to Britain. The commissar system in the army was reinforced and the purge started in the Red Army. (See also **Purges**)

The purges wiped out the skilled professional soldiers at the top and middle ranks and halved the lower levels. Commands were taken over by young, ill-prepared officers, by Komsomol reservists and by recalled retired middle-level officers. Even the loyal Voroshilov reported to Stalin that morale and discipline in the army and navy had crumbled.

The first campaign of the Red Army in Europe was the occupation of Poland from the east in 1939. Cracks in the logistical services began to show, but when Stalin launched the Red Army into war against Finland, the deficiencies were clear and he reversed his policy. The Red Army was again allowed a professional corps of officers without intrusion from political doctrinaires. On 8 May 1940 Voroshilov was replaced by Timoshenko and the titles 'General' and 'Admiral' were restored. Military Commissars were abolished and a new harsh military code introduced, which included severe punishments and instant obedience to officers, symbolised by saluting. The 1918 decrees were abandoned.

1941–45 The shock of the German attack in June 1941 caused Stalin to revise the High Command. A State Committee for Defence, the Stavka, and newly empowered commissars, to stiffen the military will by threats, were created. A number of senior Party men were sent to supervise the different fronts, co-ordinating the military, industrial and civilian activities. With Voroshilov as commander of the north-west, Stalin put Zhdanov as political supervisor; the western theatre was commanded by Timoshenko, with Bulganin as his shadow; and the south-west had Budyenny and Khrushchev.

In 1942, faced with further German advances, Stalin continued to strengthen the army. On the Stalingrad front he put Khrushchev in charge of the overall political effort, and sent his most trusted Stavka generals to command in the field. He redefined the status of the officer corps, reintroducing epaulettes to emphasise and give weight to rank and making the 'General' class a higher category. The families of the military were to have special privileges. Morale was further raised by designating specially successful units as 'Guards Regiments' and so on, recalling the glories of the old Russian army.

1945–53 With the end of the war in Europe, Stalin reasserted Party control over the army. Heroes like Marshal Zhukov were transferred out of public view and credit for the victory was given to Stalin and the Party. Zhdanov, the political head of the Leningrad victory, was deputed to bring strict Party discipline into all fields, cultural, scientific and military, too. A trusted military élite was established, with the experienced and victorious posted out of public view to the provinces. But after his death, Zhdanov's Leningrad associates were purged and again Stalin seemed to favour the military as a balance to the Party.

1953– Malenkov curbed military expansion by stressing the importance of nuclear deterrence, for by now the Soviet Union's scientists had developed thermo-nuclear weapons, and the military's budgets were cut. Malenkov used the extra funds to speed up his consumer programme. Military discontent coincided with the rise of Khrushchev. The day of Malenkov's resignation, Marshal Zhukov was made Minister of Defence.

On 11 March 1955, 11 generals were promoted to marshal and Zhukov led a move to loosen Party hold and to revise strategic thinking. But in October 1957 he was dropped (accused of 'Bonapartism') and replaced by Marshal Malinovsky; a victory for Khrushchev and the Party, but also for other army factions. The army was against reduction to a nuclear missile support role and pressed for a large army which would be able to repulse an attack, with a strong regular cadre able to cope with the technological complexity of new weapons.

The 'Brezhnev Doctrine', in which the Soviet Union maintained its dominance over the Eastern bloc, intervening overtly in Czechoslovakia and Hungary and able to show local superiority to China, was central to strategy in the 1960s and 1970s. It was maintained by successive Ministers of Defence, while the army gradually improved its weapons systems. Its position remained unchanged until the lack of success in Afghanistan, a minor local war, caused dissatisfaction in both nation and army.

In January 1986 the new leader, Gorbachev, stated the objective of total elimination of nuclear weapons. On 7 December 1988, at the United Nations, he announced a cease-fire in Afghanistan from 1 January 1989 and cuts in the Soviet armed forces. Then, on 21 March 1989, he signed a decree for the reduction of ground forces by 530,000. One officer in six (or perhaps five) to go, including officers from the two armoured divisions being returned from Germany and disbanded. The overall reductions were planned as follows: Europe 240,000; Far East 200,000; southern USSR 60,000.

Four of the 19 divisions stationed in Germany in 1989 would go and one each from Czechoslovakia and Hungary. In the Far East the cuts would mean about half the troops facing China and the bulk of the 65,000 troops in Mongolia would be withdrawn.

Red Guards

Armed bands of workers in Petrograd in 1917 became officially recognised as 'Red Guards' and were the model for other cities.

In industrialised Russia young workers often lived in barrack-like accommodation provided by the factory or in overcrowded apartment buildings. The needs of World War I had led to an increase in the number of young workers in Petrograd, not only because of production requirements but also because the frequent drafting of workers to the army drew more recruits to industry from the countryside. Housing conditions were terrible and food shortages constant; strikes and consequent police repression were common.

The revolution of 1905 had led to both workers' soviets and armed groups: in Helsinki these had been called 'Red Guards'. The situation in 1917 brought both of these into action again. On 25 February striking workers, armed only with sticks and knives, began fighting the police. The military governor found he could not rely on the army, not even the Cossacks, to support the police and units of the army began to mutiny. Weapons now came into the workers' hands.

By mid-March 20,000 men were under arms in Petrograd, organised in many different ways, and the groups began to use the name 'Red Guard'. They were not aligned to political parties, but with the confrontation in April between the Provisional Government and the anti-war factions, the Red Guards showed their strength in demonstrating against the pro-war ministers. At first the Mensheviks opposed them, since they might be a rival to the revolutionary groups of soldiers and seemed to be a power base for Lenin's Bolsheviks. A Red Guard conference in April failed to establish them as revolutionary institutions.

The Petrograd city Duma organised a militia, effectively a police force, which was to be paid by the factories' managements. Lenin and the Bolsheviks saw the city militia as policemen rather than as armed workers and opposed it, encouraging a 'Council of the Petrograd People's Militia' instead. On 10 June the Bolshevik Central Committee called for street demonstrations against the war and against the Provisional Government, but these were abandoned after Chkheidze organised another demonstration on 18 June which turned out to be dominated by the Red Guards.

In July soldiers, sailors from Kronstadt and Petrograd workers, in all certainly over 30,000, demonstrated against the war, because of low wages and in hatred of the government. The day ended in disorder, Tsereteli called on the Provisional Government to disarm the Red Guards, the Council of the Petrograd People's Militia was raided and its officials arrested. The Provisional Government published a general Militia Law for Petrograd, Moscow, Kiev and Odessa, to bring workers' armed squads under control, which provoked further antagonism. The factory managements began to refuse to pay the militiamen, adding to the confusion.

By August the Bolsheviks were building a new Red Guard organisation based on factories, with 13-man units grouped in companies and battalions (of 480 riflemen) under district commands. The structure allowed Red Guardsmen also to have representatives at each district. At this point Kerensky, leader of the Provisional Government, dismissed Kornilov, the army commander, who then seemed to launch a military coup against Petrograd. The Red Guards rallied to the defence of the Petrograd Soviet and no Kornilov attack materialised. The Red Guards drew encouragement from this and, despite the Provisional Government's opposition, began to grow in number and weapon strength. In September there were between twenty and thirty thousand Red Guards in Petrograd, mostly armed with rifles but also with machine guns and some artillery.

When the Bolsheviks saw their opportunity for a take-over in October, they underestimated the Red Guards' size and power. Although not necessarily Bolshevik themselves, they were a force to be reckoned with in Petrograd and took many local initiatives in seizing key points. They turned out to be the most dependable support for the Bolshevik seizure of power.

In other industrial cities, including Moscow, a similar pattern of soviets and workers' militias had grown since February and, similarly, after the Kornilov affair the city militias decayed and were replaced by the Red Guards. Everywhere they were factory-based young men, ready in October to take power even before Bolshevik soldiers arrived or to send forces to help in the seizure of non-industrial areas. Workers who had been with the Red Guards and returned, unemployed, to their villages were often the leaders in forming village Red Guards.

The Red Guards defended the Revolution from immediate counter-attacks and protected stores and food supplies from looting. They enforced new decrees and many became the first members of the Cheka. Detachments were sent to fight the Don Cossacks and the Ukrainian Rada, to Finland and the Urals. When the German army advanced in December, Red Guards were sent to the front. Yet they were basically factory workers on part-time volunteer duty, and this made their next role ambiguous.

On 15 January 1918 the 'Workers' and Peasants' Red Army' was decreed. Many of the Red Guards were enrolled as soldiers and brought into the army their collective spirit and acceptance of political organisation, but at senior levels professional soldiers could not accept their amateur colleagues in positions of command. The two, Red Army and Red Guards, existed side by side until, at the 9th Party Congress in 1920, Trotsky proposed territorial militias based on industrial enterprises or the like. But since, in essence, the Red Guards were a spontaneous organisation of workers, the regular soldiers, led by Frunze, used to a central command structure, objected. With the end of the Civil War, the idea and the need for the Red Guards faded, just as Trotsky's influence had.

Refusenik

Those dissidents who in the 1970s refused on principle to do military service. Some of them were Soviet Jews who had been refused permission to emigrate.

Religion

On 2 November 1917 a Declaration of the Rights of the Peoples of Russia abolished all national religious privileges and restrictions. This was aimed at the Russian Orthodox Church, the State Church of the Tsarist empire, and by removing its privileges it relieved oppressed religious groups, Jews, Armenians and others, by putting them on an equal footing. Other decrees put Church schools and teaching institutions under the authority of the Commissariat of Education, gave only civil marriages legal status, and cut all State funding of Churches.

In the constitution of July 1918 clergy were condemned with the capitalists, ex-police and criminals, being deprived of the right to hold office and to vote: it also limited the clergy's right to housing or food rations. However, the State and religion were firmly separated and religious freedom was guaranteed. This was followed by an ordinance that specified the Churches and cults as Russian Orthodox, Old-Believers, Georgian, Catholic and Protestants (all as one), Judaism, Islam and Buddhism – or any cult not listed.

The 8th Party Congress of 1919 declared the need for a programme of scientific anti-religious propaganda and the 1921 10th Party Congress urged a massive campaign. During the 1922 famine, Church possessions were often seized by the State to help meet the emergency, thus intensifying the struggle. In May Patriarch Tikhon was arrested after protesting against the seizures. In June a State-approved 'living Church' established a supreme Church administration. In July the Metropolitan of Petrograd was executed.

The disestablishment of the Church proceeded with varying degrees of vigour; abuses were later officially criticised, such as closing a house of prayer when a group of 20 citizens were prepared to take responsibility for it; stripping religious objects of their ornamentation if they were used by a proper group; searches of priests being carried out at a time when they were ministering to a group, and giving priests unseemly forced labour, such as cleaning the streets. Interpretations of the laws followed and in 1921 the teaching of religion was confined to seminaries and the like. In 1924 it was laid down that children could only have religious teaching at home.

The 12th Congress of 1923 said the NEP had allowed bourgeois clerical–nationalism to grow, meaning pan-Islam, Zionism, Roman Catholicism among the Poles and Baptist evangelism in the north-west. However, crude anti-religious tactics were warned against at this congress and the next in 1924.

In 1929 the law was further tidied. Citizens over 18 had the right to form 'religious societies' or 'groups of believers', but these were restricted to religious activities (there could be no charities, pilgrimages or reading rooms, for instance). The society had to be registered, its funds only to be collected within the group and not as fees or charges, its meetings to be held only in the registered buildings or elsewhere by specific permission. The public display of rites, ceremonies or cult objects was forbidden. Religion was in the hands of the State.

In August 1929 the continuous working week was introduced throughout the USSR with varying days of rest which were in contradiction to established religious feast or rest days: absence from work could result in loss of rations or housing rights.

The principle of religious freedom was modified in Stalin's constitution of 1936 as the right to profess but not to propagate religion. Stalin demolished the Christ the Saviour Church in Moscow in the 1930s, but in the patriotic fervour of the war of 1941 the Orthodox Church regained something of its old national importance, and the Jewish community great sympathy in the face of Nazi persecution. Apart from the recognition of the Orthodox Patriarch as a national figure, there was little change in the official attitude to religion. Nor did the post-Stalin era bring change beyond minor technical revisions of the laws. In 1953 there were 15,000 churches, reduced, through Khrushchev and Brezhnev campaigns against religion, to 6,794 by 1986.

Gorbachev appointed a new head of the Government Council for Religious Affairs,

Konstantin Kharchev, in November 1984. He agreed to the reopening of churches and mosques, ended the persecution of minor sects, like the Hari Krishnas, and oversaw the Government's part in the millennium of the Russian Orthodox Church (from AD 988). Thirty-five churches were acquired by the Orthodox Church and three monasteries returned, including the Danilov in Moscow, to be the Church's administrative HQ. A new cathedral was to be built in Moscow and six churches, used as warehouses etc., were to be restored. However Kharchev's enthusiasm was excessive for a career Party man. He had supported a plan of Patriarch Pimen for democratic elections to the Church leadership, and was accused of meddling with the Church's affairs. He tried to reduce the KGB's influence on religious committees. But worst of all, he espoused the cause of the banned Ukrainian Uniate Church. Kharchev was removed from his post in mid-1989 and replaced by the more cautious Yuri Khristoradnov.

Uniate Church or Byzantine Rite Established in the western Ukraine, it uses Orthodox liturgical forms but gives its allegiance to Rome, although distinct from the Roman Catholic Church. It was a Polish creation of 1595 to lure Christians away from the Russian Orthodox Church. As a Ukrainian nationalist Church, it suffered persecution under the Tsars.

Its leader, the Metropolitan of Lvov, had been a noted patriot for many years, standing up to Polish repression in the 1920s and 1930s and to the Germans during their occupation. The Party Secretary in the Ukraine, Khrushchev, accused them of wartime collaboration and ordered them to merge with the Russian Church. Thousands of obstinate adherents were deported, and yet four million continued in an 'underground' fashion with masses said secretly in forests and cellars. They complained of persecution, instancing the beating-up of members and the disruption of Christmas celebrations (celebrated by the old style calendar, on 7 January, of course). Their churches have been blocked by police who try to force Orthodox priests to take services. In 1986, at an ecumenical meeting in Assisi, Italy, the Uniate Cardinal (who lives in Rome) and the Orthodox Metropolitan of Kiev were the only two clerics who refused to shake hands.

True Orthodox Christians A schism from the Russian Orthodox Church from 1925 with the death of Patriarch Tikhon, who, its followers said, was murdered because of his resistance to communism, and succeeded by Metropolitan Sergei who they thought to be involved with the OGPU. They were the object of purges in 1937 and the survivors are hotly against ecumenism, which they suspect as a plot against true Churches. They survive in the shadows without official recognition, which is not surprising since they canonised Tsar Nicholas in the 1980s.

Catholics of the Armenian Rite They are to be found in the Armenian and Georgian Republics, and number well over one hundred thousand.

Newer Western Christian sects These have been enlarging their following, although figures are unreliable. Among them are the Evangelical Christians – Baptists with, in 1987, 5,000 communities uniting over half a million people with 49 new prayer houses opened since Gorbachev took office. Seventh-Day Adventists flourish and there are also secret adherents to the banned sects of Pentecostals and Jehovah's Witnesses.

Islam This had been seen as a force in opposition to Tsarism by the Bolsheviks of 1917, because many Muslims had risen in 1916 in protest against a widened conscription order. However traditional Muslims were suspicious of the Russian Bolsheviks and the application to them of the same decrees as Churches gave rise to hostility. There was a Commissariat for Muslim Affairs between 1918 and 1920, but this was abandoned and a less conciliatory attitude adopted. The 12th (1923) and 13th (1924) Party Congresses recognised that the great mass of Muslims retained their 'medieval prejudices' and that stronger campaigns against them were needed. In the Great Purge of the 1930s many Muslims were accused of being in the pay of Japan as spies and saboteurs. In 1930 it was admitted that among the Chechen and Ingush, Islam dominated: these Sunni Muslims were accused of collaboration with the Germans during World War I and their communities broken up. By 1941 it was reckoned that there were only 1,312 mosques, served by 8,052 mullahs, in the whole of the Soviet Union.

In spite of the deportations from the Caucasus, the status of Islam in the Soviet Union improved with World War II and the number of recognised mosques doubled, and in 1945 a group was permitted to make the Haj pilgrimage to Mecca, though it was years before another was allowed. Gradually the Party reverted to an anti-Islamic attitude which, before it came to a head, was dampened by the Central Committee's November 1954 decree condemning anti-religious excess. By 1959 official figures suggested that there could be 30,000,000 Muslims in the Soviet Union and, with Moscow's awareness of its neighbours in Asia and of Communist China's mishandling of its Muslims, softer approaches began.

Jews They number about two million officially and their religion is among those officially recognised. (See also **Jews in the Soviet Union**)

Republics

The USSR is the Union of Soviet Socialist Republics. The Union consists of 15 equal Union republics, the largest of which is the RSFSR. Some of the Union republics contain within their boundaries autonomous republics, autonomous provinces (oblast) and autonomous regions (okrug).

Autonomous republics inside a Union republic have their own constitution which takes their special circumstances into account. Similarly, autonomous provinces and regions are fitted into the constitutions of their republic and have their own range of special features. There are 15 Union republics (SSR), within four of these are 20 autonomous republics (ASSR).

Republics	Capital	Population
Russian SR	Moscow	146,450,000
Ukrainian SSR	Kiev	51,200,000
Uzbek SSR	Tashkent	19,564,000
Kazakh SSR	Alma Ata	16,100,000
Belorussian SSR	Minsk	10,141,000
Azerbaijan SSR	Baku	6,800,000
Georgian SSR	Tbilisi	5,298,000
Tajik SSR	Dushambe	4,969,000
Kirghiz SSA	Frunze	4,208,000
Moldavian SSR	Kishinev	4,190,000
Lithuanian SSR	Vilnius	3,682,000
Armenian SSR	Erevan	3,410,000
Turkmen SSR	Ashkabad	3,400,000
Latvian SSR	Riga	2,673,000
Estonian SSR	Tallinn	1,557,000

Right Opposition

The name given by Stalinists to those led by Bukharin, Rykov and others in 1928 to 1929 when some of the Party urged compromise with non-communists and were labelled with this description. Also known as 'Right Deviationists'. (See also **Left Deviationists**)

RKI see **Rabkrin**.

RMC
Revvoyensoviet, the Revolutionary Military Council of the republic, the top military command, 1918–34.

Romania
Population: 22,553,000
Area: 91,699 sq miles (237,500 sq km)   Capital: Bucharest (population: 1,834,000)
Romania, with 22 million people, is a predominantly agricultural country and was a monarchy. In 1940, under German pressure, King Carol ceded land to Bulgaria and Hungary and then Bessarabia (which became part of the Soviet Republic of Moldavia). It allied itself with the Axis during World War II in the hope of saving itself and the king abdicated in favour of his son. In 1944 King Michael attempted to take the country out of the war and ordered his army to put themselves under the command of the Red Army. In February 1945 Vyshinsky ordered King Michael to appoint a communist, Petru Groza, as Premier. The government formed had several parties, but by 1948 King Michael had been forced to abdicate and the Communist Party, combined with the Left Social Democrats, had a firm grip on the country.

By the time Nicolae Ceaucescu came to power in 1965 more than 90 per cent of the land was either in State farms or agricultural co-operatives. He built up a very personal dictatorship which included more than 30 members of his family and in particular his wife Elena, who was appointed deputy Prime Minister. He played a maverick role within the Soviet bloc, failing to support them on the invasion of Hungary, and remaining friendly with the Chinese.

Domestically, his rule was both brutal and disastrous. He established the Securitate, the most feared secret police in Eastern Europe, reduced the economy to penury by insisting on repaying debts to the US, which had been built up by extravagant and pointless developments. He prefered to be known as the 'Conducator', and at the end of his reign was planning to destroy 13,000 villages and replace them with agro-towns. When the momentous changes began in Eastern Europe in the spring of 1989, reaching Bulgaria in November, it was generally assumed in the West that Ceaucescu was strongly entrenched enough to hold out.

But on 17 December there was rioting in the provincial city of Timosoara which was brutally suppressed by the army and the Securitate. According to the Romanian government, more than 600 were killed and many more disappeared. On 21 December Ceaucescu appeared before a vast crowd in Bucharest and was greeted by howls of derision. He and his wife fled by helicopter, but they were captured, speedily tried and executed.

Romania is now being governed by the National Salvation Front, but elections to be held in 1990, the first properly democratic elections to be held in the country since 1937.

For events since December 1989 see the Chronology.

Romanov
The family dynasty of the Tsars of Russia from 1613 to 1917.

Rouble
The old unit of Russian currency, with 100 kopecks to the rouble, used by the Soviet Union. The gold-based chervonets (see page 125) was introduced in 1922. In 1988 the official rate of the rouble was $1.00 = 0.60 roubles, but the black market gave five

roubles to the dollar. In November 1988 'hard currency auctions' were officially held, with major importers or exporters being allowed to participate. The first result was to devalue the official tourist rate for Soviet citizens by 90 per cent, making the rate per dollar 6.25 roubles. It is proposed that in 1991 there will be a new system of convertible currency, ending the artificially high rate which has been maintained for years to the detriment of foreign trade.

RSDLP
Russian Social Democrat Labour Party.

RSFSR
Russian Soviet Federal Socialist Republic, the official name of Bolshevik Russia to 1922 when the USSR was formed; now the name of the largest of the Soviet Union's republics.

Population (1988): 146,450,000

Area: 6,593,391 sq miles (17,081,323 sq km)   Capital: Moscow (population: 8,801,000)

The RSFSR covers three-quarters of the Soviet Union's area and over half its population are in it. The RSFSR is, in effect, the core of the old Russian Empire, from the Baltic to the Pacific, including Siberia but without the Polish and Ukrainian provinces to the west and without the Central Asian conquests of the mid-nineteenth century. Some 83 per cent of the people are Russians but there are about a hundred other nationalities. In the RSFSR there are 16 autonomous republics (ASSRs):

ASSR	Capital	Population (1987)
Bashkir	Ufa	3,894,000
Tatar	Kazan	3,564,000
Daghestan	Makhachkala	1,765,000
Udmurt	Izhevsk	1,586,000
Chuvash	Cheboksary	1,329,000
Komi	Syktyvkar	1,246,000
Chechen-Ingush	Grozny	1,235,000
Buryat	Ulan-Ude	1,030,000
Mordovian	Saransk	964,000
Karelian	Petrozavodsk	795,000
Mari	Yoshkar-Ola	738,000
Kabardin-Balkar	Nalchik	732,000
North Ossetian	Ordzhonikidze	619,000
Kalmyk	Elista	329,000
Tuva	Kyzyl	290,000
Yakut	Yakutsk	278,000

There are also five autonomous regions and ten autonomous areas (containing nationalities insufficiently large to form separate republics), among them being the Jewish Autonomous Region in Birobidzhan, close to China.

Eleven RFSFR cities have populations over a million: Moscow, Leningrad, Gorky, Novosibirsk, Kazan, Kuibyshev, Sverdlovsk, Chelyabinsk, Omsk, Perm and Ufa.

After the Civil War, industrialisation under the Five Year Plans changed the population pattern of the RFSFR. Much of the redevelopment was in Siberia, where the Tsarists exiled revolutionaries: under Stalin many of the camps were set up for the victims of collectivisation and the purges. The iron and steel industry in the Urals was redeveloped, partly at the new town Magnitogorsk and partly round the coalfields of the Kuzbass, where Kuznetsk became called Stalinsk (and is now Novokuznetsk). Oil and gasfields in western Siberia, beyond the Urals, have provided half the annual Soviet output.

It is in the Soviet east that discontent has been shown. In the March 1989 elections to the Congress of People's Deputies, with a high turn-out of electors, Party Secretaries failed to be elected in many places, including the Karelian ASSR, the Jewish Autonomous Region, Sakhalin and Khabarovsk.

The coal mines of the Kuzbass, the second largest producing fields after the Ukrainian Donbass, were said to be underfinanced and with productivity well below international standards, with 50 per cent of underground work still done by hand. Its coalmining cities are among the most polluted in the world. In July 1989 12,000 Kuzbass miners came out on strike and the numbers soon increased to 100,000.

In the Yakut ASSR, with over 1,160,000 square miles (3 million sq km) but only a quarter of a million people, elections to the All-Union People's Congress of Deputies were dominated by local issues of housing, food and consumer goods and the Party candidates suffered heavily. There is no movement for independence in these deprived territories.

For events since 1989 see the Chronology.

RVS
Revvoyensoviet (See **RMC**)

S

Sajudis
The Lithuanian party of democratic activists who support perestroika. (See also **Democratic Union**)

Sakhalin and the Kuriles
The Russian Empire reached the islands north of Japan and east of Manchuria in the 1850s. Southern Sakhalin (Karafuto) was acquired from Japan in exchange for the Kurile Islands in 1875, but retaken by Japan in the treaty of 1905. After World War II the Soviet Union took both southern Sakhalin and the Kuriles back, gaining only 18,000 square miles (46,632 sq km) and less than half a million people. But the resulting territory was of great strategic importance in the north Pacific and gave it control of a valuable fishing area.

Sakhalin When Anton Chekhov visited the island in 1890, studying the large Tsarist penal colony there, he called it 'the end of the world', the northern part of Sakhalin island became an NKVD corrective camp and part of the Gulag empire. After World War II the Soviets reinforced it heavily as a defensive frontier. It was from Sakhalin in 1983 that the Soviet fighters took off to destroy the Korean airliner which had strayed off its flight path.

The original islanders, the Nivhi people, still live there, but the result of the camps, the mineral exploitation and cement factories have made the island a dismal place. In the 1989 elections to the People's Congress, the Party Secretary was voted out and a young journalist voted in. With Gorbachev's dream of developing the Far East region, there are glimmerings of hope for Sakhalin among the young.

Kurile Islands The four islands to the north of Hokkaido, Japan, annexed by the Soviet Union in 1945. Japan refuses to sign a peace treaty until they are returned, but the settled inhabitants, Russians, Ukrainians and Belorussians, are determined to remain and develop the local fishing industry. They also argue that the islands were explored and taken hundreds of years before by Russians.

Samizdat

'Self-publication', newsletters or single issues of works of literature or politics produced outside the official publication and censorship system, typed, stencilled or photocopied and distributed by individuals, usually clandestinely. The word was formed by analogy from 'Gosizdat', the State publishing house. Works published outside the Soviet Union were sometimes called 'tamizdat' or 'over there' publications.

The switches in policy and practice have meant that some authors have their work published both openly and as samizdat literature, or that sometimes samizdat becomes public. Particularly from 1966, when more effective controls were imposed after the Khrushchev 'thaw', there was a proliferation of samizdats. Solzhenitsyn is a good example of the situation. After the authorised publication of *One Day in the Life of Ivan Denisovich*, he found it impossible to get his next works, such as *Cancer Ward*, published in Russia, so the works were irregularly published abroad and in 1974 he was expelled from the USSR.

Although the samizdats of the 1960s were typically anti-Stalinist or liberal, there have also been the ultra-nationalist writers whose unapproved works have appeared by these means. (See also **Dissidents**)

Scissors Crisis

The economic crisis of 1923–24 when two divergent economic trends, shown graphically, resembled a pair of scissors. The price of food went down, the price of industrial products went up. The peasants' incomes went down and their costs went up: the result was the discontent that the NEP tried to appease.

Sealed Train

The train on which Lenin and his companions arrived at the Finland Station in Petrograd in 1917. On 10 April (in the calendar used in Western Europe) a train left Zurich in Switzerland, taking a party of revolutionaries into Germany – then at war with Tsarist Russia. A railway carriage was prepared for them, which was locked by the railway authorities (technically called a 'sealed train'), to carry them through the Rhineland, via Berlin, to the Baltic port of Sassnitz, where they were ferried across to Trelleborg in Sweden. By night train they went to Stockholm and thence into Finland, unloading their baggage at the Russian frontier, and boarding another train which took them to Petrograd.

Here they were greeted by large crowds. All day Bolshevik agitators had been touring the city, displaying slogans and putting up posters to say 'Lenin arrives today. Meet him.' At the stations were not only the crowds the Party had called for but also a deputation from the Petrograd Soviet (who had made it a practice to greet all returning revolutionaries). Chkheidze, the Chairman of the Soviet, a Menshevik and opposed to the Bolsheviks, was obliged to greet Lenin at the station.

A list of the 30 passengers was made out at the start of the journey:

Lenin and his wife Krupskaya

Georgy and Valentina Safarov (a Bolshevik who had attended the Zimmerwald conference and who would later serve on the VTsIK)

Grigory Ussievich

Helene Kon

Inès (or Inessa) Armand

Nikolai Boitsov

F Grebelsky

A Konstantinovich

E and M Mirinhov

Abraham Skovno

B Eltchaninof

Grigory Brillant (or Sokolnikov, his revolutionary name)

M Kharitonove

D Rosenblum (probably of the Bund)

A Abramovich

S Scheinesohn

Mikha Tskhakaya (or Barsov, a Georgian who had been a delegate to the 3rd Party Congress before Stalin)

M Gobermann

A Linde
M Aisenbud (probably of the Bund)
Zinoviev, his wife Zena
   Radomyslsky and their son
D Slussarev

Pripevsky (the assumed name of
   Radek)
David Souliachvili
Olga Ravich

Smolny Institute
Formerly a girls' school in St Petersburg, it became the offices of the Petrograd Soviet and from September 1917 the headquarters of the All-Russian Congress of Soviets.

SNK see Sovnarkom.

Social Democrats
RSDLP (All-Russian Social Democratic Labour Party), the Marxist party founded at Minsk illegally in 1898 when all the delegates were arrested. The second congress was therefore held in Brussels and London in 1903, where the Lenin-led 'Bolsheviks' gained a vote over the (minority) 'Mensheviks'. The Bolsheviks saw the future state as one where only workers and peasants ruled, while Mensheviks wished to include middle-class liberals as well for the sake of steady social development. By 1917 the two were effectively separate parties and in 1918 the Bolsheviks adopted the name Communists. There were also regional Social Democrat parties in Latvia and the Ukraine.

Socialist Populist see Trudoviks.

Socialist Realism
The doctrine by which Soviet arts were judged. It was first publicly defined in the statutes of the Writers' Union in 1934 as 'the basic method of Soviet imaginative literature and literary criticism', demanding from the artist 'a truthful, historically concrete depiction of reality in its revolutionary development'. The doctrine was extended to all arts, not only literature. Socialist realism was given a historical foundation, crediting Gorky and other Russian writers with conforming to it before its formulation, as were Mayakovsky, Sholokov and Fadeyev, for example. Great international writers were also named as practitioners of socialist realism, including the German Brecht, the French Louis Aragon and the Spanish Pablo Neruda. Socialist realism in the theatre was doomed to be produced by mediocre artists and bore a striking similarity to the contemporary art of Nazi Germany, idealising the human body, male or female, in relation to industrial effort.

A characteristic of socialist realism was its willingness to conform to the Party line: for instance, collectivisation was popular and any depiction of a peasant who did not like it (or any worker who did not praise a Five Year Plan) was *untypical* and therefore not part of socialist realism. This gave Party officials an entry to literary or artistic criticism, and was the basis of Andrei Zhdanov's campaign from 1946, until his death in 1948, against intellectuals.

After Stalin there was a relaxation in the witch-hunting of writers and artists, but Sinyavsky's critique of socialist realism, published abroad in 1956, was the eventual cause of his arrest and trial with Daniel in 1965 (see pages 245, and 292).

Socialist Revolutionaries (SRs)
A political party founded in the 1890s from Narodnik groups – radical intellectuals who looked to the peasants rather than the industrial workers for a revolutionary base. Early in the century the SRs had a Combat Section devoted to the assassination of key Tsarist officials. During World War I they were mainly 'Defensists' (agreeing with the war as 'Defence of the Fatherland'). Although weakly represented in the fourth

Duma, the SRs had a considerable following in the country, more so than the Social Democrats.

SR-Maximalists split from the SRs in 1905 and were similar to the Anarchists in urging revolution. They believed in terrorism as political action, many being arrested and executed when they attempted to kill Stolypin, the Minister of the Interior, in 1907. They were usually identified as being near to the Bolsheviks, with whom they collaborated in 1917, but were later persecuted by them and the party ceased to exist by 1920.

Centre-left SRs were led by Chernov, and centre-right by Gots, Avksentiev and Bresho-Breshkovskaya.

The Left Socialist Revolutionary Party, an internationalist wing formed by Kamkov and Maria Spiridonova, split from the SRs in October 1917, joining with the Bolsheviks in the Military Revolutionary Committee until March 1918 when, opposing the Treaty of Brest-Litovsk with Germany, they withdrew. In July 1918 they took part in an armed revolt against the Bolshevik government.

Soviet
'Council'. The term was commonly used in Russia prior to its adoption by the communists.

Soviet Academy of Sciences
Originating from the Academy founded in 1724 by Tsar Peter the Great, with 270 full and 540 corresponding members, it is potentially the largest single concentration of scientific talent in the world.

Sovkhoz
State farms formed originally from the land confiscated from the large estates. They were managed and staffed by paid workers and it was hoped that they would serve as model farms to instruct the peasants in proper farming methods. They were always preferable to the Kolkhoz ideologically because they represented the ideal method of socialising agriculture.

In 1940 they numbered 400; by 1962 this had grown to 8,500 and a total area of 617,750 acres (250,000 hectares). When the Virgin Lands programme got under way in 1954, the Sovkhoz was the chosen model used to undertake the vast agricultural expansion. Despite the Sovkhoz's theoretical advantages and some practical ones – there were none of the complications often found in dealing with the Kolkhoz – the results were continually disappointing. Perhaps this was because they lacked the personal involvement conferred by the private plot. (See also **Agriculture**)

Sovnarkom
Soviet Narodnikh Kommissarov (SNK) Council of People's Commissars, the all-Bolshevik body elected by the 2nd All-Russian Congress of Soviets in October 1917 which (with some Left SR members) became, from 8 November 1917, the effective government of the nation exercising legislative powers, with Lenin as its chairman. In 1946 this became the Council of Ministers.

Sovnarkhoz
Local economic councils set up in 1957 to replace centralised ministries.

Space
After World War II, advanced Soviet theoretical physics, using captured German rocket technology to advance their own pre-war work, began a race with the US to develop powerful rocketry for military purposes, especially the delivery of the new atomic bombs. Rocketry soon became more ambitious and the exploration of space

became a national goal. France, China, Japan and the UK followed in this race, but were left behind by the super-powers in achievement. The USSR had the first dramatic success with Sputnik 1 in 1957, followed that year with Sputnik 2, carrying a live dog. A third Sputnik was launched in 1958 and in 1959 Lunik 3 photographed the hitherto unseen far side of the moon.

On 12 April 1961 the Soviet Union again seized the leadership of the race into space with the single orbit of the earth by Yuri Gargarin in a Vostok spacecraft. Valentina Tereschkova then circled the earth 48 times in June 1962, becoming the first space woman.

Manned space flights concentrated on the establishment of 'space laboratories', firstly through the three-man flight of Voskhod 1 in October 1964. The first man to 'walk in space' stepped out of Voskhod 2 in 1965. At this stage Soviet progress was marred by a number of accidents, principally the death of an astronaut from Soyuz 1 on landing in 1967. In 1969 the US Apollo 11 landed on the moon and its astronauts set foot on it. The Soviets followed this in 1969 by launching Soyuz 4 and 5 to meet and dock together in space. In the next year they collected soil samples with Soyuz 16 and landed a remotely controlled vehicle on the moon from Soyuz 17.

US–Soviet collaboration in space was achieved briefly in 1975 when an Apollo spacecraft linked with a Soyuz above the earth. Although hailed at the time, this collaboration was not continued under the conditions of mutual suspicion of the Cold War.

Interplanetary travel became an objective from 1967 when Venera 4 and later rockets went towards Venus and Mars, with a Vega spacecraft putting balloon-borne instruments into the atmosphere of Venus in 1985.

Much of the use of space technology has, as with other nations, concentrated on communications satellites and the Soviet Union has used its Molniya communications satellites for this purpose since 1967. For weather forecasting their Meteor satellites have been in continual use.

The military use of space has taken a large part of the Soviet defence budget. Soviet rocket unit forces are a separate branch of the armed forces, while nuclear warheads of intercontinental missiles are probably under the guard of special KGB units. The Cosmos programme of space satellites has been largely one of military intelligence, with low orbits and recovery systems, using radar and infra-red photography.

In 1987 Energia, a powerful space vehicle launcher, was developed, but that year also saw a setback with the failure of Proton, a heavy lift vehicle. It is probable that the immense costs of space travel have caused the Soviet government to give it less priority than before and, as in the USA, the beginning of the 1990s saw a pause in development.

Spanish Civil War

In 1936 the Spanish Left was dominated by the two general trade unions, the CNT, influenced by the anarchism of Bakunin, and the UGT, Marxist but not Bolshevik. The Spanish Socialist Party had formally disassociated itself from the Comintern and Russian Bolsheviks in 1921 and a separate Spanish Communist Party was then founded. The Communist Party was small in 1933 and had been torn apart over the expulsion of Trotsky. One group had formed the Workers' and Peasants' Alliance, which became the central group in POUM (Partido Obrero de Unificación Marxisto). For the elections of February 1936, the Left came together, at the communists' suggestion, in a Popular Front. The outcome gave them 278 seats against 55 of the Centre and 134 of the Right; of the 278 Popular Front seats, the communists held 17.

When General Franco led a military rising against the government in July 1936, the reaction of Stalin and the Soviet Union was dictated more by its fear of the growth of the Nazis and their Anti-Comintern Pact with Italy, than by the opportunity to promote a communist Spain. The Comintern was brought into play and communists from other countries were encouraged to participate. In August they accepted a non-intervention agreement with France and Britain and officially banned the export of weapons to Spain. At the same time the USSR established diplomatic relations with Spain and sent an ambassador with a formidable staff. This included Berzin, who had just left his post as head of the GRU, Military Intelligence, and as Consul-General in Barcelona came Antonov-Ovseenko, a leader of the October 1917 Revolution but who had since been thought a Trotskyist.

The Spanish Civil War gave the Red Air Force an opportunity for combat experience and the first 18 Il-15 fighters were unshipped at Cartagena on 13 October 1936. Probably up to 1,500 planes were sent to Spain and up to 770 aircrew served for some time during 1936 to 1938. The Soviet aircraft outmatched the first German aircraft they met, giving the Republicans air superiority until the Messerschmitt Bf109 altered the balance in mid-1937.

At the time, socialists throughout the world saw Spain as a microcosm of world politics: fascism was being fought by the popular fronts of the world. Disappointments were bitter. From the left-wing point of view, the policy of non-intervention meant that France and Britain were allowing Germany and Italy a free hand against the Republican government. While the activities of the Soviet Union seemed as much directed against its allies as against Franco and the fascists, judging by the betrayals and purges of the anarchists and social democrats in Spain. Most of the Soviet officers sent to Spain were executed on their return, as Stalin feared they had been corrupted by exposure to Western values.

Sport

Sport has always had an important place in Party thinking in the USSR. Considerable emphasis is placed on sporting activities at school and in the work place, and is backed up by a mass physical-culture movement. State and public organisations plan sports programmes and include large sums in their budgets for this purpose. The most striking result of this has been the impressive results for the Soviet Union in the Olympics. Between 1952 and 1988 Soviet athletes won more than 1000 medals at the games. At the 1988 Olympics at Seoul they won 55 gold medals and beat the USA into third place.

The most popular sports in terms of participation are track and field events, volley-ball, skiing, football, chess and basketball.

The Soviet Union has lately produced two world-class tennis players, Andrei Chesnokov and Natalia Zvereva. Many Soviet athletes have found world fame over the last 30 years, including such names as Vladimir Kuts, Irina Press and Sergei Bubka, the amazing winner of the pole vault at the twenty-fourth Olympics at Seoul in 1988.

High achievement in sports has also been encouraged by conferring honorary titles, such as Master of Sport of the USSR, of which more than a 100,000 have been awarded, while the rarer Honoured Master of Sport has been earned by less than 2,000 people in the USSR.

There has always been a degree of international resentment concerning the amateur status of Soviet athletes, on the grounds that they are heavily subsidised by the State. It is also true that sport has been used, quite unashamedly, by the USSR as a propaganda weapon.

SRs see Socialist Revolutionaries.

Stalinism

The model of socialism in the Soviet Union questioned openly since the 20th Party

Congress and attacked under the leadership of Gorbachev. Its main features were:
- an official ideology drawn from Marx and Lenin and used as the only measure of the correctness of any policy, law or tactic;
- the insistence on a one-party system with decisions made at the top and binding on all lower organisations;
- common ownership of the means of production, whose meaning was extended to mean State ownership and central planning of the economy and thence to Party control of all institutions, the courts of law, trade unions, the Press and cultural organisations;
- the belief that citizens can be converted to conform to a collective pattern and that individualism should be strictly controlled, hence criticism of the regime became punishable;
- a cult of personality, assuming that the leader of the Soviet Union must be not only great but perfect.

Stavka

Army Supreme HQ, a term used both in Tsarist days and in the Soviet Union, when it was re-established on 10 July 1941.

Strikes

Strikes in industry, when they occurred, have never before been publicised, but in July 1989 newspapers reported that the nation's coal miners came out on strike, losing three billion roubles' worth of production and threatening fuel supplies for the winter. The number of strikes in the first half of 1989 was given as 100. In April 1989 a new draft law on trade unions was published, reaffirming the unions' duty to defend the workers' interests, but not stating clearly if there was a right to strike. This was followed in October by the Soviet Congress agreeing to a decree outlawing strikes in essential industries. However, the decree established the *right* to strike as an extreme measure, and the right was not confined to unions but could be exercised by a work-floor group; management then found to have mismanaged could be dismissed.

Supreme Soviet see Political Structure.

T

Tajik Soviet Socialist Republic

Population: 4,969,000 (59% Tajik, 23% Uzbek and 10% Russian)
Area: 54,019 sq miles (139,946 sq km)   Capital: Dushambe
Contains the Gorno-Badakhshan Autonomous Region.

The Tajik people differ from others of Central Asian Soviet republics in being Persian rather than Turkic speakers, although in Gorno-Badakhshan, high in the Pamir Mountains, the population is mainly Kirghiz. The region was incorporated in the Tsarist Empire only in 1895 (under a treaty with Britain which at that time was much concerned with Afghanistan), taking part of the territory of the Emirate of Bokhara. Bokhara was declared a Soviet republic on 1 September 1920 and the Red Army moved into Dushambe on 21 February 1921. The territory then became the Tajik ASSR within the Uzbek SSR on 15 March 1925 and came into the Soviet Union as an SSR on 5 December 1929, the seventh Union republic.

Rebel Tajiks, commonly known as Basmachis, were active in their resistance to the Soviets up to 1926 and the last armed threat from them was a brief invasion in 1931 from Afghan territory by Ibrahim Beg, styling himself as the 'Commander of the Islamic Army'. The political unreliability of some Party leaders in this affair, together with a failure to meet the collectivisation targets, led to a purge of the leadership. In 1934 and 1937 the Party was purged for harbouring among its leadership Trotskyists and Bukharinists. Unlike other victims of the purges, those from Tajikistan have not been rehabilitated.

In common with other republics, there was an upsurge of nationalism in the 1980s. In 1987 there were anti-Russian and anti-Uzbek riots in Dushambe. Since then mixed marriages have decreased in number and non-Tajiks are said to be leaving the republic.

Tatars
There are two groups of Tatars in the USSR: the Kazan Tatars, with an autonomous republic on the Volga River east of Moscow, and the Crimean Tatars.

Tatar Autonomous Soviet Socialist Republic (within the RSFSR) Population: 3,564,000
Area: 26,000 sq miles (67,358 sq km)   Capital: Kazan
The assimilated Turkic-speaking descendants of the Golden Horde formed the Khanate of Kazan, a rival to Moscow until 1552 when it was taken by Tsar Ivan IV, known as 'The Terrible'. The Muslim Tatars were subjected to religious and racial persecution, but by the end of the eighteenth century their right to their religion was recognised, as was their control of Russian trade with Asia. Further religious repression in the mid-nineteenth century only added to their religious determination. At the same time, the Tatars began to develop their education and literacy. By 1917 Tatar newspapers, in their Turkic language, were widely read and printed in Ufa, Orenburg, Astrakhan and Uralsk.

In July 1917 a United Muslim Congress was convened in Kazan and in November at Ufa, where elections were held. On 29 November the Tatars declared an autonomous state, which existed until the Bolsheviks dissolved it officially in April 1918, having decreed a Soviet Socialist Tatar-Bashkir Republic on 23 March. The Civil War prevented any realisation of local governments. However on 23 March 1919 the Bashkir ASSR was established, and the Tatar ASSR on 25 June 1920.

The Tatars felt that, by making two republics, the Russians had reduced their status to that of other small minority peoples. Dissatisfied Tatar intellectuals were purged during the 1930s. However the survival of the Tatar language, used at Party meetings and at institutes of higher education, has ensured the continued identity of the people.

Crimean Tatars
Muslim descendants of the thirteenth-century invading Mongol and Turkic Hordes, they had, in the fifteenth century, an independent state. From Ottoman rule, they passed in 1783 into the Russian Empire. Under Russian rule they were a declining subject people and there were less than 200,000 of them by the start of the twentieth century.

The Crimean Autonomous Soviet Socialist Republic was established in October 1921. After the German occupation of the Crimea in World War II, the Tatar population was accused of collaboration and treason. It was sent, under penal conditions, to Kazakhstan and Uzbekistan in 1944; the half million survivors were 'rehabilitated' in 1967 in a decree which referred to them as 'formerly resident in the Crimea'. The Crimean ASSR had been disbanded in 1946 and incorporated into the Ukrainian SSR and the land resettled.

Tauride Palace
The building in St Petersburg which housed the Tsarist Duma and in 1917 the Petrograd Soviet.

'Thaw'
The sense of cultural freedom that followed the death of Stalin.

Theatre

The pre-revolutionary theatre of Russia was dominated by the Moscow Art Theatre, founded in 1898 by Vladimir Danchenko and Konstantin Alexeyev (Stanislavsky), who in 1902 produced one of Maxim Gorky's first plays *The Lower Depths*, as well as justly celebrated productions of Chekhov, Ibsen and Hauptman.

After the Revolution and under the generous and enlightened rule of Lunacharsky, the resolution made at the 8th Party Congress 'To open and make accessible to the working masses the treasures of classic art' was implemented. The numerous theatres already in existence, the Moscow Arts, the Alexandrinsky and the Theatres for the People in Petrograd were absorbed into the system, as well as the Bolshoi in Moscow and the Marinsky in Leningrad which specialised in opera and ballet. Many new ones, the Lenkom, the Lensoviet and the Meyerhold for example, were established. In addition to these the nationalities and the republics established their own theatres: in 1938 Georgia had 39 theatres.

In Stalin's time the usual problems of censorship existed as much in the theatre as elsewhere, and as a result Soviet dramatists of note are thin on the ground. Ivanov's *Armoured Train* was a success, as were Afinogenov's *Fear* (1931) and *Distant Point* (1934). Bulgakov's *Day of the Turbins* saved the author from acute disfavour, if not worse – Stalin liked it so much he saw it 14 times. It was even produced in London in 1938 under the title of *White Guard*.

During World War II there was, of course, little new theatrical activity, though there were plays by Simonov and Rozov on popular patriotic themes.

Following Stalin's death there was, as in the other arts, a considerable loosening of official restraint on the theatre. Several new theatres have opened in the last 20 years, of which the most notable are the Taganka, the Theatre of Satire and a new Meyerhold theatre, the old having closed in 1938. This new Meyerhold is a gesture towards the rehabilitation of the theatrical martyr of the Stalin era. What really separates the Soviet theatre from the rest of the world is the degree of security given to the actor. Each theatre has a permanent company and performs a changing repertory of plays. Actors, directors and designers have a job for life.

Third World, the USSR's involvement

1917–24 The Bolsheviks' success in 1917 and their survival and victories in the Civil War sent tremors through the world. An international revolution was a threat that seemed real. On 2 March 1919, 52 leading revolutionaries met in Moscow to establish the Communist Third International, the Comintern. (The First International had been founded by Marx in 1864 and was dissolved after a split with Bakunin in 1876. The Second was a non-revolutionary movement formed in Paris in 1889 which collapsed in 1914 with the outbreak of World War I.) They believed that Europe, weakened by war, would soon go up in flames and their time would have come. The Second Comintern Congress of 1920 produced Lenin's *Theses on the National and Colonial Question* which stressed the need to support anti-colonialist forces to undermine the imperialists' world. This was at the height of Zinoviev's influence as head of the Comintern. In September 1920 he was host to 1,800 delegates of some 20 nationalities from the Middle East and Central Asia at a congress in Baku. The Red Army, under Frunze, succeeded in ejecting the traditional rulers from the subject states of the former Tsarist Empire in Khiva and Bokhara and bringing them under Bolshevik rule. In August 1920 Lenin saw the chance of carrying the revolution into Western Europe where the Red Army was advancing into Poland, but world revolution was not at hand and the Polish workers did not rise to meet their would-be liberators. The Red Army was beaten and driven back.

The development of Stalin's 'Socialism in one country' policy as against the Trotskyist 'Permanent revolution', culminating in the 13th Party Congress in 1924, put the interests of the USSR first and from the mid-1920s there was an isolationist stance towards what we now call the Third World.

1953–62 The Comintern's early dreams of world revolution had faded, but the turmoil of the post-World War II period gave new hope to dreamers of a socialist future. By the 1950s the Soviet Union had the new governments of Eastern Europe on one frontier and communist China on the other. To the south, independent India and Pakistan gave evidence of friendship. There was hope that further political advances might be made.

The main stages in Russia's involvement with the Third World were:

1955 Bandung Conference: 29 states of Asia and Africa (including communist China, but excluding the USSR) met at Bandung in Indonesia. The main theme was their dissatisfaction with the domination of international politics by the quarrel between the two super-powers, the USSR and USA, and the danger of a Sino-American war. But this was also the year in which the USSR started supplying arms to a 'non-aligned' Egypt, which was also the adversary of America's ally, Israel.

1958 The West African state of Guinea turned down France's offer of independence within a French-controlled economic pact, and at once all French aid was cut off. Ghana offered political support and the USSR made loans to support the economy. One item of totally inappropriate aid is said to have come when an entire airport and all equipment was shipped to Guinea – down to the detail of the standard snow plough for the (Russian) winter.

1961 Belgrade Conference: 35 Mediterranean and Afro-Asian countries met and agreed on the principles of Bandung and declared 'non-alignment'. This conference was an embarrassment to the Russians, since the dissident communist leader of Yugoslavia, Marshal Tito, was the host. However, the Russians were able to make use of the principle of non-alignment, tactically, as a tool against American influence and it provided them with an important voting bloc in the United Nations General Assembly.

Advances were made in relations with the Third World, but not with the full success hoped for. Often military aid was asked for rather than economic and the regimes supported did not turn out to be the friends that Russia desired. In the case of Somalia, an aid recipient turned out an enemy. In Afghanistan, increasing economic aid turned into political intrigue and involvement which culminated, in 1979, in a war from which Russia pulled out, in some disarray, with damage to its international reputation, in 1988.

In 1961 Kwame Nkrumah, the President of Ghana, toured the Soviet bloc after the Belgrade Conference and was impressed by the State-owned corporations he saw. He returned to Ghana and within five years had created some 50 State corporations, obtaining various forms of international aid for all of them. The Russians gave particular help to the State farms and the gold mines. The refinery for the gold was, however, already obsolete by the time of its delivery and added neither to Ghana's riches nor to Russia's reputation as a donor. Other offers were to train 400 military specialists and a large number of doctors. The former offer made the old officer corps nervous and was a major cause of the military coup which toppled Nkrumah in 1966. The medical training disturbed the medical profession and returning graduates were subjected to severe testing and required to take further training, discouraging subsequent students from going to the USSR.

Trades Unions

Russian industry saw its first trades unions formed in 1905, as a result of the first revolution. In 1917 they were largely dominated by Menshevik Social Democrats, but after the October Revolution they were soon taken over by the Bolsheviks. While

Trotsky and Bukharin would have incorporated unions into the state machine, there was a strong element, the Workers' Opposition, who would have insisted on their remaining a separate instrument directly under the workers' control. At the 10th Party Congress in 1921, Lenin's view prevailed and the unions remained non-government bodies with the traditional role of defending workers' rights, but operating in collaboration with management and State. Unions thus became agencies for worker mobilisation and for welfare administration, and any attempt to make them independent ended with the purge of Tomsky in 1929.

In the post-Stalinist age, in 1957, the Central Committee called for unions to participate in economic planning and in 1970 they were given a central role in the revised Labour Code, with regulations for conditions of employment. 99 per cent of all industrial workers are union members, as are members of State farms (though not collective farm workers). Unions are organised by industry, not by 'trades', hence all the workers in one factory will be members of the same union. There is a structural hierarchy, from representation at the factory departmental level to deputed representatives at an all-union level with a controlling bureaucracy of its own, publishing the unions' own newspaper, *Trud*.

Most of the functions at the local level involve collaboration with the management, arranging prizes for achieving agreed levels of production, while protecting workers' rights, particularly in health and safety matters. Unions will provide legal aid to workers in dispute with their management, but until 1988 strikes were officially unheard of and unions are not geared to a confrontational debate with management.

Trudoni
Units of a day's work.

Trudoviks, the Socialist Populists
A large group in the first Duma of Narodnik origin. They campaigned mainly for land distribution. At first many of them sided with the Kadets, and while others leant towards the Social Democrats, although they did not associate with the revolutionary aspect of socialism. Kerensky was a Trudovik from 1912–17, but then joined the SRs as a minister in Lvov's Provisional Government. The Trudoviks then ceased to have independent political significance.

TsIK
Tsentralnyi Ispolnitelnyi Komitet, the central Executive Committee elected by the Congress of Soviets.

TsKK
The Central Control Commission, the top controlling Party body, elected by the Party Congresses, 1920–34. (From 1934, see **KPK**)

Turkmen Soviet Socialist Republic
Population: 3,400,000 (68% Turkoman, 13% Russian and 9% Uzbek)
Area: 188,417 sq miles (488,127 sq km)   Capital: Ashkabad (subject to earthquakes, Ashkabad was completely destroyed in 1948 and then rebuilt).
A battleground for many Asian empires, the land lost much of its fertility and by the nineteenth century was inhabited by Turkic-speaking Sunni Muslim peoples, centred on the oases and along the rivers. The rulers were the Persians or the Khans of Khiva. In the last quarter of the century, the Russian Empire extended itself beyond Kazakhstan, taking Khiva and Merv and meeting, on the Amur–Darya River, the British sphere of influence in Afghanistan.

In 1916, like the rest of Russian Central Asia, the attempt to conscript indigenous people (formerly exempt) for military service caused riots in the towns. But when, in

1917, the Bolsheviks tried to take power, mainly through the efforts of railwaymen in Ashkabad, they met hostility and a Russian White 'Provisional Government of Transcaspia', and a Turkmen Congress were formed. When the Turkmen Congress tried to form an army from returned Turkmen cavalry, the Red Army sent units to Ashkabad to disperse them. A Turkestan ASSR was proclaimed, as part of the RSFSR on 30 April 1918, but in July the congress, with some Mensheviks and SRs and help from a British army group from Persia, established themselves in Ashkabad. This threatened the city of Tashkent, in Bolshevik control, but when the British withdrew, the Red Army under Frunze's command took the area early in 1920. In 1924 the Central Asian republics were redefined and the Turkmen SSR came into being on 27 October 1924, with its congress formally declaring its formation and entry to the USSR on 14 February 1925.

Collectivisation attempted to force nomads into farms and there was open rebellion in 1928–31. The purges of the 1930s were directed particularly against those who gave signs of nationalist opposition, or who objected to the vast cotton schemes imposed from Moscow.

When, in 1958, the First Secretary of the Party, Babayev, argued that leading posts should be filled by Turkmen, he and others of the Party were dismissed and expelled.

In 1989, after the May Day parade, 200 students rioted. The shortages of food and goods were an immediate cause, but there has been growing a Muslim-nationalist feeling against the small Russian population.

U

U2
The US spy plane shot down near Sverdlovsk in May 1960. The Lockheed U2, first flown in 1955, was designed to fly at a great height, over 80,000 feet (24,000 m), for clandestine reconnaissance. The Soviet Union went to great lengths to shoot it down and thereafter the U2 was used for lawful purposes. The pilot, Gary Powers, was put on a show trial.

Ufa Conference
At Ufa, an industrial centre in the Urals, on 23 September 1918, an anti-Bolshevik government was established by dissident members of the Petrograd Constituent Assembly. Kolchak disbanded it in December 1918.

Ukaz
Also written as 'ukase', a State decree of the Tsarist days; the term was revived in the 1936 Soviet constitution.

Ukrainian Soviet Socialist Republic
Population: 51,200,000 (74% Ukrainian, 21% Russian, 1% Jewish, 1% Belorussian)
Area: 252,046 sq miles (652,969 sq km)   Capital: Kiev (population: 2,540,000)

1917–21 The first distinctive appearance of Ukrainian nationalism is in the nineteenth century with the poetry of Tarsa Shevchenko, but in its political forms it emerged only after the establishment of Soviet Russia, and the Treaty of Versailles, which divided its people into citizens of the Soviet Union to the east, and of Poland, Romania and Czechoslovakia to the west. Political attitudes to the Soviet Union were ambivalent. On one hand there were strong Russian Pan-Slavist sympathies, on the other strong feelings of a Ukrainian identity which stressed the importance of the separate language, and the fact that the majority of the population belonged to the Greek rather than the Russian Orthodox Church.

In April 1917 the first Ukrainian Rada (council, the equivalent of soviet) was established by an academic, Mikhailo Hrushevsky. In July an administration in the city of Kiev was started under Vladimir Vinnichenko, a Marxist writer, and Simon Petlyura a journalist and amateur soldier (all 'a ridiculous farce of a few university professors and students' according to the German communist Rosa Luxemburg). They declared a Ukrainian People's Republic after the pattern of the Bolsheviks in Petrograd, but the Germans, whose armies controlled the region, threw this out and put a government based on the land-owning aristrocracy in power, as part of their new eastern order.

Early in 1918, Bolshevik troops invaded and set up another Soviet Ukrainian government. But on 3 March 1918 the Treaty of Brest-Litovsk recognised Ukrainian independence. Soviet troops withdrew and the Rada returned to Kiev, though powerless in the economic and political chaos. The Germans appointed General Pavel Skoropadsky as 'Hetman' of the Ukraine, but chaos prevailed as peasant groups fought with arms taken from the disintegrating Russian army to protect their crops, and the Germans carried out bloody reprisals to defend their supporters.

When the German Empire collapsed in November 1918, the nationalist Directorate emerged again with Vinnechenko as President and Petlyura as Commander-in-Chief, and armed forces growing rapidly to 100,000. Petlyura entered Kiev on 14 December and Skoropadsky fled to Berlin (disguised as a German officer).

On one side of the Ukraine was the new republic of Poland, anxious to extend its influence to the Dnieper, and on the other the new Soviet state threatened by the White anti-Bolsheviks. A succession of Ukrainian governments came and went, supported by either one of these powers. For a time a 'West Ukrainian Republic' was formed in Galicia, but this came under Polish rule. The Red Army finally won the military struggle for the Ukraine and the last of the nationalist governments went into internment in Poland, after a final raid into the Soviet Union in October 1921.

In spite of Stalin (Commissar for Nationalities), who would have brought the Ukraine into the Soviet state as an 'autonomous republic', a Socialist Soviet Republic was established in December 1920. The Bolshevik leaders were opposed to the old 'Great Russian Chauvinism' and encouraged an independent cultural life in the Ukraine. Hence although there was a permeation of Russian, Ukrainian sentiment was allowed to be identifiable.

1921–59 Collectivisation at the end of the 1920s hit the Ukraine heavily, where the peasants' ways of land use ran counter to the large-scale farming being introduced and large numbers were deported from the Ukraine.

Ukrainians in Poland and Czechoslovakia began to identify themselves as minority groups there and a 'Ukrainian Military Organisation' and a 'Union of Ukrainian Nationalistic Youth' were formed and joined together in 1929 as the OUN ('Organisation of Ukrainian Nationalists'). In 1938, as Czechoslovakia was occupied and dismembered by Nazi Germany, the OUN began to see its opportunity. One faction declared Ukrainians to be 'Aryan' and became the willing tools of the German Nazis. The inheritors of the People's Republic, the UNR, had by this time strong links with the Polish government and many of them moved west towards the Germans when the Russians took half of Poland in 1939, and became the unwilling pawns of the Germans.

The World War II underground in the Ukraine has usually been described in terms of Khrushchev's partisans (he was Party Secretary there from January 1938) and an underground Central Committee: there were nationalists and anti-communists and some who co-operated with the Germans, especially in west Ukraine. There was the Ukraine Insurgent Army (the UPA), the Banderists (followers of Stefan Bandera, a Ukrainian nationalist released in Poland in 1939), 'Bulba's Men', led by Taras Borvets, and the OUN followers of Colonel Andrew Melnyk, a former Austrian officer and Ukrainian nationalist. Melnyk had moved to Rome and led the OUN from there until, during the war, he was taken into Nazi custody for attempting to set up a government in Kiev.

The OUN survived as a relatively powerful underground organisation during the Soviet occupation of eastern Poland, as parts of that territory were taken into Soviet Ukraine. As the Red Army retreated in 1941, Ukrainian nationalists claim that the NKVD shot all prisoners with long sentences and, in some towns, burnt down the prisons with their inmates. The OUN members tried to establish Ukrainian nationalist governments in Lvov (Bandera) and Kiev (Melnyk), but the Germans dispersed these and jailed the leaders. They were released in 1944 in order to lead the OUN against the Russians, but the OUN were at war with both Stalin and Hitler.

Many of these groups continued after the Russian re-entry to the Ukraine in 1944 and carried on a civil war until some time in the 1950s. They may have hoped that the defeat of Nazi Germany would mean the re-establishment of small independent nations and the OUN kept hoping for a popular insurrection. The UPA forces, mainly in the western Ukraine, had been hotly nationalist and had in their campaigns killed Jews, Poles and Slovaks; there were claimed to be as many as 20,000 UPA fighters by 1944, some operating in eastern Ukraine and as many as 6,000 in Polish territory. Brezhnev played a part in the elimination of the UPA. The famine conditions of 1947–48 brought more support for insurgents and more attempts to suppress or re-educate people. It was under these circumstances that the Uniate Church was banned in 1946.

The destruction of the nationalist underground was completed in 1959 with the assassination in West Germany, where he then lived, of Stefan Bandera.

1953– The death of Stalin brought immediate changes to the Party in the Ukraine. Khrushchev said that he had restrained Stalin in his fight against the Ukrainian intelligentsia after the war, and claimed that Stalin would have deported them all to the east. Kirichenko was sent as Party Secretary, and was succeeded by Podgorny in 1957. Both were Ukrainians with considerable power in the USSR and both gave a feeling of self-esteem to the Ukraine.

At least three underground political movements were uncovered in the western Ukraine between 1958 and 1961 and their leaders either executed or given long sentences. In spite of this, there has been a continual current of dissent, particularly among academics urging the spread of the use of the Ukrainian language.

In the Gorbachev era, the Ukraine still lived in the Brezhnev climate. The Party Secretary, Vladimir Shcherbitsky, was the last of the Brezhnev-era men on the Politburo of the Soviet Union, appointed in 1972. Although he expressed commitment to perestroika, the Ukraine was still without the reforms of the Baltic states. Shcherbitsky attempted to stop the publication of a Ukrainian Narodny Rukh (Popular Front) programme before the 1989 elections. This, supported by nationalists, members of the Uniate Church and human rights campaigners, was the strongest group outside the Party. Shcherbitsky was replaced by Ivashko, a Party worker in Kiev, and was dropped from the Politburo in 1989.

In Kiev new organisations were formed, including Zelenje Svit (Green World), Hromada (Gathering) at the university, the Ukrainian Cultural Club, the Ukrainian Helsinki Union, the Ukrainian Democratic Club. In Lvov, in western Ukraine, annexed from Poland in 1939, there are many who can remember a pre-Soviet Union society; there, a 'Lion Society' was formed in 1987 to preserve Ukrainian culture.

In the March 1989 elections to the All-Union Congress, while many voters spoiled their ballot papers as a protest against the Party's ban on their election meetings, many Party candidates failed to get seats. With insufficient votes, they were not declared elected. Thus in Kiev, the Party Secretary and the mayor, although unopposed, were not elected. For events since 1989 see the Chronology.

Union of the Russian People

A political party established in 1905, avowedly nationalistic, monarchist and anti-Semitic; the open front for the Black Hundreds, who in the period up to the Revolution, with the Tsarist authorities' approval, carried out pogroms and the murder of radicals.

Uzbek Soviet Socialist Republic

Population (1988): 19,564,000 (69% Uzbek, 11% Russian and others, including the Kara–Kalpak Autonomous SSR population: 1,140,000; capital: Nukus)

Area: 157,181 sq miles (407,205 sq km)

Capital: Tashkent (population: 2,100,000). The city, of largely Russian creation, was nearly destroyed by an earthquake in 1966 and has since been reconstructed.

A former protectorate of the Persians – Persian is widely used in the towns of Bokhara and Samarkand (where the inhabitants are said to wish to be considered as enclaves of the Persian-speaking Tajikistan) – Imperial Russia conquered its dominant Khanate of Khiva in 1873 and controlled the Emirate of Bokhara and the Khanate of Kokand. With Samarkand and Tashkent, a large Russian province was carved out. The revolts of 1916 were widespread, but the 1917 Revolution gave the opportunity for Russians in the towns to take over. Largely Menshevik, but with Left SR and Bolshevik railway workers and soldiers in Tashkent, provisional governments were formed. The Muslims of Turkestan were observers of the Revolution.

Among the early campaigns of the Red Army were those to bring the land under Bolshevik control. Frunze arrived in November 1919 with instructions from Lenin to this end, and found strong Muslim and nationalist attitudes there. To the Bolsheviks, these were lumped together as anti-communist bandits, Basmachis, and therefore not to be tolerated. Moscow's power was maintained from the largely Russian city of Tashkent. The Turkestan Autonomous Soviet Republic was formed in 1918 and, with the Red Army's victories, the Bokhara and Khorezm People's Soviet Republics in 1921.

A version of the NEP was introduced to Turkestan, in an attempt to fit the local economic patterns. In 1924–25 Turkestan was divided into national units (partly as a counter to Pan-Turkic claims that the peoples of Central Asia were once united by Islam and Turkic culture). The major republic of Uzbekistan was formed in 1925 and from 1928 it featured largely in the Soviet Union's Five Year Plans.

Collectivisation of agriculture from 1931 meant intensive growing of cotton, using the best of irrigated land for this. Uzbekistan was to give the USSR independence from foreign cotton markets. But even after the de-Stalinisation process from 1953, cotton remained the centre of its planned economy.

A cotton fraud of 3 billion roubles was uncovered in 1983 and led to years of investigation. As a result, Inamzhon Usmankhodzhayev was removed from the post of Party leader in January 1988 (for 'reasons of health'), as was Akil Salimov, President of Uzbekistan's Supreme Soviet. The Party leaders of Samarkand and Bokhara were sacked in October 1988. The most spectacular of the accusations was against Yuri Churbanov, the son-in-law of Brezhnev, who was accused of taking 650,000 rouble bribes while Deputy Interior Minister (1980–83). He was arrested, tried and sentenced on 30 December 1988.

But worse than the fraud, in the long term, was the result of intensive cotton planting: irrigation that has wrecked natural water supplies, fertilisers that have chemically polluted the countryside and a monoculture which has deprived the markets of the traditional abundant varieties of fruit.

The Muslim peoples of Uzbekistan have retained their languages and customs, while outwardly conforming to Russian practices. In spite of official disapproval combined with controlled toleration, Islam is strong. The Tashkent Islamic Board, responsible for 30 million mostly Sunni Muslims in Uzbekistan, Kazakhstan and Central Asia, sacked its Mufti Shamsuddinkhan ibn Ishan Babakhan, on 6 February 1989, after an appeal to the Party Secretary, Gairat Kadryov. This was a demonstration of their rejection of Party-appointed toadies.

The 160,000 Mesketian Turks, deported from southern Georgia to Uzbekistan in 1944, were the subject of racial attacks from 3 June 1989 and 15,000 were evacuated to the safety of military camps in the Ferghana valley, where most of them live, and later taken out of Uzbekistan. Cars were burnt and the Party headquarters attacked: 87 deaths were declared, although other estimates exceeded 100, among them Tajiks and a Russian. Mesketians are seen to be active in street markets and are held responsible for shortages. A few have returned to Georgia only to find their lands long-occupied by other Georgians. Some of the blame for the Ferghana riots was put on 'holy Uzbeks', a group of religious Sunni Wahabis. Ethnic riots erupted again when Uzbeks rioted against the police demanding the release of 400 of their number arrested in Kokand by KGB troops.

The new Party Secretary, Rafiq Nishanov, is associated with those who feel that Uzbekistan has been treated as a colony, supplying raw materials to Russia. The nationalist Birlik (Unity) movement, founded in 1988, has condemned the anti-Mesketian riots and told how rumour was used to spread dissension among Sunni Muslims (who have little in common with the Shia fundamentalists of Iran) and destabilise the new regime's efforts at perestroika.

V

Vekhi Group
A group of young philosophers who broke both with Marxist thought and with other radical traditions of Russian thinking of the 1860s and 1870s. Influenced by Peter Struve, they published a book of essays in 1909 under the title of *Vehki* (*Landmarks*). Their thinking stressed the need for the intelligentsia to break away from outworn revolutionary traditions, for government to be based on the concept of law, and for the State and nation to combine into a whole. There was also a strongly religious element in their arguments.

Apart from Struve, the other members of the group were N A Berdyaev, S N Bulgakov, S L Frank, B A Kistiakovsky, M O Gershenzon and A S Izgoev.

Vekhi, which quickly went into five editions, attracted violent criticism from the Kadets, the Socialist Revolutionaries and, of course, from Lenin who accused it of being typical of the Kadet outlook. After the Revolution, of which the group profoundly disapproved, some members produced another volume of essays under the title of *De profundis*. In one of the essays, Struve calls for the overthrow of the Bolsheviks for the salvation of the State. He made a direct contribution to this idea by joining the White forces under the leadership of Denikin. The majority of the Vekhi group, Struve included, emigrated from Russia during or after the Civil War.

Vishesinskaya Mansion
The Petrograd headquarters of the Bolsheviks in July 1917.

Volost
A rural district.

VSNKh
Vesenkha, the Supreme Council of the National Economy, managing industry chiefly; established in December 1917 and operating until 1934.

VTsIK

Vserossisski Tsentralnyi Ispolnitelnyi Komitet, All-Russia Central Executive Committee of the Soviets, formed in February 1917, mainly of moderate socialists, Mensheviks and SRs. In October, a new VTsIK was elected by the Second All-Russia Congress of Soviets, with a Bolshevik majority. It was the top law-making and executive body of State power in the RSFSR from 1917 to 1936. This became the Praesidium of the Supreme Soviet.

W

Wages

There are considerable wage differentials in Soviet industry, with the highest wages going to miners and workers in the oil industry. Wages are low by Western standards, but housing, though of rather poor quality, is available at very low rents. The Party élite (see **Nomenklatura**) get not only better wages but access to privileges, such as special shops, better housing, cars (chauffeur-driven for high Party officials), holidays in special resorts and have no difficulty in obtaining higher education for their children.

War Communism

The term used to describe the policies adopted during the confusion or near-anarchy of the first years of communist rule, from mid-1918. The decree of nationalisation led to the wholesale take-over of factories and businesses and, in reaction, a chaotic decline in industry and in food distribution. Grain requisitioning was carried out by Cheka squads going out to the villages; food rationing in towns was carried out with social discrimination against the 'bourgeoisie'. Inflation (multiplying some 1917 costs by four million in 1922) was welcomed by War Communism enthusiasts as 'the dying out of money' and the breakdown of society and its replacement by a communist society.

Whites/White Russians

The name given to the anti-Bolshevik forces in the Civil War. The colour white (as opposed to red) is often associated with monarchist, loyalist or legitimist movements and derives from the colour used by the French Bourbon monarchy. 'White' is not to be confused with Belorussia ('White Russia').

White Armies

The Armed Forces of South Russia (AFSR) was a coalition of White forces:
- The Volunteer Army, set up by Alekseev in the Don Cossack region in 1917, notable for the Don campaign under Kornilov and the 'ice march', the first Kuban campaign; it was then commanded by Denikin.
- The Don, Kuban and Terek Cossack armies were formed by local provisional governments.
- The north-western army was the smallest of the White armies, being formed in October 1918 at Pskov, under German protection. In May 1919 it was in Estonia and in July, under Yudenich, it advanced towards the Petrograd suburbs, but having only 14,400 men it was much inferior to the Red Guards who faced it. In November 1919 the army was disarmed and interned in Estonia.
- The All-Russian Directory at Omsk in September 1918 formed an army, led by Admiral Kolchak. At Samara another army was formed under Chernov. It was with these armies that the Czech Legion collaborated.
- Jägers, Finns trained in the German army who took part in holding Finland against the Soviet attacks (see **Finland**).

● At Archangel, the Russian General Miller tried to raise a force, but met with no local enthusiasm, and on 21 February 1920 he evacuated himself and his followers. In Murmansk there was no White army at all and the only opposition to the Red take-over was the presence of the British army (see **Intervention**).

● At Vladivostok, an army formation took charge, under Japanese occuaption. In eastern Siberia, also under Japanese control, the Cossack commander in Trans-Baikal, Grigori Semenov, had authority over troops.

Winter Palace
An official home of the Tsar and from August 1917 the seat of the Provisional Government.

World War I
The Russian Empire had chosen to give support to Serbia in the Balkans, partly as a counter to Turkish influence and partly because it lay beyond Russia's neighbours Romania and Austria. When, on 15 June 1914, the heir to the throne of the Austrian Empire, Archduke Franz Ferdinand, and his wife were shot at Sarajevo, Austria was convinced that the assassination was inspired by Serbia. In July Austria and Serbia went to war. The Tsar decided to mobilize the army and this caused a chain of military reactions in Europe, compelling Germany towards war with Russia. On 19 July Russia and Germany declared war and Austria joined with Germany on 25 July. France and England, bound by treaties, declared war against Germany and Austria, the Central Powers, at the beginning of August.

Austria invaded Russian Poland, while the Russians went into German East Prussia and Austrian Galicia. However, the Germans defeated the Russian army at Tannenberg on 16 August, destroying a massive army that many had thought invincible.

Turkey joined the Central Powers in October, closing the Black Sea to Russia, and began an unsuccessful campaign in the Caucasus.

Russia was at this point in a state of fervid anti-German patriotism, renaming its capital Petrograd, since 'St Petersburg' sounded German. Alexandra, the Tsar's German wife, and her circle, including the priest Rasputin, became objects of public suspicion and then hatred. But the disaster at Tannenberg, with its colossal losses of men taken prisoner, and evidence that the army was running short of munitions began to change public opinion. In July 1915 the All-Russian Union of Zemstvos for the Relief of Sick and Wounded Soldiers was formed under the chairmanship of Prince Lvov. It organised hospitals and supplies, but rapidly became a focus for criticism of the government among the middle classes.

The pattern of the war continued, with defeats on the German front balanced by victories against the weaker Austrians and Turks. In July the Germans took Warsaw in Russian Poland after a campaign with over a million Russian casualties.

The Duma met in August, proposing a Defence Council to run the war, and the leaders of the central and liberal groups formed a 'Progressive Bloc', calling for a 'government of confidence'. The Tsar now cut himself off from the support of his middle classes. He took command of the armies, moving to the Stavka, and leaving Palace politics in the hands of the Empress Alexandra. His ministers offered their resignations and the Tsar prorogued the Duma.

In 1916 the army's need for men was answered by decrees for the call-up of non-Russian peoples, previously exempt. This caused a revolt in Russian Asia, the first of many popular uprisings against the war. Although the June offensive by General Brusilov seemed victorious and took half a million Austrian prisoners, there were a further million Russian casualties. The food shortages and heavy losses led to strikes in Russian cities and mutinies by soldiers at the front. Even in the Palace there was a revolt and a group of aristocrats murdered Rasputin, believing him morally evil and pro-German.

On 27 February 1917 the Tsar's cabinet resigned and the Progressive Bloc proclaimed that they had replaced the Tsarist government. A Petrograd Soviet of Workers' and Soldiers' Deputies was formed and the Tsar left the army to join his wife and family, abdicating from his throne. A revolution was under way and attention in Russia was turned away from the war, to the satisfaction of the Central Powers.

The Tsar's brother, Grand Duke Michael, was dismissed as Commander-in-Chief and replaced first by General Alekseev and then by General Brusilov, who launched a new offensive against the Germans in June. But this only led to more losses and mutinies. Kornilov replaced Brusilov, intending to bring order back to the army. But the German army continued to advance along the Baltic coast, towards Petrograd, where the October Revolution brought the Bolsheviks to power. They called for peace and in November started negotiating at Brest-Litovsk for an armistic with Germany and a peace treaty. The Germans knew they could make their own terms, and started by declaring an independent Ukraine..

In February 1918 the Bolsheviks tried Trotsky's policy of 'neither peace nor war', that is to declare the war at an end but not to accept the Austro-German annexations. The Germans ignored this and resumed the fighting, obliging the Soviets to accept their terms for peace. The Treaty of Brest-Litovsk between Russia and the Central Powers was signed in March, ceding independence to Poland, the Ukraine and Finland and accepting German claims on the Baltic. Belorussians took the opportunity to declare independence too, while the 'Democratic Federal Republic of Transcaucasia' was declared in the presence of Turkish and German troops.

This was seen in the West as a great German gain. Allied troops landed at Murmansk and Vladivostok to protect their interests. To the revolution was now added Intervention. A 'White' goverment, loyal to the Tsarist Empire, was set up in Archangel, while in the south and east other White governments and armies formed with Allied encouragement. To Intervention was added civil war.

World War I ended in November 1918 and the Soviet government denounced the Brest-Litovsk Treaty. However, peace in Europe was barely noticed in Russia, where one war had blended into another.

World War II

Always referred to in the Soviet Union as the Great Patriotic War. The Russo-German pact signed in September 1939, and Stalin's belief that Hitler could not possibly fight a campaign on two fronts, seems to have deluded him into believing that the Nazis would not move against the USSR, at least not in the immediate future. The massive German attack, which they code-named Barbarossa and launched on 22 June 1941, despite numerous reports both from intelligence sources and from his own generals in the field, took Stalin completely by surprise.

The German attack was launched on three fronts simultaneously: Army Group North driving for Leningrad via the Baltic states; Army Group Centre aiming for Moscow on the line of Minsk and Smolensk; while Army Group South's objective was Kiev and the Ukraine. Over 3,000 Russian aircraft were destroyed in the first ten days of fighting, and the Red Army, many of its best commanders killed in the purges, and with inadequate tanks and aircraft support, was in no position to resist. Leningrad was under siege within a fortnight, and on the central front the German army had reached more than 350 miles (560 km) beyond Smolensk by early August, with 850,000 Russian troops captured.

In the south, though there was stronger resistance at first, a million and a half men were captured at Kiev and at Uman in the Ukraine. By 15 October Rostov and Kharkov had been captured. By 20 October Operation Typhoon saw the German troops 40 miles (65 km) from Moscow.

In December General Zhukov, who had been brought in to defend the city, counterattacked, and the Red Army launched other attacks at Rostov, and to relieve Leningrad.

Although these were not notably successful, the temperature on the centre and northern fronts had dropped to minus 40° and the Nazi forces, unable to make further progress, fell back from the capital.

In the spring of 1942, Hitler launched his offensive in the Caucasus, partly to seize oilfields supplying fuel to the Red Army, but it became increasingly concentrated on the capture of Stalingrad. Spearheaded by General von Paulus with his 6th Army Group, a direct attack was launched in August. The city was defended street by street. Then in November General Zhukov, in overall command of armies under Generals Rokossovsky, Vatutin and Yeremenko, led an attack to retake the city. Despite desperate attempts by the German High Command to reinforce von Paulus, he was captured in February 1943 with 90,000 of his men and 250,000 in total casualties. This was effectively the turning-point in the war.

By 1943 the situation of the Red Army had improved enormously. Counting on the neutrality pact signed with the Japanese in 1941, Stalin had brought reinforcements in from the Far East, and the newly expanded industries beyond the Urals were turning out new and improved tanks and aircraft. From 1942 the USSR had received vast quantities of war *matériel*, including aircraft, and particularly motor transport from the US and Britain. The supplies came overland through Iran and by sea to the Arctic port of Murmansk, and some through the eastern port of Vladivostok. At the same time, younger and better commanders had replaced those relics of the Civil War, such as Marshals Voroshilov, Budyenny and Timoshenko. The German situation was precisely the reverse: they had suffered huge losses, partisans were tying down large numbers of German troops and Hitler continually interfered with his High Command.

The second great German defeat was the Battle of Kursk in August 1943 (see pages 164–5), the biggest tank battle ever fought. This was followed by an overall Russian offensive in which the Red Army captured Smolensk at the end of September and Kiev in early November.

All in all, German morale was very low. From January 1944 the Red Army was attacking on all fronts, and by then the Soviet High Command had a superiority of more than two to one in men, tanks and aircraft. Furthermore, the US and British landings in Italy in 1943 and in France in 1944 diverted all German reserves away from the Russian front.

At the end of the 1944, German Army Group North was trapped in a huge pocket in the Baltic states, and in August an offensive in the Balkans had led to the capitulation of Romania, together with the majority of the German armies there. By February 1945 Bulgaria, Hungary and Yugoslavia had all fallen to the Red Army. In April Marshal Malinovsky's men reached Vienna.

On 25 April the two and a half million men of the eight Soviet armies in the central sector launched an all-out attack on Berlin. They entered the Reichstag on 30 April. Hitler committed suicide in his bunker on the same day, and on 8 May Field Marshal Keitel signed the document of unconditional surrender which ended the war in Europe.

The Soviet Union had suffered enormous casualties, perhaps approaching 20 million dead and missing and the destruction of much of its industry. The Great Patriotic War had started only a few years after the terrible purges of the 1930s. But its effect, encouraged by Stalin's radio speeches, was to revive an intense patriotism which enabled the country to triumph against appalling odds.

Writers' Union of the USSR

The sole professional organisation of writers in the Soviet Union, established in 1934 on the basis of a Party decree of 23 April 1932.

In the comparatively liberal atmosphere that flourished in the immediate aftermath of the Revolution, writers were allowed to criticise the regime to some extent. But by the time Stalin had assumed power the situation had changed. In 1934, at the First All-Union Congress of Soviet Writers, Zhdanov laid down the doctrine stating that socialist realism was to be the fundamental criterion for Soviet literature and literary criticism. It was adopted as a charter by the congress and from then on all writers wishing to be published – for expulsion meant not being published at all – had to follow the line.

The union is structured on the pattern of other Soviet political institutions. It has several thousand members and a board of several hundred elected from them. The board elects its secretariat of several dozen members, with a president and First Secretary. The secretariat has its core, its bureau, which effectively runs the union.

From 1934 to 1936, the board controlling the union was headed by Maxim Gorky. Akhmatova and Zoshchenko were expelled in 1946, but after Stalin's death there was some relaxation of the rules. However Pasternak was expelled in 1958, and Solzhenitsyn in 1969. The board monitors its own members, approximately 8,000, actively encourages high standards of writing and publishes several magazines, of which the best known is *Novy Mir* (*New World*) and the newspaper *Literaturraya Gazeta* (*Literary Gazette*). Although it can be seen as a repressive instrument, its positive function can allow writers an economic and personal freedom for their work.

Y

Yalta Conference (4–11 February 1945)
The last meeting of World War II between Roosevelt, Churchill and Stalin, sorting out the political future of the world. Stalin agreed to end the Russo-Japanese Neutrality Pact of 1941 and declare war on Japan two or three months after Germany's surrender, providing: the Mongolian People's Republic was maintained; the 1904 gains by Japan against Tsarist Russia were returned, including Sakhalin, Dairen internationalised, the Soviet Union to have a naval base at Port Arthur and the railways brought back to Sino-Russian control; the Kurile Islands given to the Soviet Union.

However Stalin's demands for a seat in the United Nations for each of the USSR's republics was turned down, though the seats for the Ukraine and Belorussia were conceded.

Yezhovshchina
The Great Purge starting with the assassination of Kirov in 1934, carried out first by Yagoda and then from 1936 by Yezhov on Stalin's orders. As many as ten million people were arrested, many executed, millions held in camps, and only a few tried in public 'show trials'. The intensity of the purge ended when Beria was appointed People's Commissar for Internal Affairs in 1938. The Leninists and old Bolsheviks had mostly been destroyed and Stalin's power was absolute. Under Khrushchev and later under Gorbachev, the details of the Yezhhovshchina were made known. (See also **Purges**)

Z

Zemstvo
The local self-government unit set up in the Tsarist reforms of 1864. Each zemstvo was elected by all classes to administer education, health, roads and welfare. Their national association, the Zemstvo Union, was a major force in maintaining the fabric of society during World War I. It campaigned for social reform and was part of the revolutionary action of both 1905 and February 1917.

BIOGRAPHIES

A

Abel, Rudolf Ivanovich, 1902–71
A Soviet intelligence officer convicted in the USA and sentenced in 1957 to 30 years' jail for handing over secrets to the USSR, but exchanged in 1962 for Gary Powers, the US pilot of the U2 reconnaissance plane shot down over the Soviet Union in May 1960.

Abramov, Fedor, b. 1920–
Writer. Born in Archangel and a member of the Party since 1945, he graduated from Leningrad State University in Philology and from 1950 was head of the Department of Soviet Literature there. His works are leading examples of the 1950s' school of 'village prose' and include *Brothers and Sisters* (1958), a novel about northern peasants during World War II, *Fatherlessness* (1961) and *In Severnaya Zemlya* (1962), which deals with life on the Kolkhoz and records some of the more unedifying aspects of that life. He has also written critical works, notably his study of *The Kolkhoz in Post War Prose* (1954).

Akhmatova, Anna (Anna Andreyevna Gorenko), 1889–1966
A pre-Revolution poet who was officially disapproved of until 1940. She chose the pen-name Akhmatova from her Tatar great-grandmother. With Mandelstam, she was a member of the Acmeist group which sought precision in poetic expression and a place in the tradition stemming from Graeco–Roman literature. After her husband was executed in 1921 her poetry was refused recognition until 1940. She was again banned in 1946 when she was, with Zoshchenko, the star victim of the Zhdanov witch-hunt which involved the imprisonment of her son, condemned for 'bourgeois-aristocratic aestheticism' and her being called 'part nun, part harlot'. She continued to write; among her work was the cycle of laments entitled *Requiem*, on the Terror, and including her experience of queueing up to find news of her jailed son. Expelled from the Writers' Union but rehabilitated in 1959, she was able to travel abroad for the first time since 1912, and revisited Italy and received an honorary doctorate from Oxford University.

Akhromeyev, Sergei, 1921–
He joined the Red Army in 1939 and rose to become Chief of Staff with the rank of marshal in 1984. He resigned in 1988, because of his disagreement with Gorbachev's cutting of the armed services. In the 1989 Congress he represented Moldavia.

Alekseev, Mikhail, 1857–1918
A general who gained promotion by his administrative talent, without any influence at court. A successful commander in 1914 and 1915, he was made Chief of Staff at the Stavka (Army Supreme HQ) when Tsar Nicholas assumed command of his armies in August 1915. His ignorance of social etiquette (such as leaving the table before the Tsar in order to return to his desk) did not endear him to the aristocrats of the staff. He was Commander-in-Chief until briefly replaced by Brusilov in 1916. He attempted to serve the Provisional Government but found the intrusions of the Petrograd Soviet intolerable. The result of the 'Kornilov affair' was his enforced retirement from the Stavka and in November 1917 he quietly went south to Novocherkassk, where he tried to form the Volunteer Army in the Don Cossack State under Kaledin. He fought for a while under Denikin until he died exhausted and ill from cancer in October 1918.

Alexandra see Nicholas II.

Aliyev, Geyder A, 1923–
An Azerbaijani major-general in the KGB. He was in the Central Committee of the Party and the Politburo from 1976 until the reforms of 1989, when he was ousted.

Alliluyeva, Svetlana, 1926–
Stalin's daughter by his second wife Nadezhda. She came to the world's notice in 1967 when she took the ashes of her second husband Bradegh Singh to India and decided not to return to the USSR. She went to the USA, where she wrote two books, *Letters to a Friend* and *Only One Year*, disclosing details of her father's private life and his entourage. After a period of depression she married an American architect, William Peters, but this marriage failed and she moved to England in 1982 with her daughter. She returned to the USSR in 1984 but clashed with the authorities and left once more to live in the USA and England.

Altman, Nathan, 1889–1970
Artist. He studied at Odessa Art School and in Paris. His early influences were cubism and futurism but he soon turned to more representational styles. In 1920 he did a portrait bust of Lenin in bronze and then took up portrait painting; there is a well-known portrait of Lunacharsky. He was also involved in graphic design and did sets for Mayakovsky's *Mystery Bouffe* in 1921 and Shakespeare's *Hamlet* in 1954.

Andreyev, Andrei, 1895–
A surviving Party member since 1914 and a member of the Praesidium since 1953. He started as a member of the Metalworkers' Union and progressed through a number of Party posts, being a member of the Politburo from 1926 until 1950 when Stalin, apparently by caprice, removed him from office.

Andropov, Yuri Vladimirovich, 1914–84
Soviet leader 1982–84. Born in Ngutskaya, his father a railway official. Rising from Komsomol organiser and leader, he became First Secretary of a number of Party organisations from 1940. He was ambassador to Hungary (1953–57) at the time of the Soviet suppression of the Hungarian uprising, then head of the Party's liaison committee with overseas parties. He rose through the ranks of the Party Central Committee, as Suslov's protégé, to the Politburo Central Committee from 1967, becoming chairman of the KGB. He gained a public reputation for attacking bureaucracy when he gave the annual Lenin Birthday Speech in 1976.

He also started an anti-corruption campaign, bringing charges against Shchelokov, former Minister of Internal Affairs, and Medunov, both members of the Central Committee. In 1984 he had the director of the largest food store in Moscow tried and executed. He put new men into the Politburo, among them his protégé Gorbachev. On Brezhnev's death, 10 November 1982, he was made General Secretary. In December he became a member of the Praesidium, whose president he was until his own death from kidney failure two years later.

Antonov, A S, ?–1922
A former SR politician who led the uprising in the Tambov area, 1919–21, with 50,000 peasants and Red Army deserters, which was suppressed and the cause removed only by the implementation of the NEP. The slogan of the rising was 'Down with Communists and Jews'.

Antonov-Ovseenko, Vladimir A, 1883–1939
A regular infantry officer who joined the Social Democrats in 1903, he was jailed for his political activities but escaped in 1907 and reached Paris in 1910. Here, despite his

Menshevik sympathies, he became friendly with Lenin, and joined the Bolsheviks in May 1917.

A slim, handsome man, more like a poet than a warrior, he played a leading role in the October 1917 Revolution as a member of the Military Revolutionary Council, and he was responsible for the capture of the Winter Palace. He was a Red Army commander, most notably leading the February 1919 move into the southern Ukraine which caused the French troops, landed from Odessa, to withdraw from the Civil War.

After Trotsky's fall in 1925, he was removed from his posts and sent as ambassador to Czechoslovakia and then to Lithuania. He published a declaration in favour of Stalin (refuting the 'Testament' of Lenin) and became ambassador to Poland in 1928. He was made Soviet consul-general in Barcelona on the outbreak of the Spanish Civil War in 1936, but, like many others sent there, he was recalled in 1937, supposedly to become People's Commissar for Justice in the RSFSR. He was put on trial and (having refused to confess at a show trial) shot.

Armand (b. Stefan), Inessa or Inès 1874–1920

Paris-born daughter of a French actor and an Anglo-French mother, she became tutor to the family of a French industrialist, Eugène Armand, in Russia, one of whose sons, Alexandre, she married. In 1903 she joined the RSDLP and was arrested but escaped from detention. She met Lenin in Paris in 1909 and settled there. She was sent back to Russia, illegally, in 1912 to help with the elections to the 4th Duma, but was again arrested and again escaped, reaching Switzerland in 1913. She spent the war there, returning with Lenin on the 'sealed train'.

She played little part in the October 1917 Revolution and was part of the left-wing opposition to the Brest-Litovsk Treaty. Her main work for the Bolsheviks was directed to improving the conditions of woman factory workers. She died of cholera after a visit to the Caucasus. She was buried in the Kremlin wall.

Lenin was clearly attracted to her and was deeply affected by the news of her death. However close their friendship, there is no evidence that they were lovers.

Avilov, Mikhail, 1882–1954

Painter. Born in Leningrad and studied at the Academcy of Arts from 1905–13. An academic painter known for his battle scenes, such as *A Breakthrough on the Polish Front by the 1st Cavalry Army in 1920*. He was made People's Artist of the RSFSR in 1953 and was awarded the Red Banner of Labour.

Avksentiev, Nikolai, 1878–1943

A Right SR, a minister in the Provisional Government, who moved from Petrograd to help organise the Omsk government in Siberia, he was a member of the Ufa Directorate with Kolchak. But when he was arrested as a socialist by the Whites, he left Russia from Vladivostok in December 1918.

B

Babel, Isaac, 1894–1941

A novelist (*Red Cavalry*, 1924), short-story writer (*Odessa Tales*, 1923–4) and playwright (*Sunset*, 1928, *Maria*, 1935). Babel served for a time in a Cossack military unit, which gave him the unusual experience of a Jew working equally among a people of long-standing anti-Semitic tradition. Although much acclaimed, his polished prose and his highly individual ironic standpoint, combined with his description of the horrors of anti-Semitism and of the Polish–Soviet war of 1920, made him politically suspect. He was arrested in the Yezhovshchina – another irony since Yezhov was a personal friend – and died in a concentration camp.

Bakst, Leon, 1866–1924
Painter and scenic designer. Born in Grodno, he studied at the St Petersburg Academy of Arts and in Paris. Returning to Russia, he became a member of the World of Art group. His illustrations and paintings of the time were strongly influenced by the art nouveau movement. He was one of Diaghilev's most important designers, doing sets and costumes for *Firebird* and *Daphnis and Chlöe*. His art used themes both from classical Greece and the East. After leaving Russia in 1906, he worked in Paris, London, New York and Rome.

Bakunin, Mikhail, 1814–76
International revolutionary and anarchist, a man of imposing appearance, born to the Russian landed gentry, he went to Germany to study Hegel and became engrossed in radical politics. In 1848 he joined in the risings, first in Paris and then in Germany. He took part in a revolt in Prague and then went to Dresden, where he was arrested and sentenced to death for his part in the risings; instead he was handed over to the Austrians, who deported him to Russia in 1852. He prospered in exile in Siberia and in 1861 escaped, through America, to Europe. He became his own sort of international socialist, but he was disowned by Marx's International. Fascinated by Nechaev, he collaborated on the 'Revolutionary Catechism'. This finally alienated him from Marx, but he had a long-lasting influence on Italian and Spanish anarchists.

Barkhin, Grigory, 1880–1969
Architect. Studied at St Petersburg Academy of Arts and after graduating took up teaching there. From 1930 to 1967 he was a professor at the Moscow Architectural Institute. An excellent example of a completely establishment Soviet architect, he is remembered for his *Izvestia* building in Moscow, built in 1925, and also for the restoration of Sevastopol, rebuilt between 1943 and 1946.

Benois, Alexandr, 1870–1960
Painter and scene designer. Born in St Petersburg, the son of an architect, he worked in Paris before World War I. When he returned to Russia, he became the ideologist of the World of Art group. He was against purely formalistic trends in painting and from 1918–26 was director of the picture gallery at the Hermitage Museum. His early work showed an interest in the world of privilege, such as *The Last Promenades of Louis XIV*, painted in 1897. In 1908 he designed the sets and costumes for Stravinsky's ballet *Petrushka*. In 1921 he did the same for the Bolshoi's production of Goldoni's *Servant of Two Masters*. From 1926 he lived in Paris and was involved in theatre design work.

Berdyaev, Nikolai A, 1874–1948
A philosopher who advocated a mystical 'creativity'. He was expelled from the Soviet Union in 1922. He lived in France as an active anti-Marxist, although he had been a Social Democrat in 1905.

Beria, Lavrenti, 1899–1953
A Georgian follower of Stalin, in the Party from 1917, working in intelligence from 1921. He was First Secretary to the Transcaucasian Committee of the Party, 1932–38, acting as Stalin's agent there. In 1934 Stalin made him a member of the Central

Committee and his deputy in the Caucasus. In 1938 he succeeded Yezhov as Commissar for Internal Affairs, or head of the NKVD, and organised the Terror after the 1936–38 Yezhovshchina purge. From 1941–53 he was deputy chairman of the Council of People's Commissars (later Ministers) in charge of security. Here his empire included its own armed forces, armour and aircraft. Even the famous Moscow Dynamo football team was controlled by him. After Stalin's death he was made Minister of Internal Affairs, but he was arrested in the post-Stalin power struggle in June 1953 and shot in December after a trial in which he refused to plead guilty, went on hunger strike and begged on his knees for mercy.

According to Khrushchev he was a notorious womaniser, indeed a rapist, and an alcoholic. He once said to him, showing his overweening pride and confidence in his powers, 'Listen, let me have a man for one night, and I'll have him confessing he's the King of England.'

Berzin, Yan K., 1889–1937

Head of the 4th Bureau of the GRU, Soviet military intelligence, founded by Trotsky, from 1920 to 1935. In 1905 he led an active guerrilla force at the age of 16. Captured and exiled to Siberia, he returned to join the Red Army after the 1917 Revolution. A drinking companion of Voroshilov and holding the rank of general, he was responsible for organising the network of agents and spies beyond the frontiers of the Soviet Union. One of his main targets was China, where the political victories of the Chiang Kai-shek nationalists of 1927 had removed all main contacts. Among his emissaries was the famous German spy Richard Sorge, who later moved to Japan. In 1935 Berzin was removed from his post and replaced by General Uritski. He went to Spain as military attaché, using the names 'Goriev' and 'Starik'. He played a major part in the defence of Madrid, but with other Soviet advisers he was recalled to Moscow in 1937. Both he and Uritski were shot in 1937 and both rehabilitated in 1964.

Biryukova, Alexandra, 1929–

Central Committee Secretary for Consumer Goods, she joined the Politburo as Candidate Member in 1988, the first woman appointed for over 20 years. She trained and worked as a textile engineer until 1968, when she became secretary to the Central Council of Trade Unions.

Blok, Alexander, 1880–1921

Poet. Born in St Petersburg; his father was a professor. He graduated in 1906 in philology, and his first poems were published in 1903. In 1917 he was appointed secretary of a commission to investigate the leaders of the Tsarist regime. His celebration of the October Revolution, *The Twelve*, caused a considerable furore, featuring, as it did, 12 Red Guards, who were identified with the 12 apostles. Although widely fêted as a representative Soviet poet, he became more and more out of sympathy with what he described as the oppressive atmosphere of communist rule.

Blyukher, Vasili K, ?–1938

Marshal of the Soviet Union and Commander-in-Chief in the Far East. After fighting in the Civil War, he became Commissar for War of the Far Eastern Republic in 1921, until it joined the RSFSR in 1922. From 1924 to 1927 he was one of the principal advisers to Sun Yat-sen, the Chinese republican, using the cover name Galin. He formed the Special Red Banner Far Eastern Army in 1929, taking action against the Chinese when they seized the Manchurian railway in 1929. His fame became legendary in the Soviet Union.

On 6 August 1938 he was suddenly replaced as commander in the middle of battle, reassigned to Moscow, arrested, tried and on 9 November shot. It was the year after the other generals and Marshal Tukhachevsky had been shot, but he was one of the first to be rehabilitated after Stalin's death.

Bogdanov (Malinovsky), Alexander A, 1873–1928

A philosopher and writer on economics and scientific topics. He graduated from Kharkov University in medical science but became involved in revolutionary politics and supported the Narodniks in 1899. In 1904 he became a Social Democrat and went to Switzerland, where he met Lenin. In his philosophical writings he attacked Berdyaev and impressed many of the Bolsheviks by his arguments. He served on the editorial boards of Bolshevik publications, including *Vpered*, and then became involved in the school on Capri founded by Maxim Gorky.

Although elected to the Central Committee at the 3rd Congress, he led a non-Leninist leftist splinter group after 1905, which Lenin outmanoeuvred. He was expelled from the Party for factionalism in 1909. In Russia during the Revolution he undertook the directorship of what became the Communist Academy. He refused to become involved in Party quarrels, retained his post under Stalin and devoted himself to scientific pursuits. He was the author of several books, including two science-fiction novels. His death was apparently the result of an ill-conceived medical experiment.

Bonch-Bruevich, Vladimir D, 1873–1955

A journalist and revolutionary. Born in Moscow and a graduate of the Kursk Surveying Academy. In 1892 he became an active Marxist and emigrated to Zurich in 1896. There he continued his studies and met Lenin and the Liberation of Labour group. Back in Russia he helped set up Bolshevik publications and ran a bookshop in St Petersburg. He was on the board of *Pravda* from 1912. After the July Days, it was in his *dacha* in Finland that Lenin took refuge. In the October 1917 Revolution, he was commander of the Tauride Palace district and later held administrative posts, including the move of Sovnarkom to Moscow and reorganising Moscow's water and sewage system. His brother Mikhail was a Tsarist general recruited by Trotsky to organise the Red Army's first General Staff.

In 1931 Vladimir Bonch-Bruevich published his memoirs of 1917–18 and became Director of the State Museum of Literature in 1933. From 1945 until his death, he was Director of the Museum of Religion and Atheism.

Borodin (Gruzenberg), Mikhail, 1884–1951

The romantic Comintern agent of the 1920s and 1930s. Born in a Jewish village near Vitebsk, he joined the Bund and then became a follower of Lenin in exile from 1903. He went to Riga in 1905, from where he fled to Sweden and, in 1907, to the USA. He managed to study at Valparaiso University, Indiana, and became a teacher of English to immigrants in Chicago, mixing with American socialists there under the name of Michael Berg. In June 1918 he returned to Moscow, where Lenin employed him to deliver a letter to the Workers of America. He did not manage to get to America with the letter but got it into the hands of John Reed, who published it. In 1919, as a senior Comintern agent, he smuggled gold and diamonds into the USA to support communist movements there and in Mexico. In England as 'George Brown', in 1922 he oversaw the reorganising of the Communist Party; he was arrested and deported in 1923. About this time he began to use the name Borodin.

Later in 1923 he went to China to establish relations between the Bolsheviks and the leader of the Chinese revolution, Sun Yat-sen, and to stimulate the Chinese Communist Party. In China Borodin was at first spectacularly successful. His team included the future Marshal Blyukher, who worked with the military commander of the Chinese forces, Chiang Kai-shek. Michael Borodin seemed to be leading China into the communist world. When the Chinese nationalists won a victory in 1927, the world at first saw it as a gain for Borodin and the Chinese Communist Party (including its leader Mao Zedong). But Chiang outmanoeuvred the Communist Party and the nationalists gained supremacy. Borodin had to make his way back to Moscow in 1927.

In 1929 he was moved out of Comintern work and sent into industry. Then, in 1930, the American journalist Anna Louise Strong started the English language weekly *Moscow News*, which he ran for the rest of his life. In 1949 Stalin had him arrested because of his association with foreigners. He died in a labour camp in Siberia.

His wife Fanya, whom he had met in Chicago, followed him to Russia, went with him to China where she was imprisoned and threatened with execution, but survived him for nearly 20 years.

Bresho-Breshkovskaya, Ekaterina, 1844–1934

'The Grandmother of the Revolution', an SR who spent many years in prison or exile. When, in 1878, she was sentenced to forced labour by the Tsarist government, the reports by George Kennan, an American diplomat, made her internationally famous. She adopted Kerensky as her 'political heir', but left Russia after 1917 and lived in Prague, Czechoslovakia, the star of all the liberal White émigrés.

Brezhnev, Leonid Ilyich, 1906–82

Soviet leader from 1964 to 1982. Born in Dneprodzerzhinsk (then Kamenskoye), a steel town in the Ukraine, where his family had been steel workers for three generations. Brezhnev was the elder son, with an elder sister and a younger brother. He was still a child when the 1917 Revolution brought the Bolsheviks to power, and while the Civil War raged in the Ukraine with Red and White armies sweeping through the towns pillaging, looting and killing.

In 1921 Brezhnev graduated from high school. In 1923 he took the major step of joining the Komsomol and was chosen to study surveying at the Kursk Land Technical College. On graduation in 1927, he was drafted to the Land Department of the Kokhanovksiy raion, in Belorussia. He was just in time for the opening of Stalin's campaign for the collectivisation of the Russian peasantry.

During the winter of 1972, the Party organisations in the raions were told that they had to use extraordinary measures to obtain the grain which the peasants preferred to hoard rather than sell to the State. The methods, earlier justified because of the Civil War, included beating and threats of deportation. There can be no doubt that Brezhnev applied such methods with enthusiasm In 1929 the policy of liquidating the kulaks caused a split in the Party and the Right Deviationists, Bukharin and his associates, were purged for supporting the peasantry. The purge caused gaps and Brezhnev was promoted to fill the place of his purged superior in the Land Department. In 1929 he joined the Party and the next year, at the age of 24, was promoted to deputy chairman of the Land Management Board for the whole of the Urals. Before he went, and acting on dekulakisation orders received from his headquarters, he organised meetings at the collectives at which 'unanimous decisions' were taken to expel all kulaks. Depending upon their degree of resistance to change, they were to be deported, in extreme cases to Siberia and in lesser cases to remote districts of the oblast or beyond.

Shortly after his arrival at Sverdlosk for his new job. Brezhnev was sent to the Moscow Agricultural Academy. This promotion did not last for long. He left school and returned to work in a factory in his hometown. The reason is not known, but it seems certain to be the result of a political argument, perhaps with an influential Bukharinite. Back in Kamenskoye Brezhnev joined the local institute to complete his engineering studies. He did well there and became active in institute and local politics. In 1933 there was an appalling famine in the Ukraine. Once again the fate of the peasants was not aided by the forced collection of grain which had rapidly been instituted, and of which Brezhnev was undoubtedly a part. The mortality record for one town near Kamenskoye was 11,680 out of a population of 60,000. In 1935 he graduated with honour from the institute, and in the same year he was drafted into the army, and spent a year in Siberia, where he became a platoon sergeant in a territorial unit.

1936–39 On his return from the army Brezhnev became director of a technical college in Kamenskoye, and then was elected as vice-chairman of the Executive Committee of the city's soviet, taking the place of another victim of Stalin's purge. The purge sharpened when Khrushchev arrived in the Ukraine in January 1938 as Party Secretary. He and his NKVD chief cleared out all 'recidivist elements' and 'old followers of the Ukrainian Party'. Nationalism there remained a constant problem for the Soviet leaders. The Ukrainian Party leaders, Kossior and Postyshev, were executed, and by the beginning of May only two members of the Party and government institutions had survived. One of the people that Khrushchev picked for his new administration was Brezhnev; he appointed him head of the Dnepropotrovsk regional Party Committee's Department of Ideology and Indoctrination. In other words, he had become Khrushchev's propagandist. In this role he concentrated on Stalin's russification policy for the Ukraine; just as Russian was to be a compulsory subject in schools, so newspapers and magazines in the Ukraine were planned to be printed in Russian. He had also, more importantly, found a patron. His career from then on was to be tightly linked with Khrushchev's.

1939–45 When Hitler invaded Poland in September 1939, the Red Army, operating under the Russo-German pact, occupied eastern Poland. Brezhnev organised rallies in the territories newly added to the Ukraine to show popular support. In June 1941 the Ukraine was the first to be overrun by the German advances. In October Brezhnev was appointed First Deputy Chief of the Political Administration of the Southern Front, the Ukraine war area. The political officer for this front was Khrushchev and Brezhnev worked directly under him for much of the war. Essentially Brezhnev was a military commissar, a position abolished in 1940 but reintroduced during the chaos following the German invasion. Morale was low; there were thousands of desertions and commissars, and when necessary Beria's special NKVD units were there to keep the fronts intact. Commissars and party workers were supposed to go into action first, as an inspiration, and there are numerous stories of Brezhnev's having done so. The truth of these stories is impossible to vouch for, but it was necessary for an emerging leader to have an impeccable war record and he did.

In 1944 Brezhnev arrived in Uzhgorod in Transcarpathia to plan the take-over of the territory, needed by Stalin to act as a gateway to Czechoslovakia. He set up a People's Congress and organised support for a union with the Ukraine. He also, with help from the army and the NKVD, crushed the UPA, the Ukrainian Insurgent Army, with a ruthlessness which equalled Khrushchev's operations in Poland in 1939. Thousands were killed, many more deported.

In June 1945 he took part in the Victory Parade in Red Square. He ended the war with the rank of major-general.

1945–53 Khrushchev had returned to the Ukraine, and from his HQ in Kiev was reassembling his political team. He got Brezhnev's discharge from the army, and made him Party Secretary in the important industrial oblast of Zaporozhye, where he organised the rebuilding of the Dneproges Dam and the Zaporozhye steel works in record time. The achievement saved Khrushchev, who was out of favour with Stalin for what was regarded as his failure to meet economic targets in the Ukraine. At the same time he was being intrigued against by Malenkov. Khrushchev returned as Party Secretary in the Ukraine and in December 1947 Brezhnev was awarded the Order of Lenin personally by Stalin.

In 1950 Khrushchev, as part of his power play with Malenkov, managed to get Brezhnev appointed as Party Secretary of Moldavia to fulfil the Five Year Plan which the Party Secretary there had bungled. There he launched a dekulakisation drive on the new collective farms which he claimed had been infiltrated by subversives, using where necessary the death penalty which he had reintroduced. He turned agriculture around and then launched a Stalinist attack on the cultural front, insisting that Moldavian literature and art be ideologically strengthened. He then fought off an attack in *Pravda* obviously inspired by Malenkov.

In October 1952 Stalin's expansion of the Central Committee found a place for Brezhnev, and he also made it into the Party Secretariat. On 7 November he made his first public appearance at the anniversary parade with Stalin above the Lenin Mausoleum in Red Square.

1953–59 Following the death of Stalin in October 1953, the struggle for succession temporarily banished him into the Ministry of Defence, where he became a deputy chief of the Main Political Administration, though he continued to work in Moscow. Khrushchev, as part of his manoeuvrings against Malenkov, became his boss again.

It is generally believed that Brezhnev was involved in the plot to destroy Beria, probably in co-ordinating the actions of the Party members and the military.

Khrushchev's next ploy in his battle with Malenkov was the Virgin Lands programme. Since much of the land was in the Kazakh Republic, he attempted to get his protégé appointed there as Party Secretary. Malenkov insisted on his own man, Ponomarenko, and won. Brezhnev was made his deputy. The two men fought out the battle for power in the republic until Malenkov's final defeat and resignation in February 1955; by May Pantelimon Ponomarenko had disappeared. Drought in the Virgin Lands caused Brezhnev, and his patron, trouble in 1955, but they were fortunate in 1956 and the harvest was the best for many years. For his work there he received a second Order of Lenin. In July 1957 Brezhnev defended Khrushchev in defeating the anti-Party group which had attempted to oust him and was given a place in the Praesidium.

1960–64 In June 1961 Brezhnev was awarded the title 'Hero of Soviet Labour' for his work in the development of rocket technology and for assuring the successful flight of a Soviet man in the spaceship Vostok. He had been involved with Dmitri Ustinov and the scientist Mstislav Keldysh as a management team for the production and development of ballistic missiles since 1956. By the time of the manned flight in 1961, he had left the programme.

In May 1960 Brezhnev succeeded Marshal Voroshilov as Chairman of the Praesidium of the USSR. Until now this had been a formal appointment but he was to transform it into a vital instrument of Soviet foreign policy.

In February 1961 Brezhnev set out for Africa to put into practice the USSR's support for the 'National Democratic State', a concept that it was felt described many of the post-colonial countries in Africa and Asia. He visited Morocco, Guinea and Ghana and promised them lavish aid, in return for which they promised to take the socialist road or at least align themselves against the West. He also began to organise aid for the MPLA (the popular movement for the liberation of Angola) in Angola. In Asia he signed an arms deal with President Sukarno in Indonesia. In India he provided more than 30 million dollars worth of military equipment and when Nehru visited Moscow in December 1961, he directly backed his move to liberate Goa, Daman and Diu from the Portuguese. He was also involved in negotiations with Cambodia with the intention of limiting China's influence in Asia; economic assistance to Afghanistan was provided for the same reasons in 1963. A great deal of money was spent by the USSR in these activities; in 1961 alone, aid worth more than 500 million dollars was extended. His efforts in Yugoslavia were not so fruitful, nor were they with the Shah of Iran. In general, Brezhnev was a more polished diplomatic performer than Khrushchev and was adept at dealing with crowds.

Between 1960 and 1964 there was a fresh power struggle in the Party; this time between Frol Kozlov, the Leningrad Party chief and his associates, and the Ukrainian group headed, until his dismissal in 1960, by Kirichenko, and then by Brezhnev. The state of the power struggle between the two groups was marked by observers in terms of appointments within various Party structures, or the position in line-ups at official celebrations. The situation changed abruptly when Kozlov had a severe stroke and at the June Plenum in 1963 the two candidates as Khrushchev's successor emerged as Podgorny, Party Secretary in the Ukraine since 1957, but new to Moscow and dependent on Khrushchev, and Brezhnev, no longer trusted by his old patron, who regarded him as too ambitious and independent. In July 1964 Brezhnev was freed from his other duties to concentrate on his job in the Party Secretariat.

1964–67 During the last few years of Khrushchev's rule, Brezhnev's attitude to him was a mixture of support and criticism. He supported him on agriculture until Khrushchev proposed adding an additional layer of administration and further restricting the private plots attached to collective farms. He disagreed with him about what he saw as a soft attitude to the West on Berlin and on the confrontation with China. When the plane was sent to pick up Khrushchev from his dacha on the Black Sea – crewed incidentally by KGB men – the plot to oust the Party Secretary had been cleared by Brezhnev not only with the KGB but also with the military; Marshals Malinovsky and Grechko were both old Ukrainian friends. By the time of the 22nd Party Congress, Brezhnev's supporters in the Central Committee, with men such as Dymshits, Pavlov and Tikhonov, numbered 15. Neither Podgorny or anybody else in the Central Committee had anything like the same support.

Brezhnev, having been elected First Secretary of the Central Committee in October 1964, set about consolidating his position. He became chairman of the Constitutional Commission in December, and two years later, at the 23rd Party Congress, took the title General Secretary which only Stalin had held before. He also became chairman of the Defence Council, thus further strengthening his hold on the military. His two main rivals for power in the Party were Podgorny and Shelepin. Podgorny, as the number two man in the Party Secretariat, represented a real threat. Brezhnev attacked Podgorny's moderate policies towards the consumer industries, his foreign and defence policies, and at the December 1965 Party Plenum managed to remove him from the Secretariat and place him in Mikoyan's job as chairman of the Supreme Soviet Praesidium. During the same year Brezhnev's other rival, ex-KGB chief Aleksandr Shelepin, also made something of a bid for power by attempting to obtain a meeting with Chairman Mao to discuss Sino–Soviet *rapprochement*. He was severely criticised for acting against the collective principle of leadership, stripped of many of his jobs and replaced as deputy premier. (In 1967 he was removed from the Secretariat.) Between April and the end of 1965, half of the Central Committee chiefs had been removed and replaced by Brezhnev's candidates. Two important appointments were Konstantin Chernenko, appointed head of the General Department of the Central Committee, and Yuri Andropov, who in May 1967 replaced Semichastny as head of the KGB.

1967–71 Both in agriculture and defence, Brezhnev charted a different course from that of Khrushchev. He called for an increased capital investment, higher but stable farm prices, a reduction in income tax and greater liberty in the use of private plots.

In defence, Brezhnev took the view expressed in a speech in November 1964 that peaceful coexistence with the West could be achieved by strengthening the military power of the USSR. To back this up, defence spending for the 1966–70 Plan increased by nearly 50 per cent, and for the next two Five Year Plans by an even greater percentage. This involved recruiting more men and reinstating the separate role of ground forces which Khrushchev had merged with the rest of the defence establishment. The number of ballistic missiles was greatly increased, by 1972 surpassing the US total, and the Soviet fleet under Gorshkov was raised to super-power size and status. Malinovsky was succeeded as Minister of Defence in 1967 by Marshal Grechko, who was co-opted on to the Politburo in 1973 at Brezhnev's personal request.

1971–78 Prior to 1971 Brezhnev had taken a hard (i.e. anti-Khrushchev) line on foreign policy but he had come to realise that hostility to China was pushing them towards better relations with the USA. He was also acutely aware that the expenditure called for in the new Five Year Plan on consumer goods and defence would not be possible without Western aid, unlikely to be granted while the USSR continued in its Cold War posture. He believed that with détente the USSR, like Nazi Germany, would be able to have both guns and butter.

Brezhnev opened his campaign for détente in West Germany. He obtained recognition of East Berlin as the capital of East Germany in return for guaranteeing unlimited access of civilian traffic to West Berlin.

May 1972 produced a summit with President Nixon, and the signing of the first SALT treaty. The April 1973 Plenum in Moscow produced complete support for the policy of détente and for Brezhnev personally. But his subsequent visit to the USA, and US demands on human rights, somewhat soured the détente scene. The Helsinki Accord, for instance, which dealt with both economic and human rights issues, produced little in terms of action. Not much progress was made with new SALT talks under President Ford and though a treaty was signed with President Carter in May 1979, it was felt that things had not gone quite as intended. The Soviet invasion of Afghanistan in December 1979, denounced by all Western nations, created a sudden and complete chill in the climate of détente.

Brezhnev continued to strengthen his position in the Politburo. Shelepin, already demoted, was dropped from the Politburo in April 1975. The only opponents of any stature left were Kosygin, Podgorny and Polyansky. Podgorny was used by him as a pawn in his battles with Kosygin and was not finally removed from the Politburo until 1977. Polyansky was credited with the agricultural disasters of 1975 and dismissed. But the battle with Kosygin was long and bitter. Kosygin held on to his 'soft' doctrines on defence and industry for as long as he could, even resisting the idea of Soviet aid to North Vietnam, until the passage of his own economic reform package was threatened. Kosygin did not make the report on the 10th Five Year Plan in 1976 and as Kirilenko took over a large part of his economic empire in 1977, he was eliminated as a major player. At the same time Brezhnev appointed new members of the Politburo who were his allies, Marshal Grechko, Gromyko and Grigori Romanov. In 1978 Chernenko joined the Politburo and Tikhonov and Shevardnadze became candidate members, while Mikhail Gorbachev, a relatively unknown figure from Stavropol, was appointed as Secretary responsible for agriculture.

1978–82 In 1974 Brezhnev underwent major surgery for dental problems and he was fitted with a pacemaker. A visit to West Germany in May 1978 had to be cut short for health reasons and his television appearances had to be extensively edited. But, as is usual in the USSR, Brezhnev showed no willingness to retire and it was the chill he caught while attending the celebration of the October 1917 Revolution in Red Square that led to his death in November 1982.

Judgement on his term of office has been dominated by tales of the corruption which flourished, and his fondness for nepotism. His son Yuri, though a well-known alcoholic, had been made a member of the Central Committee; his son-in-law Yuri Churbanov was jailed for corruption in 1988 and his daughter Galina, whose liaison with a black-marketeering circus manager was notorious, was made a senior executive in Intourist.

Brodsky, Isaak, 1883–1939
Painter. Born in the Zaporozhe oblast, he studied at Odessa Art School. He started his career by painting lyrical landscapes and some portraits, but after the Revolution he became well known for the historical pictures of the revolutionary period, with

paintings such as *The Solemn Opening of the 2nd Congress of the Comintern, 1920*. His most famous picture is *The Execution of the 26 Baku Commissars in 1925*. He also painted a well-known portrait of Maxim Gorky. He was appointed professor and director of the All-Russian Academy of Arts in Leningrad and was awarded the Order of Lenin for his life's work.

Brodsky, Joseph, 1940–

The winner of the 1987 Nobel Prize for Literature. Born in Leningrad of Jewish parents, he stopped attending school and was sent to a labour camp at the age of 24. In detention he continued to write poetry and on his release in 1972 became well known internationally. He was exiled and went to the USA, where he found teaching posts in colleges. His reputation spread and at the age of 44 he was the second youngest ever recipient of the Nobel Prize.

Budyenny, Semion, 1883–1973

Marshal of the Soviet Union. A dragoon sergeant in the Tsarist army, he joined the Red Army in 1918 and during the Civil War campaigned with Stalin. Starting as second in command to No. 1 Socialist Cavalry Regiment, he became the most successful cavalry commander of the Civil War. He led his First Cavalry Army both in Poland, where he was involved in the controversial attack at Lvov, and in the final victory over Wrangel in 1920.

In 1937 he was given command of the Moscow military district and in 1940 made First People's Commissar for Defence, and at the outbreak of war in 1941, Stalin appointed him to the Stavka of the High Command. In September 1941 he was posted to the reserve armies and later sent to the western Caucasus theatre, returning to Moscow in 1942. In January that year Budyenny was made commander of cavalry and a member of the Supreme Military Council.

From 1947 and 1953 he was Deputy Minister of Agriculture for Horse Breeding. While there he developed a special breed of riding horses, known as the Budyenny breed.

He was known for a frank and rather coarse manner and, like some other Civil War comrades of Stalin, was not highly thought of by his professional colleagues. Konev called him 'completely incompetent'. He was said to have killed his first wife in a fit of temper.

Bukharin, Nicholas Ivanovich, 1888–1938

Communist Party leader and thinker. A Bolshevik from 1906, forced to live abroad in Western Europe from 1911, where he met Lenin and Stalin. He moved from country to country: he was in the USA in 1917, and returned to Russia via Japan. He joined the October 1917 Revolution in Moscow, seeing it as the beginning of a world revolution, calling for a 'holy war in the name of the proletariat'. His logical mind tried to fit all problems within a system and in 1918, with Preobrazhensky, he produced the popular *ABC of Communism* and was editor of *Pravda* in 1917. Lenin regarded him as 'the greatest and most valuable theoretician in the Party'.

He saw 'War Communism' as a natural step towards socialism but soon accepted and advocated the NEP. The 'scissors crisis' and the failure of the German revolution in 1923 separated him from Trotsky and found him in support of Stalin's 'socialism in one country'. He became Stalin's spokesman and at the 15th Congress declaimed against the expelled 'Left Opposition', declaring 'the iron curtain of history is about to fall'.

Then, in 1928, support of the peasantry and of the neo-capitalist doctrine of the NEP made him vulnerable to attack by Stalin. He was expelled from the Politburo (but left on the Central Committee). With Tomsky and Rykov, Bukharin recanted his errors, admitting his responsibility for the 'Rightist Opposition' of 1928–29. However, in February 1934, Bukharin became the editor of *Isvestia* and in August he was among the leading speakers at the 1st Congress of Soviet Writers. In 1936 the Politburo sent him to France to meet other socialists and collect material for the Marx and Lenin Institute.

In January 1937 he ceased to edit *Isvestia* and in February he received notice of his forthcoming expulsion from the Central Committee, and he went on hunger strike in protest. With Rykov, he was accused of being a spy and saboteur and arrested. In March 1938 Bukharin, with Yagoda, Rykov and others, was tried for treason, and of having been a party to the murders of Kirov, Gorky and Menzhinsky. He was found guilty and shot. The trial convinced the American special ambassador Joseph E. Davies, who attended it with an interpreter, that Stalin had uncovered a real nest of traitors. Bukharin's last wish was to write a note to Stalin, using an old nickname, 'Koba, why do you need me to die?' Stalin kept the note in his desk for the rest of his life.

In 1988 Bukharin was rehabilitated.

Bulgakov, Mikhail, 1891–1940

Writer. Born in Kiev, he studied medicine at Kiev University and graduated during World War I. In 1919 he took up a career as a writer. He worked as a freelance journalist and also wrote short stories, somewhat influenced by Gogol. His first major work was the novel *The White Guard*, which was dramatised under the title of *The Day of the Turbins*. The play was banned for political reasons, but it was saved by Stalin, who thought highly of it. It is said that he attended 14 performances, claiming that it illustrated perfectly the inevitable nature of revolutionary forces. He did not complete his novel *The Master and Margarita*, generally regarded as his masterpiece, until 1938 and it was not published until many years after his death. He lost his sight in 1939 and died the following year.

Bulganin, Nikolai A, 1895–1975

Party Leader 1955–57. In 1918 he joined the Cheka, and in 1922, having established a reputation for his grasp of economic issues, he was appointed to the VSNKh. In 1927 he was put in charge of the Moscow electric plant and in 1931 became chairman of the Moscow City Soviet and worked with Kaganovich, then Khrushchev. Also on the City Soviet at this time were Malenkov and Yezhov. He continued to rise through the ranks of the Party until 1938, when he became Deputy Premier. He was Minister of Defence 1947–49 and 1953–55, gaining the rank of marshal, and had a place in the Politburo from 1952–58. He was appointed chairman of the Council of Ministers (and thus head of state) after Malenkov's fall in 1955.

For a brief period he and Khrushchev appeared to act in concert as joint leaders and travelled the world together: to Yugoslavia in 1955 and India, Burma and Afghanistan in 1956. In 1957 Bulganin was a member of the Anti-Party group which attempted to get rid of Khrushchev. The others were dismissed immediately; he was allowed to remain until 1958, when he was expelled from the Praesidium.

Bunin, Ivan, 1870–1953

A poet and novelist who opposed the 1917 Revolution and went to live in Paris from 1919. He was awarded the Nobel Prize for Literature in 1933, the first Russian to receive the prize. This reflected not so much his literary quality as a demonstration of anti-Bolshevism.

C

Chagall, Marc, 1887–1985

Born near Vitebsk, he studied art at St Petersburg with Bakst, among other artists, and from 1910 to 1914 lived in Paris. At the outbreak of World War I he returned to Russia and was conscripted into a camouflage unit. After the Revolution, Lunacharsky made him Commissar for Fine Arts in Vitebsk, where he opened an art school. His liberal views on art conflicted with Malevich and he moved to Moscow. There he worked on scenery for the Yiddish Theatre until, in 1922, he left Russia, going first to Berlin and then to Paris. He is known for his vivid use of colour and the strong and unusual arrangements of his figures in space. Many of his images are based on a Jewish childhood in a small Russian village.

Chaikovsky, Nikolai V, 1850–1926

A veteran Narodnik revolutionary, he returned from exile 1918 as a 'Defensist' to join the anti-Bolsheviks in Archangel. He led the Provisional Government there and was named as one of the original five members of the Ufa conference, until he left for Paris in January 1919, announcing his support for Kolchak, but retiring from the political struggle.

Chapayev, Vasily I, 1887–1919

The most famous of the Bolshevik leaders of semi-independent peasant armies. A simple man capable of inspiring his unruly and illiterate followers, he was picked out for officer training in 1915 and later rose to command a Red Army cavalry division. He was the subject of a romantic Soviet film, *Chapayev*.

Chebrikov, Viktor, 1923–

A Ukrainian security officer with the rank of colonel general. In the headquarters of the KGB in 1967, he succeeded Andropov as chairman in 1982. He was appointed to the Politburo in 1983, becoming a full member in 1985. In 1987, with Ligachev and the conservatives, he openly criticised Gorbachev's glasnost policy and after the Party Conference in September 1988, he was moved sideways to head a commission on legal reform, being replaced as head of the KGB by Kryuchkov. In September 1989 he was dropped from the Politburo.

Chernenko, Konstantin, 1911–85

Born in central Siberia, a Komsomol (1929) and a Party member (1931), he was active in the purges of kulaks, probably as a member of the NKVD during the 1930s. He was with the NKVD in World War II and a post-war aide to Brezhnev in Moldavia. Brezhnev was responsible for his rapid promotion from head of the Secretariat of the Praesidium of the Supreme Soviet in 1964, to Secretary of the Party Central Committee, in 1976, then to the Politburo in 1978 and to run Brezhnev's own personal staff. In February 1984 he succeeded Andropov, on his sudden death, as General Secretary and on 11 April as President of the Praesidium. Chernenko was backed by the 'old men', Tikhonov, Gromyko and Marshal Ustinov. He seemed to let affairs revert to the days before Andropov and the campaigns against bureaucracy and corruption lapsed. His ill health, obvious at the start of his period of office, soon led to his death in March 1985.

Chernov, Viktor M, 1876–1952

The founder of the Socialist Revolutionary Party, he was in exile in Switzerland and England until 1917. He returned to be Minister of Agriculture in the Provisional Government from May 1917. In the July Days the angry marchers arrested him as soon as he appeared to speak, but he was rescued by Trotsky. 'Take power, you son of a bitch, when they give it to you!', growled one of the mob. But Chernov's mild rational ways had no place in the Revolution and he continued to hope for a solution through the Constituent Assembly. When it met after the October 1917 Revolution, his presidential speech was ineffective. He moved to Samara in 1918 to head an SR government. He emigrated in 1920 to France and then to the USA.

Chicherin, Georgy V, 1872–1936

An aristocrat who served in the Tsarist diplomatic service, but he joined first the Socialist Revolutionaries in 1905, and then the Bolsheviks and as a result was forced to leave Russia. He returned in January 1918 and took over from Trotsky as Commissar for Foreign Affairs in March. The American diplomat George Kennan described 'the gigantic disorder of his office, his apparel and his working habits; his near-sightedness; his ill-health and hypochondria; his aversion to daylight and fresh air; his limitless pedantry and inability to delegate detail; his love of music in general and Mozart in particular. Aesthete and book-worm turned revolutionary, animated by faith always close to despair, slaving day and night to execute the hectic diplomacy of the young revolutionary state.'

He successfully made treaties establishing the Soviet Union's relations with her neighbours, the Baltic states, Finland, Poland, Persia and Afghanistan in 1920–21. In 1921 he achieved recognition with Britain for the Soviet Union through a trade agreement, and in 1922 signed the Treaty of Rapallo, establishing relations with Germany. Stalin was then not concerned with foreign affairs and Chicherin was allowed to remain in his post until 1930, when he was succeeded by his assistant Litvinov. He spent his remaining years in quiet obscurity.

Chkheidze, Nikolai S, 1864–1926

A Social Democrat from Georgia who became the Menshevik leader in the Duma from 1907 and the first president of the Petrograd Soviet. He warned delegates to the All-Russian Congress of Soviets against a Bolshevik take-over in June 1917. He became president of an assembly to establish an independent republic in his native Georgia, where he had spread Marxism in the 1890s. When the Soviet republic was established there in 1921, he escaped to France. Trotsky wrote a letter to him in 1913 with adverse comments on Lenin which Stalin published after Lenin's death as part of his proof of Trotsky's treachery.

Churbanov, Yuri, 1937–

The son-in-law of Leonid Brezhnev, having married his daughter Galina in 1971. He came to the world's attention as a militia general posted to Murmansk in 1982, but relieved of his post and rank as general in February 1985. He was then put on trial by the Soviet Supreme Court in September 1988 with others from Uzbekistan for corruptly receiving over one million dollars during his period of office as First Deputy Minister of the Interior, 1978–82, and he was sentenced on 30 December to 12 years' hard labour in a camp. He was said to have used his position to block probes into corruption in Uzbekistan during the period in office of Sharaf Rashidov, the Uzbekistan Party Secretary, and above all to have covered up the three million rouble Uzbek cotton fraud between 1976 and 1983.

D

Dan (Gurvich), Fedor I, 1871–1947

An early Menshevik leader, on the first Executive Committee of the Petrograd Soviet in 1917, but the Bolsheviks had him arrested in 1921 and he emigrated in 1922, first to Berlin, then to Paris and, in 1940, to the USA. He was active in maintaining Menshevism overseas.

Daniel, Yuli, 1925–88

A dissident writer, arrested in September 1965 and put on trial with Sinyavsky in 1966 for having published abroad without permission. Daniel's publications were short stories. They were 'secret' writers of parodies of Soviet life, little known in the USSR, but read abroad. The trial was in the hands of Andropov, then head of the KGB, who, unusually in a show trial, allowed them to plead not guilty and had them tried on the charge of libelling the State. That fiction could be judged a libel made the case a notorious travesty of justice. Daniel had a five-year sentence, but was freed in 1970 and exiled to Kaluga until 1979. He then lived in Moscow where some of his work was published before his death.

Denikin, Anton I, 1872–1947

A leading White general in the Civil War. His father had risen from serfdom in Siberia to become an army officer and Denikin was a general commanding an army group for the Tsar in 1917. He first led the Volunteer Army, based in the Kuban and northern Caucasus in 1918, and defeated Ordzhonikidze's 11th Red Army in January 1919 on the southern front. In June his army entered Kharkov, in the Ukraine, and cleared the Soviet forces out of the Don country. Hoping for victory, he put himself under the authority of Admiral Kolchak, in command of the 'Armed Forces of Southern Russia', taking Odessa and Kiev in August. But Budyenny's Red Army Cavalry outfought Denikin's in October and, with revolts by the peoples of Dagestan and the Kuban behind his lines, his army was driven into retreat.

Kolchak resigned in favour of Denikin in January 1920, and although he made new agreements with the Don Cossacks for the 'Government of South Russia', he was forced to retreat into the Crimea, where in April he handed over to Wrangel, resigned and sailed to Constantinople and thence to England. He lived in France for many years but died at Ann Arbor, Michigan, in 1947.

Deutsch (Deich), Lev G. 1855–1941

The founder with Plekhanov of the Marxist 'Liberation of Labour' group in 1883. From 1876 he was an active terrorist and was extradited from Germany in 1884. After 16 years' imprisonment, he escaped from Siberia in 1901 and became a leader of the Social Democrats, working with Lenin on *Iskra*, a Menshevik and a 'Defensist' during the war. He left politics after 1917, living in Western Europe and the USA. He wrote several works on the history of radicalism in Russia.

Diaghilev, Serge, 1872–1929

Theatrical impresario. A flamboyant figure with an amazing talent for discovering and encouraging talent. He studied at the St Petersburg Conservatory under Rimsky Korsakov, and in the 1890s was involved with Benois in founding the World of Art group. In 1907 he organised the Russian Seasons Abroad with composers such as Rachmaninov, and singers, like Chaliapin. In 1909 he had his first combined opera/ballet season and created a sensation by commissioning Stravinsky to write the music for *Firebird* (1910), *Petrushka* (1911) and *The Rite of Spring* (1913). Later he used

Prokofiev, together with great choreographers, such as Fokine, Léonide Massine and Balanchine.

His first famous dancer was Nijinsky, and he also persuaded artists such as Benois and Bakst to design sets and costumes for him. He had discovered that there was a huge appetite for Russian ballet in the West and in 1913, with his Diaghilev Ballets Russes, he toured the world, playing in London, Rome and the USA.

Dimitrov, Georgi, 1882–1949

The Bulgarian head of a secret communist network in Germany, he was arrested after the Reichstag fire in 1933 and put on trial by the Nazis, who had just come to power. He defended himself so energetically against Goering, who had undertaken the prosecution, that he made Goering look like the guilty party. Although acquitted, he was held until international pressure had him released. He went to the Soviet Union and stayed there until 1946, when he was installed as Premier of Bulgaria. He was General Secretary of the Comintern from 1935.

Dobrynin, Anatoly 1919–

Ambassador in Washington from 1962 to 1985, when Gorbachev brought him back to advise on the summit talks with US President Reagan. In 1986 he was head of the Central Committee's International Department, until replaced in 1988 by Alexander Yakovlev.

Dudintsev, Vladimir, 1918–

An author and journalist whose Not by Bread Alone (1956), criticising Soviet society, was his most successful work, published by the official liberal periodical Novy Mir in the year of the 21st Party Congress. But it was later attacked as anti-Soviet by the government.

Dymshits, Veniamin, 1910–

An engineer and Party figure. From 1931 till 1950 he was involved in the construction of metallurgical plants, including an involvement with Brezhnev in the reconstruction of the Zaporozhstal iron and steel works in 1946. From 1950 to 1953 he ran the central administration for construction in the lead industry. By 1959 he had risen to being the first deputy chairman of the State Planning Commission of the USSR and shortly after was made chairman. At the 24th Party Congress he was elected to the Central Committee of the CPSU.

An ally of Brezhnev's in the power struggle for succession, he was made chairman of the newly established Council of the National Economy (Sovnarkhoz) in 1965, and was hailed in the West as the new economic tsar. The only Jewish member of the Politburo.

Dzerzhinsky, Felix, 1877–1926

Of Polish–Lithuanian aristocratic origins, he had joined the Socialist Revolutionaries as a youth and was exiled to Siberia in 1897; he escaped in 1899, was recaptured but escaped again in 1902, this time reaching Berlin. There he joined the Social Democrat Bolsheviks and was closely associated with Rosa Luxemburg. However he was arrested again in Poland in 1905 and was continuously in jail until the Revolution of 1917 freed him. Lenin used his skills on the Revolutionary Military Council and in December 1917 asked him to organise the Cheka, which in 1923 became the OGPU. He was also Commissar for Transport in 1921 and director of the Economic Council from 1924 until his death. His political stance remained strongly on the left, opposing the Brest-Litovsk Treaty and the principle of self-determination for nationalities, which put him close to Stalin in the matter of the russification and the occupation of Georgia.

Hard, even harsh, he was generally accepted to be incorruptible, though blindly obedient to the Party. He died of a heart attack at a Central Committee meeting and was succeeded as head of the NKVD and OGPU (as it had become) by Menzhinsky, who was, not surprisingly, suspected of poisoning him.

E

Ehrenburg, Ilya G, 1891–1967
A poet and novelist who spent much of his life in Paris after escaping there in 1906, returning to Russia only for the years 1917–21. He was, for a time, a member of the Supreme Soviet and twice a winner of the Stalin Prize. Several of his novels were set abroad, in France or America: *The Fall of Paris* (1942), *The Storm* (1947) and *The Ninth Wave* (1951). His novel *The Thaw* (1954–56), departing from the norms of socialist realism with an ideologically neutral standpoint, was the symbol of cultural liberalism of the post-Stalin 1950s. When called on by the Writers' Union to denounce Pasternak, he replied, by telephone, 'Ilya Ehrenburg has gone away and will not be back for some time.'

Eisenstein, Sergei, 1898–1948
Film director. Born in Riga, the son of an architect, he studied civil engineering and during the Civil War worked on the Red Army's propaganda trains. After the war he became interested in the theatre, studied under Meyerhold and directed a number of productions. In 1923 he made his first film, *The Wise Man*, and then, in 1925, *Strike*, in which the masses are shown as a revolutionary force in history.

In 1925 Eisenstein made *The Battleship Potemkin*, frequently acknowledged as one of the greatest films ever made, with its theme of revolution as a struggle for freedom and dignity. In 1928 his *October: Ten Days that Shook the World* was criticised by the Party as showing formalistic elements, referring to its visual style. In 1929 he made *Old and New* about the land collectivisation programme. Between 1929 and 1932, out of favour in the USSR, he worked in France and Mexico, where he made the uncompleted *Que Viva Mexico*. In 1938 he made a public confession of errors and was allowed to direct *Alexander Nevsky*, a patriotic film about the defeat of the German knights in the Middle Ages, for which he received the State Prize of the USSR in 1941. In 1945 he made *Ivan the Terrible*, a study of despotism and the use of power. The film was in two parts and the second could not be shown until 1958, after Stalin's death and ten years after Eisenstein's.

Engels, Friedrich, 1820–95
A German businessman and political philospher. He was an associate of Karl Marx. He retired comfortably from business and lived mostly in England from 1842. With Marx, he was the author of *The Communist Manifesto*, and completed *Das Kapital* after Marx's death.

Enver, Pasha, 1881–1922
A leading Turkish general who came to political power in Turkey but fell when Kemal Atatürk took over there. He offered to take Central Asia – and India – for the Bolsheviks in return for their helping him back to power in Turkey. He went to the Emirate of Bokhara for this purpose in 1921, but left the Bolshevik cause and sided with their Basmachi enemies, styling himself Commander-in-Chief of All the Armies of Islam. He captured Dushambe in February 1922, so controlling the old Kingdom of Bokhara. He was killed in battle on 4 August 1922 by the Red Army.

Eremenko, Andrei I, 1892–1970

An example of the Red Army's generals who survived Stalin's purges and whose skills won World War II. Of Ukrainian peasant stock, he became a cavalry sergeant, was selected for the Frunze Military Academy in 1935 and was a general at the outbreak of World War II. Transferred from the Far East in July 1941 as a deputy commander to Timoshenko, he took over the Bryansk front in September. In the 1942 winter offensive he commanded the 4th Shock Army in the north-west. Stalin sent him to the new south-east front near Stalingrad in August 1942, soon renamed the Stalingrad front, with Khrushchev as his political adviser. Eremenko held the southern perimeter of the besieged Germans in the city, and resisted the relief attempts from the south. His command was renamed the south front and after the fall of Stalingrad in 1943, he was sent first to take Rostov and then north to the Baltic front to retake Smolensk and south again to the Crimea and finally back to the Baltic for the last attack on East Prussia. His account of Stalingrad (published in 1961) is of importance, although he implies that he and Khrushchev were the real planners of the victory. He was promoted to marshal in 1955 and was on the Central Committee in 1956.

Esenin, Sergei Alexandrovich, 1895–1925

An 'Imagist' poet who affected the appearance of a peasant in the literary salons of the Tsarist Empire. He welcomed (but did not understand) the Revolution of 1917. After publishing *Memoirs of a Hooligan* (1918), he left Russia. He was briefly married to the American dancer Isadora Duncan, but returned to Russia where he could not adapt to a changed world and hanged himself.

F

Fadeyev, Alexander A, 1901–56

Writer and Party activist. Born in Kalinin, his family were professional revolutionaries. He fought in the 1917 Revolution and Civil War as a Bolshevik. At the age of 19 he took part in the suppression of the Kronstadt rising and was twice wounded. He wrote several novels concerning the Civil War and *The Rout* (1927) was hailed by critics as portraying the men of the Revolution from within. He wrote *Leningrad in the Days of the Blockade* about the famous siege, and in 1945 *The Young Guard*, a romantic tale about a group of underground members of the Komsomol and their gallant exploits against the Nazis. It received the State Prize of the USSR and was filmed in 1948.

Fadeyev was a member of the Central Committee of the CPSU from 1939–56 and from 1954–56 secretary of the Writers' Union. He led campaigns against unorthodoxy in literature and was implicated in the purges of writers in the 1930s. His best-known book, *The Young Guard*, was itself criticised for failing to show the Party's leading role.

A dedicated alcoholic, he killed himself after Khrushchev's revelations about Stalin and his crimes at the 20th Party Congress.

Fedin, Konstantin, 1892–1977

A prolific novelist from a middle-class background. After release from being a prisoner in Germany in World War I, he edited a newspaper during the Civil War and joined a group of young writers disclaiming ideological purpose. He changed his ways and wrote several novels about Soviet life which conformed to the later doctrine of socialist realism, including *The Desert* (1923) and *The Peasants* (1925). Between 1928–49 he wrote *The Rape of Europe*, which is concerned with the falsity of the world of bourgeois values.

During World War II he wrote the trilogy *First Joys* and *An Unusual Summer*, and beween 1961 and 1965 *The Bonfire*, which deals with the origins of the 1917 Revolution and the psychological effects on those involved in it. He was First Secretary of the Writers' Union from 1959 and its chairman from 1971. Fedin was responsible for the attacks on Pasternak and for the suggestion that Sinyavsky be tried (according to Solzhenitsyn). While the *Great Soviet Encyclopedia* says of Fedin: 'The humaneness of the new world is the main theme of the work of Fedin.'

Feokotistov, Konstantin P, 1926–
A designer of spacecraft, from the first Soviet satellite to Gagarin's flight and later developments. He flew and carried out experiments in Voshkod I (1964) and has made other space flights himself.

Fotieva, Lidia A, 1881–1975
Involved in revolutionary politics before the age of 21, she emigrated to Switzerland in 1904 and helped Lenin's wife Krupskaya with work for the Party. After the 1917 Revolution she became Lenin's devoted private secretary until his death in 1924. She was also on the Secretariat of the Council of People's Commissars of the RSFSR until 1930. From 1938 she was on the staff of the Central Lenin Museum.

Frunze, Mikhail V, 1885–1925
He joined the Social Democrats in 1904, while a student at the St Petersburg Polytechnic, siding with the Bolsheviks. That year he was arrested and banished from the city. He continued his political activities and was a leader of the Moscow uprising in December 1905. He had been a delegate to the 1905 3rd Party Congress in London in 1905 and was a delegate to the 4th in Stockholm in 1906. From 1907 to 1914 he was imprisoned. Rearrested in 1915, he escaped to Chita and joined the All-Russian Union of Zemstvos, working on the western front.

In February 1917 Frunze led revolts and military mutinies in Minsk, Belorussia, becoming the Chief of Staff of the armed forces there after the 'Kornilov Affair'. He took charge of putting down the Yaroslav rebellion in July 1918 and then was put in command of the Southern Army Group against Kolchak, although dismissed by Trotsky in 1919. He was Red Army commander in Crimea and the Ukraine from February 1920. From there he immediately took command in Central Asia of the Turkestan Army Group, capturing Khiva and Bokhara, using Red Army soldiers recruited from peoples of the Caucasus. In September 1920 he led the campaign against Wrangel on the southern front. He was then made commander of the Red Army in the Crimea and the Ukraine, where he ended both the Petlyura and Makhno rebellions.

In 1924 he was deputy chairman of the Military Revolutionary Council and a member of the TsIK. He was also a candidate member of the Politburo and commandant of the Military Academy (later named after him). With Tukhachevsky and Gusev, he was involved in the reorganisation of the Red Army. Together they elaborated the 'Doctrine of Proletarian War', which denounced centralism as inhibiting the army's potential for manoeuvre.

Frunze was a practical leader and a first-rate underground tactician militant with the outward appearance of a senior military man. But his championship of one-man command and his obvious ambition made the Central Committee suspicious of him, and when he died during minor surgery for an ulcer, his death was strongly rumoured, and asserted by Trotsky, to have been a murder ordered by Stalin. His wife committed suicide shortly afterwards. He was twice awarded the Order of the Red Banner and his ashes are interred in a wall of the Kremlin.

Furtseva, Ekaterina, 1910–74
A Party member from 1930 and on the Central Committee from 1952. She was on the Praesidium from 1957 to 1961, Minister of Culture from 1960 until her death, and the first woman to join the Politburo, but she was ousted as a result of Kozlov's intrigues. Gossip suggested that she had been Khrushchev's mistress: she was certainly one of his fervent supporters. Her later years were clouded by the scandal of the luxurious dacha she had had built for herself.

G

Gagarin, Yuri, 1934–68
The first man to orbit the earth in a space capsule, in 1961. He was killed in an air crash and was given a State burial.

Gamarnik, Yan B, 1894–1937
A military leader during the Civil War and chairman of the RVS from 1934. He learnt of the arrests of officers and on 31 May 1937 killed himself. The news of his death (or his reported absence from committees) told others of the beginning of the military purge.

Gapon, Father Georgy, 1870–1906
A Ukrainian 'worker priest' who led the demonstration on 'Bloody Sunday', 22 January 1905. He had built a large, but loosely organised association, for a while linked to the police, which he wanted to use peacefully. He escaped to Geneva, but fame came to Father Gapon and he was courted by politicians and publisers. He now had money and he began to spend it lavishly, visiting Monte Carlo. Back in Russia he was suspected of being an informer and was killed by the SR 'Combat Section', their hit squad.

Ginsburg, Alexander, 1936–
A dissident writer. After two spells in labour camps for his non-confirmist behaviour, he was charged by the KGB in 1964 with possessing subversive literature. The case was dismissed at the trial, but another arrest and trial in 1968 aroused world interest and protest at his five-year sentence.

Goncharova, Natalia, 1881–1962
Painter and scenic designer. Before World War I she was involved with the progressive art movements that produced such exhibitions as The Jack of Diamonds, Donkey's Tail and Target. Her work was much influenced by the cubist and futurist movements and, with Larionov, she started the rayonist movement. In 1915 she moved to Paris and worked in the theatre, carrying out designs for Diaghilev and others. She died in Paris.

Gorbachev, Mikhail Sergeevich, 1931–
Born of peasant stock in the Caucasian village of Privolnoye in the Krasnogvardeysk district of Stavropol Krai, which lost perhaps one-third of its population during the artifically created famine of 1932. His maternal grandfather was a kulak who was temporarily deported during the 1937 purge. As a youth he worked on the local collective farm, and then obtained entry to Moscow State University where, from 1950 to 1955, he studied law. He had joined the Komsomol while still at school and in 1950 became a candidate member of the CPSU. After graduating from university, where

he shared a room with Zdenek Mlynar, later one of the organisers of the Prague Spring movement in 1968, he joined the Komsomol organisation in Stavropol. He spent the next six years there, being promoted to First Secretary of the Stavropol Komsomol committee in 1960.

Gorbachev at this time married Raisa Titorenko, a fellow student at university who had read philosophy. She was offered a job teaching philosophy at the Stavropol Agricultural Institute, and is obviously a remarkable and forceful woman who has had a considerable influence on his career. In 1962 he joined one of the supervisory agricultural units that were part of Khrushchev's new deal for agriculture. He spent five years there and also studied for a degree in agro-economics. He qualified in 1967 and in 1970 became First Secretary of the Stavropol kray committee of the CPSU. At the 24th Party Congress in 1971 he was elected a full member of the Central Committee.

Stavropol is a fertile area and Gorbachev had considerable success with agricultural production there. In this he was helped by having the patronage of Fedor Kulakov who was then head of the agriculture department and became Secretary for Agriculture on the Central Committee. He had also attracted the favourable attention of Yuri Andropov and Mikhail Suslov who, both suffering from kidney disorders, were used to taking the waters at Kislovodsk, a well-known spa used by privileged Party members. Kislovodsk was under Gorbachev's jurisdication and the two men had been greeted at the station by the enthusiastic young man on several occasions. So, after Kulakov's somewhat mysterious death in July 1978, it was not surprising that they backed him for Kulakov's job on the Central Committee in Moscow.

In Moscow Gorbachev set to work to deal with the complex problems of agriculture, while Raisa was appointed to a readership in philosophy at the State University. There was a very bad harvest in 1979–80 which in no way affected his standing and in October 1980 he was made a full member of the Politburo. Perhaps it was felt that he needed all the available backing to deal with the layers of bureaucracy which now existed there. The harvest in 1981 was the worst since 1975 and 46 million tonnes of grain had to be imported. In 1982 the Food Programme – a total review of agriculture – was published. It was comprehensive but contained no real elements of reform. The 1982 harvest, though not brilliant, was adequate and Brezhnev's death drew attention away from the Secretary for Agriculture's possible shortcomings.

By March 1983 Andropov was General Secretary and Gorbachev was generally recognised as his main assistant. Andropov had little time to pursue his campaign against corruption, for by February 1984 he was dead and the obviously frail Chernenko had temporarily taken over in the Kremlin.

Chernenko had time to repeal some of Andropov's reform measures: there was a crack-down on dissidents. It was the time in which the Nobel Prize-winning physicist Andrei Sakharov and his wife Elena Bonner, the prominent Jewish activist, were exiled to Gorky. Although Gorbachev was still prominent in the Politburo, he was only really backed by Nikolai Ryzhkov and Yegor Ligachev.

On December 10, 1984, at a Moscow conference on ideology, he used the word *glasnost* for the first time to describe the conditions which should accompany socialist democracy. Later in the month, Gorbachev, as chairman of the Supreme Soviet's Foreign Affairs Committee, visited London to an enthusiastic welcome and made a great hit with Mrs Thatcher, though in practical terms he was unyielding on Afghanistan and on human rights issues. At the beginning of 1985 Chernenko died and in March Gorbachev was declared General Secretary.

General Secretary Gorbachev's supporters on the Politburo, Nikolai Ryzhkov, Viktor Chebrikov and Yegor Ligachev, were older and more experienced than he and did not owe their progress in the Party to him. He made Ryzhkov Chairman of the Council of Ministers, but did nothing about the others. Grigory Romanov, an old rival, disappeared into retirement after an inspection trip Gorbachev made to his power base, Leningrad, in May 1985. At the end of 1985 Viktor Grishin also stepped down, partly it is said because Chebrikov had let it be generally known that Grishin's daughter-in-law's father was Beria. Gorbachev at the same time promoted Edvard Shevardnadze to the post of Foreign Minister; as a Georgian he was not an entirely popular choice.

The situation in the USSR that Gorbachev inherited was immensely depressing. The economy was in terrible shape: apart from the production of defence material and space technology, it resembled a Third World state rather than an industrial super-power. The standard of living was low; infant mortality high; even life expectancy was declining. He seems to have believed that perestroika (the restructuring of the economy and the Party) and glasnost (openness) would right the situation quickly.

With Leonid Abalkin, a radical economist and now Deputy Prime Minister, he introduced the New Economic Mechanism in the summer of 1987. This brought in a new system of 'self-accounting' to State enterprises, which was related for the first time to profitability. It also gave permission for a limited form of entirely private enterprise in the shape of co-operatives. The first foundered because no attempt was made to take the more radical step of changing the system whereby 90 per cent of all production was allocated to the State, nor to change the source of materials. The co-operative movement attracted savage criticism on the grounds that its members were profiteers who were charging outrageous prices. After two years the situation has, if anything, deteriorated. There was a good harvest in 1989, but output is stagnant; millions of days have been lost due to strikes; the money supply is increasing and so is inflation.

The new two-stage Six Year Plan calls for price reforms in 1991 plus increased production of food and consumer goods, and for 1993–95 an increasingly market-based economy. The new property laws coming into effect in July 1990, under which peasants will be granted private land which they will be able to leave to their heirs, are expected to boost agricultural production, as will the end of Gosagroprom, the bloated agricultural bureaucracy set up in 1986 which failed to increase production. Over 900 joint ventures have been arranged, including one with Fiat which will increase the production of cars by 25 per cent. A unified tax system is also planned and even the introduction of a Stock Exchange.

Perestroika also applies to the political situation and here Gorbachev's plans have been constantly modified by the extraordinary speed of change in the satellite states of East Europe and in some of the republics of the Soviet Union. The major changes, the establishment of the Congress of People's Deputies to take the place of the Supreme Soviet, and the Party's abrogation of its role as the 'leading and guiding force of Soviet society', which it held under Article 6 of the constitution, have been the most striking. The latter decision was urged by a demonstrating crowd of 150,000 in Red Square. Multi-party elections have been held in the RSFSR and elsewhere and Party members have done very badly in many of them.

The internal problems in the republics, such as in Georgia in April 1989 and in Azerbaijan in January 1990, have been dealt with harshly by Gorbachev – not at all like his reasoned performance in the Baltic states, where in March 1990 Lithuania announced its departure from the Soviet Union.

Internationally Gorbachev has had an easier time than at home. He has been able to make bold and decisive gestures which have earned him plaudits around the world. This started with his speech to the United Nations in December 1988 when he said 'today the preservation of any kind of closed society is hardly possible'. He declared a cease-fire in Afghanistan and at the same time began the process of disarmament, which was emphasised by a January 1989 cut of 14.2 per cent in the military budget and the withdrawal of half a million men from Europe and Asia. He established warm relationships with Presidents Reagan and Bush, and in December 1989 had an audience with Pope John Paul II.

Mikhail Gorbachev's revolutionary changes have won him praise but also a great deal of criticism from both sides. From conservative elements in the Soviet Union, such as Yegor Ligachev and Anatoly Gidaspov, leader of the Leningrad Party, has come harsh criticism. They went along with him at first, but now, alarmed at the possible disintegration of the Party and the Soviet Empire, as well as the loss of their long-held privileges, they would like to call a halt. From the radicals, of which Boris Yeltsin is a good example, has come another sort of complaint. They believe that he is not radical enough, either politically or economically, and that the country will slip into chaos through inertia.

Gorbachev has now sought a new role for himself as President of the Republic, a position to which the Congress of Deputies voted him on 14 March 1990. This post, until it becomes elective in four years' time, gives him more power than Stalin legally possessed. He has declared that in the power vacuum left by the apparent disintegration of the Party, strong leadership is needed to prevent disaster. He has demonstrated amazing political skills in achieving what he has to date. He will need all his skill and a large measure of good luck to continue successfully 'riding the tiger' of the new Soviet Union. For events since March 1990 see the Chronology.

Gorky, Maxim (Alexei Maximovich Peshkov, 'Gorky' bitter), 1868–1936

After a childhood as an orphan and a poor wandering student (revealed in *Childhood*, 1913, *My Apprenticeship*, 1918 and *My Universities*, 1923), his first collected tales in 1898 made him a famous writer. He supported the Bolsheviks and lived in exile (on Capri) from 1906 to 1913. In 1917, opposed to the seizure of power, he set up a non-Bolshevik left-wing group. He again lived in Italy from 1921 to 1928, then returned to Russia and headed the Writers' Union, being called the founder of 'socialist realism' and becoming a friend of Stalin. Perhaps he shared with Stalin a contempt for peasants. His article 'On the Russian Peasantry' (1922) paints them as boorish sub-humans who hoard food while the townsfolk starve. His death on 16 June 1936 was claimed to have been caused by Trotskyists or right-wing elements and was used as a reason for the purges of the period.

Gorshkov, Sergei, 1910–88

Commander-in-Chief of the Red Navy 1956 to 1985. He joined the navy in 1927 and served mostly in the Black Sea, commanding a destroyer squadron in 1945. His rise to command the navy in 1956 came under Khrushchev, who had dismissed a fleet commander for resisting demands for economies. But the débâcle of the Cuban missile crisis of 1962 reversed the Soviet position. Khrushchev was ousted and the new leadership felt the need for a strong navy to project their power globally. Under Brezhnev, Admiral Gorshkov was given the new rank of admiral of the fleet of the Soviet Union and planned a new Soviet naval strategy (set out in his book *The Sea Power of the State* 1976). From a small coastal defence force using conventional naval artillery, he built a fleet of missile-launching submarines capable of striking at any point of the world. He also ensured that Russia had a massive conventional fleet with big surface ships and aircraft carriers whose world cruises and courtesy visits to Third World countries boosted Soviet prestige, while striking fear into her rivals. But after Brezhnev's death his position weakened as rivals for promotion debated his strategic concept. Why, they argued, was a big fleet necessary when submarines with intercontinental missiles could hit America without leaving port? Under Gorbachev new economies were introduced and the world role of the Soviet fleet was allowed to diminish. Gorshkov died three years after his retirement.

Gots, Abram, 1882–1937?, and Mikhail 1875–1906

Wealthy brothers who did much to organise the SRs, Mikhail died of cancer and Abram was exiled from 1906 until 1917. He returned as an SR leader in the Petrograd Soviet. He was one of the main people accused in the 1922 show trials of the SRs. He was probably shot in a camp in Alma Ata.

Grechko, Andrei A, 1904–76

Marshal and Minister of Defence from 1967 until his death. He joined the Red Army as a youth in 1919 and was selected for training at the Frunze Military Academy and later the General Staff Academy. After commanding an army during World War II, he had command of the Soviet forces in East Germany, 1953–57. He rose under Khrushchev, commanding the land forces of the USSR, 1957–60, then succeeding Konev as commander of the Warsaw Pact forces, 1960–67. He had joined the Communist Party in 1928 and became a member of the Politburo in 1973. His study of the armed forces of the Soviet Union (1974, published in English in the USSR in 1977) describes the invincibility of Soviet arms, its record in World War II and its abilities in a nuclear age.

Grishin, Viktor, 1914–

A surveyor by profession and a Party worker. He spent his early years working in the railway industry in Serpuklov, where he also became First Secretary of the Committee of the CPSU for the city. In 1950 he moved to Moscow, where he ran the machine-building department of the Moscow Committee of the CPSU. In 1956 he became president of the All-Union Central Council of Trade Unions. In June 1967 he was promoted to First Secretary of the Moscow City Committee of the CPSU.

Grishin was elected by the 19th, 20th and 22nd Party Congresses to membership of the Central Committee and was made a member of the Politburo in 1971. He was a serious candidate for the post of General Secretary after the death of Brezhnev, but it is believed that his opponents spread rumours (generally believed) that his son's wife was the illegitimate daughter of Beria, thus removing him as a serious threat to Gorbachev.

Gromyko, Andrei A, 1909–89

Born near Minsk, he joined the Party in 1931. As head of the US Department in the Ministry of Foreign Affairs and an attaché in the Soviet Embassy in Washington in 1939, he began a diplomatic career unlike any other in the Soviet Union. He served as ambassador in Washington, 1943–46; he was present at the Teheran, Yalta and Potsdam conferences. He returned to the Soviet Union in 1946 as a Deputy in the Supreme Soviet. He was the USSR's permanent delegate to the UN Security Council, 1946–49, where his use of the veto to stonewall Western proposals made him famous as 'Mr Nyet'. Gromyko was ambassador to Britain, 1952–53, Deputy Foreign Minister in 1953 after Stalin's death, then Foreign Minister, 1957–85. He was finally the titular President of the USSR from 1985 until 1988, when he retired from that post. In 1989 he stepped down from the Central Committee with other old-guard Party men. He was now an old, tired man whose life among the communist élite had made him remote from life's realities. He was given a formal State burial, in keeping with his character, cool and passionless.

Guchkov, Alexander, 1862–1936

The leader of the Moderate Liberals after 1905 and founder of the Octobrists. He was the leader of the majority in the 3rd Duma. He was the Duma's chairman on military affairs, urging reform then and during World War I. He became Minister of War in the Provisional Government of 1917. He went to Pskov to obtain the Tsar's abdication, leaving Russia for Paris in 1918 after the October 1917 Revolution.

He had a taste for duelling and fought twice while leader of the Duma: once being jailed for wounding an opposing Deputy and once contemptuously firing in the air in a duel with a colonel he thought a spy for Germany.

H

Hoover, Herbert C, 1874–1964

The 35th President of the USA (1929–33). His place in Russian history arises from his work as chairman of the American Relief Agency. He had headed the American Relief Commission in Europe from 1914 to 1919 in World War I and transferred his efforts to Russian famine relief after this. He became US Secretary of Commerce in 1921.

I

'Ilf and Petrov': Ilya Fainzilberg (1897–1937) and Yevgeny Petrovich Katayev (1903–42)

Satirical writers, *The Twelve Chairs* (1928), *The Golden Calf* (1931) and *Little Golden America* (1936). As satirists they naturally fell under political suspicion, but their world-wide popularity ensured their survival.

Ilichev, Leonid F, 1906–

A conservative or neo-Stalinist who was deputy chief and chief editor of *Pravda*, 1950–58. He was head of the Press Department of the Foreign Ministry from 1953, head of the KGB, 1958–61, Secretary of the Party Central Committee, 1961–65, and Deputy Foreign Minister, 1966–8.

Ilyushin, Sergei V, 1894–1977

Aircraft designer famous for the Il–2 Stormovik and the later Ilyushin airliners.

Ioffe, Adolf, 1883–1927

A Menshevik who was with Trotsky in Vienna in 1908. He was on the Brest-Litovsk Treaty negotiating team. The Germans were struck by his naïve optimism. In common with Trotsky, he had the illusion that by announcing 'No peace, no war' Russia had ceased to be at war and that there would be peace. Ioffe was later ambassador to Germany, Switzerland and China. He killed himself when Trotsky was expelled from the Party.

K

Kaganovich (Kagan), Lazar M, 1893–

A Bolshevik from 1911, he moved upwards through Party posts, becoming Secretary of the Ukrainian Party in 1925 and adopting the Stalinist policy of 'russification' there. His zeal in the Ukraine led to the purging of many Ukrainian communists, but Stalin bought favour there by dismissing him in 1927. A member of the Politburo from 1930 and a loyal Stalinist, he was in charge of collectivisation and the 1933–34 Party purge as chairman of the Commission of Party Control. He was People's Commissar for Railways from 1936–44 and headed several other commissariats.

With Malenkov and Molotov, in 1957 he tried to oppose Khrushchev. He failed and was expelled from all his posts. The old Stalinist hardliner lives on in retirement into the Gorbachev era.

Kaledin, Alexie, 1861–1918

A Tsarist general whose World War I reputation as a successful cavalry leader gave him great fame. Resigning from the army because of the 1917 Revolution, he became leader of the Don Cossack State and proclaimed Ataman on 25 October 1917. His attempt at a counter-revolution failed and he shot himself in January 1918.

Kalinin, Mikhail I, 1875–1946

He joined the Social Democrats in 1898 and was arrested the next year. This was the beginning of a series of arrests and deportations. He joined the Bolsheviks in 1906 and was elected mayor of Petrograd after the 1917 October revolution. He succeeded Sverdlov as president of the VTsIK in 1919 and in 1923 became president of the TsIK of the USSR. He was Chairman of the Supreme Soviet and so remained titular President of the Soviet Union for the rest of his life, a dummy noted only for his loyalty.

Kamenev (Rosenfeldt), Lev Borisovich, 1883–1936

A student radical, he had been arrested many times before the 1905 revolt. In 1902 he visited Paris and met the *Iskra* group. In 1908 Lenin asked Kamenev to join him in Geneva to edit the Bolshevik paper *Proletary*. He became a leading propagandist overseas until, in 1914, he was assigned to take charge of *Pravda* in St Petersburg. After World War I broke out, he was arrested and in May 1915 deported to Siberia – to the same settlement as Stalin.

In April 1917, back in Petrograd, he took over the editorship of *Pravda*, in which he fought against the 'April Theses' of Lenin. In October, with Zinoviev, he voted against an armed uprising. They then demanded conciliation and a coalition with other socialists. Although Lenin was firmly opposed to their ideas, he needed support and Kamenev, elected president of the TsIK, was given the chance to continue working for the Bolshevik cause. Although he was with Trotsky at the Brest-Litovsk negotiations, he was given little to do in the Civil War. Trotsky saw Zinoviev as an agitator, excited by the moment, while he saw Kamenev as thoughtful and analytical.

In 1922, during Lenin's illness, Kamenev was one of the three, with Zinoviev and Stalin, who opposed Trotsky. As Stalin took over the Party machine, Kamenev lost the support of his Moscow Party, which he had been running, and by the 15th Party Congress in 1927 his political career, like Zinoviev's, had sunk. Together they submitted to Party discipline and denounced the Trotskyites in January 1928. They hung on until Stalin had them expelled from the Party in 1932. Readmitted after self-criticism the next year, they showed their support for Stalin at the 1934 17th Party Congress.

Then they were arrested in 1935 after the Kirov murder and sentenced to imprisonment. In July Kamenev was retired, and again the next year put on a public show trial with Zinoviev, accused of an alliance with the Nazis. He was executed in August 1936. His sentences were annulled by the Soviet Supreme Court in June 1988.

Kamkov, Boris D, 1885–1938

An SR 'internationalist'. One of the organisers of the Left SR in the 'July Days' of 1917. After three years' imprisonment he left politics and worked as a statistician. In 1938 he was swept up in the purge, put on public trial and shot.

1 Petrograd, 1917. Members of the Red
Guard at a May Day demonstration.

△ 2 Lenin addressing a demonstration in
Moscow, 1920. Trotsky waits his turn to
speak on the steps. After 1927 Trotsky was
painted out whenever the photograph was
used.

▽ 3 Military leaders of the Civil War 1918-20.
Left to right: Semion Timoshenko, Semion
Budyenny and Kliment Voroshilov.

△ 4 17 March 1921. An attack on the rebels of
Kronstadt, across the ice.

◁ 5 1927 cartoon from *Krokodil*, satirising the Nepmen, who made money from the New Economic Policies introduced by Lenin in 1921.

◁ 6 Anatoly Lunacharsky, Commissar for Education and the Arts in 1930, addressing a rally at the Young Pioneers Stadium, Moscow.

◁ 7 Sergei Kirov, Secretary of the Leningrad Party, murdered under mysterious circumstances in 1934.

△ 8 Nikolai Yezhov, People's Commissar for State Security (NKVD), and Joseph Stalin on the anniversary of the founding of the Cheka.

△ 9 Funeral of Maxim Gorky in Red Square,
Moscow, 1936. Left to right: Lazar
Kaganovich, Andrei Zhdanov, Georgi Dimitrov, Vyacheslav Molotov, Joseph Stalin
and Genrikh Yagoda.

▽ 10 Sergo Ordzhonikidze, People's Commissar for Heavy Industry, 1937.

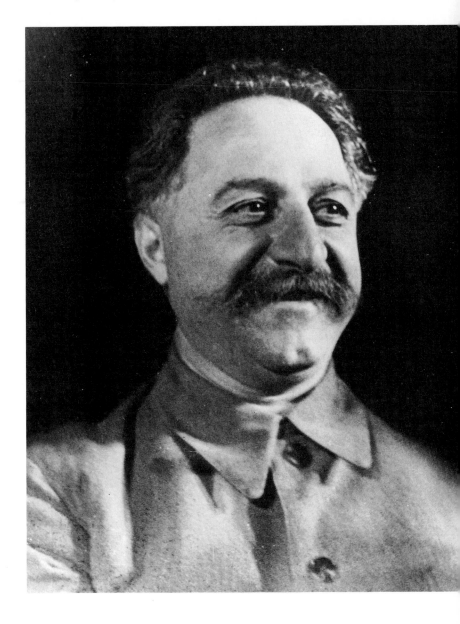

△ 11 Hitler's Foreign Minister, Joachim von Ribbentrop, his assistant Gaus, with Stalin and Molotov, meet for the signing of the Nazi–Soviet non-aggression pact in August 1939.

12 Berlin, May 1945. Soviet soldiers cele- ▷ brate the capture of Berlin on the Reichstag building.

◁ 13 Homecoming. An old man and a boy return to their village at the end of World War II.

▽ 14 Party leaders surround Stalin's bier in the House of Unions, Moscow, March 1953. Left to right: Vyacheslav Molotov, Kliment Voroshilov, Lavrenti Beria, Georgy Malenkov, Nikolai Bulganin, Nikita Khrushchev, Lazar Kaganovich and Anastasy Mikoyan.

15 Red Square, Moscow, 1964. Left to right: Alexei Kosygin, Marshal Malmousky, Leonid Brezhnev, Wladyslaw Gomulka, Secretary of the Polish Party, Anastasy Mikoyan, Chou En-lai, Foreign Minister, People's Republic of China, and Nikolai Podgorny.

16 Nikita Khrushchev meets President Kennedy at the June 1961 summit meeting in Vienna.

17 An aide supports Leonid Brezhnev as he reviews a guard of honour at Budapest airport, 1979.

18 Mikhail Gorbachev, in Berlin 1989, taking
part in the 40th anniversary celebrations of
the Republic.

Kandinsky, Wassily, 1866–1944

He was born in Moscow but studied art in Munich. He moved to Berlin but then went back to Munich, where he helped to found the Blaue Reiter movement. His work developed in a more abstract direction and he is generally recognised as a major influence in the development of abstraction in painting. He returned to Russia after the 1917 Revolution and held posts under the Commissariat for Popular Culture. He was among the organisers of the Museum of Pictorial Culture in Petrograd. In 1921 he founded the Academy of Arts and Sciences, but after the Civil War he returned to Germany, taught at the Bauhaus for a time and, when Hitler took power in 1933, settled in Paris.

Kantorovich, Leonid, 1912–86

Nobel Prize-winning economist. His work on linear programming has played a major part in the world's economic planning. He was Professor of Economics at Leningrad from 1934 to 1960, surviving all the purges.

Kapitsa, Peter, 1894–1984

A physicist who worked at Cambridge University from 1924, where he became a professor and in 1929 the first foreigner to be a member of the British scientific academy, the Royal Society. He was detained in Russia on a visit there in 1935 and was made director of the Institute for Physical Problems, continuing to do important research. He was awarded the Order of Lenin and two Stalin Prizes. For his work on low-temperature physics, he received a Nobel Prize in 1978.

Kaplan, Fanya (also known as Dora), d. 1918

On 30 August 1918 Kaplan shot Lenin in the neck and shoulder as he left the Michelson plant in Moscow, where he had been addressing the workers. She was a Socialist Revolutionary who had spent 11 years in prison for trying to kill a Tsarist official in Kiev. Freed in 1917, she worked as a milliner, but dedicated herself to the revolution and believed that Lenin had betrayed it by abandoning the Constituent Assembly. Taken first to the Lubyanka, she was soon taken for interrogation in the Kremlin. She had no useful information and on 3 September 1918 she was shot in prison.

Katayev, Valentin, 1897–

Son of a teacher from Odessa. From 1915 until 1917 he fought in the Russian army, then joined the Red Army and fought against Denikin. He wrote several short stories about this era in *Notes on the Civil War*, which contained a mixture of heroics and satire. A satirical play, *Squaring the Circle*, followed in 1928.

In the 1930s he turned towards heroic and ideological themes in such books as *I am the Son of the Working People* (1937) and *Son of the Regiment* (1945). His great success was the Odessa-based novel which began with the publication of the widely read *The Lonely White Sail* (1936), filmed in 1937, and developed slowly into the huge four-part novel *The Waves of the Black Sea* (1961). His writings were based on current society, *Time, Forward* (1933) being on a construction team during the Five Year Plan. Katayev's other claims to fame lie in his being the first Soviet author to own a refrigerator (in the mid-1930s) and only to have joined the Party in 1958. His younger brother wrote under the name Petrov with his collaborator Ilf (see page 255).

Kautsky, Karl, 1854–1938

A German socialist who was secretary to Engels in London from 1881. He opposed the Bolsheviks in Russia but supported the Mensheviks in Georgia. His writings drove Lenin to fury, and he devoted his convalescence in 1918 to a book attacking Kautsky. Kautsky lived in Austria until his last year, when he escaped from the German Nazis to the Netherlands.

Kerensky, Alexander, 1881–1970

A Russian politician who entered the 4th Duma in 1912 as a moderate socialist, gaining some fame for his defence of the Armenian Dashnaks. He later joined and led the Socialist Revolutionaries and Bresho-Breshkovskaya made him her 'political heir'. In 1917, under the Provisional Government, he was first Minister of Justice and then of War. In July he was made Prime Minister. He attempted a military offensive against Germany in 1918, but its failure led to disaffection in the army and the October 1917 Revolution. Although he survived an apparent attempt at overthrow by the army commander, Kornilov, he was thrown out by the Bolshevik take-over in November. He went into exile in France, Australia and finally the USA.

It was an odd coincidence that both he and Lenin were from Simbirsk and that Kerensky's father should have been Lenin's school teacher.

Khachaturian, Aram, 1903–78

Composer. Born in Tbilisi, he studied music at the Gresin Music Academy, which he entered in 1922, and then at the Moscow Conservatory from 1929. His Symphony No.1, his diploma piece, was written in 1935 and this was followed by the Piano Concerto in 1936 and his 1st Violin Concerto which won him a Stalin Prize in 1940. In 1939 he was elected vice-president of the Organising Committee of the Union of Soviet Composers. In 1942 he wrote the music for the ballet *Gayaneh* which contains the well-known Sabre Dance. Equally well known is his music for the ballet *Spartacus*. In 1947 his *Sinfonya Poema* was criticised for its formalism, in the time of Zhdanov when this implied corrupt Western influence. In spite of this he was awarded the Order of Lenin.

He wrote numerous film scores. His music is valued for the way in which it often uses Armenian and Georgian folk tunes and for his deep understanding of the Russian academic tradition exemplified by Rimsky Korsakov.

Khrushchev, Nikita Sergeyevich, 1894–1971

1894–1941 Born in 17 April at Kalinovka in Kursk province, he came of peasant stock. In 1908 his father, unable to make a living on the land, moved his family to Yuzovka (later Stalino and now Donetsk) in the Donbas area of the Ukraine, where he had obtained work in the coal mines. Khrushchev, at the age of 15, was taken on as an apprentice fitter in a mining facilities company. In 1912 revolutionary groups were fomenting strike activity in the mines and as he was known to be involved he was fired, though he quite soon obtained a job as a fitter in another of the mining companies.

During World War I, as a mine worker he was exempt from call-up and married for the first time. His wife Yesofrina had two children, a boy and a girl, before dying from typhoid at the end of the war.

Miners' strikes in the Donbas continued throughout the war, right up to the February 1917 revolution. After the Revolution, though still not a member of the Bolshevik Party, Khrushchev was elected to one of the revolutionary committees. They had been formed to confront the various forces threatening the hold of the Revolution on the Ukraine. The Cossack army of Kaledin was defeated by the Donets Proletarian Regiment, of which Khrushchev was a member in 1918, but the regiment was then threatened by the Germans who, after the Treaty of Brest-Litovsk, had proclaimed a Ukrainian republic. At this stage he joined the Bolshevik Party but, as the Germans were now occupying the area, had to escape eastwards and join the Red Army. From then until the end of the Civil War he was involved in minor political work in the Red Army, fighting on the Tsaritsyn front and then joining the army of the Kuban which broke the White army at Krasnodar, and he was present when the White forces surrendered at Sochi in May 1920.

After the Civil War Khrushchev returned to the Donbas and became involved in the immense work of reconstruction which took place under Lenin's NEP policies. He was appointed political leader of one of the three major mining sections, and secretary of the Party cell of the recently established technical college. In two years the Donbas was back to half its pre-war production, and in 1924, at the age of 30, Khrushchev was elected Secretary of the Raikom, the Party of the area. He also got married for the second time.

By 1927 Khrushchev had attended a Party Congress as a full delegate and the output of coal from the Donbas had exceeded pre-war levels. His ascent of the Party hierarchy was about to begin. In 1928 he came to the attention of the General Secretary of the Central Committee of the Ukrainian Communist Party, S V Kossior, and he was selected as one of the first students for the Industrial Academy which had opened in Moscow.

He quite soon came to dominate the academy politically, being responsible for purging it of its 'Right Deviationist' elements, supporters of Bukharin. Amongst them was Nadezhda Alliluyeva, Stalin's wife, who became friendly with Khrushchev, which he later claimed had influenced Stalin's attitude to him. It was while he was at the academy that he encountered Kaganovich, who was now a member of the Politburo. Kaganovich wanted a competent, tough and politically sound administrator to cleanse the Party organisation of any rightist tendencies. Khrushchev was appointed First Secretary of one of the Moscow districts and by 1934, at the age of 39, he was Kaganovich's deputy in the capital. When Kaganovich was made People's Commissar for Transport, Khrushchev took over as First Secretary in Moscow. There he was part of a group which included Bulganin, chairman of the Moscow Soviet, Malenkov running the Organisation Bureau of the Party Committee, and Yezhov, later to be the dreaded activist of the purges.

Khrushchev made a considerable contribution to the building of the Metro in Moscow, the main section of which was opened in 1935. In carrying out this work, much of it using forced labour, he showed the determination and ruthlessness for which he was to become well known. For his work in Moscow, he received the Order of Lenin, his first decoration. He also became very friendly with Bulganin and both men were often invited to dinner by Stalin. Khrushchev himself has recorded 'I was literally spellbound by Stalin, by his attentiveness, his concern ... I was overwhelmed by his charm.'

During the Terror – starting in 1934, and from 1937 when Stalin began to remove a large proportion of the old guard Bolsheviks, their associates and families – Khrushchev, despite his later denunciations of Stalin's tyranny, did nothing to protect his old friends. In fact, there are numerous speeches on record in which he showed himself eager to denounce anyone who had fallen from Stalin's favour or whom he believed to stand in his way. In 1938 he received his reward, being elected to the Praesidium, and becoming a candidate member of the Politburo.

In 1938 Khrushchev was appointed acting First Secretary of the Ukrainian Communist Party as part of Stalin's purge of the Party there. He went to work with a will. Indeed six months after his arrival, only three members of the 1937 committee were left. He wrote: 'The successful, triumphant crushing of the fascist agents – all those contemptible Trotskyites, Bukharinites, and bourgeois nationalists – we owe to the personal effects of our leader above all, to our great Stalin.'

At the beginning of 1939 Khrushchev was concerned with developing the industry and agriculture of the region and then, later in the year, with the absorption into the western Ukraine and Belorussia of parts of Poland occupied after the Russo-German pact. This involved seizing landlords' estates and collectivisation on a massive scale, and the deportation of 'unsympathetic' elements to Siberia and elsewhere. Much of this work was carried out by I A Serov, People's Commissar of Internal Affairs for the region, who became a valued colleague and friend, as did Zhukov who was appointed commander of the Kiev special military district.

On 22 June 1941, German troops crossed the border and attacked the frontier guards. World War II had begun.

1941–53 Khrushchev's role during the war, both on the Ukraine front and at Stalingrad, was as a Political Commissar on the Military Councils of the area. His official rank was lieutenant-general. He had some disagreements with Stalin, particularly at the beginning of the war when he, in common with Zhukov and others, believed that Kiev should be abandoned. They were forced to submit to Stalin's will.

In 1944, when the Ukraine had effectively been cleared of German troops, Stalin once again appointed him First Secretary of the Ukraine and also chairman of the Council of Commissars. It was obvious that, despite his relatively low profile during the war, he was still in favour. He devoted his energies to rebuilding the shattered agriculture and industry of the area, which proceeded steadily during 1945, but in 1946 agricultural output was hit by a devastating drought which caused widespread famine. Unable to meet the State's procurement demand, Khrushchev appealed to Stalin, who replied with an abusive telegram and followed this by appointing Kaganovich in his place as First Secretary. Khrushchev was careful to collaborate fully with Kaganovich and the situation was saved by a record harvest in 1947. In 1948 the harvest was even better and Khrushchev was re-elected First Secretary. But within a year he had left the Ukraine and taken up a new role in Moscow as First Secretary of the Moscow obkom.

In Moscow, for the next three years he was mostly concerned with applying his new theories about agriculture to the Moscow oblast. He amalgamated the small collectives to form larger units and, since this was successful, he obtained the approval of the Central Committee. He then came out with a grandiose scheme for the creation of agro-towns. These were to be vast farming communities with populations of 12,000 each, complete with apartment blocks, schools, restaurants and swimming pools. The scheme was a fantasy; there were no resources available to create it and it was ended by a critical article in *Pravda*. Shortly after this, in October 1952, the 19th Party Congress was held which increased the members of the Praesidium to 25 plus 11 candidate members. A little later, and in contradiction to the spirit of the congress, Stalin formed a new Bureau of the Praesidium, consisting of Malenkov, Beria, Bulganin, Khrushchev and himself. This was all part of the succession game that Stalin was playing, a game which became suddenly terrifying with the announcement on 13 January 1953 that State Security had uncovered the 'Doctors' Plot'. Stalin even made the suggestion that Voroshilov was an English agent. There seems little doubt that Stalin was planning the destruction of the remains of the old guard, certainly Molotov and Mikoyan. On 3 March Stalin had a severe stroke and on 6 March he was dead. The battle for the succession, long flourishing underground, now came out into the open.

1953–55 All former members of the Politburo and the other powerful State organs were invited to a conference in the Kremlin. A new Praesidium was elected, with Malenkov as Chairman of the Council of Ministers, Beria in charge of the MVD and MGB (Internal Affairs and State Security) and Bulganin at the Ministry for the Armed Forces, with Khrushchev as Secretary of the Central Committee in Moscow. Essentially, power was held by this triumvirate until July, when Beria was arrested on the orders of the other two, accused of being a careerist and a traitor, tried and shot. At the same time the MVD was neutralised by the arrest of its senior staff and Beria's confederates were dealt with in the same way.

The second triumvirate now consisted of Malenkov, Khrushchev and Bulganin. Khrushchev had been elected to the Party Secretariat of the Central Committee in March and in September he was elected First Secretary of the Communist Party of the Soviet Union.

In August 1954 Malenkov made his bid for power with a policy calling for the rapid development of light industry and the food industry at the same rate as the heavy industries. Khrushchev counter-attacked with a speech in which he demonstrated the appalling condition of agriculture, and in February 1954 he launched his great plan for the cultivation of the Virgin Lands. In his role as Secretary of the Central Committee, he started travelling all over Russia, and attended congresses in Poland and Czechoslovakia. In December 1954 he went to China and negotiated a deal with Mao Zedong by which Russia was to supply China with capital goods.

By late 1954, Malenkov's position had been heavily undermined and in February 1955 he resigned as Chairman of the Council of Ministers and was replaced in the triumvirate by Zhukov. In November Khrushchev and Bulganin flew to India, an event which received world-wide Press coverage, equalled only by the detonation of another hydrogen bomb, this time in the stratosphere.

Domestically, Khrushchev's concern with agriculture continued to dominate the political scene. While 1955 was a good year for agriculture in general, the Virgin Lands programme was affected by a severe drought.

1956 The 20th Party Congress opened on 14 February 1956. The trials of Beria and his associates, though only reported in outline, had caused a profound interest in the darker events of Stalin's regime. A Central Committee commission had produced a report on the cult of Stalin, and some prisoners had been released. Rebellions broke out at a number of camps and were brutally suppressed. Khrushchev suggested to the Praesidium of the Central Committee that they should include a section on the 'cult of personality' at the congress. The idea was rejected by members of the Politburo.

At the congress Khrushchev introduced several novel, even revolutionary, ideas: that peaceful coexistence was possible, even that the transition from capitalism to socialism could be a gradual one. He talked of the destruction of the Beria gang, but made no mention of Stalin.

He then proposed to the Praesidium that, as a delegate, he should make a speech about Stalin. A compromise was reached. It was agreed that he could make the speech, but as Secretary and at a closed session to be held after the election of the new Central Committee. Obviously many members were fearful of their chances of re-election. The speech was delivered on the morning of 25 February to an audience of 1,500 delegates, including a hundred party members newly released from jail and rehabilitated.

It revealed the conflicts between Lenin and Stalin at the end of the former's life, hinted at Stalin's involvement in the murder of Kirov and blamed Stalin for the disasters at the beginning of World War II. It blamed him for the repressions of the post-war period, and claimed that before his death he was planning new assaults on the Party. The speech was carefully planned. It made no mention of the destruction of the left and right opposition in the 1930s nor, more significantly, of the destruction of the kulaks and the mass deportations. It was essentially concerned with Stalin's attacks on the Party, not on the people. It also managed to implicate and therefore discredit some of Khrushchev's Politburo rivals, particularly Malenkov, but also Kaganovich, Molotov and Voroshilov.

The effects on Russia and the communist world were startling: monuments to Stalin were pulled down all over Russia, towns were renamed, Stalingrad became Volgograd, and pro-Stalin riots in Georgia had to be put down with casualties running into hundreds. Only Togliatti, leader of the Italian Communist Party, asked whether it might be possible that there was some profound flaw in the very nature of the Soviet system.

Khrushchev set up special commissions to examine the cases of the prisoners in the camps and by the summer of 1956 several million prisoners had been released; posthumous rehabilitation was also declared on a similar scale. On the other hand, it was also noticeable that very few members of the NVKD-MGB were punished for their treatment of prisoners. In Khrushchev's words, 'We must not carry out a St Bartholomew's Eve Massacre'. He added that if all those who had participated in Stalin's crimes were to be brought to book, more people would have to be imprisoned than had just been rehabilitated and released. Some cautious freeing of the cultural life of the nation was allowed, but he was always willing to attack anyone who went too far in this direction.

At the beginning of 1956 foreign policy dominated the agenda. Mikoyan was dispatched to China to grant further economic aid. Khrushchev and Bulganin visited Britain and met the queen. Relationships with Tito were improved by his visit to Moscow. In Eastern Europe the situation was not so happy. The speech attacking Stalin at the 20th Party Congress had caused crises in the Parties of Poland and Hungary. In Poland workers were demonstrating and farms were being decollectivised. In Hungary the unpopular Party leadership had been ousted and Imre Nagy was bringing non-communists into his government. Nagy's government demanded the withdrawal of Soviet forces stationed there. Soviet tanks and troops crushed the Hungarian opposition and imposed a pro-Soviet government.

At the same time in Egypt, President Nasser's seizure of the Suez Canal led to an attack by Britain, France and Israel; this ceased only when pressure was exerted by the United States. The Suez situation made it hard for the West to take a firm line about the Soviet Union's action in Hungary. There is no doubt that Khrushchev's position in the Politburo was in danger after the 20th Party Congress speech and that the conservative elements were looking for an opportunity to attack him. The troubles in Poland and Hungary could be directly linked to his speech and, aside from the strategic necessities of the situation, he was involved in protecting himself.

1957–58 In 1957 it was decided to restore to their homelands the many national groups who had been deported under Stalin. This was carried out on Khrushchev's orders despite the opposition of Molotov, Malenkov and other conservative elements in the Politburo. They were given further reason to intrigue against him when he introduced the idea of reorganising the central administration of government by introducing Economic Councils (Sovnarkhozes) to oversee ministries. He also, rashly, declared that the Soviet Union would, within a few years, equal the production of the USA in meat, milk and butter. In June, at a three-day meeting of the Praesidium, a list of charges was levelled at him, including economic 'voluntarism' and wilful action. It was the intention of the plotters, the conservative element, to replace him with Molotov as First Secretary. Khrushchev, with support from Mikoyan, Suslov and Kirichenko, defended himself on the grounds that he could only be removed by a Plenum of the Central Committee. It was not possible for the plotters to arrest him as he was backed by the army (Zhukov) and the KGB (Serov). The Plenum was called and overwhelmingly supported him. Molotov, Malenkov, Kaganovich and Shepilov lost their seats on the Praesidium; Malenkov was made manager of a power station, Molotov was sent as ambassador to Mongolia and Kaganovich to manage a factory. Shortly after this, Zhukov, despite his support, was replaced as Minister of Defence by Malinovsky.

1958–61 At the beginning of 1958 Khrushchev was in a powerful position. He had dealt with the opposition and was appointed Chairman of the Council of Ministers, while still holding, like Stalin, the position of First Secretary. He now concerned himself with reorganising the educational system and at the end of 1959 sanctioned cuts in the armed services and deprived officers of the militia and the MVD of some of their privileges. Also in 1958, and much less to his credit, he was behind the vicious campaign directed at Boris Pasternak for publishing *Dr Zhivago* outside Russia. In May 1960 changes were made in the Central Committee and Kosygin, amongst others, was elected.

In foreign affairs Khrushchev quarrelled with Tito again and cancelled commercial credits to Yugoslavia, while relations with China cooled somewhat. In September Khrushchev visited the United States, gave a speech at the United Nations and went to Hollywood, where he was greeted with enthusiasm. In May 1960 a summit meeting with President Eisenhower was cancelled as the result of the U2 spyflight. In September 1960 Khrushchev attended a meeting of the United Nations. He lost his temper several times and interrupted the UK Prime Minister Macmillan by taking off his shoe and banging it on his desk. Macmillan asked for a translation.

Agriculture In 1958 the harvest was good and in January 1959 an extraordinary 21st Congress was held to discuss the new Seven Year Plan. It was proposed, among other things, to increase industrial production by 80 per cent and the chemical industry by 300 per cent. There were to be massive increases in electronics manufacture, and light industry was also to be specially favoured. In agriculture, Khrushchev had the striking idea of closing the Machine Tractor Stations and selling their machinery to the collective farms. Many of the farms could hardly afford to buy the machines and others had no ability to service them. The net result was less use of machinery and a decline in production.

In January 1961, because of the obstinate failure of the agricultural programme to deliver the results expected, another Plenum of the Central Committee was convened. The decision was now taken to reorganise the Ministry of Agriculture and those of all the republics. They were no longer to be concerned with the organisation of production but with the scientific aspect of farming and the dissemination of information to the farms. Khrushchev and his advisers, who still included Lysenko, believed in the elimination of fallow in crop rotation and this was put into operation throughout the country: it proved to be mistaken. Also mistaken was his action in introducing a new layer of administration into agriculture, whose work would be to supervise a larger group of collectives. By the end of 1962 industrial production had increased by 9.5 per cent but agricultural production had risen by only 1.2 per cent and in the Virgin Lands erosion had written off several million hectares of land. In 1963 the harvest was again very disappointing and at a Plenum of the Central Committee, Khrushchev asked for a huge increase in the production of fertilisers and herbicides.

1961: Berlin and Cuba In April 1961 Yuri Gagarin circled the earth in the spaceship Vostok I and received a hero's welcome in Moscow, while Khrushchev was again awarded the Order of Lenin. In America relations with the new communist government in Cuba were tense and President Kennedy authorised a landing by Cuban émigrés: the fiasco known as the Bay of Pigs. This led to closer military co-operation between Cuba and the USSR. In June, Kennedy met Khrushchev in Vienna for general discussions, including the security of entry into West Berlin which the Soviets wished to hand over to the East Germans and which led to the building of the Berlin Wall. Hardly had this crisis been solved when the infinitely more serious Cuban missile crisis blew up. In July 1962 Castro's brother Raoul arrived in Moscow seeking military aid, including medium-range missiles with nuclear warheads and bombers with nuclear capacity. By October the hardware had been dispatched and the launching pads were being constructed in Cuba. Meanwhile US intelligence had reported this to the White House and Kennedy promptly issued a statement warning that the USA would not tolerate the setting up of ground-to-ground missiles in Cuba. Khrushchev ignored this and continued to send weapons. On 22 October Kennedy went on television to tell the American people that he had ordered a complete blockade of Cuba and had placed the armed services on alert, ready to invade and occupy the country if the missile bases were not removed. On 24 October two Soviet vessels approached the line of the blockade, while in Cuba work went on to prepare the missiles and the airstrip for the Russian bombers. On 26 October Khrushchev responded to Kennedy's messages and proposed that if Kennedy would raise the blockade, he would remove or destroy the missiles there. The crisis was over.

In 1962 Sino–Soviet relations also underwent a change for the worse again, starting with a series of articles in Chinese papers attacking the integrity of the Soviet Communist Party. In the Chinese Press, Khrushchev himself was constantly referred to as the great revisionist.

22nd Party Congress In October 1961 at the 22nd Party Congress, Khrushchev once again raised the matter of Stalin's crimes, and this time he specified the members of the anti-Party group who had attempted to prevent his making them public. As a result, a resolution was passed calling for the removal of Stalin's remains from the mausoleum in Red Square. That night the coffin was placed in a deep hole outside the walls and several dumptrucks unloaded tonnes of cement on top of it. There were further rehabilitations of Stalin's victims, and more freedom to discuss such matters in the media, which culminated with the Praesidium approving the publication of Solzhenitsyn's *One Day in the Life of Ivan Denisovich*.

By 1964 there was a good deal of discontent in the USSR. The Seven Year Plan was not producing results. Food was scarce, as were many consumer goods, and prices had risen. The armed forces were smarting under the reductions in their pensions and privileges, and the peasants were unhappy about curtailment of their right to earn money from their private plots. Khrushchev had now grown accustomed to wielding the reins of power and seemed unaware of the groundswell of discontent. In April he celebrated his seventieth birthday and it was announced that the title Hero of the Soviet Union had been conferred on him.

1964: the Final Year Khrushchev spent much of what was to be his last year in power in foreign travel. In May he went to Hungary, and then visited Egypt to celebrate the inauguration of the Aswan Dam with Nasser. In June he began a three-week tour of Scandinavia and took his family. He also went to Czechoslovakia, as well as welcoming endless visitors to Moscow, including Nelson Rockefeller and President Sukarno of Indonesia.

On 12 October 1964 the Praesidium of the Central Committee was summoned to meet with the object of removing Khrushchev from all his official positions. The plot had been hatched by Suslov and Shelepin, but they were supported by both Brezhnev and Malinovsky, and by the time of the meeting only Mikoyan supported Khrushchev. He was summoned to Moscow from his holiday dacha by Brezhnev. The meeting, at which Khrushchev took the chair, specified the reasons for their discontent and asked for his resignation. He refused at first and the meeting broke up, but the next day he agreed and at the second meeting Brezhnev was elected First Secretary and Kosygin Chairman of the Council of Ministers. A report was read out, itemising Khrushchev's faults and shortcomings. It accused him of: taking hasty and ill-considered decisions; encouraging unnecessary administrative changes in government; taking sole credit for his country's achievements; ignoring the authority of the Praesidium and treating the members with disdain; applying foolish theories in the field of agriculture; treating Russia's allies in cavalier fashion, ignoring some and being recklessly generous with others.

Many of these charges were certainly true and such was the atmosphere of the meeting that when the resolution was put to the Plenum, 'That N S Khrushchev be released from his duties because of his advanced age and poor health', it was passed unanimously. Khrushchev himself, when he returned to his home, said, 'Well, that's it. I'm retired now. Perhaps the most important thing I did was just this: that they were able to get rid of me by simply voting, whereas Stalin would have had them all arrested.'

His retirement was spent in a fairly modest dacha at Petro-Dalneye on the outskirts of Moscow. He lived there with his wife and spent a good deal of time with his grandchildren. He was also allotted a flat in Moscow, which he rarely used. He was paid a pension of 400 roubles a month and an ancient car was put at his disposal. He started work on his memoirs, dictating them into a tape recorder and they were published in the West in 1971. It was not clear by what route they were taken there. Khrushchev himself denied any part in it when he was summoned to explain himself to the chairman of the Party Control Commission.

On 11 September 1971, he died of a heart attack. He was buried without the elaboration of a State funeral in the cemetery of Novo-Dyevichy. It has been said of him that at least he left his country a better place than he found it.

Kirilenko, Andrei, 1906–

A Party member from 1931. An engineer and Secretary of the Central Committee from 1966 who was considered as an alternative successor to Brezhnev, but whose power dwindled when Brezhnev gave his support to Andropov.

Kirov, Sergei K, 1886–1934

A Social Democrat Bolshevik in 1906, he was jailed and was in Siberia in 1917. He moved with the 11th Red Army to Baku and to the Caucasus in 1919 and was elected as a delegate to the 10th Party Congress. From May 1920 to February 1921, he was the Soviet ambassador to Georgia, preparing the way for the invasion. In April 1923, at the 12th Party Congress, he became a full member of the Central Committee.

In December 1925 he was sent to Leningrad to cleanse the Party of its association with Zinoviev, a task which took several years. In July 1930 Stalin made him a full member of the Politburo. In the next few years he may have opposed some of Stalin's wishes, particularly the proposed shooting of Ryutin, an opponent of Stalin's policies, and the special rations given in Leningrad. Also, in January 1934, the 17th Party Congress greeted his candidature for the post of General Secretary with loud applause. On 1 December he was shot. His murderer was named as a young communist, Nikolayev. Stalin used the murder as a justification for another purge of the Leningrad Party in which thousands of opponents were shot or deported to camps. The murder is a mystery and a source of speculation still. Had Kirov in fact been involved in an anti-Stalin movement? Did Stalin engineer the murder and use it to destroy others? Kirov was officially treated as a hero after his death.

Kokoshin, Fedor F, ?– 1918

A lawyer member of the Kadet Party in 1st Duma. A conservative to the right of most Kadets, he was in the Provisional Government and urged Kerensky to accept Kornilov's proposals for drastic military powers. After the October 1917 Revolution, in January 1918, while a prisoner in the Marinsky Hospital, he was shot by a group of sailors.

Kolchak, Alexander V, 1874–1920

Admiral commanding the Black Sea fleet from 1916. Overthrowing the Ufa Directory, he led a government in Siberia, based at Omsk, as 'Supreme Ruler', with the blessing of France and Britain from late 1918. He failed to keep the support of his troops, the people of the region or the strong Czech Legion and lost power in December 1919. He was captured at Irkutsk and executed.

Kollontay, Alexandra, 1872–1952

The first woman ambassador in the world. Her mother was a wealthy heiress and her father an aristocratic Tsarist officer, both of whom had liberal and intellectural connections. Born before the marriage, she was given her father's name, Domontovitch. Her marriage to Vladimir Kollontay in 1893 did not last long, but she later claimed that she became a socialist when on a trip with him she saw workers' housing and among the houses, unnoticed and uncared for, a dead child. A supporter of Lenin from 1901, she joined the Bolsheviks. She insisted that the Social Democrats had to support women workers and found her political base among St Petersburg women textile workers. She was part of the 'Workers' Opposition' voicing popular complaints that the urban workers had not gained from the Revolution.

Madame Kollontay was a feminist in a party unaware of feminism (since the Russian bourgeoisie had already accepted a great deal of the principles of women's rights and the working classes had not yet come to face the need for them). She was made People's Commissar for Social Security in October 1917 and pushed through a series of decrees and declarations on women, including, in December, the abolition of religious marriage and making marriage and divorce a purely civil matter. Her role thereafter became that of the token woman and she was moved out of the centre of power to become the Soviet ambassador, to Norway in 1923, Mexico in 1927 and then Sweden from 1930–45, where her position in a neutral country had importance in negotiating peace with Finland.

Her well-groomed appearance and her declared opposition to the conventional institution of marriage led many to assume that she devoted her life to sexual pleasure. In fact, she stressed the 'self-preservation of the individual' and that women's lives should be realised to their fullest potential.

Konev, Ivan S, 1897–1973
Marshal of the Soviet Union, he joined the party in 1918. A taciturn and guarded man, he survived the army purges of the 1930s and in April 1941 his 19th Army in the Caucasus was moved to the western border of the USSR to face the brunt of Hitler's June invasion. In the retreat he was given command of the west front, the principal defence of Moscow, and made deputy to Zhukov. His thrust into the German lines to the north of Moscow in November 1941 marked a turn in the tide, followed by the great counter-attacks. In the 1943 Battle of Kursk, his steppe front took the offensive and captured Kharkov. He commanded the Ukrainian front, sharing (or disputing) the honour of taking Berlin with Zhukov in 1945.

He succeeded Zhukov as Commander-in-Chief of the Soviet ground forces from 1946 to 1956. He was First Deputy Defence Minister in 1956, commanded the Warsaw Pact forces from 1955 to 1960 and Soviet forces in Germany during the critical period of building the Berlin wall, 1961–62.

Kornilov, Lavr G, 1870–1918
A war hero after his daring escape from capture by the Austrians in 1915, he was made general commanding the Petrograd Military District in 1917 and was responsible for the Tsar's arrest. He led an army in Kerensky's offensive and when it was broken by the Germans, he maintained its discipline. Kerensky made him Commander-in-Chief. Thinking he was acting in the best interests of the Provisional Government, he mobilised troops to remove the Bolsheviks from Petrograd, but Kerensky misunderstood his moves and had him arrested, accusing him of planning a military coup. This became known as 'the Kornilov affair'.

Kornilov escaped to the Don to join Denikin, but he was killed in action by an enemy shell shortly after.

Korolev, Sergei P, 1906–66
An aeronautical engineer who led Soviet rocket development from 1933 and developed the rockets that led to intercontinental ballistic missiles. He played a leading role in the Vostok and Soyuz space programmes.

Kossior, Stanislav V, 1889–1939
He joined the Party in 1907, and was exiled to Irkutsk in 1915, returning to Petrograd in February 1917. He was then sent to German-occupied Ukraine, where he had charge of Party work and prepared for an armed uprising. At the time of the

Brest–Litovsk Treaty in 1918, he joined the left-wing communists and led an underground party when Denikin ruled the area. From 1921 he held various Party posts in the Ukraine and in Siberia. Kossior was a candidate member of the Politburo from 1927 and a full member from 1930 and he became General Secretary of the Party in the Ukraine. But his adherence to Leninism and his belief in internationalism was not wanted in Stalin's day. In January 1939, when Khrushchev went as acting Party Secretary to the Ukraine to clear out nationalists and dissenters, his beliefs led to his downfall, arrest and execution.

Kosygin, Alexei N, 1904–80

A Leningrad textile engineer and Party worker who was promoted by Zhdanov in the 1938 purge to be chairman of the Leningrad Soviet. His Party career prospered and by 1952 he was a member of the Central Committee, the Politburo and Minister of Light Industry, although he had lost Zhdanov's patronage at his death in 1948. He continued under Khrushchev, becoming chairman of Gosplan in 1958. In 1964 he was elected Chairman of the Council of Ministers, taking Khruschev's place, while Brezhnev took the post of Party General Secretary. He held this post, effectively Premier of the Soviet Union, under Andropov.

Kozlov, Frol, 1908–65

Party worker. He joined the CPSU in 1926 when a textile worker in Leningrad and began his Party career, becoming Party Secretary there, where he was an associate of Zhdanov. He rose in 1957 to be Chairman of the Council of Ministers of the RSFSR. Kozlov mobilised the Leningrad Party to support Khrushchev when he was challenged by the anti-Party group in 1957, and as a reward was appointed Khrushchev's deputy. In 1960 he was appointed Secretary to the Central Committee of the CPSU and began to mount a serious challenge to Brezhnev as Khrushchev's successor, firing a number of people from the Secretariat, including Furtseva, as part of his campaign. In 1961 he fell out with Khrushchev on Yugoslavia and agriculture, and in 1963 launched an attack on Brezhnev in the pages of *Pravda*. He suffered from a stroke in 1964 and his removal from the Politburo in the same year signalled Brezhnev's victory in the leadership struggle.

Krasin, Leonid B, 1870–1926

An old communist who, although he had broken with Lenin in 1909, had political importance while his industrial expertise was used in building the Soviet economy. From 1900 he worked in Baku as an engineer in the expanding oil fields. His technical skills were also used in setting up secret printing presses.

Under the cover name of Zimin (winter), he was the chairman of the Party Congress in London at which the Bolshevik faction emerged. He returned as an engineer to take charge of the St Petersburg lighting system, but he was forced to flee when the authorities found out his political background. In 1918 he undertook to head the commission organising supplies to the Red Army and was made Commissar for Trade and Industry. He was twice ambassador to Britain and also to France. He died in England.

Krasnov, Petr N, 1869–1947

The last of the Cossack romantics: a Don Cossack Tsarist general and novelist! With his Cossacks he supported Kerensky at the time of the Kornilov affair in 1917, but his men and the revolutionaries began to parlay and for a time it was uncertain who was guarding whom. Krasnov engineered Kerensky's escape, which ended in America.

He was elected Ataman of the Don Cossacks and took dictatorial power, approached the Germans for help, made an alliance with the Skoropadsky government of the Ukraine, called in the Volunteer Army and raised a force of 40,000 Cossacks. By

August 1918 the Red Army and the Bolsheviks were driven out. Krasnov encouraged a counter-Bolshevik terror and preached 'Don for the Don Cossacks'. Krasnov's rule became unpopular as food shortages increased. In December 1918 whole regiments began to desert to the Red Army. In February 1919 Krasnov resigned.

He left Russia for Germany. The Nazis chose him to lead the puppet Cossack state in World War II, but by then he was an elderly man leaning on a stick. The Cossack prisoners paid him little attention and called him 'Grandad'. He was handed over to the Russians by the British, who found him with other Cossack troops in Austria in 1945. He was executed in January 1947 after being tried for fighting against the Soviet Union, espionage and terrorism.

Kropotkin, Peter, 1842–1921

A prince and an anarchist, who had a reputation also as an explorer in Manchuria and Siberia and was secretary of the Russian Geographical Society. He was linked to extreme revolutionaries and imprisoned in 1874, escaping to Western Europe in 1876. Although he did not approve of communism, or of the Bolsheviks, he returned to Russia after the 1917 Revolution for the last years of his life. This act seemed to give a blessing to the Revolution and he was held in great esteem.

Krupskaya, Nadezhda K, 1869–1939

A teacher from the class of poor official gentry, who worked with Lenin and went with him into exile, marrying him in 1898. She later became Vice-Commissar of Education, and a member of the Central Committee and the Praesidium of the USSR.

She supported Zinoviev in 1925–26, but 'capitulated' to Stalin. Her humiliation by subjection to Stalin was nearly absolute. She was obliged to stand by, in posts of minor dignity, while he exterminated the old Party. Her book *My Life with Lenin* became her main task: the role of Lenin's widow.

Kryuchkov, Vladimir, 1924–

Trained as a diplomat, his first posting abroad was as third secretary to Moscow's embassy in Hungary, where Andropov was ambassador, 1955 to 1959. He evidently impressed Andropov during the Hungarian rising and the consequent Soviet repression in 1956, for when Andropov became chief of the KGB in 1967, he brought in Kryuchkov, then working in the Central Committee. Kryuchkov soon rose to be head KGB man in New York in the 1970s and head of all KGB foreign operations in 1978, with the rank of general. He became chairman of the KGB, in succession to Chebrikov, in September 1988.

Kryuchkov's style is in contrast to the KGB's past. He is courteous and cultured; he was the first KGB chief to receive the US ambassador in his office and has appeared in a film showing the modern, suave KGB. Gorbachev appointed him a full member of the Politburo in September 1989.

Kulik, Grigory I, 1890–1950

Marshal of the Soviet Union. From being a sergeant in the Tsarist army, he rose, with Budyenny, in the Red Army. Like others of his background, he was promoted beyond his abilities and training. Stalin even gave him the job of running the main ordnance directorate for the whole Red Army (having remembered his being in charge of a few guns at Tsaritsyn). An old cavalryman, he opposed the introduction of the T34 tank. He was dismissed for gross inefficiency in 1941 and lucky to survive. From marshal he was demoted to major, but near the end of his life promoted to major-general by Stalin.

Kun, Bela, 1886–1937
Hungarian communist. A prisoner of war from the Austro-Hungarian army in Russia, he led the Hungarian Communist government from March to August 1919, until it was suppressed ferociously by a counter-revolutionary force. This led, in 1920, to the right-wing government of Admiral Horthy. He escaped by way of Vienna to Russia. An object of suspicion to Stalin as a man with potential allies, he died in the Great Purge.

Kuusinen, Otto, 1881–1964
An old Party member from 1904, he was a member of the Finnish revolutionary government of 1918. He was made head of the short-lived puppet 'Finnish government' set up in the USSR in 1939. From 1940 he was chairman of the Praesidium of the Finno-Karelian ASSR Supreme Soviet.

Kuznetsov, Anatoly, 1929–79
Author. He lived under the German occupation of the Ukraine in World War II. His story of the lives of young workers, drawn from his own experiences on hydro-electric stations, brought him fame. He wrote a sensational novel on the Nazi massacres at Babi Yar in Kiev, also called *Babi Yar*, which the poet Yevtuskenko took as a theme. But the censorship of his novel infuriated him and he defected from the USSR in 1969, while on a visit to Britain. He became well known for his broadcasts to Russians from Western Europe. He died of a heart attack in London.

L

Landau, Lev D, 1908–68
A physicist who received the Nobel Prize in 1962 for his fundamental research in the superconductivity and superfluidity of liquid helium. Educated at Baku and Leningrad Universities, he became head of physics at Kharkov University. An internationally leading figure in space technology, nuclear physics, plasma physics, stellar energy and low-temperature physics, he also helped make the first Soviet atomic bomb.

Larionov, Mikhail, 1881–1964
Painter and scenic designer. Born in Moldavia, he went to Paris in 1906 to study and was much influenced by the fauvist and neo-primitivist movements. He returned to Russia and, with his friend Natalia Goncharova (an exact contemporary) helped to organise the trio of exhibitions Jack of Diamonds (1910), Donkey's Tail (1912) and Target (1913). He also developed the abstract theory of painting known as rayonism. In 1915 he went to Paris and worked for Diaghilev, designing for opera and ballet. Later in life, he returned to genre paintings and still-lives. He died in France.

Lazo, Sergei, 1894–1920
A young communist from the Amur region who joined the Southern Maritime province committee formed in January 1918 to replace the overthrown Vladivostok Soviet. He was made commander of the partisans and then leader of the military–revolutionary staff. The Provisional Zemstvo Government gave him charge of the Military Council. When the Japanese decided to attack the Provisional Government in April 1920, it was decided not to resist but that troops should take to the hills with their weapons. Lazo and other council members were captured by the Japanese, who disposed of them by burning them in a locomotive boiler.

Lenin (Ulyanov), Vladimir Ilych, 1870–1924

Childhood and Youth Born in Simbirsk on 22 April 1870 in the old Tatar kingdom on the banks of the Volga. Lenin's father, whose family were of nomadic Chuvash origins, was a school teacher, a kind and pious man who became director of the province's educational organisation and therefore, under the existing system, a nobleman. His mother, loving but determined, came from a prosperous bourgeois family of mixed German and Swedish descent with a fair-sized estate near Kazan. Lenin was the third surviving child of their six children.

He was educated at the grammar school in Simbirsk and he and his brothers and sisters led a peaceful and happy middle-class life.

Everything changed when Lenin was 16. His father died of a brain haemorrhage and shortly afterwards his brother Alexander, to whom he was devoted, became involved in an unsuccessful attempt to asassinate Tsar Alexander III and, despite all his mother's efforts, was hanged on 20 May 1886. On the 22 June Lenin passed his finals at the grammar school with the highest possible marks and a glowing testimonial from the headmaster, Fyodor Kerensky (father of the future prime minister).

He entered Kazan University to read law in August 1887. Up to this point he had, despite his brother's fate, shown no interest in revolutionary politics. But in the summer he read Chernyshevsky's *What is to be done?*, a novel written when the author was a political prisoner. The hero of the novel is Rakhmetev, one of the 'new men' who was prepared to live a life of the greatest privation in order to bring about a new society where all men would be free. The book had an extraordinary effect on several generations of revolutionaries and Lenin was to prove no exception. Later in the year he took part in student demonstrations, was expelled from the university in December and placed under surveillance by the political police at his mother's estate at Kokushkino, where he continued to study law.

In 1890, through his mother's influence, he was allowed to take his finals at St Petersburg University and was awarded a first-class degree. In 1893, aged 23, Lenin moved to St Petersburg and started work in the office of a lawyer there.

The Revolutionary Contemporary accounts agree that he had now changed profoundly. He seemed much older than his years and was almost completely bald. He had started reading Marx and Engels after he was expelled from university and by now had become a serious revolutionary. When he arrived in St Petersburg he immediately sought out revolutionary circles in the city, where he was known by the name of Nikolay Petrovich.

In February 1894 he met a young girl, Nadezhda Krupskaya, who had joined one of the study circles. She came from the same background, though her parents were now impoverished. She seems to have greatly admired him from the first and was content to act as his secretary, to code and decode his messages and generally look after him from then until the end of his life, though they were not married until 1898.

In March he wrote his first extended work, *What the Friends of the People Are: How They Fight the Social Democrats*, an attack on the Narodniks.

In April Lenin went to Geneva and met Plekhanov and Axelrod and then to Paris, where he met and talked with Paul Lafargue, Marx's son-in-law. He completed his European trip by staying in Berlin before returning to St Petersburg. In December Lenin, with many other Social Democrats, was arrested and spent a year in jail before, as a result of his mother's influence, being exiled to Shushenskoye in southern Siberia.

In Shushenskoye he lived in the house of a well-off peasant, Apollon Zyrianov. He thoroughly enjoyed his time there, fishing, talking to the peasants and endlessly reading. He wrote the important pamphlet 'The Tasks of the Russian Social Democrats', which spelt out his ideas concerning an insurrectionary movement led by the Social Democrats among the factory workers. On 13 March 1898 the 1st Congress of the All-Russian Social Democratic Labour Party (RSDLP) met in Minsk and Lenin declared himself a member. In May Krupskaya and her mother arrived in Shush-kenskoye and the couple were married in July and moved into their own house.

In February 1900 Lenin returned from exile but left Krupskaya, who had to remain in exile for a further year. He returned to Psovsk but then went, illegally, to St Petersburg where he and Martov were arrested with their pockets full of subversive literature, but he was soon released.

Exile Lenin went to Switzerland to visit Axelrod and Plekhanov, with whom he quarrelled about an article he had written for the new publication *Iskra*. He then moved to Munich, where he arranged for the printing and distribution of *Iskra* and where he was joined by Krupskaya in March 1901. Shortly after this he began work on his book *What Is To Be Done?* in which he outlined his policies and beliefs at some length. He demonstrated the influence of Nechaev when he wrote of 'this powerful and secret organisation rising up to destroy the autocracy'. He stressed that this movement could not be democratic, that one man or a very small number of men must take all the ultimate decisions. Shortly after the book was published, the German printers decided that it was unsafe to continue printing *Iskra* and Lenin convinced the editorial board that they should move it to London. Lenin and Krupskaya rented an apartment at 30 Holford Square, obtained a reader's ticket for the British Museum and found a printer for *Iskra*. They were soon joined in London by Martov and Vera Zasulich. At this point Leon Trotsky arrived from Russia at the beginning of his long exile and he and Lenin spent some time walking around London together. He recognised Trotsky's qualities but at this time he and the younger man were not close.

He was still arguing with Plekhanov and when the editorial board voted to take *Iskra* back to Switzerland, Lenin had such a severe attack of shingles that he was confined to bed.

Bolshevik and Menshevik On 30 July the 2nd Congress of the RSDSLP opened in Brussels, was closed by the police and moved to London. It was at this congress that the split in the party took place. Martov wanted a 'broad' party, open to anyone who supported any of its organisations, and Lenin wanted a 'narrow' party confined to those who had worked for one of the organisations. Plekhanov and Trotsky supported the side getting the minority vote, the Mensheviks. Lenin, though he continued the battle and was now the leader of the majority group, the Bolsheviks, was profoundly depressed and in poor health again. In November he resigned from the editorial board of *Iskra*. In the summer of 1904 he abandoned his revolutionary activities and with Krupskaya went off to the mountains to recover his health. In September they returned from their holidays and Lenin planned a new revolutionary newspaper, *Vpered* (*Forward*), with his new supporters, including Bogdanov and Lunacharsky. In the first edition of the new paper he wrote an article forecasting a popular uprising in Russia. Within three weeks Bloody Sunday, the massacre outside the Winter Palace, had sparked off the 1905 revolution.

The 1905 Revolution The main events of the 1905 revolution took place without any participation from Lenin. When Lenin finally arrived in St Petersburg in October, via Sweden, he was closely shadowed by the Okhrana and crossed the border to Finland to escape them. While he was there, the uprising in Moscow took place. For the next two years Lenin and Krupskaya lived mostly in or near St Petersburg, though he made occasional trips to Finland and Denmark for conferences or meetings. There were attempts at unifying the RSDLP from time to time, but Lenin was still determined to maintain his Bolshevik principles and also to remain in charge. At the end of the year he travelled to Tammerfors, where the 1st All-Russian Bolshevik Conference was held. In April 1907 he was arraigned at a special party tribunal for an article he had written against the Mensheviks. He defended himself vigorously and was not expelled from the party. He proclaimed that it was permissible to use any weapons against opponents who had caused a split in the party because 'every split is a great crime against the party'.

5th Party Congress In May he travelled to London, where the 5th Party Congress took place. It was attended also by Trotsky, Zinoviev, Kamanev and – on one of his rare trips out of Russia – Stalin, also Rykov and Voroshilov and on the Menshevik side Plekhanov, Martov, Axelrod and Dan. Lenin was in impressive form and attacked the Mensheviks for siding with the bourgeois, the Kadets, and the Duma. He accused Trotsky of being a Menshevik in disguise.

Exile Again In January 1908 Lenin and Krupskaya once again left Russia and returned to Switzerland. They were to spend the next nine years in Europe. In Geneva he wrote *Materialism and Empirio-Criticism*, a philosophical study, and in December they moved to Paris. When they arrived in the French capital, the RSDLP decided to launch a new magazine, the *Social Democrat*, and in order to remain on the editorial board, which included Martov, Lenin was forced to agree to a much modified policy with talk of armed insurrection played down. Then, in the spring of 1910, Lenin, to everyone's surprise, developed a close friendship with an attractive Frenchwoman, Inessa Armand, wife of a rich industrialist who had abandoned her husband for the pleasures and perils of revolutionary politics. The relationship lasted for many years and was important to both of them. Krupskaya, who always put her husband's happiness first, was said to have been quite prepared to step aside and let them marry, an idea which Lenin, at heart a domestic bourgeois, strongly resisted.

In the spring of 1911 Lenin set up a school for the training of underground workers near Paris. Zinoviev and Kamenev lectured on the history of the party, while Inessa Armand lectured on political science and ran a communal kitchen in her dining room.

In January 1912 a conference of the Bolsheviks was held in Prague at which Lenin asserted his dominance over the party. In June he believed there to be signs of an insurrection in Russia and he moved to Cracow in Austrian Poland, where he hoped to be able to influence events more easily. There he met Bukharin for the first time.

In Cracow, Krupskaya's health deteriorated and they took a cottage in the Tatra Mountains, but finally Lenin had to take her to Berne, where she was operated on for goitre. For the next two years they spent the winters in Cracow and the summers in the mountains, except for occasional trips to attend conferences or meetings in Paris, Berlin or Brussels.

World War I At the outbreak of war, Lenin was in Novy Targ, Galicia. The Austrian authorities searched his house and arrested him. He was freed on appeal by sympathisers in Austria. He returned to Cracow and then travelled to Berne via Vienna. He and Krupskaya were to spend the next three wartime years in Switzerland, either in Berne or Zurich, short of money as usual and living in uncomfortable circumstances most of the time.

Plekhanov and Kautsky had come out in support of the war and Lenin attacked them for this. In his *Tasks of Revolutionary Social Democracy in the European War*, he called the war a 'bourgeois, imperialist, dynastic war' and proposed as a slogan 'For the Socialist Revolution' and as an immediate goal 'A Republican United States of Europe'. Their neighbours and closest associates at this time were the Zinovievs and Inessa Armand.

At Zimmerwald in September 1915, Lenin declared that the task was to turn 'the imperialist war between peoples into a civil war' but his motion was defeated.

On 15 March 1917, after lunch, Lenin was getting ready to return to the library as usual when a friend ran in to announce news of a revolution in Russia.

Revolution Lenin's initial reactions to the February revolution were much concerned with the possibility of a counter-revolution headed by the Tsar, though he clung firmly to the necessity for the Bolsheviks to carry out propaganda for an international proletarian revolution and for the seizure of power by a Soviet of Workers' Deputies.

But Lenin's main concern now was how to leave 'this accursed Switzerland' and return to Russia. In wartime all normal means of transport were impossible. But it was Martov's plan which finally succeeded. He suggested approaching the German government and arranging an exchange of Russian exiles for German internees. The plan was adopted: to deliver Lenin and his Bolsheviks to Russia would hasten the collapse of Russia. The 'sealed train' with Lenin and his party arrived at the Finland Station in Petrograd on 16 April at 11 pm, to be greeted by enthusiastic crowds, representatives from the Petrograd Soviet, the Baltic fleet and a band playing the *Marseillaise*. Addressing the crowds from the turret of an armoured car, he shouted 'Long live the world-wide Socialist Revolution!'.

The April Theses The morning after his arrival it was decided to hold a meeting of the Bolshevik delegates to the All-Russian Conference of Soviets of Workers' and Soldiers' Deputies at the Tauride Palace. The address he gave at the conference, which was recorded as he delivered it, became known as the April Theses. The singular nature of many of these statements led to his being attacked not only by Mensheviks, which was to be expected, but also by many of his own Bolsheviks. Questions were also asked as to how he had managed to travel through Germany on the sealed train. Could he have been subsidised by the German High Command? This suspicion continued to haunt Lenin for many years, though it has been proved untrue.

By the time of the next Party Conference in May, Lenin had overcome most of his critics but the situation was anarchic. Only Kerensky, now Minister of War in the Provisional Government, seemed to have any authority. There were Mensheviks in the government, but the Bolsheviks were not asked to join and in any case would have refused.

By June the Bolshevik programme was rapidly increasing their support. After the Bolshevik failure to take the initiative in the workers' demonstrations in the July Days and the Provisional Government's action against them, Lenin was in imminent danger and, rather than face his accusers, he took refuge in a village near Petrograd and then moved to Finland. In August the Petrograd Supreme Court indicted him for treason and the organisation of an armed uprising. At the 6th Party Congress Lenin was elected to the Central Committee with Zinoviev and Trotsky. They were all either in prison or in hiding.

Lenin then published *State and Revolution* in which he argued that after the proletarian revolution there would be a period of transition before the ideal communist state could be established, and this would be the dictatorship of the proletariat. 'When the ideal state comes into existence there will be no need for it any more – it will wither away.'

On 9 October Lenin returned to Petrograd and on the 10th a meeting was held in the apartment of Nikolay Sukhanov at 32 Karpovka; twelve of the 21 members of the Central Committee were present. Lenin accused them of lacking courage and foresight and demanded an immediate uprising. A vote was taken: ten of the committee were in favour; two, Zinoviev and Kamenev, were against.

The October Revolution On the morning of 25 October the Bolshevik forces went into action and seized the key points in the city. On the 26th, Lenin attended the 2nd All-Russian Congress of Soviets of Workers' and Soldiers' Deputies. Lenin was elected chairman of Sovnarkom, the Council of People's Commissars, and on 27 October issued the Decrees on Peace and on Land, calling for immediate peace and proclaiming the end of private ownership of land.

While Trotsky organised the defence of Petrograd, Lenin proceeded with the work of government. To a large degree it was government by improvisation. As he later wrote, 'revolutions are the locomotives of history. Drive them at full speed and keep them on the rails'. On 26 October he signed a decree ordering elections to be held on

11 November. But when the Constituent Assembly met in January 1918 and the Bolshevik motions were defeated, Lenin promptly withdrew them from the assembly and called for the dissolution of the assembly on the grounds that it represented the 'old relationship of political forces'. This was formally the end of democratic government in Russia.

The peace negotiations with the Germans at Brest–Litovsk were being conducted by Trotsky and Lenin only got the party to agree to acceptance of the quite onerous terms on the grounds that he could not afford to fight a revolutionary war, or depend on the revolution taking place in Germany which Trotsky and others were relying on. Nevertheless he had to threaten resignation in order to get his own way.

In March he moved the centre of government to Moscow and lived first in the Hotel National and then in an apartment in the Kremlin, with Trotsky as a near neighbour. They arranged that the Kremlin bells should play the *Internationale*.

Invasion and Civil War The Soviet republic was in danger, with White troops menacing Petrograd. Trotsky, as Commissar for War, was responsible for defending the new Soviet republic. But Lenin introduced the most draconian punishments for anyone involved in resistance to the government. Red Terror became a principal instrument of rule. In July 1918 Left SRs assassinated Count Mirbach, the German envoy to the Kremlin, and the Socialist Revolutionaries' Deputies were arrested. Lenin sent a telegram to Stalin telling him that 'the Left SRs who have launched an uprising against us must be mercilessly suppressed'. In August there was an attempt to assassinate Lenin by another Left SR, Fanya Kaplan. He was shot in the neck and shoulder, but by October was well enough to speak in public again. His attempted assassination was followed by a mass wave of terror, the Petrograd Cheka alone executed more than 500 immediately.

The worst year of the Civil War was 1919. Lenin still had hopes of European revolutions breaking out and they were given temporary substance in Hungary and Bavaria by the setting up of 'soviets' there. But they were soon crushed, as Rosa Luxemburg and Karl Liebnecht's Spartacists had been in Berlin. In March, Lenin established the Third International, the Comintern, and declared optimistically 'The ice is broken. The Soviets have conquered throughout the whole world.' By the end of the year the Interventionists had withdrawn and the outcome of the Civil War seemed less in doubt.

At about this time Lenin developed a plan for the electrification of the country, declaring that 'Communism is the Soviet government plus the electrification of the whole country.' In February 1920 he delivered a report to a meeting of the All-Russian Central Executive Committee denying that the Bolsheviks had remained in power by the use of terror and claiming that 'we have renounced capital punishment'.

In April, war broke out between Russia and Poland and, against Trotsky's advice, Lenin ordered the Red Army to advance on Warsaw. The campaign was a failure and the disaster was compounded by Stalin taking Lvov, ignoring the overall plan. This was not the first time that Stalin had gone against Trotsky, indeed he had been attempting to poison Lenin's mind against him for some time. Lenin was forced to mediate between them, but on this occasion he supported Trotsky completely. On 12 October a peace treaty was signed with Poland and on the same day Lenin attended the funeral of his friend Inessa Armand, who had died of cholera contracted in the Crimea in August. Lenin was grief-stricken.

New Economic Policies (NEP) In 1921 peace returned to Russia, the enemies of the Soviet republic, both external and internal, had been mostly defeated, but as Lenin admitted in a letter written in February, 'It is quite useless to work on vast bureaucratic schemes of state economy. We are beggared. This is what we are – starving, destitute beggars.' Suddenly there was a new opposition. In March the sailors at Kronstadt called for free elections and the return of small-scale enterprise. This rebellion was ruthlessly suppressed, but Lenin realised that the policies of War Communism could not continue without the entire economy breaking down and with it the government. So at the 10th Party Congress the 'Workers' Opposition' was attacked and the measures known as the New Economic Policies were introduced. This was almost immediately followed by the most appalling famine caused by widespread crop failures on a scale not seen for 30 years.

Conditions in the country improved with a good harvest in 1922 and the new measures to encourage the peasantry to sell their crops. Small-scale industry and commerce had made a wider range of goods available, but Lenin was obsessed with the 'swamp of bureaucracy' which was strangling the country. It was perhaps one of the reasons for making the fateful decision to appoint Stalin as General Secretary during the course of the 11th Congress in April 1922.

Illness In April Lenin had a small operation to remove one of the bullets that had lodged in his body after Fanya Kaplan's assassination attempt, but on 26 May he suffered from a stroke and was kept at Gorky until September, when he returned to work at the Kremlin. He was supposed to work no more than five hours a day, but actually worked ten and held meetings on the days he was not supposed to work. On 31 October he attended a meeting of the All-Russian Central Executive Committee and in November spoke at a session of the Moscow Soviet, where it was noticed that his speech was slurred. In December he had a further stroke and his right side was paralysed. His doctors ordered him to bed for a complete rest.

Visitors were forbidden but he was allowed to dictate for five or ten minutes daily. He started to write his letters to the Party congress which became known as his 'Testament'. A variety of topics were covered but it mainly concentrated on his fears about the future leadership of the Party and the possible split which he saw developing from a struggle between Trotsky and Stalin. Of Stalin he wrote, 'Comrade Stalin having become General Secretary has unlimited authority ... and I am not sure that he will always be capable of using that authority with sufficient caution. ... Comrade Trotsky ... is personally perhaps the most capable man in the present Central Committee but he has displayed excessive self assurance. ... These two qualities of the two outstanding leaders of the present can inadvertently lead to split'. In further instalments of his 'Testament' he suggested increasing the number of recognised nationalities. In doing so, he criticised Stalin for his repressive actions in Georgia. He also sent a note to Trotsky asking him to look into the Georgian situation. In January he added a note to his previous comments on Stalin saying that 'Stalin is too rude ... which becomes intolerable in a Secretary General. That is why I suggest that the comrades think about a way of removing Stalin from that post.'

In March 1923 he learned of Stalin's abusive telephone call to Krupskaya, in which Stalin attacked her for allowing Lenin to discuss political matters, and he wrote to Trotsky asking him to raise the matter of the Georgians at the Plenum of the Central Committee and to Stalin to decide whether he wished to apologise or break off relations with him.

Death On 10 March he suffered a third stroke but by October was well enough to be driven into Moscow.

On 21 January 1924 he had a further stroke, lost consciousness and died at 6.50 pm. On the 23rd the body was moved to Moscow and on the 27th, against his wishes, it was placed in a mausoleum in Red Square. Thousands of mourners from all the regions of Russia flocked to Moscow to pay their last respects to their leader. And at the 2nd All-Union Congress of Soviets, the anniversary of his death was announced as a national day of mourning.

Ligachev, Yegor K, 1920–

An engineer by profession and a graduate of the Moscow Aviation Engineering Institute. A member of the CPSU since 1944. After World War II he worked as an engineer before joining the Komsomol and working for it in Novosibirsk. Several years of Party work followed this, at the end of which he became Secretary of the Novosibirsk obkom. In 1961 he went to Moscow to work in the Central Committee, dealing with Party publications. In 1965, after Brezhnev's reorganisation of the Party apparatus, he was sent back to Siberia as First Secretary of the Tomsk region. He stayed there until 1963 and built a reputation as a hard but fair Party leader. Andropov, who had a high opinion of Ligachev's integrity, brought him back to Moscow as head of the organisational department of the Central Committee. In 1985 he became a full member of the Politburo. Although he supported Gorbachev's election to General Secretary, he does not owe his political rise to Gorbachev and is regarded as being strongly to the conservative side of the Party. In the summer of 1987, with Chebrikov then head of the KGB, he published a warning against too radical changes and played a leading role in the dismissal of Boris Yeltsin. He survived the 1989 reshuffle of the Politburo and held his post as chairman of the Central Committee Commission for Agriculture. For subsequent events see the Chronology.

Litvinov, Maxim (Genokh Koissevich, Meier Wallach), 1876–1951

A Social Democrat from 1898, he joined the Leninists in 1901. After the 1905 revolution, he moved to London where he worked in an office. He married Ivy Low, a London journalist linked with the Bloomsbury intellectual set. In 1917 he was appointed the Soviet representative in Britain. He was arrested but released in exchange for the head of the British diplomatic mission to St Petersburg, Bruce Lockhart (see below).

He was Deputy Commissar for Foreign Affairs from 1921 to 1930, often representing the Soviet Union abroad at international conferences. He became Commissar in 1931, but Stalin replaced him with Molotov in 1939 when he wanted to deal with Nazi Germany, either because he was too closely associated with Western Europe or because as a Jew the Nazis would not talk to him.

He was reappointed Deputy Commissar in 1941 and was ambassador to Washington in 1941–43.

Lockhart, Sir Robert Bruce, 1887–1970

The first British diplomat to head a special mission to the Bolshevik government in 1918. The Soviets assumed immediately that he was a spy. He spoke fluent Russian and made friends with the leaders, such as Trotsky. He was imprisoned in the Kremlin, September–October 1918, on suspicion of being behind the Mirbach assassination, but released after British protests and threats of retaliation. He was exchanged for Litvinov.

He had been the paymaster of the British agent in Russia, Sidney Reilly. Together they had arranged help for White agents and planned the assassination of Lenin. The attempt by Dora Kaplan on Lenin pre-empted them. For his work in Russia, he was decorated and given a knighthood. After 1922 he worked for a bank and as a journalist, writing his memoirs in 1933.

Lukyanov, Anatoly I, 1930–

Vice-President of the Supreme Soviet and deputy to Gorbachev. A lawyer who has worked for years in Moscow for the Central Committee and the Supreme Soviet. He joined the Politburo in September 1988. Congress ratified his position as vice-president in May 1989 by a huge vote after Deputies had quizzed him intently on his role in the suppression of Hungary in 1956 and Czechoslovakia in 1968, and of his attitude to the

Baltic states and to deported peoples like the Ingush. They seemed assured that he would support perestroika.

Lunacharsky, Anatoly V, 1875–1933
The reforming Commissar for Education and the Arts. As a student in Zurich he met Rosa Luxemburg and was associated with the left thereafter. Back in Russia he was arrested and on release in 1902 he returned to Switzerland, joining Bogdanov. He met Lenin in Paris in 1904 and took on the editorship of *Vpered* and *Proletary*, magazines intended for clandestine circulation in Russia. Late in 1905 he went back to Russia. Because of his philosophical outlook, he was now attacked by Lenin, in *Materialism and Empirio-Criticism*. He returned to Switzerland in 1914.

In 1917 he went to Petrograd, joining Trotsky and moving towards the Bolsheviks again. His power of oratory impressed many and he became deputy mayor of Petrograd. After the October 1917 Revolution he became a member of Sovnarkom and Commissar for Education and the Arts. He successfully campaigned against illiteracy and the 1917 rate of 65 per cent illiteracy was reduced by the end of his time to a negligible figure. In 1930–32, before his death, he was with Litvinov as the Soviet representative at the League of Nations.

Luxemburg, Rosa, 1870–1919
Founder of the Communist Party in Germany. A Social Democrat agitator in Russian Poland, she moved to Berlin in 1898. She joined with Lenin in the 1906 'Unification' Congress in Stockholm, but she was soon at loggerheads with him because of his hostility to Mensheviks. From 1910 she devoted herself to socialism in Germany. She was killed by soldiers after the failure of the 1919 communist rising, and is remembered as one of the great martyrs of communism.

Lysenko, Trofim D, 1898–1976
The geneticist whose theories were promoted by Stalin as Marxist, ideologically correct and therefore 'true'. Of Ukrainian peasant origin, he specialised in low-temperature seeds, especially for Russia's Arctic zones. His 'neo-Lamarckian' argument stated that heredity was not determined by chromosomes or DNA, but could be modified by environment and, furthermore, that acquired characteristics could be inherited. He was made president of the Academy of Agricultural Sciences in 1938, but dismissed in 1956, after Stalin's death, having been denounced by Khrushchev for falsifying statistics and issuing diplomas to favourites. Khrushchev, however, also defended him and Lysenko returned to official favour in 1958 and was reinstated as the academy's president in 1961 until his final dismissal in 1963. The geneticist Vavilov who had founded the academy and whose theories were internationally accepted, but ran counter to Lysenko's, was arrested and died in detention in 1942.

M

Maisky, Ivan M, 1884–1975
A leading Menshevik in 1917, he held anti-Bolshevik posts until he left the Mensheviks in 1919, joining the anti-Bolshevik government in Samara. He was therefore expelled from the Party. His talents were turned to diplomacy, being employed in the Ministry of Foreign Affairs from 1920. He was ambassador to Britain, 1932–43, and Deputy Commissar for Foreign Affairs with Litvinov, 1943–46, when he retired to private life.

Makhno, Nestor I, 1889–1935

Ukrainian guerrilla leader. He was born to a peasant family but, imprisoned in Moscow in 1908 for his anarchist associations, he found the opportunity to educate himself. Released by the revolution in February 1917, he returned to his village and became the revolutionary leader of the area. The advance of the German army in the Ukraine made him take up arms and he led his local group not only against the Austrians and Germans, but against the landowners and the Ukrainian governments of Petlyura and Skoropadsky. This extended his fighting area widely and became the rallying point for all insurgents in southern Russia north of the Sea of Azov. He was a pure anarchist dedicated to the destruction of all governments and parties. Although he co-operated with Red forces for a time, he quarrelled with his Bolshevik collaborator, Grigorev, and shot him. In 1919, with the French occupation of southern Russia, he built up his peasant army to reach 40,000 men. As a Ukranian nationalist, he attacked Denikin's White Volunteer Army in the rear, leading to its defeat. Makhno was absolute in his anarchism and direct in his dealings: when Wrangel sent him an envoy to discuss co-operation, Makhno had the man shot.

In November 1920 the Red Army, under Frunze, broke up his army and he escaped from Russia, reaching Romania in August 1921. Sick and in poverty, he went on to Paris, where he stayed for the rest of his life.

Maklakov, Vasily A, 1870–1957

A Kadet of the right. A lawyer and a member of the Duma from 1905, he was sent to France as ambassador by the Provisional Government in 1917. He gave open support to Kornilov's calls for military action against the Bolsheviks and welcomed Nikolai Chaikovsky and the terrorist Boris Savinkov to the White 'Russian Political Conference' in Paris in 1919. He became the leader of Russian political émigrés in France.

Malenkov, Georgy M, 1902–79

A young loyal communist from 1920, he was on the Central Committee during the purges. During World War II he was a member of the committee in charge of military equipment and joined the Politburo in 1941. In 1950, at the 19th Party Congress, he declared that the Soviet grain problem was finally solved (bringing him in direct conflict with Khrushchev's expertise).

After Stalin's death he was head of the collective leadership of the Soviet Union, but it did not take long for Khrushchev to supplant him. He admitted his policy errors and when, in 1957, with Voroshilov and Molotov he attempted to challenge Khrushchev, he was expelled from the Central Committee and assigned to the management of a far-off electric power station. His last 12 years of retirement were spent in Moscow.

Malevich, Casimir, 1878–1935

Painter. Born in Kiev, he studied at the Moscow School of Painting, Sculpture and Architecture. He took part in the trio of progressive exhibitions before World War I with Larionov and Goncharova. Like them he attempted to combine the principles of cubism and futurism but later he developed a new geometrical abstract style of his own which he called suprematism. He denied the social purposes of painting.

He taught at the People's School of Art in Vitebsk from 1919–22 and in Leningrad from 1923–27. In the early 1930s he attempted to get in the mainstream of socialist realism with the painting *The Girl with a Red Staff*, which he produced in 1932. However he is remembered for his most absolute abstract painting: a white square on a black background.

Malinovsky, R I, 1898–1967
A Tsarist infantry NCO in the Red Army from 1920; tough, even brutal, with little formal education, he rose to be a marshal of the Soviet Union. Commanding the Ukrainian front in World War II, he ended in command of the trans-Baikal front, moving his force rapidly against the Japanese in 1945. He became Commander-in-Chief of land forces in 1956 and then succeeded Zhukov as Minister of Defence until his death.

Maltsev, T S, 1895–
A well-known figure in Soviet agronomy. Born to a peasant family, he became director of a testing station at the Zavety Lenina Kolkhoz, where he developed a new system of ploughing without a mould-board, combined with shallow disc tillage. Used in the Kurgan oblast, this produced high yields and in 1935 he was made a Hero of Socialist Labour. His method was less successful in lighter soils which tended to be subject to erosion.

Mandelstam, Osip, 1892–1938
Poet. Arrested in 1934 after reciting a satirical poem about Stalin, his wife appealed to Bukharin who was powerless, but spoke to Stalin. Stalin asked Pasternak who said Mandelstam was harmless but a good poet: Mandelstam was simply banned from Moscow. Arrested again in 1938, he died in the NKVD's hands.

His widow Nadezhda Mandelstam was also a major poet and her memoirs, *Hope Against Hope* and *All Hope Abandoned*, published abroad in the 1970s, are a revealing account of intellectual life in the Soviet Union. She recounts how they were reduced to begging to avoid starvation in the 1930s, being officially out of favour. Yet discreet help came from the intellectuals of the official Establishment. In 1956 she received a printed notification from the Supreme Court that her husband's death had been due to a regrettable oversight. He was rehabilitated.

Mannerheim, Carl G E, 1867–1948
A baron and general in the Tsarist Russian army, commanding the Guards who retook Helsinki after the 1917 Revolution. Regent of Finland, 1918–19, he fought the Soviet army and ensured Finland's independence. He was made president of the Defence Council, 1931–39, after threats of a fascist party take-over and promoted to marshal in 1933. In 1939, when the Soviet Union attacked, he assumed supreme command. The Finnish defence line on the Karelian isthmus became known as the 'Mannerheim Line'. Allied to Germany in the war against Russia, he corresponded personally with Churchill before Britain, with regret, declared war on Finland (the USA was not at war with Finland and retained a legation there during the war). In 1942, at the age of 75, he was made Marshal of Finland and continued in command of the army. He declined to accept command of the German troops in Finland, since that would have made him one of Hitler's subordinates, preferring to keep Finland's military operations limited and clear of Hitler's grand strategy. He became President in August 1944 and obtained a cease-fire with the Soviet Union on 4 September 1944. He finally declared war on Germany in March 1945 and resigned as President a year later.

Manuilski, Dmitri Z, 1883–1959
An old guard Bolshevik, one of those who returned with Lenin in the sealed train and who died in retirement. He was a radical activist from 1904, being several times arrested and deported until leaving for France in 1907, where he worked with Antonov-Ovseyenko and Trotsky as a journalist.

After the October 1917 Revolution, he had several posts, including Secretary of the Ukrainian Party from 1921 to 1923. He worked for the Comintern Secretariat from 1922, imposing its will on the German and French Communist Parties. Stalin had confidence in his ruthless methods (hidden under a convivial exterior) and used him to replace Bukharin as Secretary to the Comintern. He was then appointed deputy to the Bulgarian Dimitrov, and, unofficially, Stalin's man in the Comintern. In 1945 he was made Ukrainian Foreign Minister when that republic was given a full seat in the United Nations. He held this post until he retired – already out of favour but allowed to withdraw peacefully – in 1952.

Marchenko, Anatoly, 1938–86
A leading dissident of the Helsinki groups. First imprisoned as a 'hooligan' in 1957, he escaped from the camp and tried to reach Iran through Kazakhstan. He was retaken and put in a maximum security prison in Moscow. Released, due to ill-health, in 1966, he lived among dissidents and wrote of his experiences. Arrested again in 1968, he was exiled to Siberia. He was released but suffered constant surveillance and harassment, and was back in a labour camp in 1981. He went on hunger strike in 1986 in protest against brutality to prisoners and shortly afterwards his death was announced.

Martov, Yuly (Y O Tsederbaum), 1873–1923
From a Jewish Odessa family, he suffered from Russia's anti-Semitism and his rebelliousness had him exiled to Siberia in 1893. He advocated taking Marxism to the workers by being involved in their struggle for better conditions, rather than by intellectualising and lecturing the élite. Although he and Lenin were confined to Siberia, it was due to his activity that the Russian Social Democrat Labour Party (RSDLP) was founded. With Lenin, he started the Union for the Liberation of Labour in October 1895, and he was also a founder of the *Iskra* group. In 1903 he would not accept Lenin's proposals for a tightly run organisation of dedicated revolutionaries and the RSDLP split on the vote, Martov's faction being the minority, the Mensheviks, with Moscow as his stronghold.

He became the official leader of the Mensheviks in 1917, when he returned from exile, racked with tuberculosis. In October he led the Constituent Assembly as an 'internationalist' against Kerensky, but when he attempted to check the Bolsheviks and persuade them to negotiate, Trotsky replied, 'Go where you belong: into the trash bin of history.' He left Russia in 1921 and died an exile in Berlin.

Marx, Karl, 1818–83
German political philosopher, the founder of modern socialism. He published *The Communist Manifesto* with Engels in 1847. Expelled from Prussia, Marx lived in London from 1849, supported by the richer Engels. He completed the first volume of *Das Kapital*, the classic work of Marxian communist theory, in 1867; it was completed after Marx's death by Engels. He was the founder of the International Workingmen's Association in 1864, the 'First International', but conflicts with the anarchism of Bakunin led to its disintegration in 1876.

Maslyukov, Yuri, 1937–
Having graduated as an engineer from Leningrad, his career led him through management to be head of the Technical Department of the Ministry of Munitions and then, in 1982, into Gosplan. In 1988 he became chairman of Gosplan, at the same time he was made an alternate member of the Politburo and a deputy chairman of the Council of Ministers. In 1989 Gorbachev, as he strengthened his Party support, made him a full member of the Politburo.

Mayakovsky, Vladimir V, 1893–1930
Futurist poet and dramatist. Born in Georgia, he joined the RSDLP in his youth, although he never became a Communist Party member, and was imprisoned in 1909. In 1918 he wrote the first Soviet play, *Mystery Bouffe*, which was staged by Meyerhold.

In 1924 he wrote his famous poem *Vladimir Ilich Lenin*, and also *Hymn to the Attacking Classes*. His poem *Lost in Conference* attacked the hordes of bureaucrats whom he saw as strangling the Revolution. It was approved of by Lenin but did not increase his popularity in the Party. Pasternak was his friend and an admirer of his less public poetry. On a visit to the USA in 1925, he wrote a cycle of poems on America, praising in *Brooklyn Bridge* its engineering achievements.

In 1930 out of favour and dogged by personal problems, he committed suicide. Ideologically he was always regarded as sound (and accepted as a practitioner of socialist realism). After his death Stalin treated him as the poet laureate of the Revolution. He had the advantage during the Great Purge, the Yezhovschina, of being already dead, otherwise he would have been a certain candidate for elimination.

Medvedev, Roy and Zhores, 1925–

Twin brothers, born in Tblisi, who have played a part in modernising Russian political attitudes and persuading the world of the value of changes in the 1980s.

Zhores, as a biologist, fell foul of authority when he criticised the Lysenko regime and wrote about the censorship of private mail. He was arrested in 1970 and put in a psychiatric hospital. Following international protests, mainly organised by his brother Roy, he was allowed to emigrate to Britain in 1973. He has written on recent events in the Soviet Union and in support of perestroika.

Roy's main work as a historian has been to publish hitherto unrevealed aspects of Stalinism and of its successors. Published abroad, his academic reputation is high.

Menzhinsky, Vyacheslav R, 1874–1934

Head of the OGPU, an aesthete, dilettante, poet and painter and a Bolshevik from 1903. The son of a rich lawyer, he was accustomed to a luxurious life-style. He was out of Russia from 1907 to 1917, when he returned in time for the October Revolution. He was Commissar for Finance from October until March 1918, then consul in Berlin up to November 1918. He went to the Ukraine as a Cheka official and from July 1920 was in charge of the Cheka in the Red Army. From September 1923 he was deputy chairman of the OGPU (as the Cheka had become), succeeding Dzerzhinsky as chairman in July 1926.

Menzhinsky, known as 'the Poet of the Cheka', was responsible for the brutal enforcement of such programmes as collectivisation although, never in good health, he delegated much to his deputy, Yagoda, who succeeded him.

Merkulov, Spiridon and Nikolai (dates unknown)

The entrepreneurial brothers from a peasant family in the Amur valley who led the National Democratic Union formed of 'conservative socialists' in the Russian Far East in 1920. Spiridon had been a specialist on the region for the Tsarist Ministry of Agriculture and Nikolai was a Vladivostok industrialist. They owned a newspaper and exercised great influence. Using the Far Eastern Constituent Assembly, elected in 1920, and with Japanese support, they planned an anti-Bolshevik coup. By late 1921 they were under suspicion of corruption and of diverting supplies for their family profit. In May 1922 they declared the assembly dissolved and led their own government with the help of the last of the Imperial navy, but by August they had been ousted and Spiridon was sent off to Canada with 30,000 roubles as a pay-off. Nikolai retained an official position until October 1922, when he left, with others, for Japan.

Meyerhold, Vsevolod, 1874–1940?

Actor and theatrical director. Born at Penza and a member of the CPSU from 1918. After studying at the Music and Drama School in Moscow, he joined the Moscow Arts Theatre, where he acted for several years. Dissatisfied with the classical theatre, in 1902 he left to start a theatre of his own, the Society of New Drama. He experimented there with his theories of non-conventional, stylised drama. In 1905 he worked with Stanislavsky who was developing his famous and revolutionary methods of training for actors, and then went to St Petersburg to work with Kommissarievsky's theatre there.

After the 1917 Revolution he developed the idea of the so called 'theatrical October', a style which incorporated political messages into dramatic texts without sacrificing entertainment values. He directed the Meyerhold Theatre from 1920 till 1938. He was an early mentor of Eisenstein in experimental film work. Meyerhold had always suffered attacks from the authorities for 'formal' elements in his work, which was regarded as a failure to work within the guide-lines of socialist realism. He was arrested during 1938 and either vanished into the camps with his wife or was executed. Their exact fate is unknown.

Mikoyan, Anastasy I, 1895–1978
An Armenian brought up in Azerbaijan and a Party member from 1915. He was the sole survivor of the 26 Baku Commissars shot in 1919 by the anti-Bolshevik Musavet Party. He was a leading figure in the events of 1920 when the Red Army occupied Transcaucasia. He was on the Central Committee from 1923 and in 1925 the youngest-ever member of the Politburo. He replaced Kamenev as Commissar for Commerce in 1926. He took over Supplies and then Food until 1938. He raised huge sums of hard currency, reputedly over one hundred million dollars, through his sales of art treasures to Calouste Gulbenkian, the oil millionaire, and Andrew Mellon, the American financier. Mikoyan studied American food products and introduced a whole range of ice-creams to the Soviet Union.

He was on the Council of Ministers and the Supreme Soviet, whose Chairman (President of the Soviet Union) he was, 1964–65. He was one of the few of Stalin's Politburo both before and after World War II, but after Stalin's death he moved towards Khrushchev and with Suslov went to Hungary in 1956 to determine Soviet policy there. Although a supporter of Khrushchev and seen to have high status, during the early 1960s his power was declining.

He was a survivor and died peacefully in retirement. Once when seen going out of a house into heavy rain, without coat or umbrella, he is reported to have said, 'Don't worry, I can dodge between the raindrops.'

Milyukin, Pavel N, 1859–1943
A Russian historian, a founder of the Kadets. A member of the 3rd and 4th Dumas, he opposed the Tsar's war policies and joined the Provisional Government as Foreign Minister, February to April 1917. He fled in October 1917 and, after co-operating with the White armies, settled in Paris, where he edited anti-communist Russian papers until the German occupation of Paris in 1940.

Mirbach, Count Wilhelm von, 1871–1918
The German envoy to the Kremlin, shot and killed by Cheka men in association with Left SRs under Maria Spiridonova in July 1918. He was the representative of the German government still at war in the west and prepared to pay money to the Bolshevik government to encourage it not to pursue the war.

Moiseyev, Mikhail, 1882–1955
General commanding the Far East district from January 1987 who succeeded Marshal Akhromeyev as Chief of Staff of the armed forces and First Deputy Minister of Defence when the latter resigned in December 1988.

Molotov ('The Hammer'), Vyacheslav M Scriabin, 1890–1986

A Bolshevik from 1906 and exiled for his activities. In 1917 he was editor of *Pravda*, and a colleague of Stalin from 1921. Molotov held high office from the beginning. He was a member of Politburo, 1926–57, and Chairman of the Council of People's Commissars (Premier of the Soviet Union), 1930–41. Then from 1939 to 1941 he was Foreign Minister, replacing the Jewish and less abrasive Litvinov in order to sign with Ribbentrop the Soviet–German Pact. After Stalin's death, his power waned and an attempt to outmanoeuvre Khrushchev in 1957 led to his dismissal from the Central Committee and exile to Mongolia as ambassador until 1960. At the age of 94 he was readmitted to the Communist Party.

He looked like the perfect 'faceless bureaucrat'. Churchill described him as a man who 'perfectly represented the modern conception of a robot. ... His smile of Siberian winter, his carefully measured and often wise words, his affable demeanour, combined to make him the perfect agent of Soviet policy in a deadly world.'

N

Nechaev, Sergei G, 1847–82

Claiming to be the leader of a large revolutionary movement and hunted by the police, he went to Switzerland in 1869. There he met other exiles. He fascinated Bakunin, producing either with him, or in imitation, the Revolutionary Catechism which influenced a generation of young Russian revolutionaries, including Lenin. It is reflected in Bernard Shaw's *Man and Superman* and is still a key to understanding the idea of a 'revolutionary'.

'The revolutionary is a doomed man,' it starts. 'The revolutionary can have no friendship or attachment. ... He should not hesitate to destroy any position, any place or any man in the world. ... The filthy social order can be split up into several categories. The first category comprises those who can be condemned to death without delay.'

Extradited from Switzerland for murder in 1872, he spent his last years in close confinement in the Peter and Paul Fortress in St Petersburg.

Nekrasov, Viktor, 1911–87

Soviet writer. He won a Stalin Prize in 1945 with his first novel, on the Battle of Stalingrad in which he had taken part. In 1962 his essays *Both Sides of the Ocean* gave views of Europe and the USA that angered Khrushchev. His later defence of Solzhenitsyn led to Nekrasov's expulsion from the Writers' Union in 1972. He went to France in 1974, where he became a leading figure among exiled dissidents.

Nicholas II, Romanov, 1868–1918

Tsar of Russia from 1894. He succeeded his father, Alexander III. The revolution of 1905 forced him to summon a Duma. His reign survived because of the gestures of reform made under Stolypin. His Tsarina, Alexandra Feodorovna, a granddaughter of England's Queen Victoria, anxious for the health of their sickly son, brought the family under the charlatan Rasputin's influence from 1906. This alienated many of the aristocracy, particularly when war against Germany came and the German-born Tsarina and Rasputin were suspected of treachery. Nicholas took command of the armies in the face of the defeats of 1915.

When the February 1917 revolution came, he abdicated in favour of his brother Michael in March 1917, although his brother did not take the throne, handing authority to the Provisional Government under Prince Lvov. Under Bolshevik rule he was sent with his family to Ekaterinburg under guard. On 16 July 1918, when it seemed that White troops were approaching, he, the Tsarina and their four children were shot and their bodies thrown in a marsh.

O

Oistrakh, David, 1908–74
Violinist. An international prize-winner in the 1930s, he became professor at the Moscow Conservatory. He died, on tour, in Amsterdam.

Oistrakh, Igor, 1931–
Violinist son and pupil of David Oistrakh who has also become an internationally renowned musician.

Ordzhonikidze Grigory (Sergo) K, 1886–1937
A political activist from Georgia and a close associate of Stalin. From early in his career, he was a Bolshevik. This was confirmed in 1910 when he made his way to Paris and mixed with Lenin's Bolshevik colleagues. Sent on a mission to Russia, he was arrested and exiled to Yakutsk in Siberia.

In the Civil War he was the political commissar in Voroshilov's army and in February 1921 he joined with Stalin in plotting the invasion of Georgia (which took most other Party leaders by surprise) and was the commander of the military force. In 1922 he was the Politburo's representative in Georgia, where he urged the unpopular official line that it should merge into the Transcaucasian Republic. In the course of this, he beat up a Georgian communist leader, provoking an angry reaction from Lenin, who compared him to a Tsarist bully. 'Sergo' was Stalin's instrument and responsible for the russification of Georgia; his methods disturbed Lenin and led to his viewing Stalin in a different light.

Stalin appointed him to the Politburo in 1930, and in 1932 he was made Commissar for Heavy Industries.

In 1933 he is believed to have resisted, with Kirov, Stalin's programme of terror and to have opposed the persecution of Bukharin. In 1937 Molotov attacked Ordzhonikidze's powerful commissariat for its protection of 'saboteurs'. Shortly after this he commited suicide or was murdered, it is not clear which. He was never denounced or criticised during Stalin's regime. His mistake may have been to have tried to block the rise of a younger and even more ruthless Georgian, Beria.

P

Pasternak, Boris, 1890–1960
A poet and novelist whose parents were famous Russian artists, his father a painter and his mother a pianist. In 1957 the publication abroad, in Italy, of his novel *Dr Zhivago* and the award of the Nobel Prize for Literature led to his dismissal from the Soviet Writers' Union. Although in disgrace when he died, his funeral in Moscow was attended by a large crowd. In 1988 his expulsion from the union was, posthumously, cancelled and the novel published in the USSR.

Peters, Jacob, 1886–?
Born in 1886 in Courland, he worked in London from 1909 to 1917, where he was a

member of the British Labour Party. He was arrested with others in December 1910 for the murder of three policemen at Houndsditch in London, tried at the Old Bailey and acquitted. There is also some possibility that he was the 'Anarchist', known as Peter the Painter, hunted by the police and the object of the spectacular 'Sidney Street Siege' led personally by the Home Secretary, Winston Churchill, who brought in the army in an unsuccessful attempt to capture him. In 1917 he was sent back to Russia by his communist colleagues in London, where Dzerzhinsky used him to infiltrate the Ministry of Foreign Affairs. In 1919 he was appointed Chief of Internal Defence of Petrograd and stamped out the revolt ruthlessly, sending some 3,000 hostages to Moscow. There is an account of him wearying of endlessly signing death warrants, unread. In October 1920 he left Russia for a period (his wife was English), but in 1923 he was elected a member of the Party Central Committee and was 'Commandant' of the Kremlin until 1937, when all trace of him ceases. He was presumably shot in the purges, but the latest edition of *The Great Soviet Encyclopedia* gives neither date nor cause of his death.

Petlyura, Simon V, 1879–1926

A Ukrainian journalist specialising in social matters who became the Rada Secretary for Military Affairs. Jailed for the four months of the Skoropadsky regime, he re-emerged as a Ukrainian military leader. His troops, however, were diminished by the defection of Makhno's peasant army to the Bolshevik cause. In 1919 he made a deal with the Poles and the next year co-operating with Pilsudski, he retook Kiev on 25 April 1920. The Red Army, however, retook the city in June and Petlyura's campaign ended with his flight from the Ukraine.

Petrov, Yevgeny P (Katayev), 1903–42

One of the pair of authors known as 'Ilf and Petrov' (see page 255). He was the younger brother of the novelist Valentin Katayev.

Pilsudski, Josef, 1867–1935

A Polish socialist, exiled by the Tsarist government to Siberia, 1887–92, he agitated for Polish independence. In 1914, in World War I, he led an anti-Russian 'Polish Legion' supported by the Austrian Empire. Interned by the Germans in 1917, he was released to command the Polish army after the Treaty of Brest-Litovsk. In 1918 the new Poland elected him chief of state and dictator until the constitution of 1922. As Marshal of Poland in 1920, he led the campaign against the Bolsheviks, defeating the Red Army and taking Kiev in 1920, with French help, when the Red Army tried to take Warsaw. Although not head of state, he retained dictatorial powers until his death.

Plekhanov, Georgy V, 1857–1918

A Narodnik and the leading philosophical Marxist in Russia. He left Russia in 1880, living mostly in Geneva, Switzerland. He founded the Social Democrat Party and collaborated with Lenin, but sided with the Mensheviks after 1903. During World War I he took a strongly patriotic and 'Defensist' position and opposed the Bolshevik revolution.

Podgorny, Nikolai V, 1903–83

A Party member in the Ukraine from 1930. Minister of Food in 1940, he rose to be the All-Union Minister and First Secretary of the Ukraine Party Central Committee, 1963–65. He was then appointed Secretary of the USSR Central Committee and Chairman of the Supreme Soviet Praesidium (President of the USSR) from 1965 to 1977, when Brezhnev pushed him into retirement.

Preobrazhensky, Evgeny A, 1886–1937

An active Bolshevik from early in his career. Living to the east of the Urals, he saw the revolution there threatened first by the arrival of the Czech Legion and then by the armies of Kolchak. He was elected to the Central Committee, taking a hard left-wing position. In 1920, as one of the three Party Secretaries, he campaigned for democratisation, but this brought him into conflict with both Stalin, who opposed his ideas, and Zinoviev, who felt he had a monopoly in this field. In 1926 he was a leading figure in the 'New Opposition' and was expelled from the Party and exiled to Siberia the next year. He capitulated to Stalin and was readmitted to the party in 1929, only to be expelled again. In 1936 he was a witness for the prosecution against Zinoviev and then himself arrested. He vanished from history.

Prokofiev, Sergei, 1891–1953

Composer and pianist. Born in the Ukraine to middle-class parents, he was a child prodigy who wrote his first piano piece at the age of 5 and entered the Leningrad Conservatory at the age of 14. Here he met Miaskovsky, who became a life-time friend, and they both became involved with the World of Art group who were arranging concerts featuring the music of Schoenberg, Strauss and Stravinsky. In 1914 he won the Rubinstein Award at the conservatory with a performance of his own First Piano Concerto. He spent the summer of 1917 outside Petrograd, writing his First Violin Concerto.

In 1918 Prokofiev left Russia and went to the USA, where he gave concert performances and tried, unsuccessfully, to write operas, including the brilliant *Love of Three Oranges*, which was not actually performed until 1926. He abandoned America for Paris, where he worked with Diaghilev and Stravinsky in the theatre and wrote his Third Piano Concerto.

In 1933 he returned to Russia, where he spent the rest of his life. His relationship with the authorities was complex and unhappy, though he was not shown the harsh treatment that some artists received. But like every other composer, he was subject to the control of the Union of Soviet Composers, and he was certainly not free to indulge in the experimentation that was common in the West. His Cantata for the 20th Anniversary of the Soviet Revolution was not performed until 1966. He wrote the music for Eisenstein's *Alexander Nevsky*, and in 1944 his most successful work, the superb Fifth Symphony. In 1948 the harsh decree from the Central Committee which attacked the work of Soviet artists for being riddled with formalist perversions did not spare him. He attempted to regain favour with an opera based on the life of a well-known war hero, but it was badly received. Prokofiev died in Moscow in October 1953 on the same day as Stalin.

Pyatakov, Grigory (Yuri) 1890–1937

The leader of the Ukrainian Communist Party who set up a secret government in Kursk in December 1918 and led Red troops into an attack on the Ukraine. Stalin accused him of being part of the Trotsky conspiracy and he was executed after a trial in 1937. His sentence was annulled by the Soviet Supreme Court in June 1988.

R

Radek, Karl Bernhardovich (Sobelsohn), 1885–1939 (1941?)

Brought up in Polish-speaking Galicia, then part of the Austrian Empire, he became a socialist in his youth. He travelled to Switzerland and Germany, writing and translating for a living. He entered Russia (without a word of the language) in 1905 and was imprisoned and sent back to Austria in 1907. He joined Lenin and Zinoviev in

Switzerland and returned with Lenin in the 'sealed train' to Petrograd in 1917.

A brillant, often outrageous man, looking like a cross between a professor and a bandit according to Bruce Lockhart, he worked in the Commissariat for Foreign Affairs, specialising in Central Europe. He took part in the Brest-Litovsk negotiations, got himself into Germany in December 1918 and helped found the Communist Party there. Imprisoned in Berlin, he turned his cell into the unofficial embassy of the Bolshevik government. On his return, he was given the position of Secretary of the Comintern. Involved with the attempted communist take-over in Germany in 1923, accompanied by Larissa Reisner, he was held responsible for its failure and lost his post.

Something of a political turncoat, he tried to reconcile the left opposition with Stalin's views, though he remained consistently hostile to Zinoviev. His career was not advanced by his apparently cynical changes of belief, even when events proved him right. In December 1927, with 74 others, he was expelled from the Party for opposing its line: he made a prompt about-turn and with Preobrazhensky joined in a declaration against 'right opportunism' and was readmitted. From 1929 to 1936 he was Stalin's adviser on foreign affairs. In 1936 he worked with Bukharin on the new Soviet constitution, and that year he joined in condemning Zinoviev and Kamenev, calling for their deaths. That year he too was arrested, and accused of maintaining contact with Trotsky. Sentenced to ten years' imprisonment, he disappeared and at some point died of a heart attack, or perhaps was murdered by fellow prisoners.

He had his sentence annulled by the Soviet Supreme Court in June 1988.

Raskolnikov, (Ilia) Fyodor Fedorovich, 1892–1939

The illegitimate son of a priest, who became a socialist as a student, and worked for *Pravda* in St Petersburg, with Molotov and Stalin. He joined the Tsarist as a cadet navy during the war and sailed with the fleet in the Pacific. When the February 1917 revolution broke out, he rejoined *Pravda* and was sent to Kronstadt, becoming vice-chairman of the Kronstadt Soviet on 17 March. He was one of the leaders of the Kronstadt sailors who demonstrated in Petrograd in the July Days, and with Trotsky secured the release of Chernov.

The failure of the demonstration landed him in the Kresty Prison until the October Revolution. As an assistant in the new Commissariat for Naval Affairs, he ensured the scuttling of the fleet at Novorossiysk in June 1918, and commanded the Volga naval flotilla which captured Kazan that August. In December 1918 he commanded a destroyer in the Baltic which met a British naval force; his ship was grounded and he was taken as a prisoner to Brixton in London, until May 1919, when he was exchanged for captured British officers. He then took command of a Caspian–Volga flotilla, which was in action until 1920, when he was appointed 'Commissar-Commander' of the Baltic fleet. 'In March 1921,' he wrote, 'I demobilised myself and was appointed ambassador to Afghanistan.'

This revolutionary romantic was married to the beautiful Larissa Reisner and was in tune with neither the old guard Bolsheviks nor the newly rising Stalinists, preferring the world of writers and artists. In 1930 he resumed a diplomatic career and was ambassador to Estonia, Denmark and Bulgaria, where, in 1937, he noticed that his own volume of memoirs was on the list of banned books in the Soviet Union. He therefore ignored an order recalling him and went to France. On 12 September 1939 he died in Nice under unexplained circumstances. His book *Kronstadt and Petrograd in 1917* (Moscow, 1925) was reprinted in 1964, but as an émigré he has never been fully rehabilitated.

'Rasputin', Gregori, 1871–1916

A mystic living at the Tsar's court from November 1905, and believed to have healing power over the Tsar's son, sick with inherited haemophilia. He was despised for his peasant manners and hated for his influence by the men of the court (but he had an effective sexual attraction for many of the ladies). He was suspected generally of working for the Germans and was murdered by courtiers, after many attempts, in December 1916. The name 'Rasputin' means the profligate.

Reed, John, 1887–1920

An American journalist, the hero of the 1982 film *Reds* and author of *Ten Days that Shook the World*, published in March 1919, the well-known account of the October Revolution.

Reed was the son of an Oregon judge who became a journalist after Harvard and went to Russia as a war correspondent in 1917. Impressed by the Revolution, he worked for the Bureau of International Revolutionary Propaganda from December 1917. In 1918 the Bolshevik government proposed him as their consul in New York, but this was unacceptable to the US government. Reed helped to found the US Communist-Labour Party. He returned to Russia, joining the executive committee of the Comintern in October 1919. He died of typhoid while on a mission in Baku.

Reilly (Rosenblum), Sidney (Sigmund), 1874–1925(?)

Born in Odessa, he led a wandering life, marrying in England as Sidney Reilly. In World War I he obtained an arms-purchasing agency to sell weapons to Russia. Recruited by the British secret service, he was sent to Russia in 1918 and forced into hiding in the wave of terror that followed the Mirbach assassination. Reilly escaped through Sweden to London, where he set to work to support Savinkov's Paris-based anti-Bolshevik operation. In the course of this, Reilly passed on the 'Zinoviev letter', forged correspondence implicating the British Labour government with the Comintern. Working independently from the British secret service, Reilly went back into the Soviet Union on the invitation of 'the Trust', a supposed group of dissidents. He was captured by the OGPU and vanished.

Reisner, Larissa M, 1895–1926

The daughter of a communist professor, she was brought up in Germany in intellectual circles. She completed her education in Russia and began writing poems and political articles, involving herself with workers' movements and in particular the Kronstadt sailors. With the October Revolution, she took to arms and fought with the Red Army, being made a commissar. With her husband, Fyodor Raskolnikov, she saw action with the Volga and Caspian flotilla and later joined him in the Soviet embassy in Afghanistan.

Their marriage broke up when they left Afghanistan in 1923; Raskolnikov had ill-treated her and she went to live with Karl Radek (who later wrote her biography). She then went to Germany on a mission to encourage the communist rising in Hamburg. Back in Russia, she continued writing, but the malaria she had contracted on her travels led to her death at the age of 31.

Rokossovsky, Konstantin K, 1896–1968

Marshal of the Soviet Union. He joined the Red Guards in 1917, then in 1919 became a member of the Party and joined the Red Army. Among the purged army officers of 1937, he was released early in 1939. He was an outstandingly successful and heroic commander during World War II, commanding armies outside Moscow in 1941, Stalingrad in 1942, at Kursk in 1943 and at the final entry to Berlin in 1945, when he was promoted to marshal of the Soviet Union.

Although of Polish origin, he had been raised in Russia and spoke Polish with a heavy accent; nevertheless he was given command of the Polish army in 1949, until the Polish leadership removed him in 1956. There were suggestions that he had prepared to take over the government in Moscow's interest. His last military employment was as officer commanding the Transcaucasian military district.

Romanov
The family name of the ruling Tsars of Russia. The heir-apparent, Alexis, was killed with the rest of the family in 1918.

Rozanov, Sergei Nikolaivich, ?–1920
A White general appointed by Kolchak to establish military control in the Far East in July 1919. His cruel administrative methods and his reliance on Japanese support alienated other Russians. When Kolchak fell, he put himself under the protection of the Czechs who handed him over to his opponents in Irkutsk, where he was executed in February 1920.

Rybakov, Anatoly, 1911–
Author of children's books. His first book, *The Dagger* (1948), won a Stalin Prize in 1951 and was filmed in 1958. Several of his succeeding books were also turned into films. His *Children of the Arbat* (1987) shattered the Soviet literary world on its publication. He had been preparing this work for years but had hesitated to publish it. It concerns Kremlin intrigues in the 1930s and implies that Stalin had ordered the murder of Kirov.

Rykov, Alexei, 1881–1938
An early Bolshevik with moderate leanings who advocated coalitions with other socialists in 1917. A member of the Politburo, he succeeded Lenin as the chairman of Sovnarkom (the Council of People's Commissars) from 1924 until 1930. He was accused of being in the 'Right Opposition' and recanted. He was put on a show trial and executed in the purges.

Ryzhkov, Nikolai, 1929–
From the Urals; he started as a mine-worker, then qualified as an engineer in 1959. He worked in industry in Sverdlovsk and had close contact with Kirilenko. In 1974 he went to Moscow to the Planning Commission of the Supreme Soviet and in 1979 was made first deputy-chairman of Gosplan. Under Andropov he became Central Committee Secretary and has been in the Politburo since 1985, becoming Premier and Chairman of the Council of Ministers under Gorbachev in succession to Tikhonov.

S

Sakharov, Andrei, 1922–89
Nobel Peace Prize winning physicist, a member of the Soviet Academy of Sciences at the age of 22, awarded the Order of Stalin and the Order of Lenin, and made a Hero of Socialist Labour. He is known as the father of the Soviet hydrogen bomb.

In the Khrushchev era he became outspoken, calling for coexistence between the USA and the USSR and for a nuclear test-ban treaty. In 1968 he published, as a samizdat, *Thoughts on Progress. Peaceful Co-Existence and Intellectual Freedom*, which resulted in internal exile in Gorky. Released in December 1986, he decided to get a nomination to stand for Congress in 1989 from the Academy of Sciences and would not accept any lesser body, turning down the support of members of 'Memorial', a group commemorating the victims of Stalinism. He was, in the event, elected. In the Praesidium of the Congress he became the focus of the new opposition.

Sakharov, Vladimir, 1944–

A diplomat who defected to the USA in 1971 and is the source of several personal stories about contemporary Soviet leaders.

Savinkov, Boris, d. 1924

An old SR terrorist, involved with the assassinations of the minister Plehve in 1904 and the Grand Duke Sergei in 1905. He was a Deputy Minister of War under Kerensky but broke with his party in September 1917, supporting Kornilov. He was in touch with British intelligence through the diplomat Bruce Lockhart and worked with Sidney Reilly. He set up his own military organisation, the 'Green Movement', which organised brief, abortive risings in Rybinsk, Murom, Kazan, Kaluga and Vladimir and most importantly, in July 1918, in Yaroslav. He fled to Paris but kept his groups in action from a Warsaw base as head of a 'Russian Political Committee'. In 1924 he was decoyed into the Soviet Union and put on trial. He died in prison, possibly by his own hand.

The English novelist and one-time spy, Somerset Maugham, described him as 'a genial likeable fellow'. Winston Churchill met him in 1919 and thought him 'a terrorist for moderate aims', but the British Foreign Office wrote him off as 'most unreliable and crooked'.

Scharansky, Natan, 1948–

A prominent campaigner for Jewish rights. Graduating in Moscow as a computer specialist, he was married in 1974, and his wife emigrated to Israel but he was refused permission to travel. His campaign for the right to emigrate led to his arrest in 1977 and sentencing to 13 years' imprisonment on charges of anti-Soviet agitation. Released in 1986 in an exchange of spies, he went to Israel. His memoirs, *Fear no Evil*, were published in 1988. He was proposed as Israeli ambassador to the UN in 1989.

Semenov, Grigori Mikhailovich, 1890–1946

A Cossack Ataman who, as Tsarist military commander, continued to control Trans-Baikal until 1920, working with the Japanese Interventionist forces. An ambitious and energetic leader, his ruthlessness lost him support among other anti-Soviet soldiers and politicians. His own Cossacks deposed him in June 1921 and in September he left for Japan, leading anti-Soviet intrigues there and in Manchuria, where he led a pan-Mongol movement with Japanese support. At the end of World War II he was captured and taken to Moscow, where he was tried in August 1946 and executed.

Semichastny, Vladimir Y, 1917–

Having risen through Party ranks from the Komsomol, he was made chairman of the KGB in succession to Shelepin in 1961, holding the post until 1967, when the powerful Yuri Andropov took over.

Serov, Ivan A, 1905–

Head of the KGB (chairman of the State Security Committee) after Stalin's death and Beria's removal. Rumoured to have been responsible for the Katyn Forest massacre in 1940, he was in charge of the removal of the Crimean Tatars and others in 1943–44. Malenkov gave him the KGB post in 1954, but his brutal past caused him to be replaced by Shelepin in 1958. 'Like other high-ranking executives in the security apparatus, Serov had a long record of crime and abuse of power, but he was devoted to Khrushchev and was prepared to act promptly on any order that he received from him,' wrote the historian Medvedev.

Shcherbitsky, Vladimir V, 1918–

A Party member from 1941, after World War II he held a succession of high Party posts. Under Brezhnev he became Ukrainian First Secretary and a member of the Praesidium of the USSR Supreme Soviet from 1972. He was honoured twice as 'Hero of Socialist Labour' in 1974 and 1977 and awarded the Lenin Prize in 1982. The last member of the 'old guard', he survived Gorbachev's 1988 rebuilding of the Politburo and stood unopposed for a seat at Dnepropetrovsk, his first Party post, in the 1989 Congress election. He was dropped from the Politburo in September 1989.

Shelepin, Aleksandr N, 1918–

From a Komsomol organiser, and its First Secretary in 1952, he was made chairman of the State Security Committee (the KGB), 1958–61. At the 22nd Party Congress he spoke out against Stalin's atrocities. He was one of the younger men of the time and received rapid promotion, moving to be Central Committee Secretary, a member of the Politburo and deputy chairman of the Council of Ministers. In June 1967, after the defection of Svetlana Alliluyeva, he was demoted to a post in charge of trade unions.

Shevardnadze, Edvard A, 1928–

A Georgian, responsible for an attack on corruption in Georgia. His party career was in Georgia, becoming First Secretary in 1972. He gained popularity there when he ruled that Georgian not Russian should remain the official language of the republic. He joined the Central Committee in 1976, and the Politburo in 1978. In July 1985 he succeeded Gromyko as Foreign Minister, visiting China in February 1989. For subsequent events see the Chronology.

Shliapnikov, Alexander G, 1884–1937

A Bolshevik leader in Petrograd during World War I, and on the Executive Committee of the Petrograd Soviet in 1917. He held commissar posts in the Soviet government, but from 1920 he led the Workers' Opposition Group in the Bolshevik Party, criticising the centralised bureaucratic control of industry. He was expelled from the Party in 1933 and presumably arrested and shot in 1937.

Schmidt, Dmitri, ?–1937

A Ukrainian Jew who had been a Civil War cavalryman and in 1936 commanded the Red Army's only heavy tank brigade: he was the first to be shot in the military purge.

Sholokhov, Mikhail, 1905–84

Nobel Prize-winning novelist. He was born near Rostov and worked as a house painter and driver. In the mid-1920s he wrote several collections of Cossack stories of which the first, *Donskie Rasskozy*, attracted a good deal of attention. His immense novels, *The Quiet Don* (1928–40) (also known as *Quiet Flows the Don*) and *Virgin Soil Upturned* (1932–60), brought him fame and prizes – the Lenin Prize in 1960 and the Nobel Prize in 1965. His success also brought him a large house in the country, a luxurious flat in Moscow, even a private aeroplane.

However, there has been well-founded criticism of his work claiming that he took much of the material from the diary of another Cossack writer, Fedor Kriukov, who was killed in the Civil War. He took a highly aggessive attitude to fellow writers who appeared to dissent in any way from the Party line. He joined in the attacks on Pasternak and demanded the death penalty for Sinyavsky and Daniel during their trial in 1965.

Shostakovich, Dimitri, 1906–75

Soviet composer. Born in St Petersburg, he helped support his widowed mother and family by playing the piano in a local cinema. He studied at the Petrograd Conservatory and wrote his First Symphony in 1926. In 1936 he was attacked by the authorities for his opera based on a novel, *Lady Macbeth of Mtsensk*, and in order to justify himself to the Union of Soviet Composers produced his immensely popular Fifth Symphony. In 1940 he was awarded the Stalin Prize for his Piano Quintet. In 1942, during the war, he produced his Seventh Symphony, dedicated to the city of Leningrad then under siege. After its performance in Moscow and Leningrad, a score was flown at once to the USA, where it was given a highly publicised performance by Toscanini with the NBC orchestra.

After the savage assault on composers by Zdhanov in 1948, Shostakovich compromised by writing simpler, accessible music for public performance, one work from this period was entitled *The Sun Shines on our Motherland*, and more complex and private works, such as the Violin Concerto which was not performed until after Stalin's death. In Khrushchev's time he was inclined to side with the authorities in criticising experimentation and his Twelfth Symphony was dedicated to the memory of Lenin. He was declared People's Artist of the USSR in 1954 and awarded the Order of Lenin in 1956.

He maintained his contact with young artists, and his 13th Symphony (1962) was inspired by Yevtushenko's poem on Babi Yar.

Sinyavsky, Andrei, 1925–

A literary critic and dissident, arrested in September 1965 and put on trial with Daniel in 1966. They were 'secret' writers of parodies of Soviet life, little known in Russia, but read abroad. The trial was in the hands of Andropov, then head of the KGB, who, unusually in a show trial, allowed them to plead not guilty and had them tried on the charge of libelling the State. That fiction could be judged a libel made the case a notorious travesty of justice and attracted much adverse publicity in the West, but while it reflected the conservative reaction of the time in the Party, it also lost the respect of the more able writers. Sinyavsky was given a seven-year sentence, but he was released and emigrated to France.

Skoropadsky, Pavel P, 1873–1945

A Tsarist officer from a wealthy Ukrainian family, promoted to general in 1912. In February 1917 he renamed his Russian command the 1st Ukrainian Corps. He was nominated head of the Free Cossacks in October and in March 1918 he became head of the Ukrainian state under German protection. In December 1918, wearing German uniform, he escaped from a further Ukrainian revolt to Germany. He lived there until his death.

Skvortsov-Stepanov, Ivan, 1870–1928

A Social Democrat in Moscow from 1896. The first Soviet Commissar for Finance. He edited *Das Kapital* in Russian, but Lenin described him as 'only a theoretical Marxist'.

Sokolnikov, Grigori, 1888–1939

Deputy-Commissar for Finance in 1921. The paradox of a 'Bolshevik financier' who arose from the collapse of the Soviet economy in 1921. There was a massive budgetary deficiency and the currency was becoming valueless. Sokolnikov set out guide-lines in the 1922 11th Party Congress to attack the problem by backing the paper money with internationally accepted gold and thus forcing State trusts to be measured by their market values. The gold-backed unit of currency, the chervonets, equivalent in value to the Tsarist 10-rouble gold piece, was successful and the financial crisis was overcome.

Sokolnikov had been a Bolshevik since 1905, although he had disagreed with Lenin over his treatment of Mensheviks. In 1918, since other leaders would not commit themselves, he was the Russian signatory to the peace of Brest-Litovsk. At the peak of his career he was on the Politburo, but in 1925 aligned himself with Zinoviev, Kamenev and Krupskaya in the 'new opposition'. He lost his ministerial post in January 1926 and was sent as ambassador to London, 1929–32. At the Party Congress in January 1934 Kaganovich mocked him as an arrogant enemy of the working class and forced him to recant his former views. He was arrested in July 1936, tried and sentenced in the following January. He did not survive life in the camps. His reputation was rehabilitated in 1989.

Solomentsev, Mikhail S, 1913–

A factory worker and engineer who has held many Party posts in the USSR, including Chelyabinsk, Karaganda, Kazakhstan, Rostov. A member of the Central Committee since 1961, the Politburo in 1983 and chairman of the Party Control Commission until 1987.

Solzhenitsyn, Alexander, 1918–

Soviet author and critic of the regime. Born in the northern Caucasus, his father already dead, he was brought up by his mother, who was the daughter of a rich farmer. He graduated from Rostov University in maths and physics in 1941, and spent the war as an artillery officer in the Red Army. He was decorated for bravery but in 1945 was arrested in East Prussia by the NKVD for making disparaging remarks about Stalin. He was sentenced to eight years' imprisonment, the first five of which were spent working in a special research institute run by state security. He used his experience in his book *The First Circle*. The rest of his sentence was spent in a camp in Kazakhstan, which he wrote about in *One Day in the Life of Ivan Denisovich*. In the camps he fell ill with cancer but recovered and wrote of this in *Cancer Ward*. He was exiled to Siberia.

The editor of *Novy Mir* got special permission from Khrushchev to publish *One Day in the Life of Ivan Denisovich* in 1962 and Solzhenitsyn immediately became an international celebrity. He soon ran into trouble in the USSR and was the subject of constant harassment and persecution, and after 1966 he was no longer allowed to be published at home. He won the Nobel Prize for Literature in 1970 but was not allowed to attend the award ceremony. When *The Gulag Archipelago* was published in France he was expelled from the country in handcuffs and deported to Germany.

In 1976 he went to live in the USA, where he was hailed enthusiastically, until it was discovered that his views were those of a right-wing monarchist. He is currently engaged in writing a mammoth work, *The Red Wheel*, set in Russia during World War I and the revolutions of 1905 and 1917.

Spiridonova, Maria, 1884–1941

The most famous Russian woman revolutionary leader. In 1905, as an SR activist, she shot the brutal Tsarist governor of Tambov and was captured, beaten and raped by his Cossack guard, then sentenced to life imprisonment, which she served in hard-labour camps. At the outbreak of the February 1917 revolution she was appointed mayor of Chita and celebrated this office by blowing up the town jail. She returned to Petrograd in 1917 and with Kamkov founded the break-away Left SR faction. In July 1917 'the little peasants' General', with her pince-nez spectacles, dark hair pulled back and simple blue dress, led workers, soldiers and Kronstadt sailors on the march against the Provisional Government.

She was the Bolshevik-supported candidate for the presidency of the Assembly in January 1918 (when the Centre-Left SR Chernov was elected). She was arrested after the Left SR revolt in July 1918. Thirteen others were executed, and although she admitted ordering the murder of the German ambassador, she was sentenced to only one year's imprisonment by the Moscow Revolutionary Tribunal, then ordered to be sent to a sanitorium (possibly the earliest case of the use of mental hospitals for imprisoning dissidents), but eventually exiled to Soviet Central Asia. She never ceased to demonstrate her opposition to the Bolshevik government, was arrested again in the 1930s and died in a prison camp, possibly in 1941.

Stakhanov, Alexei G, 1906–1977
A coal miner whose output of 12 tonnes a day so far exceeded the standard that he was praised by Stalin and held up as a model for workers, establishing the 'Stakhanovite Movement'. His production figures were almost certainly rigged and the objective of a sevenfold increase could not be maintained anywhere without loss of quality.

Stalin, (Djugashvili) Joseph Vissarionovich, 1879–1953
Stalin was born on 21 December 1879 in the small Georgian town of Gori, the fourth child – the previous three had died in infancy – of Ivanovich Djugashvili, a peasant turned cobbler and his wife Ekaterina. His father's business failed and he got a job in a shoe factory, dying when his son was 11. Stalin's mother brought him up on her wages as a washerwoman, it is claimed that his father had subjected him to fearful beatings when drunk.

At the age of 9 he was sent to the ecclesiastical school at Gori and at the age of 14, with the aid of a scholarship, he went to the Theological Seminary at Tbilisi, where he spent the next five years training to be a priest in the Greek Orthodox Church.

Georgia was socially regressive, the freeing of the serfs took place later than in the rest of Russia. At the same time, because many of the liberals and later revolutionaries were deported to the province, it was a breeding ground for radical ideas and movements. The Seminary itself was frequently accused of harbouring such ideas.

Stalin was a good pupil, well read in the Russian classics and an excellent debater, though it is claimed that he disliked being beaten in an argument. He was soon in trouble with the authorities for reading subversive literature. In 1898 he joined 'Mesame Dasi' (the 'Third Group'), an illegal Social Democratic Group in Tbilisi. He later wrote 'I became a Marxist because of my social position, but also because of the harsh intolerance and Jesuitical discipline that crushed me so mercilessly at the Seminary.' In May 1899 he was expelled from the seminary for not attending examinations, though Stalin claimed it was for spreading Marxism. He got a job as a clerk in the observatory but was now actively involved in the Social Democratic movement and helped to organise the first May Day Parade in the Caucasus. The following year the Okhrana came to arrest him and, taking a false identity, he entered the political underground from which he was not to emerge until the 1917 Revolution.

He became a wanted Socialist agitator, living under a variety of assumed names and organising strikes, the distribution of literature and endless meetings. He impressed the local leadership sufficiently to be elected a member of the Social Democratic Committee of Tbilisi in 1901. At this point he was sent to the oil town of Batumi to carry the socialist message to the workers and it was here that he took the nickname 'Koba', meaning indomitable in Turkish. In April 1902 he was arrested by the Okhrana and spent 18 months in jail before being exiled to Novaya Uda in the Irkutsk province of Siberia. In his absence he was appointed a member of the All-Caucasian Federation of the Social Democratic Party. By the beginning of 1904 Stalin had escaped from his confinement in Siberia and reappeared in Tbilisi.

The split between the Bolsheviks and Mensheviks had just occurred and Stalin took the side of Lenin and the Bolsheviks and in an article published shortly after his return to Tbilisi, he stressed his view of the need for complete uniformity of views inside the Party. He took only a local role in the 1905 revolution, but he had become a leading figure among the Bolsheviks of Georgia and had married Ekaterina Svanidze from an active Marxist family there. Ekaterina died in 1907, leaving a son, Yakov, to be brought up by her family.

At a Party conference at Tammerfors in Finland in 1905 he met Lenin for the first time and was disappointed by the fact that Lenin did not stage-manage his entrance to the conference, which Stalin wrote 'seemed to me rather a violation of certain essential rules'. He attended the 4th Party Congress in January 1906 in Stockholm where he disagreed with Lenin about land nationalisation – he wanted to divide the land of the large estates amongst the peasants – and the 5th Congress in London in June 1907. In London he met his great rival Trotsky for the first time.

Amongst his Party duties was being co-ordinator with the 'fighting squads' who were raising money for the cause by robbing banks and hijacking treasury vans. Stalin turned his attentions to labour politics in Baku, and organised a series of strikes by the oil workers. During this period he met many of the people with whom he was to become closely involved, including Sergo Ordzhonikidze, later Commissar for Heavy Industry, and Voroshilov, then secretary of the oil workers union and later to be a marshal of the Soviet Union. That year both Stalin and Ordzhonikidze were arrested by the Okhrana and exiled to Vologda province, from where he rapidly escaped and returned to Baku. In March 1910 he was again arrested and returned to Vologda. This time he completed his sentence.

In 1912 Lenin, at the 6th Party Congress in Prague, proclaimed his final break with the Mensheviks. Ordzhonikidze was elected to the Central Committee and Stalin was co-opted on to it by Lenin. In the general round-up of suspects following the assassination of Stolypin, Stalin was once again deported to Vologda from where, inevitably, he escaped and made contact with the Bolshevik Deputies to the Duma. He then prepared the first issue of *Pravda*, published on 22 April 1912. At the end of December Stalin left Russia for six weeks, the longest trip abroad he was ever to make. He went to Cracow for a meeting with Lenin, who sent him to Vienna and suggested he write an essay on 'The Problems of Nationalities and Social Democracy' which appeared under the name K Stalin. In Vienna he met Bukharin, who was working on a scholarly thesis on economics, and Leon Trotsky again, who was later to write of the 'glint of animosity' in Stalin's yellow eyes directed at himself. There was good reason for the animosity. Trotsky, a brilliant and famous figure in the movement, had criticised the employment of the fighting bands which Stalin had organised and was attacking Lenin's disruption of the Social Democratic Party.

Stalin returned to St Petersburg at the end of February and was betrayed by Roman Malinovsky, an Okhrana informer on the Central Committee (he was also the leader of the Bolsheviks in the Duma). This time he was exiled to northern Siberia where he spent four years hunting, fishing and reading. World War I had broken out and the imposition of martial law made it safer to stay in exile. He wrote to his future mother-in-law Olga Alliluyeva asking for picture postcards to relieve the dull ugliness of the landscape. It is the only known non-political letter of his.

In 1917 Stalin, Kamenev and others returned from Siberia and were welcomed in the capital. In the absence of Lenin and other senior members of the movement, Stalin took over the editorship of *Pravda* and was, in essence, for a brief time the leader of the party. At the end of March an All-Russian Conference of Bolsheviks was held and Stalin presided over it. He took a comparatively moderate stance and was prepared to support a motion suggesting reunification with Mensheviks who would be 'anti-Defensist', against the war. It was this stance that brought Trotsky over to the Bolsheviks.

Lenin's arrival at the conference after his journey across Germany in the 'sealed train' had a shattering effect. His 'April Theses' urged the Bolsheviks towards a seizure of power. Stalin, who as editor of *Pravda* had been taking a quite different attitude, rapidly moved into line with his master once more. At a further national conference of Bolsheviks in April, Stalin was elected to a new Central Committee with Lenin, Zinoviev, Kamenev, Sverdlov and others. Stalin was assigned the difficult and arduous task of organising the party groups in the various soviets that were springing up all over the country.

After the July Days Lenin was forced to go into hiding and Trotsky was arrested. Stalin once again took over temporary leadership, but relinquished it in August when the leaders had been released. In October, against the wishes of Kamenev and Zinoviev, the Central Committee decided on an insurrection, the main planning for which was the work of Trotsky. An immediate excuse for the rising was provided by the Provisional Government closing the printing presses of *Pravda*. And in the early morning of 25 October 1917 the Bolshevik forces went into action. Throughout the whole of the October rising, Stalin remained very much in the background. Trotsky's view was that Stalin's essential caution kept him on the fence until he could see how it was all going to turn out. Stalin wrote 'The revolution is incapable either of regretting or burying its dead.' Prophetic words indeed.

After the October Revolution Stalin supported Lenin completely and on 26 October became a member of the new government, as Commissar for Nationalities. With Lenin and Trotsky, he resisted the inclusion of other parties in the government.

In March 1918 Stalin left Petrograd for the new seat of government in Moscow. With him came his new wife, the 16-year-old Nadezhda Alliluyeva, daughter of the family he had lodged with in Tbilisi. From a small room in the Smolny Institute, Stalin now had an office in the Kremlin and he set to drafting a constitution for the new Russian Soviet Federative Socialist Republic, which was adopted in July. Stalin foresaw an integrated 'Great Russian' state, and he had no sympathy with nationalists, being particularly keen to force the Ukraine away from its aspirations of independence.

The Civil War In June 1918 Stalin went to Tsaritsyn to supervise the movement of food supplies, but with the Don Cossacks and the Volunteer Army to the south, he required a strong armed escort. By July, seeing the priority lay in defending the Revolution, he decided to take charge of the north Caucasian military district, turning himself into a military man and gathering support. The old Baku committee reassembled; Voroshilov was the commander of the Tenth Army, Budyenny was commanding a cavalry troop and Stalin's old friend Ordzhonikdze was a political commissar with the Tenth Army. The Tsaritsyn group soon began a fierce conflict with Trotsky who, as Commissar for War, resented Stalin making decisions about his front without referring them to him. A battle raged around Tsaritsyn for some time before the White armies were repulsed, for which both Stalin and Trotsky were later to claim the credit. The Tsaritsyn affair served to increase the bitterness between the two men but also served to magnify the importance of the city for Stalin, with momentous consequences during World War II.

Stalin's military adventures went on into 1919, acting as the political eyes and ears of Lenin and the Central Committee from Estonia to Kharkov. He also gained permission for Budyenny to lead the highly successful independent '1st Cavalry Army'.

Russo–Polish War In May 1920 the Russo–Polish war opened with the seizure of Kiev by Marshal Pilsudski. When the Red Army repulsed the attack, Stalin sided with Lenin in urging an invasion of Poland which they hoped would incite a revolution among the working class. The Red Army under Tukhachevsky were advancing on Warsaw when Pilsudski counter-attacked. Budyenny, commanding the southern front, was ordered to attack but, encouraged by Stalin, he changed direction to take Lvov and the Red Army, its forces divided, was soon in full retreat. On this issue both Trotsky and Tukhachevsky were once again in bitter conflict with Stalin.

His native Georgia, formally independent and under a Menshevik government, was the subject of Stalin's attention in late 1920. Ordzhonikidze, designated Party boss for Transcaucasia, received instructions, bypassing Lenin, to 'defend' the Soviet republic against Georgia. In July 1921 Stalin visited the Caucasus and Georgian Menshevism was brutally suppressed.

War Communism and the NEP During the period which followed the Civil War Stalin had little to contribute in a theoretical sense; all attention both in the country and in the world outside was focused on Lenin and Trotsky. The Party was often referred to as the Lenin/Trotsky Party but Stalin was in fact steadily accumulating power. He had been appointed Commissar of Nationalities in 1917, Commissar of Rabkrin (the Workers' and Peasants' Inspectorate) and one of the five original members of the Politburo in 1919. As Commissar of Nationalities he was responsible for dealing with almost 50 per cent of the population, from the Ukraine to the furthest fringes of Russia. He used his position to build allies just as he used his command of Rabkrin to build up a unique understanding of the machinery of government. In the Politburo he was the liaison officer with the Orgburo and he became a member in April 1920.

Then on 3 April 1922, following the 11th Party Congress, he was elected to the new post of General Secretary of the Party's Central Committee, with Molotov and Kuibyshev as assistants. The Secretariat prepared the agenda for Politburo meetings and was responsible for the appointments of Party functionaries and their careers. It is said that Lenin spoke to his intimate circle about some misgivings concerning the last appointment. 'This cook can only serve peppery dishes', he is reported to have remarked. But the sheer drudgery of the work had not tempted any of the other more brilliant figures in the Party. There was little concern about the concentration of power in Stalin's hands because he was regarded as Lenin's assistant.

But at the end of May 1922 Lenin suffered the first of the three strokes that were finally to kill him. In October, when Lenin was convalescing, he received a visit from Stalin, anxious to put his side of the case concerning Trotsky's criticism of the Inspectorate, and his methods of dealing with the opposition in the Ukraine and Georgia. Lenin gave him his full support then, but in December, having received many more complaints about the General Secretary and having had a second stroke, he dictated a memorandum in place of a will in which he spoke of his fears about a split in the Party and talked of the enmity between Stalin and Trotsky. Of Stalin he wrote 'Comrade Stalin having become General Secretary has concentrated enormous power in his hands; I am not sure that he always knows how to use that power with sufficient caution.' Of Trotsky he wrote 'he displays too far-reaching self confidence and a disposition to be too much attracted by the purely administrative side of affairs.'

With Lenin incapacitated, Stalin was pushing the constitutional reform of the Union of the Republics through the 10th All-Russian Congress of the Soviets and on 30 December 1922 'USSR' became the official name of the country. Lenin, who had learnt more about Stalin's methods in Georgia, dictated a postscript to his Testament concerning the succession. 'Stalin is too rude,' he wrote, 'and this fault becomes unbearable in the office of General Secretary. Therefore I propose to find a way to remove Stalin from that position and appoint to it a man more patient, more loyal, more polite and more attentive to comrades.' He then launched a public attack on the Inspectorate and promised to take up the case of the opposition in Georgia. He had also learnt of an abusive telephone call to his wife from Stalin and wrote a letter breaking off personal relations with him. On 9 March Lenin had the third and final stroke. Stalin was at a critical point in his life. If Lenin recovered he would launch an attack on him at the forthcoming 13th Party Congress, at which Stalin had suggested to Trotsky that the latter took Lenin's place. Stalin was careful to make all sorts of concessions to critics of his motions for the congress and also got the Politburo to agree not to show Lenin's notes on the Georgian situation to the congress.

At the same time, with Zinoviev and Kamenev, he formed a triumvirate in the Politburo with the express purpose of defeating Trotsky in the leadership struggle. The other members, Bukharin and Tomsky for example, were unwilling to back

Trotsky. Battle was now joined between the triumvirate and Trotsky, who appealed to the Party and particularly the younger members, talking about degeneration in the old guard of the Bolsheviks, and the new monolithic structure of the bureaucrats – i.e. the Secretariat – who no longer wished for debate. Stalin countered this by appealing to Lenin's rules against factionalism in the Party. At the conference in January Stalin attacked Trotsky as the mouthpiece of the 'petit bourgeois intelligentsia', while his group claimed to represent the proleteriat. The conference voted against Trotsky's motions and condemned the opposition on the grounds of 'petit bourgeois deviation from Leninism'.

Three days later, on 21 January, Lenin died. The emergence of the Leninist cult took formal shape at his funeral and the subsequent exhibition of his embalmed body in the mausoleum in Red Square. Stalin and other members of the Politburo arrived at Lenin's home in Gorky within three hours of his death and on 27 January he helped to carry the bier into the crypt of the mausoleum. Trotsky had gone for medical treatment to the Caucasus and did not return for the funeral. He later claimed that Stalin had not informed him of the date.

Stalin also survived the reading of Lenin's personal attacks on him at a plenary session of the Central Committee in May. Zinoviev assured the committee that in this case Lenin's strictures on the nature of the General Secretary had proved to be baseless. Both Zinoviev and Kamenev, believing themselves superior in intellect and imagination to Stalin, felt they had nothing to fear from him, whereas Trotsky's charismatic personality and oratorical brilliance frightened them. During the next three years the power struggle between the various factions in the Politburo continued. The most important issues were the controversy over Stalin's 'Socialism in One Country' versus Trotsky's theory of 'Permanent Revolution'. Stalin supported the view that, although at some unspecified date in the future, revolution would undoubtedly take place in all capitalist countries, with determination it was possible to build a socialist society in Russia. Trotsky and his followers believed that a truly socialist society could only be built in co-operation with the revolutionary proletariat of the advanced countries.

The second great debate arose from the policies of the NEP which had caused new alignments to arise within the Politburo. Supporting the Leninist, moderate neo-capitalist policies of the Right, as they came to be known, were Bukharin, Rykov and Tomsky. On the Left were Zinoviev and Kamenev, unhappy with the NEP on the grounds that it was the road back to capitalism. Stalin for the moment supported the Right.

After the 14th Congress in December 1925 Molotov, Voroshilov and Kalinin were elected to the Politburo, all supporters of Stalin, while Zinoviev and Kamenev, with the Leningrad delegates, voted against the Central Committee's report and were heavily defeated. Stalin sent Kirov to Leningrad to deal with the opposition stronghold there. In the spring of 1926 Zinoviev and Kamenev threw in their lot with Trotsky. Voroshilov had been appointed as Commissar of War to replace Trotsky but his deputy Lashevich, an associate of Zinoviev, was now denounced by Stalin for having attempted to form an opposition party in the army. As a result Zinoviev was expelled from the Politburo and then, in October 1926, Stalin expelled Trotsky.

Essentially the opposition had been crushed, though Trotsky and Zinoviev were still members of the Central Committee. The General Secretariat refused to allow publication of their statements intended for the next congress and they printed them in secret. For this they were expelled from the Central Committee. In December 1927 Trotsky was deported to Alma Ata, while Zinoviev, Kamenev and the remainder of the opposition made a declaration renouncing their views. Having rid himself of the Left, Stalin now took on his recent allies, the Right. With the help of Molotov, Voroshilov and Kalinin and two new members, Kuibyshev and Rudzutak, Stalin was able to start removing Bukharin's supporters from key points in the Party. He described them as the 'Right Opposition' and in April 1929 first mentioned Bukharin as their leader. In January 1929 the Politburo agreed to deport Trotsky from Russia. Stalin then removed the remainder of the Right Opposition from their important positions, and by the end of the year they had all submitted. The cult of Stalin was visibly forming and beginning even to overshadow the cult of Lenin.

1929 The Second Revolution The 1928 crisis in the grain supply threatened not only the food supply to the towns but also the great new plans for the industrialisation of the country. Stalin acted decisively and ruthlessly. He decided that the agricultural sector must be industralised and the kulaks must be dispossessed to provide equipment and capital for the collectives. He also took the optimistic but fairly moderate ideas outlined in the industrialisation plans and transformed them. He talked about getting an increase in production of 50 per cent in a year. In agriculture he succeeded in exploiting the peasant in order to finance his industrial plans, but at the most appalling cost in human misery. Millions were deported and uncountable numbers died of disease and starvation. In industry extraordinary results were achieved in the heavy industrial sector, though the interests of the consumer were virtually ignored. In 1931 in a speech to business executives, he revealed the thinking behind his actions. 'We are fifty to a hundred years behind the advanced countries. We must make good this lag in ten years. Either we do it or they crush us,' he said. One of the ways in which this was achieved was by the use of forced labour from the vast labour camps peopled by rebellious peasants and other dissidents.

The Purges On the night of 8–9 November 1932 Stalin's wife Nadezhda killed herself. Some change came over Stalin. He had always shown some disinclination to punish those who opposed him. He refused to take drastic action against Trotsky though urged to by Zinoviev. But there were signs of opposition in the Party and in the country and in June 1934 Stalin signed a decree to the effect that a whole family would be held responsible for the treason of any of its members. Stalin also reorganised the political police, replacing the GPU by the NKVD. Everything changed abruptly when, on 1 December 1934, Kirov was assassinated in Leningrad, it is now generally believed on Stalin's orders. Immediately Zinoviev and Kamenev were arrested and sentenced to penal servitude and in the spring of 1935 Zhdanov was sent to Leningrad as governor, where he instituted a reign of terror in which thousands of suspect Party members in Leningrad and other Russian cities were deported to camps in Siberia. Stalin's control over the USSR was now not only aimed at political opponents, the whole field of philosophy, literature, history and art were brought under the strictest control.

In 1936, after a short pause, the purges began again with a series of show trials, including not only most of the better-known members of the opposition, but in 1937 a large number of senior army officers. All were charged with an incredible list of crimes, including attempting to assassinate Stalin and other members of the Politburo.

Two of the men charged, Yagoda and Yezhov, were the chiefs of the NKVD who had provided the evidence against the other accused.

Most were shot, having confessed to all the crimes with which they were charged. By the end of 1938 Stalin had destroyed most of the Bolshevik old guard, some of whom could have formed an alternative government, and he had crippled the army. He had also terrified the country into the complete acceptance of his will. To settle accounts with his main opponent, Trotsky, took a little longer. In August 1940 Trotsky, who had settled in Mexico, was killed in his office by an ice pick wielded by an NKVD trained assassin.

Foreign policy Until 1939 Stalin's view of foreign policy can be summed up by his statement to the 16th Congress in June 1930: 'We do not want a single foot of foreign territory, but we will not surrender a single inch of our territory either.' In China he supported Chiang Kai-shek until the Chinese leader, fearful of the power of the communists, broke off relations with the USSR. Stalin correctly predicted the Wall Street crash and the onset of the depression. But he underestimated the strength of the German Nazi movement when it came to power in 1933. He began to search for anti-Nazi coalitions which, because of the distrust felt for him by Western politicians, led nowhere. He involved the USSR in the Spanish Civil War, but even there did little for his reputation by conducting a witch-hunt for Trotskyites and traitors among the Spanish Republicans.

In April 1939 Stalin made diplomatic moves in two directions: a pact with Britain and France and an approach aimed at a *rapprochement* between Germany and Russia. In August Hitler, who was about to invade Poland, began to make active advances for a non-aggression pact. This was signed by Molotov and the German Ribbentrop on 23 August. The secret protocol attached to the pact included the partition of Poland between the two powers and made Finland and the Baltic states part of the Russian sphere of influence. Both parties to the pact were attempting to win time and freedom of action, but Stalin seems to have overestimated the military strength of France, Poland and England and underestimated the might of the German war machine. In April 1941 Stalin entered into a pact of neutrality with Japan which was to prove of vast importance during the forthcoming struggle with Nazi Germany.

The goodwill between the new allies did not last long. Though Stalin had been warned specifically by Churchill that the Germans planned to attack the USSR in June, he paid no attention, even though there were 150 German divisions massed on the frontier. On 22 June Hitler launched Operation Barbarossa, a full-scale attack on the Soviet Union.

World War II During the whole of World War II Stalin played a key role in the day-to-day conduct of the war. The Stavka, the Red Army's nerve centre, was controlled from his office in the Kremlin, where he stayed even when the Nazi armies were in the suburbs in December 1941. He was constantly in touch with all the fronts and armies but he rarely overrode his generals' plans. However he did take Voroshilov's and Budyenny's commands away from them at the beginning of the war when they had suffered appalling defeats at the hands of the Germans and revealed themselves as incapable of dealing with modern mechanised warfare. Stalin broadcast messages to the Russian people, reminding them of past victories over Napoleon and calling for them to be prepared to make sacrifices against the invading Germans who were out to restore Tsarism and the rule of the landlords.

He also made alliances with both the United States and England and obtained vast quantities of supplies from the Allies, of which the most significant feature was transport. In 1942 the focus of the campaign shifted south to Stalingrad which the Germans were determined to take. It became the most significant battle of the war more for personal than strategic motives: to Hitler because of its name; to Stalin because of his past associations with the city. The Red Army counter-attacked and then surrounded the Germans who finally surrendered in February 1943. Though there were hard and vicious battles to come, it was Stalingrad that signalled the final defeat of the German invasion. After the battle Stalin took the title of marshal.

During 1943 the Russians recaptured a sizeable portion of the territory occupied by the German armies during the invasion and in November Stalin met Churchill and Roosevelt at Teheran. He called, as he had done in 1942, for a second front in France, while Churchill, anxious to limit Russia's power in the Balkans, proposed landings in southern Europe. Stalin won the day and Operation Overlord was agreed on for May of the following year. By the time the three met again, at Yalta in February 1945, the situation had changed dramatically. The Red Army had swept the Nazi armies off Russian soil and were poised on the Oder for the final assault on Berlin, and the Allied armies in the west were dealing with Hitler's last desperate offensive in the Ardennes.

At the Yalta Conference Churchill and Roosevelt obtained Stalin's agreement to join in the final assault on Japan but without informing him of their development of the atomic bomb. It is now known that Stalin had already been informed of this by his intelligence staff. When officially informed about it at the Potsdam Conference in August 1945 he was non-committal, realising the implications for the balance of power. By the time of Potsdam Roosevelt had died and half-way through the conference Churchill, defeated in the post-war election, had been replaced by Attlee. Signs of conflict between the wartime allies were appearing over the dividing-up of Germany, and Stalin's policy in the Balkans. But Stalin was still concerned enough about public opinion in the West to agree to send Molotov to the first assembly of the United Nations.

Victory and the Fruits of Victory Stalin was proclaimed Hero of the Soviet Union and Generalissimo after the great Victory Parade in June 1945. His task was then to rebuild a shattered nation which had suffered appallingly from the war, with 20 million casualties, most of the cities and towns in European Russia destroyed, and much of its population homeless. His plan for rebuilding the USSR was as ruthless as the first Five Year Plan. Agriculturally, the peasants were to go on suffering by increasing the compulsory quotas from collective farms to provide cheap food for industry, and industrially the emphasis was once again almost entirely on rebuilding heavy industry at the expense of consumer goods. However he had one resource previously denied him. As the result of Russian victories at the end of the war, there were conquered nations, such as East Germany, which could be plundered of both resources and labour. Even more important were those countries within the Soviet Union's sphere of influence which could be linked economically for its benefit.

To make this effective Stalin inspired and co-ordinated communist take-overs in the countries of eastern and central Europe and when this was achieved virtually sealed the Eastern bloc off from the West. The Iron Curtain of Churchill's speech had come to pass, and extended not only to frontiers but even to the airwaves. The wartime revival of old themes, such as Mother Russia, and the restoration of traditional regimental titles, such as Guards and Cossacks, and the celebration of the victorious generals were dropped, indeed many of the troops returning from Europe were shipped straight to labour camps. Stalin was fearful of their experience of the West and the possibility that they might start to demand a better life from the government. What the average worker in Russia received was the harshest and most stringent direction of labour and discipline, under which the punishment for the most trivial offence was deportation to the Gulag. While the ex-Commissar for the Nationalities ordered the uprooting of entire nations, like the Crimean Tatars, accused of collaboration with the Nazis, and their deportation to Siberia.

Then, in March 1947, President Truman in a speech to both houses of Congress declared America's support for the Greek government fighting communist insurgents and offered help to any country fighting communism. The Cold War had been declared. America launched the Marshall Plan which Stalin rejected for Eastern Europe. He then founded the Cominform, essentially a revival of the old Comintern, and tightened his grip on Eastern Europe. In Czechoslovakia a few days after a Communist take-over, Masaryk, the Foreign Minister, who had been resisting Stalin's demands, was found dead on the pavement under his office windows.

Stalin announced a blockage of Berlin, hoping to drive the Western powers out of the city. But he had underestimated the strength of the Allies' air power and Berlin was kept supplied from the air. Another blow was the breach with Marshal Tito of Yugoslavia and this inspired similar stirrings in some other Eastern bloc countries, which resulted in a succession of show trials on the Soviet model, followed by executions all over Eastern Europe.

In China Mao Zedong had come to power. He was an old comrade and a formal treaty was signed in February 1950. It was to be followed shortly afterwards by the attack over the 38th Parallel by the communist North Koreans on their fellow countrymen. China became directly involved in the conflict but Stalin could see no profit for the USSR in the war.

The USSR had exploded its first atomic bomb in 1949 and in 1953 its first hydrogen bomb. Industry had achieved astonishing feats, reaching a 50 per cent increase on pre-war production figures in 1952 but agriculture was disastrous. Between 1949 and 1953 the average grain harvest was less than it had been in 1913.

In Stalin's last years in the Kremlim his suspicious and devious nature became more and more pronounced, climaxing in the famous Doctors' Plot, which has led many to believe that he was about to launch another wave of terror against the remainder of the old guard in his entourage. Khrushchev related that at the 19th Congress in 1952, Stalin launched a savage attack on Molotov and Mikoyan and claimed that Voroshilov was a British agent. On 6 March 1953 Stalin's death was announced. He had suffered a brain haemorrhage and a stroke six days earlier. He was 73. His bier was carried into Red Square and buried in the mausoleum next to Lenin.

It did not remain there for long. After the 20th Congress in 1956, as a result of the speech by Khrushchev denouncing Stalin as a bloody tyrant, the body was removed and is now buried outside the walls of the Kremlin.

Ekaterina Svanidze Stalin's first wife (d. 1907). Their son Yakov was born in 1906 and raised in the Caucasus by her parents.

Nadezhda Alliluyeva Stalin's second wife (1901–32). He knew her family in Baku. She was in Petrograd with her father in 1917, joined the Party and they married in 1918. She was expelled from the Party in 1921 as non-active, but Lenin intervened and she was reinstated. She studied at the Industrial Academy where she met Nikita Khrushchev and introduced him to Stalin. She killed herself in 1932 the night after having spoken out to a small gathering about the miseries being suffered in the country.

Stolypin, Peter A, 1862–1911
Stolypin was a provincial, simple and direct man. In the revolution of 1905, while he was governor of Saratov, his personal coolness restored order. Once, during a riot when an agitator seized him by the arm, Stolypin asked him to hold his coat while he carried on, in the face of shooting.

He was the Tsar's prime minister from 1906 and made some moderate reforms, seeking to build a class of peasant farmers as a counter to the Duma liberals and revolutionaries. He promoted the breaking up of the mir (peasant communes) and the migration of peasants to Siberia. He introduced a property qualification for the Duma and planned social improvements, but he governed by decree under 'Article 87' without using the Duma and ordered courts martial throughout the country to deal with any rebel, having many peasants hanged. In hunting intellectual suspects, he encouraged anti-Semitism and the murder gangs of the Black Hundreds.

His home was bombed in 1907, and he survived only to be assassinated four years later in a Kiev theatre.

Stravinsky, Igor, 1882–1971
Composer. His father was a singer and his mother was from a wealthy family. He was not successful at school but was passionate about music and encouraged by Rimsky Korsakov, whose youngest son was a school friend. In 1907 his first work, Symphony in E, was performed privately.

Diaghilev heard his next work the *Scherzo fantastique*, and commissioned a score for the ballet *Firebird*, which was performed at the Paris Opera in 1910. This was followed by *Petrushka* in 1911 and in 1913 by *Rite of Spring*, also produced in Paris, which, though vastly successful, created a huge scandal. Stravinsky spent World War I in Switzerland, and when the news of the February 1917 revolution reached him, his initial reaction was one of delight, but by October he realised that it would be impossible for him to return to Russia.

He spent the years between 1920 and 1939 living in Paris, and continued to write ballet scores: *Pulcinella* in 1920 and *The Wedding* in 1923, which was based on the Russian village weddings of his childhood. In 1928 he broke with Diaghilev and in 1934 became a French citizen. In 1939 he went to America and settled in Hollywood with a group who became known as The Hollywood Exiles and included such eminent figures as Aldous Huxley, Bertolt Brecht and Arnold Schoenberg.

He divided the remainder of his life between Europe and America. He continued writing: *The Canticum Sacrum*, much influenced by Schoenberg and serialism, in 1956, and a new ballet, *Agon*, in 1959. In 1962 Stravinsky was invited to return to the USSR, where he gave three concerts in Moscow and two in Leningrad. They were an enormous success and he proclaimed himself more pleased by these concerts than anything else in his musical life. He died in New York and is buried in Venice.

Struve, Peter Berngardovich, 1870–1944

A writer on history, politics and economics. He was at first influenced by Marxist thought, and was responsible for the manifesto of the foundation congress of the Russian Social Democratic Labour Party in 1898. However, he soon came to believe in an evolutionary rather than a revolutionary view of Marxism, broke with the Social Democrats and helped to found the Liberation of Labour movement. In 1906 he joined the Kadet Party and was elected to its Central Committee.

But Struve's real commitment was to the idea of liberty. He was awarded an honorary doctorate from Cambridge University and elected to the Russian Academy of Sciences in 1917. The Revolution disturbed him profoundly and the Bolshevik coup in October drove him to support the Whites, whom he believed to be on the side of liberty. When Wrangel was defeated he went to Prague, where he became Professor of Political Economy at the Russian Juridical Faculty at the university. From there he went to Belgrade and then spent the last two years of his life in Nazi-occupied Paris. He liked to describe himself as a 'liberal conservative'.

Sukhanov, Nikolai, 1882–1940

A Menshevik supporter of the October 1917 Revolution, but arrested with other Mensheviks in 1931 and died in prison.

Suslov, Mikhail A. 1902–82

A Party official from 1921 with a reputation for intellectual rigour. In 1944 he was made Chairman of the Politburo in Lithuania and editor-in-chief of *Pravda* from 1947. He was appointed to the Politburo in 1952.

He insisted on the total dominance of Russia and the Russians in the Soviet world, not simply by reason of military force, but through cultural domination. With this purpose, in 1956 he went to Budapest just before the rising was crushed, in 1958 he went to Prague to question Dubček's ideology and in 1981 to Poland at the time of the 'Solidarity' strikes. Always strong on correct Party lines, in October 1964 he led the attack on Khrushchev, but in 1970 it was Suslov who stopped Brezhnev combining the posts of head of Party and government. When this survivor of Stalin's regime, the grand old man of the Politburo, died, Andropov succeeded him in his posts.

Sverdlov, Yakov M, 1885–1919

An activist in the Bolshevik underground in Russia from the early days. Released from exile in a remote part of Siberia in 1917, he made his way to Petrograd where he became Secretary to the Party Central Committee and Head of State as Chairman of the VTsIK, the Central Executive Committee of the Soviets. His organising ability made him, in effect, the Central Committee's first General Secretary, before the post existed. In the 1917 'July Days', when other Bolshevik leaders were either in hiding or under arrest, he was the Party leader. He died in the 'Spanish' influenza epidemic at the time, caught while travelling in the Ukraine.

T

Tarkovsky, Andrei, 1932–86

Film director. Born in Moscow, the son of a poet. He graduated from film school in 1961 and made *Ivan's Childhood*, his first feature film, the next year. It dealt with the heroism of an orphan boy in World War II and won an award at the Venice Film Festival. His next film, *Andrei Rublev*, a realistic account of life in fifteenth-century Russia, attracted a great deal of disapproval from the authorities and was banned, though it won a prize at the Cannes Film Festival. In 1972 the science fiction picture *Solarus*, again won international acclaim but found little favour at home. He then made the even more unorthodox *Mirror* in 1975, and *Stalker* in 1978. This was shown only for a few weeks in Moscow and shortly after Tarkovsky left to make a film in Italy, *Nostalgia* (1983). In 1984 he was deported and stripped of his citizenship. His last film was the impressive but obscure *Sacrifice*, shown in 1988. He died in Paris and his films are now hailed as triumphs of cinematic art in the Soviet Union.

Tikhon, V I Belavin, 1865–1925

Archbishop of the Russian Orthodox Church in Moscow, elected to the post of Patriarch (which had been abolished since Peter the Great) under the Provisional Government in 1917. He at once asserted his authority by refusing to recognise the newly elected head of the Georgian Orthodox Church. He spoke out against the Bolsheviks in January 1918 and protested against the seizure of Church property in 1919. Seeing the reality of the situation, the failure of the Whites and the danger of the Red Terror, he urged his clergy to co-operate with the regime. Resisting the seizure of the Church's treasures, he was jailed in May 1922. Priests less hostile to the Bolsheviks then formed the rival 'Living Church'. He was released in 1923 after he recanted his anti-Bolshevik past. After his death it was two years before his successor, Stragorodsky, was elected (having also been jailed) and he was not installed until 1943.

Tikhonov, Nikolai, 1905–

An old Party member, loyal to Brezhnev and Chernenko, he retired as Premier in 1985 and was succeeded by Ryzhkov.

Timoshenko, Semion K, 1895–1970

A marshal of the Soviet Union, he began his career as a peasant conscript to the Tsarist army in World War I. Timoshenko joined the Red Guard in 1918 and was involved in the defence of Tsaritsyn (later Stalingrad), where he made the acquaintance of Stalin. He became a member of Budyenny's Cavalry Corps and later commanded the 4th Cavalry Division, taking part in the defeat of Wrangel in 1920.

After the Civil War he continued to serve in the Red Army, being commander of the northern military district in 1937 and commander of the Kiev military district in 1939. In January 1940 he commanded the north-western front in the Russo-Finnish war and in May 1940 he was made People's Commissar for Defence. On 22 June 1941, at the outbreak of war with Germany, Stalin made him Commander-in-Chief. In July he was relieved of this post but appointed to the 'Stavka', the High Command.

During World War II Timoshenko held a series of commands. He was in charge first of the southern, then the south-western fronts. In the early days of the Stalingrad campaign he was appointed to head this front but was removed a short time later. In 1943 he co-ordinated the Volkov and Leningrad fronts and from 1944 to the end of the war was responsible for the Ukraine.

After the war Timoshenko held appointments in military districts. He was a candidate member of the Central Committee of the Party from 1952 until his death. He was well known for his blunt and outspoken manner, but remained a favourite of Stalin's to the end. Under Khrushchev, in 1960 he was quietly put on the shelf as an inspector general of the Ministry of Defence.

Tomsky (Efremov), Mikhail P 1880–1936

A working-class militant from St Petersburg. A printer by trade, he tried to organise a union which ended with his arrest and deportation to Tomsk (hence the cover name 'Tomsky'). In 1917 he made his way from Siberia to Moscow and, when Lenin returned, to Petrograd. He remained a trade unionist and was president of the Congress of Trade Unions from 1919. Because of his standing in the Party, he was one of the eight pall bearers at Lenin's funeral; his popularity with workers and his administrative ability made him of great use to Stalin. His antipathy to the left-wingers, including Trotsky, put him among the 'right-wing bloc' in 1925. In 1928, with the 'left' opposition destroyed, Tomsky found himself, with Bukharin and Rykov, a trio in opposition to Stalin, uring a slow-down in the collectivisation process. Despite warnings, they refused to give way and in 1929 were condemned by the Central Committee, Tomsky being expelled from the Politburo and from his union presidency.

Tomsky went through a process of self-criticism at the 16th Party Congress the next year and regained some of his status. When he heard that Vyshinsky had started inquiries about him, in November 1936 he killed himself. Bukharin later, at his own trial, was to name him as the link between the conspirators of the 'Right Opposition' and a group in the Red Army.

Trotsky (Bronstein), Lev Davidovitch (Leon), 1879–1940

One of the major figures in the Bolshevik Revolution. Born 26 October 1879 at Yanovka, a small village near Kharkov, the fifth child of a prosperous Jewish farmer. Educated at the St Paul School in Odessa, he felt 'an intense hatred of the existing order, or injustice, of tyranny' from an early age, as he declares in his autobiography *My Life*.

His father wished him to become an engineer but stirred by the self-sacrifice of a girl student in Petrograd in 1897, he decided to take up revolutionary politics. He formed a commune of students and workers, but in 1898 they were betrayed to the Tsarist police and he with many others was imprisoned in Moscow and then exiled to Ust-Kut. There he married for the first time, Alexandra Lvovna, a member of the South Russian Workers Union. During his exile he began his literary career, writing for an Irkutsk paper and studying Marx, Engels, Plekhanov and Lenin.

In 1902 Trotsky left his wife and two daughters in their place of exile and escaped, with her blessing, to Europe in order to work for the revolutionary paper *Iskra*.

In the autumn of 1902 Trotsky arrived in London, by way of Paris, and established a relationship with Lenin there and later in Paris. At the 2nd Congress of the Social Democratic Party in London, the Party divided into the Menshevik (minority) and Bolsheviks (majority) factions. Trotsky, not approving of Lenin's ruthless authoritarianism, sided with the Mensheviks. In the revolution of 1905 Trotsky played a dominant role in the St Petersburg Soviet, elected chairman while at the same time writing for three papers, *The Russian Gazette*, *Nachalo* (*The Beginning*) and editorials for *Izvestia* which was the official organ of the soviet. During this period he married his second wife, I. N. Sedova, also a political activitist.

On 3 December he was arrested with other members of the soviet and spent the next 15 months in prison. The regime was customarily relaxed and he was able to continue writing pamphlets and books and reading the European classics. Trotsky escaped from Berezov in January 1907 and left Russia via Finland for a foreign exile that was to last for ten years.

First Exile After attending the Social Democratic Congress in London in 1907, Trotsky settled in Vienna with his wife for the next seven years, mostly to keep in touch with the political situation, for the German Social Democratic Party was regarded by the Russian revolutionaries as a model, with Bebel and Kautsky as its intellectual gurus.

In 1908 be began publication of *Pravda* in Vienna, which was smuggled into Russia by members of the underground Seamen's Union. His chief contributor was A A Ioffe who later played an active part in the 1917 Revolution. He also travelled in the Balkans and continued to study economics and mingle with both Menshevik and Bolshevik factions of the Party.

Immediately after the outbreak of World War I in August 1914, Trotsky and his wife moved to Zurich and entered into the life of the Swiss Socialist Party. In November 1914 he went to France as a war correspondent and settled down in a borrowed house at Sèvres, attending from there the conference at Zimmerwald.

In 1916 Trotsky was deported from France. He spent a few weeks in Spain with his family, sailed for New York and arrived there on 13 January 1917.

In New York he met Bukharin, but by 27 March, with news of the February revolution, he was on his way to Russia with his family as passengers on a Norwegian boat. But, at a request from the Provisional Government, they were held at a camp in Halifax in Canada for a month. Finally, in May, they arrived in Petrograd, where he was briefly imprisoned but when released made chairman of the Petrograd Soviet as he had been 12 years earlier. Despite the Bolsheviks imprisoned by Kerensky, their numbers were growing in the soviet and were increased by the threat of a right-wing coup headed by General Kornilov.

Revolution At the Congress of the Soviets on the evening of the October Revolution Trotsky, replying to Martov who was urging the revolutionary party to form a coalition with the Mensheviks and SRs, said 'Your part is over. Go to the place where you belong from now on – the trash bin of history.'

At the first meeting of the Party Central Committee, at Trotsky's suggestion, ministries in the newly formed government were called People's Commissars, and the government the Soviet of People's Commissaries. Lenin proposed him as the chairman, which he rejected, as he also turned down the Commissariat of the Interior because of his Jewish origins, and the capital that might be made from this by their enemies. Finally he accepted the job of Foreign Affairs. In doing so he became involved, much to the fury of the Western Allies, in separate armistice talks with the Germans and their allies at Brest-Litovsk.

The negotiations were complex and on 7 February Trotsky announced to the startled Germans and their allies that the Russian armies had been demolished. This was an expression of his 'neither peace nor war' policy, the merits of which he thought he had convinced Lenin. On 6 March, under threat of Lenin's resignation, the treaty was signed. Later in the year Trotsky made a public appreciation of Lenin's part in the Brest-Litovsk decision. He said 'Only Comrade Lenin maintained stubbornly, with amazing foresight, that we had to go through with it to tide us over until the revolution of the world proletariat. And now we must admit that we were wrong.'

Civil War By August 1918 the fate of the Revolution hung in the balance, threatened by external and internal counter-revolutionary forces. Trotsky, who had been appointed Commissar of War and chairman of the Supreme War Council, VVS, moved to Moscow with Lenin and the rest of the government and started to fit out the armoured train which was to become his command post and indeed almost his home for the next two and a half years. It contained a secretariat, a printing press, a telegraph station, a radio station, a library, a garage and even a bath. It also included a squad of handpicked troops armed with machine guns and their own transport. As Trotsky wrote, 'We were constructing an army all over again and under fire at that.' His first mission with the train was to Sviyazhsk on the Kazan front, where the Czech Legion had just taken Kazan. His inspiring leadership and, where necessary, ruthless discipline restored the situation and on 10 September Kazan was recaptured. Two days later Simbirsk was recaptured by the First Army commanded by Tukhachevsky, one of the many former Tsarist officer 'specialists' whose use by Trotsky met with a great deal of opposition from the ultra-left in the Party and led to Trotsky's first direct clash with Stalin. This took place at Tsaritsyn where Stalin and Voroshilov ignored the commander of the southern front, an ex-Tsarist officer, and then Trotsky's direct orders. He appealed to Lenin, who directed Stalin to give in, which he did with ill grace but then attempted to stir up trouble by claiming that Trotsky was recruiting a faction hostile to Lenin.

In March 1919 Stalin was appointed to the Politburo along with Trotsky, Lenin, Kamenev and Krestinsky, but he was also appointed to the Orgburo, the administrative arm of the Party Central Committee. His fatal grip on the levers of power was beginning.

Stalin soon caused trouble for Trotsky by persuading Lenin to overrule his decision to remove the commander on the eastern front. Trotsky returned to Moscow and admitted that he had been in the wrong, but when the Politburo supported the commander, he resigned from all his posts. Lenin was so appalled by the consequences that he persuaded the other members to change their minds. Fully in charge now and with Lenin's total support, Trotsky reorganised the southern front and planned an October offensive on the forces of Denikin. Then he returned to Moscow and persuaded the Politburo to implement his plan for total mobilisation in order to save Petrograd, which Lenin had been seriously thinking of abandoning. Arriving in the city in October, he threw himself into the battle, actually chasing the retreating troops of an infantry regiment back into action. He stopped Yudenich's White forces at the Pulkovo Heights outside Petrograd and on 22 October drove them back to the Estonian frontier. A month later Kolchak was defeated in Siberia. Trotsky was awarded the Order of the Red Flag.

The Red Army, now an efficient fighting force, recaptured Kiev from Pilsudki's Poles in June 1920, but Trotsky was against the attempt to reach Warsaw where Lenin hoped to rouse the workers to revolt. He was proved right and the situation was worsened by Stalin's mistimed attempt to capture Lvov. But by the end of November a peace treaty had been signed with Poland and Wrangel had been defeated and driven off Russian soil. The Revolution was once again safe.

War Communism In 1920 the economic situation in the country was grave, the peasants were cultivating no more than they needed for their own survival and industrial production was down to a third of what it had been before the war. In certain parts of the country famine was rife. Trotsky had been given the job by Lenin of restoring the railway system. He came back from his tour of inspection in the Urals convinced that the system of expropriation from the peasants would never provide the huge increase in food supplies needed. He suggested to Lenin and the Central Committee a form of progressive tax on agricultural produce which would make it profitable for the peasant to cultivate more land and sell more grain. His suggestions were turned down by the committee. Appointed as economic spokesman at the 9th Party Congress, he therefore suggested the only logical alternative, militarisation of the labour force and the trade unions. He personally put the railway workshops under martial law, provoking a storm of protest from the extreme left. Then in February 1921, following a week of strikes and protests in Petrograd, the tragic Kronstadt revolt took place.

Although it was quickly put down, the committee realised that a crisis point had arrived and at the 10th Party Congress in March 1921 Lenin put forward his proposals for a New Economic Policy (NEP) which mirrored almost exactly those which Trotsky had suggested a year earlier.

NEP The new policies had an instant and dramatic effect. The harvest of 1922 was back to about three-quarters of the pre-war average and smaller industrial enterprises increased output by more than 50 per cent. It was not enough for Trotsky who insisted that full-scale economic planning was necessary, though Lenin remained unconvinced.

In April 1922, just after the 11th Party Congress had dispersed, Stalin was designated General Secretary at Lenin's suggestion and at the same time, and not coincidentally, Trotsky was asked to become deputy chairman of the Soviet of People's Commissars. He refused, perhaps because there were already two deputy chairmen and he regarded the offer as a slight. Then on 26 May Lenin had a stroke, losing the power of speech and the use of his right arm and leg.

The struggle for leadership Lenin's illness immediately raised the question for the first time of who would succeed him as the Party leader. This led to the formation of the Stalin, Zinoviev and Kamenev triumvirate, whose immediate purpose was to prevent the emergence of Trotsky in this role. He was, after all, a hero of both revolutions, a brilliant orator and thinker with a huge popular following. Zinoviev was envious of Trotsky and Kamenev feared his extremism. Stalin felt about Trotsky much as Zinoviev did, but his jealousy and envy were more extreme, as his ambition was greater.

Lenin was sufficiently recovered by September to ask Stalin to bring up the matter of Trotsky's appointment to the deputy chairmanship again. Stalin, disturbed by the growing closeness between the two men, telephoned Krupskaya, Lenin's wife, and coarsely abused her for allowing Lenin to write to Trotsky 'against doctor's orders'. Lenin knew nothing of this, but had a second stroke in December.

Later when he had learnt of Stalin's attack on his wife and also of the actions taken by Stalin in Georgia, he asked Trotsky to take charge of the inquiry into the whole affair. Lenin also wrote to Stalin asking him to apologise for his rudeness to Krupskaya on threat of breaking off relations with him. Stalin made his apologies to Lenin before, on 10 March, he suffered the third and final stroke from which there seemed little likelihood of recovery.

The 12th Party Congress was due shortly and the triumvirate was anxious to know whether Trotsky would use Lenin's papers on the Georgian affair. Trotsky declared himself against the idea of removing Stalin from the Politburo but declined to deliver the keynote speech at the congress lest it be thought that he was seeking to replace Lenin as leader. During the congress, Stalin secured agreement to increase the size of the Central Committee, many of them being his own candidates.

After the congress 46 members of the Party, some of them close associates of Trotsky, wrote to the Central Committee complaining of the growth of bureaucracy in the Party, for which they were condemned for fractionalism. In October he got soaked through while duck shooting near Moscow, and contracted a fever which lasted on and off for several months. Occurring at this time, it is difficult to resist making a connection between the illness and the extreme stress under which he was now living. He rallied sufficiently to attack his opponents with a letter in which he accused them of attempting to terrorise the Party. Zinoviev called for his expulsion from the Party, but Stalin, recognising the depth of feeling which Trotsky could arouse, was more cautious. Then in January 1924 his doctors advised him to visit a Black Sea resort to recuperate. While there he received the news of Lenin's death. He planned to return to Moscow for the funeral but Stalin told him, quite falsely, that he would not be in time for it, and he remained in Tiflis.

Just before the 13th Party Congress on 22 May, Lenin's Testament was presented to a joint meeting of the Central Committee and heads of the delegations. Despite its crushing references to Stalin and its call for him to be replaced as General Secretary, the Politburo decided to suppress it. Trotsky could only sit there in impotent rage. Zinoviev, adding insult to injury, called for a recantation of his views. He refused. In July he lost his place on the Executive of the Comintern to Stalin.

Permanent Revolution In the autumn of 1924 a massive campaign of denigration was launched at Trotsky, aiming to diminish his role in the Revolution and more specifically to attack him on vital ideological matters: firstly on his theory of permanent revolution, by which he meant that socialism would be impossible to construct in Russia without the transformation of other Western societies by the same route; secondly, on his statement that the peasantry was naturally bourgeois in attitude and would have, of necessity, to be led by the proletariat.

Although all these doctrines had been regarded as perfectly respectable, if debatable, in the past, statements denying them could always be found in the writings of Lenin, who was by now being turned into the icon of the Revolution. In December Stalin produced his own theory, largely based on an article of Lenin's which suggested that because of the unequal development of capitalism, socialism might develop in only a limited number of countries at first, perhaps only one. Stalin called his policy – it became the orthodox view – socialism in one country.

In January 1925 the Central Committee met and removed Trotsky as Commissar of War, though he was allowed to remain on the Central Committee and the Politburo. He was appointed to the Electro-technical Development Board where he suggested harnessing the Dnieper for power generation, which Stalin sneered at, only to adopt the idea himself, ten years later.

The leadership battle continues The triumvirate was beginning to break up. Zinoviev, aware now of the menace of the General Secretary, launched an attack on his new doctrine in *Leninism* and, with Krupskaya, demanded a free debate on the Bukharin policy of indulging the peasantry. It was refused and at the 14th Party Congress he was attacked by a packed meeting. In January Stalin sent Kirov to Leningrad to purge the Party there and to take over from Zinoviev as chairman of the Leningrad Soviet. In April Zinoviev and Kamenev arranged a meeting with Trotsky and suggested an alliance against Stalin. He left for Germany for medical treatment almost immediately. When he returned to Moscow, he and his followers, calling themselves the United Opposition, organised small meetings, frequently disrupted by local officials and Party members loyal to Stalin. In a letter to the Central Committee Trotsky put the opposition's point of view, asking for a rapid industrialisation programme, an end to the socialism in one country idea, and greater democracy in the Party. In reply, the Politburo ejected Zinoviev and he and Kamenev persuaded Trotsky to make a truce with Stalin, which he did, holding fast to his criticism but promising to cease all factional activities. On 23 October, the day before the meeting of the 15th Party Congress, Stalin broke the truce by denouncing the opposition as Social Democrat deviationists. Trotsky rose to his feet and, pointing to Stalin, declared 'The First Secretary poses his candidature to the post of Grave Digger of the Revolution'. Stalin rushed from the room, slamming the door behind him. Stalin denounced his views at the congress and Trotsky replied in masterly fashion, but the congress stood by Stalin and reaffirmed their strictures on the opposition.

In April 1927 Trotsky had a final opportunity to demonstrate what he considered as the 'criminal character' of Stalin's support for Chiang Kai-shek which led directly to the massacre of the Chinese communists in Shanghai. But it was too late. Almost the last official moves of opposition in the Party were made by Trotsky and Zinoviev in Leningrad at a meeting held to celebrate the introduction by the Politburo of a five-day working week, which the opposition held to be a fraud. A week later the Central Committee, meeting in an extraordinary session, expelled all the opposition leaders and Trotsky and Zinoviev were removed from the Party. At the 15th Party Congress in December, Zinoviev and Kamenev decided to capitulate and on 12 January 1928 the GPU informed Trotsky that on account of his counter-revolutionary activities he would be deported to Alma Ata in Turkestan.

Exile He was determined that his exile would be seen for what it was and so locked himself into his house with Natalia and their two sons. He even forced the GPU to carry him on to the train. After complaining to Moscow, he was given a four-roomed apartment in the town. He immediately set himself up as the headquarters of the opposition, writing endless letters and sending telegrams. He was appalled by what he heard of events in Moscow. Bukharin, Stalin's ally on the right of the Party, had been disposed of as efficiently as his previous allies and had submitted to the Party will. Almost all of Trotsky's supporters had now been virtually exiled or had submitted.

Trotsky's daughters by his first marriage were ill. Nina died in a sanatorium and Zina was suffering from consumption. Trotsky himself was ill with a recurrence of the fever he had had for the previous two years. On 16 December a special representative of the GPU arrived to give him an ultimatum: desist from directing the opposition or be exiled from the country. Trotsky refused and on 20 January 1929 he was handed a letter which sentenced him to deportation from the USSR on the grounds of provoking anti-Soviet actions, and preparing for an armed struggle against the Soviet power.

Deported Trotsky refused to sign a confirmation of his deportation order but by 22 January he and his family were on their way to Constantinople, which had been selected as his place of exile. They arrived on 12 February and the GPU escort handed him the sum of 1,500 dollars 'to enable him to settle abroad'. He eventually found a house to rent on Prinkipo Island and set about applying for visas to various European countries. He was turned down successively by Germany, Norway, France and England.

Trotsky settled down to his usual political existence. He found a printer in Paris to produce an Opposition Bulletin which circulated in Europe widely, though few copies reached the Soviet Union. He also wrote *My Life, an Attempt at an Autobiography* and started work on the massive *History of the Russian Revolution*.

Although Trotsky continued to denounce Stalin's tactics and his principles, he had little success in building a serious opposition outside the USSR, partly due to the ruthless suppression of his associates. His daughter Zina, with whom Trotsky had a difficult relationship, arrived with his son Lyova. Zina stayed with them for a time but Lyova was sent to Germany. Trotsky, who had correctly forecast the rise of the Nazis, had hopes of the working class rising in armed resistance, though he denounced the German Communist Party for its tactical liaison with the Nazis. In January 1933 Trotsky was devastated by the suicide of Zina in Berlin. In July some of his French admirers persuaded the government to allow him a residence permit. He found a house in Barbizon but it was an unhappy situation, with severe restrictions on his freedom of action and harassment by the police and the Press.

In December 1934 the assassination of Kirov and the massive purge of the Leningrad Party signalled the prelude to a campaign of terror, and within weeks Zinoviev and Kamenev were on trial, though at this time they were given only relatively short prison sentences. But the assault on Trotsky's family began with the arrest of his son Sergei. It was to continue until they had all been eliminated.

Norway Knowing that he was outstaying his welcome in France, Trotsky managed to get a six months' visa from the new Labour government in Norway. Then, on 15 August 1936, the first of the great show trials was announced. Kamenev, Zinoviev and 14 others were to stand trial. At the centre of the accusations was the charge that Trotsky and his son Leon Sedov had been the chief conspirators and that the German Gestapo were involved.

Trotsky promptly denounced this as 'the greatest foregery in the world's political history' but the accused, prompted by torture or threats to their families, confessed to a man. Zinoviev indeed said that he had been second only to Trotsky in the group which killed Kirov and planned to kill Stalin. Guarantees from Stalin that they would be freed if they made their confessions were followed by the firing squad. Trotsky's attempts to defend himself by giving interviews and statements were cut off by the Norwegian government under pressure from the Soviet Union.

In December 1936, and much to his relief, Trotsky was informed that Mexican admirers of his led by the artist Diego Rivera had persuaded the Mexican President to grant him asylum.

Mexico, the final chapter Trotsky and Natalia had hardly been made welcome by the Riveras at their house in a suburb of Mexico City when a second show trial opened in Moscow, this time with 14 less well-known defendants but with more specific and absurd accusations involving Trotsky as arch conspirator. Now he was accused of conspiring with the German and Japanese governments and promising them the Ukraine and the eastern maritime provinces in return for being made ruler of Russia when the country was inevitably defeated. Trotsky heard that his son Sergei had been executed, accused of organising the mass gassing of workers at a factory in Siberia where he was working. Then in May Marshal Tukhachevsky and five other prominent generals were tried and executed, the beginning of the purge in the army which Trotsky had created. Then early in February 1938 his son Lyova, who had been working for Trotsky in Paris, was admitted to hospital for an operation for appendicitis. He died on the 16th. Poisoning by the GPU has been suspected but not proved

For Trotsky, the horrors in Moscow continued. In March Bukharin, Rykov and Krestinsky were arraigned. Bukharin was accused of planning, with Trotsky's assistance, the murder of Lenin in 1918. Yagoda, who as head of the GPU had been in charge of the whole apparatus of repression and torture, was also charged with being a tool of Trotsky. Bukharin defended himself bravely; the others confessed to all charges. Eighteen of the accused were shot immediately. Late in 1938 Trotsky fell out with Diego Rivera and moved to a house in Coyoacan paid for by admirers in New York.

In January 1940 Sylvia Angelof, a New York Trotskyist, arrived to work for the family, bringing with her a man known as Frank Jacson but whose real name was Ramon Mercader, son of a Spanish communist named Caridad who was the mistress of a senior GPU official. Mercader had been trained by the GPU and he now infiltrated himself into the Trotsky household.

In May there was an armed raid on the house, using machine guns and explosives, in which Trotsky and his family escaped uninjured. However one of the guards, a young American, disappeared with the raiders and was later found shot dead. The affair was hailed by pro-Stalinist factions as a put-up job but no one was ever charged. Then in August Jacson/Mercader, who had been on a trip to New York, suddenly started to take an interest in politics and asked Trotsky to look at an article he had written. He returned on 20 August and, while Trotsky was reading the article in his study, drove an ice pick into his head. Trotsky struggled with him but then fell to the ground. He was rushed to the hospital but died on the evening of 21 August. Mercader was tried and sentenced to 20 years. In 1960 he was released, made a Hero of the Soviet Union and wound up in Czechoslovakia as a radio repair man.

Trotsky's body lay in state for five days and 300,000 people filed past the coffin. A brief note appeared in *Pravda* which said that he had been killed by a disillusioned follower.

Tschaikovsky see **Chaikovsky**.

Tsereteli, Irakly G, 1882–1959

A very active, tall, stylish and dominating Menshevik from Georgia. He returned from exile in Siberia to become a member of the Petrograd Soviet and Minister of Posts and Telegraphs in the first Provisional Government up to July 1917. He demanded strong action and called for the disarming of the Bolsheviks. He left the government and moved south to form the Menshevik Georgian government in 1918 and emigrated in 1919.

Tukhachevsky, Michael N, 1893–1937

A Tsarist Guards officer of noble ancestry who was made a prisoner of war by the Germans, and escaped through Switzerland in 1917. He joined the Bolsheviks in 1918 and was an early Red Army officer; by May 1918 he was Military Commissar for the Moscow region. In September he led the successful counter-attacks on the Czech Legion at Simbirsk. As an army commander under Frunze, he played a leading role in the campaigns of 1919, and his rapid advance beyond the Urals towards Omsk led to the complete rout of Kolchak's troops. In February 1920 he was in the Caucasus as commander of the south-east front, where his organisation of the Red Army and his swift advance led to the disintegration of Denikin's army.

With Frunze, he began to develop a Marxist 'Doctrine of Proletarian War' hostile to the Tsarist tradition of centralised control, which depended on exploiting partisans and using the maximum offensive mobility possible. In July he had charge of the western front against Poland, but the failure of co-ordination between the armies led to the Red Army's defeat. His study of the campaign laid blame on the lack of command skills in the south-western front, where Stalin preferred to strike independently at Lvov, leaving a gap between the armies which the Poles exploited. Stalin would never forgive him.

Tukhachevsky was the army commander when the Kronstadt rising was put down in 1921. He held senior army posts and was one of the five officers promoted to marshal in 1935. His modernisation and mechanisation plans for the Red Army were frustrated by his superior, Voroshilov, who was Stalin's crony and who still dreamt of cavalry battles. Among his aims was the development of a parachute landing force to drop in advance of the army – though Tukhachevsky saw their role as bringing the oppressed proletariat out in arms against the capitalist oppressors. His outspokenness did not help his reputation among Stalin's friends.

In the purge of the army, he was one of the first to be arrested, interrogated and shot, accused of a conspiracy with Nazi Germany (he had, of course, been involved in the many secret training operations with Germany in the 1920s and 1930s). He was one of the first to have his reputation rehabilitated, in 1958.

Tupolev, Andrei N, 1888–1972

Aircraft designer. He studied under the pioneer of aircraft design, Zhukovsky, in Moscow and established an aircraft design bureau in 1916. His rival in design, Polikarpov, preferred a small innovative work group, while Tupolev, concentrating on the design and mass-production of large multi-engined aircraft, developed a huge, hierarchial organisation. Arrested in the purge of 1938, on the ridiculous charge of having sold the plans of the Messerschmitt 109 to the Germans, he continued to work in OGPU detention during the war until he was released and rehabilitated in 1943. His major aircraft designs were the Ant–25, a single-engined monoplane which broke world records for long-range polar flights from the USSR to the USA in 1934, the Tu–4 bomber of 1947, copied from USAAF B–29s that had force-landed in the Soviet Union during the war, and the jet airliners Tu–104 and Tu–114.

U

Ungern-Sternberg, Baron Roman Nicolaus Fedorovich, 1887–1921
A Baltic German baron who, as a former Cossack officer, led White Russian and Mongol forces on the Chinese borders in 1920 with Japanese support. He had a dream of a Greater Mongolia which would liberate Russia from communism (and from Western decadence). He fought his brief war with savagery and sadism. In 1921 he declared himself Emperor of all Russians, but his grandiose, mad schemes collapsed and he was taken and killed by the Red Army

Uritski, Semeon Petrovich, d.1937
He helped suppress the 1921 Kronstadt mutiny, leading cavalry across the ice. He became head of the 4th Bureau, Military Intelligence, GRV, in 1935 in succession to General Berzin, and he too was arrested in the purge and shot. But, with Berzin, he was rehabilitated in 1964.

Ustinov, Dmitri, 1908–84
Held the rank of marshal as Minister of Defence, having been a technical specialist in gunnery and military engineering. He reached general rank, then became Minister for the Defence Industry, 1941–63, and finally Brezhnev's Minister of Defence in 1976 after Marshal Grechko. He also was deputy chairman of Gosplan, 1955–57, chairman of the Dniepetrovsk ferrous metalurgy industry, 1957–60, and was on the Central Committee from 1966 and a candidate member of the Politburo in 1978.

V

Valentinov (Wotsky), Nikolai, 1879–?
A friend of Lenin who wrote perceptively about him. His father was a journalist and Nikolai joined the Bolsheviks in 1903. But in 1904 he moved to the Mensheviks and strove to introduce his brand of 'revisionism'. He left Russia for the USA in 1930.

Vasilevsky, Alexander M, 1895–
A marshal of the Soviet Union. In the Tsarist army he had risen from a conscript temporary officer to staff captain before joining the Red Army. An early graduate of the General Staff College, in 1941 he was appointed to the Stavka, heading the operations department, later becoming Chief of the General Staff (even though he was for long periods absent with active field commands) and always in close touch with Stalin. Seeing the German advance on Stalingrad, he made the overall plan for its defence and took charge of the three Stalingrad fronts in November 1942, which led to the massive German defeat and his promotion to marshal. His final command was in the north, where he oversaw the armies clearing the Baltic and Prussia. He was then given command of the brief 1945 war against Japan. In 1948 he became Chief of the General Staff again and in 1949 Minister of Defence, replacing Bulganin until the death of his patron Stalin, when he retired from public life.

Vlasov, Andrei A, 1900–1946
Major-general. Joining the Red Army in 1919, he became a military adviser to Chiang Kai-shek. Commander of the 37th Army in the Ukraine and then the 20th Army outside Moscow. A soldier of promise, he was captured with his 2nd Shock Army in June 1942 after it had been overrun during the German advance and holding out in the forests since March. He was used as a propaganda tool by the Germans. Given the

title 'Chairman of the Committee for the Liberation of the Peoples of Russia' in 1944, he raised an army from prison camps to fight on the German side. He surrendered to the Americans in 1945. They handed him back to the Soviets, who hanged him.

Voroshilov, Kliment E, 1881–1969

Marshal of the Soviet Union. A steel worker and an early member of the Bolsheviks, he was a comrade of Stalin from the Civil War, who gave him command of the Soviet troops at Tsaritsyn although he was without any previous military experience. He fought with Stalin on the southern front and became a commander in Budyenny's cavalry. Described by Trotsky as a 'hearty and impudent fellow, not overly intellectual but shrewd and unscrupulous', he acquired a reputation among White forces for cruelty and atrocities.

After the Civil War Stalin used him as his spokesman on even minor military matters, though Voroshilov was known to consult Stalin on even minor military details. During the early 1930s the German General von Manstein met him on official liaison visits, and described him as 'more of a politician than a soldier'. He resisted Tukhachevsky's plans to modernise the army. Appointed marshal in 1935, it was he who approved Stalin's liquidation of the rest of the General Staff, Tukhachevsky, Blyukher and the others. In 1938 he was appointed chairman of the main military council, the RKKA, and in 1941, on the outbreak of war, became a member of the Stavka. In July he was appointed to the State Committee of Defence.

In 1943, with Molotov, he was Stalin's close companion at the Teheran Conference. The British Field Marshal Alanbrooke said of him 'With his squat figure, bluff manner and uncultured speech he seemed a typical Russian peasant'. He was also something of a showman, riding out to inspect Cossack troops on a white horse. Konev said of him 'A man of inexhaustible courage but incapable of understanding modern warfare'.

Although a member of the Central Committee of the Party from 1921 to 1961 and of the Politburo from 1926 to 1952, by 1948 he had fallen from favour with Stalin who was toying with the idea, typical of the last years of his rule, that Voroshilov was an English agent and had forbidden him to attend Politburo meetings or to receive any documents. After the death of Stalin in 1953, he was President of the Praesidium of the Supreme Soviet, nominally President of the USSR, until removed by Khrushchev in 1958. He was loaded with honours and buried in Red Square.

Voznesensky, Andrei, 1933–

Poet. Many of his works have been translated into English, particularly *Anti-Worlds* (1966) and *Nostalgia for the Present* (1978).

Voznesensky, Nickholas A, 1903–48

Head of Gosplan during World War II, he recommended allowing the peasants to cultivate their own plots and to put the State retail network at their disposal. He publicly launched the 5th Five Year Plan in 1946. He was arrested in 1948 and was shot.

Vyshinsky, Andrei, 1883–1954

Stalin's prosecutor in the purge trials. Of Polish extraction, he had joined the Social Democrats in 1903 but remained a Menshevik until 1920. Vyshinsky was a lecturer in law at Moscow University and was eventually made rector of the faculty. He became a prosecutor in 1928 and ensured his place in Stalin's favour with the trial of German and Russian engineers accused of sabotage in 1929. As prosecutor general in the Metro-Vickers trial of 1933, on the question of the truth of the charges, he made the classic statement that 'We have our own reality', suggesting some special form of Soviet legal truth. He specialised in hurling abuse at the accused: 'human garbage', 'scum!' or (his favourite) 'reptiles!'. Among his sneering attacks, there was a certain degree of anti-Semitism, when he referred to Jews as 'people without a fatherland'. He prosecuted Zinoviev, Kamenev and 14 others in August 1936 on charges of sedition and in 1937 Marshal Tukhachevsky. In 1938 Bukharin, Rykov and Yagoda were subjected to his rage and were shot within three days of the trial's end.

Vyshinsky, seen by some contemporary observers as a clear-minded academic, was also the model for Roland Friesler, the hanging judge of the Nazi 'People's Courts'. In 1940 he was sent to Latvia, recently occupied by the Soviet Union, to introduce Soviet methods of government. In 1947 he succeeded Molotov as Foreign Minister and introduced his particular brand of diatribe to the United Nations General Assembly, deliberately alienating the Western democracies. He died in New York.

W

Witte, Count Sergei, 1849–1915

The Tsarist official who, in October 1905, attempted to establish a constitutional government. He had been in charge of the state's finances and had stabilised them, creating an enormous gold reserve and encouraging foreign enterprise and railway development, particularly the Trans-Siberian. He negotiated, with the intervention of the US President Theodore Roosevelt, the treaty to end the Russo-Japanese war in 1905. He drafted the Tsar's October Manifesto and became 'President of the Council of Ministers', the Tsar's Prime Minister. He introduced fresh laws to deal with the status of the new Duma, most notoriously 'Article 87' which allowed the government at any time to declare an emergency, and to issue edicts without reference to the Duma.

But, however able this masterful, insensitive and egocentric man was, the left and the right, the liberals and the Tsar, attacked him and he resigned in May 1906.

Wrangel, Baron Peter, 1878–1928

This tall, lean Tsarist general was a baron from an old German Baltic family. As a cavalry officer he had served in the 1905 Russo-Japanese war with distinction; had been commander of the Tsarevich's Own Regiment of Cossacks, and in 1914 in World War I had enhanced his reputation at the early Russian victory of Gumbinnen. In 1918 Wrangel resigned his commission and went to the Crimea, choosing to serve under Denikin. After a series of defeats, Wrangel quarrelled with Denikin and left Russia, but when Denikin lost the confidence of his fellow generals, they elected Wrangel to succeed as Commander-in-Chief in April 1920. That month, as the Polish army drove into the Ukraine, capturing Kiev, he led his army out of the Crimea and fought until November. Then, driven back to Perekop, he was finally defeated and had to evacuate the remnants of his army, 130,000 men in 126 boats, to Turkey. He tried to keep an anti-Bolshevik force in existence, but gave up the attempt in 1925 and left Yugoslavia for Belgium, where he died. He was taken back to Belgrade for burial in the White Russian church there.

Y

Yagoda, Genrikh, 1891–1938

A Lodz-born son of a chemist who joined the Red Army and the Party. In 1930 he became head of the labour camps organisation. Menzhinsky brought him into the NKVD as his protégé, where he revised the overseas networks and tightened control within the NKVD itself. He took over from Menzhinsky in 1934 – until he was removed and shot after the first great show trial in 1936.

Yakovlev, Alexander S, 1906–89

A leading aircraft designer of the Soviet Union. He was born in Moscow and trained at the Zhukavosky Aircraft Engineering Academy. He started by designing gliders, but in 1927 his Air–1 appeared (at first to a chorus of suspicion from rivals) to take a world record by flying the 800 miles (1,300 km) from Sevastopol to Moscow in 15 hours 30 minutes. He graduated from the academy in 1931, first joining the Polikarpov Bureau, but then, in 1937, setting up his own aircraft design bureau in Moscow.

In 1938 he designed the Air–22 high-speed reconnaissance aircraft which, after modification, was picked to be put into mass production in 1939, and Yakovlev was awarded the Order of Lenin and a premium of 100,000 roubles. He was ordered by Stalin to produce a prototype of an interceptor fighter within six months and did so. This was the Yak–1, manufacturerd with a wooden wing and steel tubular body, his motto being 'Simplicity not primitiveness'. The plane carried a 20 mm cannon and two 7.62 machine guns and had an excellent performance, comparable to the Spitfire or the Messerschmitt Bf109. It was succeeded by modified versions, the Yak–3, 7 and 9.

In 1940 Yakovlev was made Deputy People's Commissar of the Aircraft Industry. His later successful designs included the Yak–15, the first Soviet jet fighter, and in 1958 the Yak–28, the first supersonic tactical bomber. During his life he supervised the design and production of 75 aircraft types, including, from 1944, helicopters, trainers and a vertical take-off and landing plane. His last plane was the commercial Yak–42 which entered Aeroflot service in 1980.

Yakovlev was awarded numerous decorations, including eight Orders of Lenin and in 1972 he received the Lenin Prize. In 1974 he was made a member of the French Legion d'Honneur.

Yazov, Dimitri, 1923–

An infantry officer during the war, starting with officer cadet training and rising to second in command of a company by 1945. He worked his way up, attending the Frunze Military Academy in 1956, the General Staff Academy in 1967. He became a divisional, corps and then army commander in 1974, with command of the Central Asian and Far Eastern military districts in 1980. Associated with Gorbachev's policies, and the withdrawal from Afghanistan, he became a candidate member of the Politburo and Minister of Defence in 1988.

Yeltsin, Boris N, 1931–

An 'anti-establishment radical'. An engineer, graduate of Sverdlovsk University, becoming First Secretary in the Sverdlovsk Region from 1976 to 1985. He was transferred to Moscow as Central Committee department head for construction in 1985. In 1986 he went into the Politburo as a Kirilenko follower and was taken over by Andropov. He became Moscow Party Secretary, but was removed in 1987 after a conflict with more conservative elements. Ligachev attacked his reforms at the Party Conference in July 1987 but Gorbachev allowed Yeltsin to speak. For the 1989 elections to the new Congress he preferred to stand for the Moscow constituency, opposed by the manager of the 'Zil' limousine factory, rather than his old power-base Sverdlovsk and was elected with a triumphant majority.

In 1989 his popularity increased and in 1990 he was elected President of the RSFSR. For this and later events, see the Chronology.

Yevtushenko, Evgeny, 1933–
Poet. Born in the Irkutsk region of Siberia, he went with his father on geological expeditions in the Altai mountains. His poems were published from as early as 1952 and he has been the recipient of many prizes, both Soviet and international. He has been seen as a product of the post-Stalin thaw and his poem on Babi Yar, the slaughter of Jews in Kiev by the Nazis, achieved considerable fame for him. He was elected a member of the Congress of People's Deputies in 1989.

Yezhov, Nikolai I, 1895–1939?
A St Petersburg metal worker who joined the Party in 1917 and was with the Red Army until 1921, then filling Party posts in various parts of the Soviet Union. In 1927 he became a member of the Central Committee, having responsibilities in 1929–30 for the 'liquidation of the kulaks as a class'. He was at the 17th Party Congress, and in charge of its Industrial Department. He became Secretary to the Central Committee and chairman of the Central Control Commission of the Party in 1935, rooting out corruption and red tape. He followed Yagoda as head of the NKVD in 1936. On Stalin's orders he launched the terrible purges. Nicknamed 'the Iron Commissar' by some and 'the Dwarf' by others, he gave the period of terror its name 'Yezhovschina'. In 1938 he was abruptly removed from his post and made Commissar for Water Transport, then arrested. He was, presumably, shot by his former employees. He had moved his way up steadily, showing no sign of viciousness – only loyalty to the Party and a Spartan discipline. Yezhov always wore a simple tunic and kept his head shaved in the Civil War style.

Yudenich, Nicholas N, 1862–1933
The general of the White army in command of the Baltic area. With British advisers, he moved from Estonia to Petrograd, whose suburbs he reached in September 1919. The Petrograd Red Guards defeated him and he retreated as his army disintegrated. He left Russia immediately and went into exile.

Z

Zasulich, Vera Ivanovna, 1849–1918
A girl student who, as an ardent admirer of Nechaev, was used by him to spread the rumour of his great conspiracies. She shot at General Trepov, the military governor of St Petersburg, was tried, acquitted and became an exile and an internationally known revolutionary heroine. With Plekhanov, she was the founder of the 'Group for the Emancipation of Labour'. Lenin met her in Geneva in 1900, where she lived with Martov, a fellow socialist. She was a co-editor of *Iskra* and worked with the Bolsheviks in their founding days.

Zhdanov, Andrei A, 1896–1948
Made Secretary of the Leningrad Party after the assassination of Kirov in 1934 and led Stalin's witch-hunt there. Secretary to the Central Committee, he was marked by his adherence to a strict Party line and his extreme nationalism, which manifested itself in his antagonism to any Western influence in art or literature. Although he was crudely dictatorial in his methods, he favoured a decentralisation of authority. After his death in 1948, Stalin became convinced that he had been murdered and a number of Jewish doctors were arrested in 1953 in an episode which later became known as the Doctors' Plot: they were released after Stalin died.

Zhukov, Georgi K, 1896–1974
Marshal of the Soviet Union. Mobilised into the cavalry in 1915, he became a much-decorated NCO. He joined the Red Army cavalry in August 1918, and was wounded at Tsaritsyn in 1919. After officer training, he fought against Wrangel as a lieutenant in 1920 and from 1920–23 in actions against kulaks. He had senior officer training at the Moscow Frunze Acacemy in 1929–30, becoming Assistant Inspector of Cavalry and in 1933 taking command of the 4th Cavalry Division. In 1936 or 1937 he was in Spain, returning in 1937 as commander of the 3rd and 6th Cavalry Corps. In June 1939 he had command of Soviet–Mongolian troops; his August offensive against the Japanese ended in victory.

In autumn 1939 he was deputy commander of the Ukrainian military district, then in June 1940 commander of the Kiev special military district, and led troops into Romanian Bessarabia. From January 1941 he was Chief of the General Staff, becoming in March a Commissar of Defence. From July, after the German attack, he took command of the reserve army, in September of Leningrad, and in October of Moscow. In February 1942 he had the Western army group, being promoted to marshal in January 1943. He led the Red Army in its advance into Germany and received the German surrender in Berlin in 1945.

After the war Zhukov, although a popular hero, was given a remote posting by Stalin. However, in 1955 Khrushchev showed his gratitude for his support by making him Minister of Defence, only to sack him in 1957. Brezhnev rehabilitated his reputation in 1964, honouring him with the Order of Lenin, but gave him no further employment.

Zhukovski, Nikolai, 1847–1921
The 'Father of Russian Aviation'. A lecturer in mechanical engineering in the Moscow Higher Technical College who had studied the theory of flight and had already set up an aerodynamic laboratory before the Wright brothers' first flight. With Andrei Tupolev, he worked on designing a bomber for the Red Army. Although his project was a failure, his work team was the foundation for the Soviet Union's future in aircraft design.

Zinoviev (Radomislsky, born Hirsch Apfelbaum), Grigory, 1883–1936
From southern Russia, he was a Social Democrat from 1901. He was a member of the Bolshevik Central Committee, 1907–27, and was close to Lenin in exile from 1907. He returned with Lenin in April 1917, but opposed his call for an armed rising. He was head of the Party's Petrograd organization, 1918–26, and head of the Third International, the Comintern, 1919–26. In 1924 a letter in his name, addressed to the British Communist Party and purporting to be a secret directive from the Comintern, was published: it was a forgery but the effect was to destroy the reputation of the Labour Party then in power in Britain. After Lenin's death, with Kamenev and Stalin, he formed a triumvirate, but was soon allied with Trotsky and Kamenev against Stalin, as a leader of the United Left Opposition, 1926–27. He was expelled from the Party for this, but having acknowledged his errors he was readmitted in 1928 but was finally expelled again in 1932. He was arrested in 1934 and accused of complicity in the murder of Kirov, tried in 1935 and given a jail sentence. He was tried again in August 1936 and executed. His sentence was annulled by the Soviet Supreme Court in June 1988.

 **MAPS**

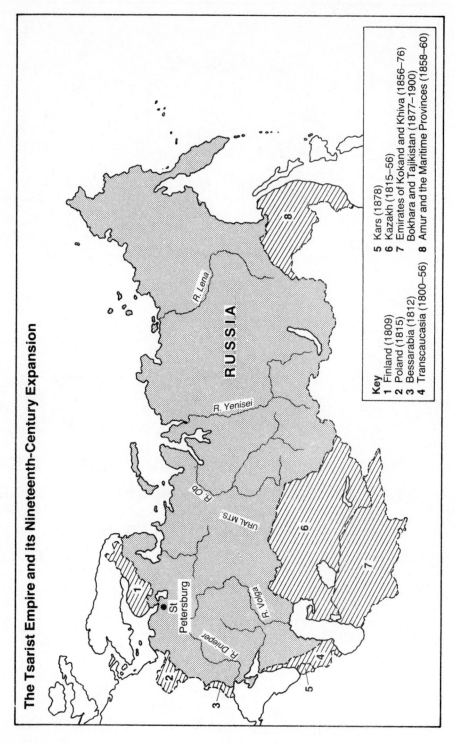

The Tsarist Empire and its Nineteenth-Century Expansion

Key
1 Finland (1809)
2 Poland (1815)
3 Bessarabia (1812)
4 Transcaucasia (1800–56)
5 Kars (1878)
6 Kazakh (1815–56)
7 Emirates of Kokand and Khiva (1856–76)
  Bokhara and Tajikistan (1877–1900)
8 Amur and the Maritime Provinces (1858–60)

RUSSIA

St Petersburg

R. Lena
R. Yenisei
R. Ob
URAL MTS.
R. Volga
R. Dnieper

321

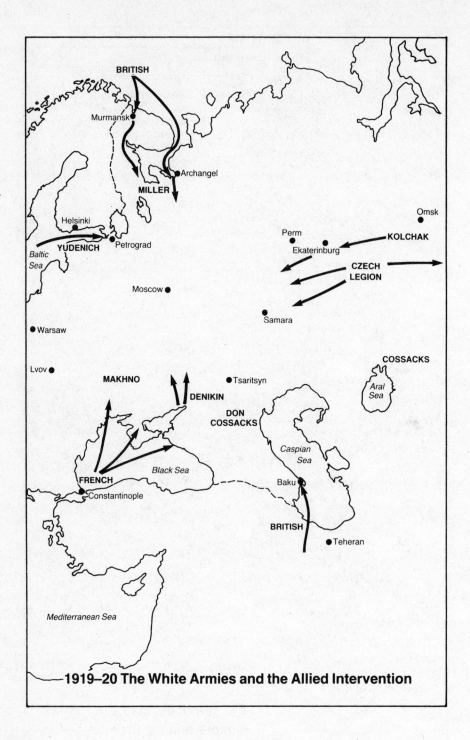

1919–20 The White Armies and the Allied Intervention

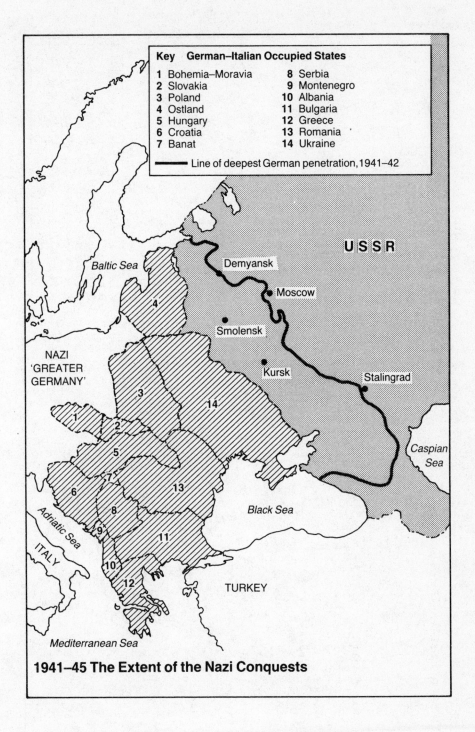

Key   German–Italian Occupied States

1 Bohemia–Moravia
2 Slovakia
3 Poland
4 Ostland
5 Hungary
6 Croatia
7 Banat

8 Serbia
9 Montenegro
10 Albania
11 Bulgaria
12 Greece
13 Romania
14 Ukraine

▬▬ Line of deepest German penetration, 1941–42

Baltic Sea

USSR

Demyansk

Moscow

Smolensk

NAZI
'GREATER
GERMANY'

Kursk

Stalingrad

Caspian
Sea

Adriatic Sea

ITALY

Black Sea

TURKEY

Mediterranean Sea

1941–45 The Extent of the Nazi Conquests

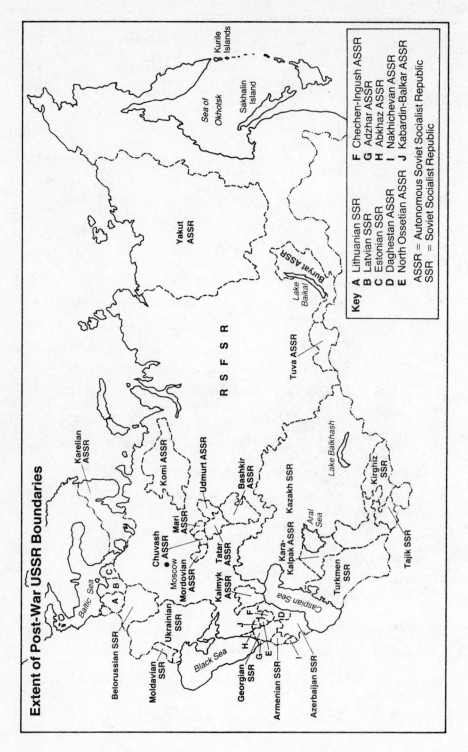

Extent of Post-War USSR Boundaries

Key
A Lithuanian SSR
B Latvian SSR
C Estonian SSR
D Daghestan ASSR
E North Ossetian ASSR

F Chechen-Ingush ASSR
G Adzhar ASSR
H Abkhaz ASSR
I Nakhichevan ASSR
J Kabardin-Balkar ASSR

ASSR = Autonomous Soviet Socialist Republic
SSR = Soviet Socialist Republic

Kurile
Islands

Sea of
Okhotsk

Sakhalin
Island

Yakut
ASSR

R S F S R

Buryat ASSR

Lake
Baikal

Tuva ASSR

Karelian
ASSR

Komi ASSR

Udmurt ASSR

Bashkir
ASSR

Kazakh SSR

Lake Balkhash

Kirghiz
SSR

Mari
ASSR

Chuvash
ASSR

Moscow

Mordovian
ASSR

Tatar
ASSR

Aral
Sea

Kara-
Kalpak ASSR

Tajik SSR

Baltic
Sea

A
B
C

Belorussian SSR

Ukrainian
SSR

Kalmyk
ASSR

Turkmen
SSR

Caspian Sea

Moldavian
SSR

F

J
H
G
E
D

I

Black Sea

Georgian
SSR

Armenian SSR

Azerbaijan SSR

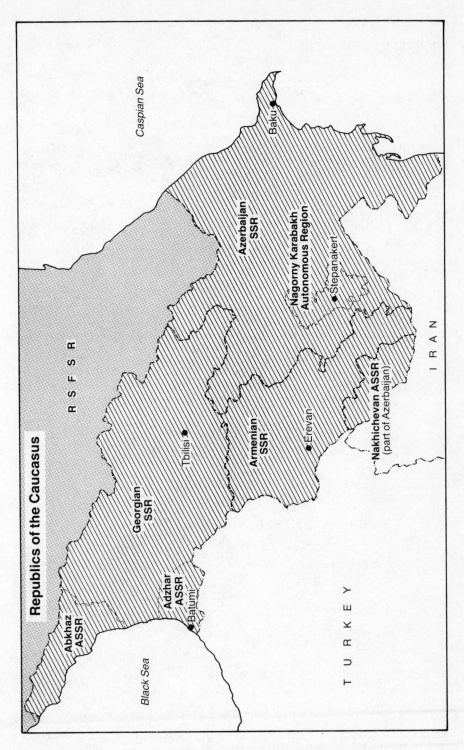

Republics of the Caucasus

Caspian Sea

Baku

Azerbaijan
SSR

Nagorny Karabakh
Autonomous Region

Stepanakert

R S F S R

Tbilisi

Armenian
SSR

Erevan

I R A N

Nakhichevan ASSR
(part of Azerbaijan)

Georgian
SSR

Adzhar
ASSR

Batumi

Abkhaz
ASSR

Black Sea

T U R K E Y

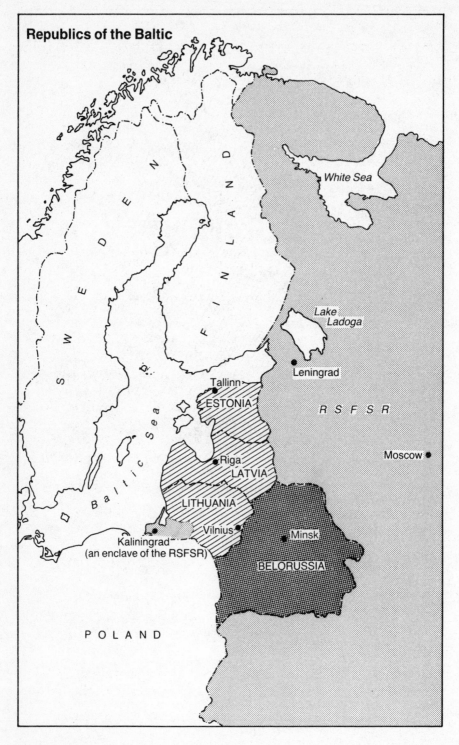

Republics of the Baltic

SWEDEN

FINLAND

White Sea

Lake Ladoga

Leningrad

Baltic Sea

Tallinn
ESTONIA

RSFSR

Riga
LATVIA

Moscow

LITHUANIA

Vilnius

Minsk

Kaliningrad
(an enclave of the RSFSR)

BELORUSSIA

POLAND

Major Industrial and Agricultural Areas

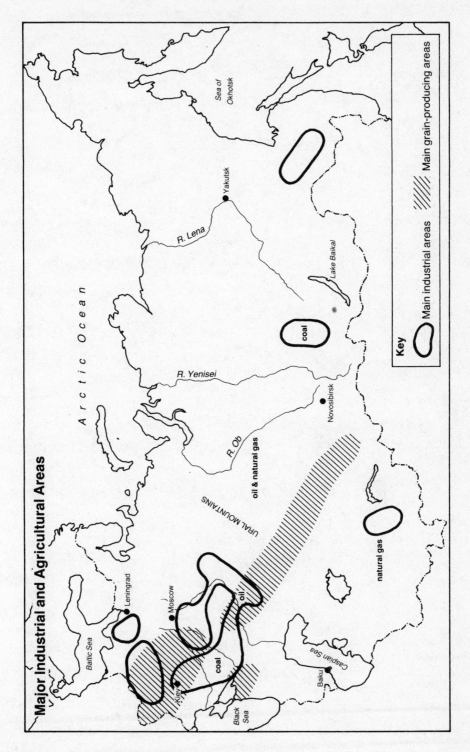

Key

Main industrial areas

Main grain-producing areas

Arctic Ocean

Sea of Okhotsk

Yakutsk

R. Lena

Lake Baikal

coal

R. Yenisei

Novosibirsk

R. Ob

oil & natural gas

URAL MOUNTAINS

Leningrad

Moscow

Baltic Sea

coal

oil

natural gas

Kiev

Black Sea

Caspian Sea

Baku

Akmolinsk now Tselinograd, in
Kazakhstan, since 1961

Aleksandropol now Leninakan

Alma Ata formerly Verny

Andropov formerly and now Rybinsk

Arkhangelsk Archangel

Ashkabad formerly Poltoratsk
1919–27

Berdyansk known as Osipenko
1939–58

Bobriki now Novomoskovsk

Chapayevsk in the Kuibyshev oblast,
formerly Ivashchenkovo, then
Trotsk from 1919–27

Chistyakovo now Torez

Chkalov now Orenburg

Detskoye Selo now Pushkin

Dnepropetrovsk formerly
Ekaterinoslav

Donetsk formerly Yuzovka (after the
nineteenth-century Welshman John
Hughes who founded a coal mine and
iron foundry there), then Stalin from
1924 and Stalino, 1935, and Donetsk
from 1961.

Dorpat Tartu

Dushambe sometimes 'Dushanbe',
known as Stalinabad 1929–61

Dzaudzhika now Ordzhonikidze

Ekaterinodar now Krasnodar

Ekaterinoslav now Dnepropetrovsk

Erevan Yerevan

Frunze formerly Pishpek (capital of
the Kirghiz SSR) until 1926

Gorky formerly Nizhny Novgorod
(Gorky's birthplace)

Hayastan Armenia, in the Armenian
language

Ivano-Fankovsk formerly, 1945–62,
Stanislav, in the Ukraine, spelled
Stanislau to 1919 and, in Polish,
Stanislawow 1919–45

Izhevsk now Ustinov

Kalinin formerly Tver

Kaliningrad formerly Königsberg

Khelmitsky formerly Proskurov,
until 1954

Khodzhent now Leninabad

Kirov since 1936, formerly Vyatka

Kirovograd in the Ukraine, was
Elizavetgrad to 1924, then
Zinovievsk until 1936. It was called
Kirovo between 1936 and 1939

Klaipëda Memel

Königsberg now Kaliningrad

Krasnodar formerly Ekaterinodar

Kuibyshev formerly Samara

Kuznetsk now Novokuznetsk

Lemberg the German name for Lvov

Leninabad in the Tadjik SSR,
formerly Khodzhent or Khojend, to
1936

Leninakan in the Armenian SSR,
Aleksandropol to 1924

Leningrad changed from the
German-sounding St Petersburg in
WW1 to Petrograd and changed to
Leningrad in 1924 after Lenin's
death

Leninskoye a village in the Jewish
Autonomous oblast, Khabarovsk,
RSFSR, was Mikhailovo-
Semyonovskoye, then Blyukherovo
until 1939

Lugansk now Voroshilovgrad

Lvov *see also* Lwow and Lemberg

Lwow the Polish spelling (*see also*
Lemberg) of Lvov

Mariupol known as Zhdanov
1948–89

Mary formerly Merv

Memel Klaipëda

Merv now Mary, since 1937

Molotov now, as formerly, Perm

Molotovsk now, as formerly,
Severodvinsk

Nikolskoye now Ussuriysk

Nizhny Novgorod now Gorky

Novoazovsk Novonikolyevka to 1935 and Budyonnovka 1935–66

Novokashirsk a suburb of Kashira, Moscow oblast, until 1935 was Ternovsk, from 1935–57 Kaganovich

Novokuznetsk Kuznetsk to 1931, Stalinsk 1931–61

Novomoskovsk Bobriki to 1934, Stalinogorsk 1934–61, near Tula

Novosibirsk Gusevka to 1903 and Novonikolayevsk until 1925

Ordzhonikidze formerly Vladikavkaz until 1932, then Dzaudzhika 1944–54

Orenberg known, 1938–57, as Chkalov

Osipenko now Berdyansk

Perm known as Molotov 1940–57, in the Urals

Petrograd now Leningrad

Pishpek now Frunze

Poltoratsk now, as formerly, Ashkabad

Proskurov now Khmelmitsky

Pushkin formerly Tsarskoye Selo, then Detskoye Selo 1917–37

Reval the German form of the Russian Revel, the Estonian name Tallinn is now used

Rybinsk known as Shcherbakov, 1946–57, later Andropov

St Petersburg now Leningrad

Samara now Kuibyshev

Shcherbakov formerly and now Rybinsk

Severodvinsk known as Sudostroy 1918–38 and Molotovsk 1938–57, in the north-west of the RSFSR

Sovetsk formerly Tilsit

Stalin now Donetsk

Stalinabad Dushanbe, known as Stalinabad 1929–61

Stalingrad formerly Tsaritsyn, now Volgograd

Staliniri now Tskhinval

Stalino now Donetsk

Stalinogorsk now Novomoskovsk

Stalinsk now Novokuznetsk

Stanislav now Ivano-Frankovsk

Stavropol now Tolyatti

Sudostroy now Severodvinsk

Sverdlovsk formerly Ekaterinburg (or Yekaterinburg), 1924

Tallinn formerly Reval

Tartu Dorpat

Tbilisi formerly called Tiflis

Tolyatti (Togliatti, the Italian communist) formerly Stavropol

Torez (Thorez, the French communist) since 1964, formerly Chistyakovo, in the Ukraine.

Tsaritsyn now Volgograd

Tsarskoye Selo now Pushkin

Tselinograd since 1961, formerly Akmolinsk; Tselino = Virgin soil

Tskhinval capital of South Ossetian Autonomous oblast in Georgia, formerly Staliniri 1934–61

Tver now Kalinin

Ussuriysk Nikolskoye to 1926, Nikolskoye-Ussuriysk 1926–35 and Voroshilov 1935–57

Ustinov formerly Izhevsk in the Udmurt ASSR

Verny now Alma Ata

Vilna Wilno (Polish), Vilnius (Lithuanian)

Vladikavkaz now Ordzhonikidze

Volgograd formerly Tsaritsyin and from 1925 Stalingrad

Vorshilov now Ussuriysk

Voroshilovgrad formerly Lugansk, to 1935, renamed Lugansk 1970 but later reverted to Voroshilovgrad

Vyatka now Kirov

Yerevan Erevan

Yuzkova later Stalino, now Donetsk

Zhdanov Mariupol, known as Zhdanov 1948–89

Note: In 1988 a number of places named after either Brezhnev or Chernenko reverted to their original names. See also Adrian Room, *Place-Name Changes Since 1900*, Scarecrow Press, Metuchen, NJ, USA, 1979.

≡ BIBLIOGRAPHY ≡

Aganbegyan, Abel, *The Challenge – Economics of Perestroika*, Hutchinson, London, 1988

Akiner, Shirin, *Islamic Peoples of the Soviet Union*, Kegan Paul, London, 1983

Amnesty International, *Prisoners of Conscience in the USSR*, Quartermaine House Ltd, London, 1975

Armstrong, John A, *Ukrainian Nationalism*, Ukrainian Academic Press, Colorado, 2nd edn 1980

Auty, Robert and Obolensky, Dimitri, *An Introduction to Russian Art*, Cambridge University Press, 1980

Ball, Alan M, *Russia's Last Capitalists, the Nepmen, 1921–29*, University of California Press, Berkeley, 1987

Boyd, Alexander, *The Soviet Air Force since 1918*, Macdonald and Jane's, London, 1977

Breslauer, George W, *Khrushchev and Brezhnev as Leaders*, Allen and Unwin, London, 1982

Brown, Archie and Kaser, Michael, (eds), *Soviet Policy for the 1980s*, Macmillan, London, 1982

Brun, Capt. A H, *Troublous Times*, 1931 (probably published in Tashkent 1917–19)

Carr, E H, *The Bolshevik Revolution*, 3 vols, Macmillan, London, 1953

Central Committee of the CPSU(B) (ed), *History of the Communist Party of the Soviet Union (Bolsheviks)*, Moscow, 1941

Chorley, Katherine, *Armies and the Art of Revolution*, Faber & Faber, London, 1943

Clark, Ronald W, *Lenin, the Man Behind the Mask*, Faber & Faber, London, 1988

Cohen, Stephen F, *Bukharin and the Bolshevik Revolution*, Oxford University Press, 1980

Cole J P, *Geography of the Soviet Union*, Butterworth, London, 1984

Conolly, Violet, *Beyond the Urals*, Oxford University Press, 1967

Conquest, Robert, *The Great Terror*, Macmillan, London, 1968

Conquest, Robert *Stalin and the Kirov Murder*, Hutchinson, London, 1989

Crankshaw, Edward, *Khrushchev*, Collins, London, 1966

Dallin, David J, *Soviet Russia and the Far East*, Yale University Press, 1949

Daniels, Robert V (ed), *The Stalin Revolution*, D C Heath, Lexington, 1972

Deacon, Richard, *A History of the Russian Secret Service*, Muller, 1972

Dyker, David A (ed). *The Soviet Union under Gorbachev*, Croom Helm, London, 1987.

Dziewanowoki, M K, *A History of Soviet Russia*, Prentice Hall, New Jersey, 2nd edn 1985

Erickson, John, *Stalin's War with Germany*, 2 vols, Weidenfeld & Nicolson, London, 1975

Eudin, X J and Fisher H H, *Soviet Russia and the West 1920–1927*, Stanford University Press, 1957

Fairhall, David, *Russia Looks to the Sea, the Expansion of Soviet Marine Power*, Deutsch, London, 1971

Feis, Herbert, *Churchill–Roosevelt– Stalin*, Princeton University Press, 1967

Ferro, Marc, *The Bolshevik Revolution, a Social History*, Routledge & Kegan Paul, London, 1980

Fleischhauer, Ingeborg and Pinkus, Benjamin, *The Soviet Germans*, Hurst, London, 1986

Footman, David, *Civil War in Russia*, Faber & Faber, 1981

Frankland, Mark, *The Sixth Continent*, Hamish Hamilton, London, 1987

Getty, J Arch, *Origins of the Great Purges*, Cambridge University Press, 1985

Getzler, Israel, *Kronstadt 1917–1921*, Cambridge University Press, 1983

Gorbachev, Mikhail, *Perestroika*, Collins, London, 1987

Goudever, Albert P van, *The Limits of Destalinisation in the Soviet Union*, Croom Helm, London, 1986

Hart, B H Liddell, *History of the Second World War*, Cassell, London, 1970

Haupt, Georges and Jean-Jacques Marie (trans, C I P Ferdinand and D M Bellos), *Makers of the Russian Revolution*, Allen & Unwin, London, 1974

Heller, Mikhail and Nekrich, Aleksandr (trans. Phyllis B Carlos), *Utopia in Power, the History of the Soviet Union from 1917 to the Present*, Hutchinson, London, 1986

Hill, Ronald J, *Soviet Union*, Francis Pinter, London, 1985

Hingley, Ronald, *Russian Writers and Soviet Society, 1917–1978*, Weidenfeld & Nicolson, London, 1979

Hosking, Geoffrey, *A History of the Soviet Union*, Collins/Fontana, London, 1985

Jacobs, Dan N. *Borodin, Stalin's Man in China*, Harvard University Press, 1981

Jukes, Geoffrey, *The Soviet Union in Asia*, Angus & Robertson, Sydney, 1973

Kapur, Harish, *Soviet Russia and Asia 1917–1927*, University of Geneva, 1965

Katz, Zev with Rogers, Rosemary and Harned, Frederic (eds), *Handbook of Soviet Nationalities*, The Free Press, New York, 1975

Kilmarx, Robert A, *A History of Soviet Air Power*, Faber & Faber, London, 1962

Kolarz, Walter, *Russia and her Colonies*, George Philip, London, 1952

Kolkowicz, Roman, *The Soviet Military and the Communist Party*, Westview Press, Boulder & London, 1985

Laquer, *Europe since Hitler*, Penguin, London (rev edn) 1982

Levytsky, Boris, *The Uses of Terror, the Soviet Secret Service 1917–1970*, Sidgwick & Jackson, 1971

Levytsky, Boris (compiler), *The Stalinist Terror in the Thirties*, Stanford University Press, 1974

Lincoln, W Bruce, *Passage through Armageddon*, Simon & Schuster, New York, 1986

Longworth, Philip, *The Cossacks*, Constable, London, 1969

Lubachko, Ivan S, *Belorussia under Soviet Rule 1917–1957*, University Press of Kentucky, 1972

Luckett, Richard, *The White Generals*, Longman, London, 1971

McAuley, Mary, *Politics and the Soviet Union*, Penguin, London, 1977

McCauley, Martin, *The Soviet Union since 1917*, Longman (History of Russia series), 1981

McNeal, Robert H, *Stalin: Man and Ruler*, Macmillan, London, 1988

Marshall, Richard H, jr (ed), *Aspects of Religion in the Soviet Union, 1917–1967*, University of Chicago Press, Chicago.

Mawdsley, Evan, *The Russian Civil War*, Allen & Unwin, Boston, 1987

Medvedev, Roy, *Khrushchev*, Blackwell, Oxford, 1982

Medvedev, Roy, *On Stalin and Stalinism*, Blackwell, Oxford, 1979

Medvedev, Roy, *The October Revolution*, Constable, 1979

Medvedev, Roy, *Nikolai Bukharin*, Norton, New York, 1980

Medvedev, Zhores, *Andropov*, Blackwell, Oxford, 1983

Medvedev, Zhores, *Gorbachev*, Blackwell, Oxford, 1986

Medvedev, Zhores, *Soviet Agriculture*, Norton, New York, 1987

Mett, Ida, *The Kronstadt Uprising* Solidary, London, nd (1987?)

Mezhenkov, V (ed), *Soviet Scene 1987*, Collets, London, 1987

Michel, Henri (trans. D Parmée), *The Second World War*, Deutsch, London, 1975

Miler, R F and Rigby, J H and T H, *Gorbachev at the Helm*, Croom Helm, London, 1987

Misiunas, Roland J and Taagepera, Rein, *The Baltic States*, Hurst, London, 1983

Morris, L P, *Eastern Europe since 1945*, Heinemann Education, London, 1984

Mosley, Nicholas, *The Assassination of Trotsky*, Michael Joseph, London, 1972

Munting, Roger, *The Economic Development of the USSR*, Croom Helm, London, 1982

Murphy, Paul J, *Brezhnev*, McFarland, Jefferson NC, 1981

Nekrich, Aleksandr M (trans. George Saunders), *The Punished Peoples*, Norton, New York, 1978

Nove, Alec, *An Economic History of the USSR*, Penguin, London (rev edn) 1982

Novosti Press Agency, *USSR Yearbook '88*, Novosti Publishing House, Moscow, 1988

Novosti Press Agency, *USSR Yearbook '89*, Novosti Publishing House, Moscow, 1989

Pares, Sir Bernard, *The Fall of the Russian Monarchy*, Cape, London, 1939

Paxton, John, *Companion to Russian History*, Facts on File, New York, 1983

Payne, Robert, *The Life and Death of Lenin*, W H Allen, London, 1964

Pearson, Michael, *The Sealed Train*, Putnam, New York, 1975

Radkey, Oliver H, *The Sickle under the Hammer*, Comumbia University Press, New York, 1963

Raleigh, Donald J, *Revolution on the Volga, Saratov in 1917*, Cornell University Press, Ithaca, 1986

Rauch, George von, *A History of the Soviet Union*, Pall Mall Press, London, 5th edn 1967

Read, Anthony and Fisher, David, *The Deadly Embrace*, Michael Joseph, London, 1988

Ripka, Hubert, *Eastern Europe in the Post-war World*, Methuen, London, 1961

Robottom, John, *Modern Russia*, Longman, London, 2nd edn 1972

Ro'i, Yaacov (ed), *The USSR and the Muslim World*, Allen & Unwin, London, 1984

Saikal, Amin and Maley, William, *The Soviet Withdrawal from Afghanistan*, Cambridge University Press, 1989

Salazar, General L A S, *Murder in Mexico*, Secker & Warburg, London, 1950

Schmidt-Häuer, Christian, *Gorbachev – the Path to Power*, I B Tauris and Pan Books, London, 1986

Schwarz, Boris, *Music and Musical Life in Soviet Russia, 1917–1970*, Barrie & Jenkins, London, 1972

Seaton A, *The Russo-German War 1941–1945*, Barker, London, 1971

Seaton, Albert and Joan, *The Soviet Army, 1918 to the Present*, Bodley Head, London, 1986

Segal, Ronald, *The Tragedy of Leon Trotsky*, Hutchinson, London, 1979

Serge, Victor and Trotsky, Natalie, *The Life and Death of Leon Trotsky*, Wildwood House, 1975

Seton-Watson, Hugh, *Nationalism and Communism*, Methuen, London, 1964

Shapiro, Leonard, *The Origin of the Communist Autocracy*, Macmillan, London, 1977

Shapiro, Leonard, *Soviet Treaty series,*

2 vols, Georgetown University Press, Washington, 1950–55

Shapiro, Leonard, *The Communist Party of the Soviet Union*, Random House, New York, 1960

Shapiro, Leonard, *1917: the Russian Revolutions and the Origins of Present Day Communism*, Maurice Temple Smith, London, 1984

Shukman, Harold (ed), *The Blackwell Encyclopedia of the Russian Revolution*, Blackwell, Oxford, 1988

Silverlight, John, *The Victors' Dilemma, Allied Intervention in the Russian Civil War*, Barrie & Jenkins, London, 1970

Smith, Canfield F, *Vladivostok under Red and White Rule*, University of Washington Press, Seattle, 1975

Staar, Richard F, *Communist Regimes in Eastern Europe*, Hoover Institution Press, Stanford CA, 1982

Steele, Jonathan and Abraham, Eric, *Andropov in Power*, Robertson, Oxford, 1983

Strobe Talbot, T R, *Khrushchev Remembers*, Deutsch, London, 1971

Tatu, Michel (trans. Helen Katel), *Power in the Kremlin*, Viking, New York, 1969

Veen, Hans-Joachim (ed), *From Brezhnev to Gorbachev*, Berg, Leamington Spa, 1987

Voline (Vselvolod Mikhailovich Eichenbaum), *The Unknown Revolution, 1917–1921*, Black Rose Books, Quebec, 1975

Wade, Rex A, *Red Guards' and Workers' Militias in the Russian Revolution*, Stanford University Press, 1984

Walker, Martin, *The Waking Giant*, Michael Joseph, London, 1986

Warner, Oliver, *Marshal Mannerheim and the Finns*, Weidenfeld & Nicolson, London, 1967

Werth, Alexander, *Russia at War, 1941–1945*, Barrie & Rockliffe, London, 1964

Westwood, J N, *Endurance and Endeavour, Russian History, 1812–1986*, Oxford University Press, 3rd edn 1987

Wildman, Allan K, *The End of the Russian Imperial Army*, Princeton University Press, 1980

Wistrich, Robert, *Trotsky, Fate of a Revolutionary*, Robson, London, 1979

Zaleski, Eugène, (trans MacAndrew and Nutter), *Planning for Economic Growth in the Soviet Union, 1918–1932*, University of North Carolina Press, Chapel Hill, 1971

INDEX

Credits

The black-and-white illustrations are reproduced with kind permission of the following:
Novosti Press Agency: 1, 3, 4, 6, 7, 9, 13, 16, 18
David King Collection: 2, 5, 10, 12
Popperfoto: 8, 11, 14, 15, 17

The tables and information on pages 127, 145, 146, 147, 188, 189 are reproduced by kind
permission of NPA.